NO JOE BLOGGS

First Published in Great Britain 2014 by Mirador Publishing

Copyright © 2014 by Joe Morris

First edition: 2014

A copy of this work is available through the British Library.

ISBN: 978-1-910530-24-5

Mirador Publishing
Mirador
Wearne Lane
Langport
Somerset
TA10 9HB

NO JOE BLOGGS

BY

JOE MORRIS

Dedication

This book would not have been possible without the help of the following my wife Beverley and daughter Rachel for their patience and my son Sam for all his help on the computer. I have a special thanks to Ian Warner for proof reading this book. He did a great job.

Joe Morris.

Part 1:
The beginning.

And then it happened. No trumpets, no fanfares but nonetheless very special. My glorious hour, my glorious morning. 23rd November 1962. My first appearance on the silver screen. My first day on Planet Earth. The day of my birth, that momentous day, that first entrance into the big, wide world, my introduction to London, England and society. I'm not sure whether there were any earthquakes, hurricanes or political scandals. It was a day rather like any other. It was wintry but nothing extraordinary happened but it was significantly my day.

23rd November 1962 did though mark one other special newsworthy occasion, a notable event on the BBC. The day of my first birthday coincided with the first episode of that national treasure Doctor Who with William Hartnell as the good Doctor.

But all the attention was elsewhere. At the Royal London Hospital in Whitechapel, the heart of London's East End, it was time for me to let out that first tentative yell, that first yearning for adventure, that first very first and admittedly primitive attempt at speech, a cry from the heart, a passionate longing to live life to the full.

For this is the story of me, my family, an affectionate tribute to my parents, growing up in the respectable Essex suburb of Ilford, the Seventies, living and experiencing life in all its pastel shades and nuances. It is the story of a very humble child, his grandparents, their struggles, trials and tribulations, triumphs and successes. It is quite literally a triumph against all of the odds, emerging victorious in the face of disaster and adversity.

It is the story of my quirky observations of the London that I grew up with during the 1960s, a very fond if imaginary account of my mum and grandparents surviving the Second World War nightmare, how she fought back and defeated the evil forces, a Holocaust survivor with her dignity intact.

I've written about my late and wonderful dad, who suffered tragically and terribly with a mental illness he had no control over. But he was my dad and that's all that mattered. I'll always remember and always love him.

There is no plot or narrative to my story. It is heartfelt, confessional, hopefully funny and quirky, vividly illustrating life in late 1962 and the decades that followed. I had no book manual for life, there were no coaching manuals telling me how to behave. It was all off the cuff and very natural.

It is a story about observations, bite sized stories, cute little anecdotes, quaint reminiscences and wonderful childhood memories. I can remember them as if it were yesterday.

But metaphorically, I start my autobiographical voyage in my grandfather's barber shop in Upton Park. He was the one who cut the hair of those legendary World Cup winning heroes Bobby Moore, Geoff Hurst and Martin Peters. My grandfather was the one who announced quite emphatically to the rest of the world that West Ham had won the World Cup.

Now my grand-dad was the voice of authority and he knew what he was talking about. So here I am at the beginning of my personal journey. Right at the point where my grand-dad cheered and celebrated England's finest hour and I made my debut. I can never thank my grand-dad enough. I may have only been a fresh faced three year old with idealistic eyes but this is where it all started. Time to go back to that barber's shop in Upton Park and it's over to you Jack, my grand-dad.

Part 2: My grandfather –
Hammer through and through and an armchair fanatic.

This is a story that might make you chuckle with delight or move you to uproarious laughter. In fact if he were alive today, I'm sure my grandfather would shake my hand, smile knowingly and ooze with appreciation.

My grandfather was the gentleman from whom I inherited my enduring support of West Ham United. He was the man who introduced me to the wondrously fascinating game that is football. He was the man who sighed despairingly when the Hammers were beaten and would then just sit forlornly in his armchair until the rest of the classified football results were read out on World of Sport.

But, for my grandfather, the highlight on a Saturday afternoon was his weekly helping of the memorable Wrestling. Now Wrestling was the only sport that came from a draughty town hall in Northern England. It was the only sport that showed enormous men in leotards performing ridiculous routines in a dusty wrestling ring.

Of course it was preposterous nonsense and we all know that wrestling will always remain the province of showbiz and the old fashioned fairground booth. Still my grandfather – rest his soul– embraced the whole spectacle with all the warmth of an old friend.

Wrestling was complete escapism for my dear grandfather, a joyous distraction from the week's toil and drudgery. To the outsider, of course, wrestling might have seemed a frothy and frivolous past- time but to my grandfather, it was the most satisfying and exhilarating of any TV sporting programme in the world.

My grandfather, for as long as I can remember, was an industrious barber who took inordinate pleasure in cutting hair and styling it to the point of perfection. For years, he worked tirelessly and diligently in a barber's shop called Kelly's in Upton Park.

Without any shadow of a doubt though, I'll always treasure some of the funnier stories about my grandfather. My mum, who, like her dad, was fluent in Yiddish, would revel in the telling and re- telling of some magical moments.

There was the occasion when, after the final whistle had gone in the 1966 World Cup Final, my grand-dad, accompanied by his triumphant colleagues, raced out of the shop and happily proclaimed that West Ham had won the World Cup. His colleagues voices could be heard the length of the Barking Road. The mood of celebration and jubilation was unashamedly obvious.

Now here's another misty eyed recollection from my grand-dad's repertoire of stories. I've always craved a claim to fame. My grand-dad, wait for it, cut the hair of the fabled 1966 World Cup trio of Bobby Moore, Geoff Hurst and Martin Peters. No, I hear you cry sceptically not Moore, Hurst and Peters. Yes, those immensely talented West Ham players who jigged and skipped around the old Wembley Stadium with the World Cup firmly in their hands.

The point is though, my grand-dad cut the golden locks of three of England's finest footballers, family men with wives and children. Every time the Hammers graced us with their presence on a Saturday afternoon, my grand-dad would produce his trusty scissors, shaving brush and comb.

To this day, my mum has in her possession the very scissors, comb and shaving brush that my grand-dad used. Now I know my mum attaches a great deal of sentimental value to this priceless keepsake and will always cherish it. But he was a proud man and for most of his life my grand-dad cut, styled and crimped the hair of all and sundry.

He did have one customer who regularly had his hair cut in their Gants Hill home but the image of three of English football's finest asking my grandfather for a haircut is one to savour. Jack, for that was my grand-dad's name, I'll have a short back and sides please.

On the subject of my grandfather, here's another tale. My parents once persuaded my grandparents to join me, my brother and my mum and dad to go on holiday. I think they were reluctant to commit themselves but they eventually succumbed to the charms of the Costa Blanca with its sinuous flamenco dancers, paella for tea and beachside restaurants that were still open for business at midnight.

Anyway, I'll never forget the way he would gently ease his way into the hotel swimming pool and just abandon himself to rest and relaxation. Here was a man who had endured all of the horrors and abominations of the Second World War splashing around almost ecstatically, content in the knowledge that he and my lovely grand-ma were having the time of our lives.

Nothing would give my grand-dad more pleasure than to see his grandchildren at play, enjoying the heat of the Spanish sunshine. The Seventies saw the package holiday boom to Spain at its peak. And my grandparents were in their element. Never in their wildest dreams did they ever think that one day they would find themselves rubbing shoulders with Spanish restaurant waiters. It was their holiday of a lifetime.

Part 3:
Memories from my childhood.

It wasn't funny at the time but, on reflection, I can now acknowledge that this little cameo was absolutely hilarious.

My mum, eagerly expecting her second child, was rushed into hospital for that inimitable day of birth. Soon, the auspicious day arrived and my wonderful brother came into the world. Springtime, in all its pristine beauty, had well and truly arrived. The crocuses, bluebells and tulips were in full bloom and my brother was born on the 21st March 1969, the year Neil Armstrong took those first steps on the Moon.

On arrival back at home, my dad, who had just arrived home from work, walked up to the house bursting with sheer elation. At that moment, the embarrassing discovery was plain for all to see. My parents had locked themselves out and pandemonium broke out.

Trouser pockets were frantically searched, coats thoroughly searched but, frustratingly to no avail. On reflection, this incident was a source of enormous amusement but when I think back to that day, I'm not sure how we managed to get back into the house. Still it remains one of my favourite childhood memories.

What happened next will live in my memory bank for many a decade. My mum, dad and I knocked on the door of our neighbours, who were a very kindly, elderly couple. Now it has to be said that they were the most charming neighbours you could wish for. How they loved pottering about in their immaculate, well-manicured garden.

On this occasion, they were charm personified. We walked through their kitchen and out into their showroom garden. At the time, we had this very strong wooden fence which seemed to withstand everything. We then proceeded to climb over the fence, wedged open the kitchen window and squeezed our way into the house.

With the benefit of hindsight, I can now see the funny side of that day but I'm sure my parents and I with the new baby must have thought differently. Why did they leave the house without a key and how did we smuggle our way through a kitchen window? To this day, I've no idea how we managed it but the operation proved a successful one. The jokes and laughs around the dinner table seemed to reverberate around the neighbourhood.

I can't remember how old I was – probably six or seven – but I can distinctly remember a summer's day during the 1960s. Yours truly was blissfully playing in my mum and dad's back-garden when my mum had a brainwave.

For ages, my mum had set her heart on an apple tree for our garden. For years she had lovingly watered and pruned the most stunning row of roses you're ever likely to see. But now she was determined to have a small apple tree outside the kitchen. I don't think my mum was ever heavily into horticulture but she did like her roses and one which immediately springs to mind was the much cherished Blue Moon.

Anyway, the point is that one morning, my mum set out quite purposefully for the shops to get some seeds for her apple tree. My grand-ma had been invited around for tea and happily gave her hearty approval to the idea of an apple tree.

Eagerly digging for the right place, she scraped a hole in the ground and dropped the apple seed into the earth. How thrilled she was. Ah, but she hadn't bargained on a mischievous and rebellious son who was about to wreck her plans.

Yours truly, in a childish outburst of sheer naughtiness and petulance, decided to stand on the dirt patch before gleefully destroying the apple seed. I trampled on the patch of earth, kicked the seed away and in an unforgivable act of cruelty, my mum's wondrous vision of an apple tree had been sabotaged.

What followed was like something out of a silent movie or a Whitehall farce. My wonderful grand-ma and my mum launched into the most unforgettable chase around the garden. Suddenly, my grandma and mum had turned into Olympic athletes. They ran after me for what must have seemed like an eternity, before finally catching their little darling and delivering the appropriate punishment.

I'll always remember my childhood. During the school summer holidays, my school friend and I would spend countless hours doing our utmost to catch tadpoles in what can best be described as a narrow stream. From the earliest hour, we would take our jam jars and patiently wait for that golden moment when both newts and tadpoles would suddenly wriggle their way into the jar.

I can also recall the school summer holidays for another unforgettable reason. It was the hottest summer of 1976 and Britain resounded to the music phenomenon that was Philadelphia soul. We strutted our funky, flamboyant stuff until the small hours of the morning.

But to those with fond recollections of that summer of 76, the enduring memory will always be the glorious weather. From late April until the August Bank Holiday, Britain basked in the most remarkable heat wave since the late 1940s.

Day after day, the mercury would suddenly rise on our thermometer in quite the most delightful fashion. It was almost as though somebody had hung out a warm blanket for the best part of four months. The skies were a flawless blue, the sunshine had switched on its most radiant smile and Britain revelled in almost 100 degrees of heat. It was undoubtedly one of the warmest and hottest summers that I can remember.

Needless to say, my local park and countless others across the country spent most of that summer bathing in the local lido. Now, sadly, lidos are no longer the fashionable attractions that they used to be. But for me, outdoor swimming was the only activity that mattered and I must have swum every conceivable stroke until deep into the late afternoon.

But yours truly was determined to make the most of this balmy, beautiful heat. At roughly 11.00 in the morning, I would grab hold of some swimming trunks, wrap a towel around the trunks and throw myself enthusiastically into the pool. By now, the pool itself was a sea of bodies. Children were laughing and screaming with uninhibited joy while parents looked on with paternal and maternal pride.

When I look back now, I'm sure ours was the most fortunate and privileged generation. The 70s was one continuous sequence of hope, opportunity and Sunday afternoons at Lyons Corner House in Marble Arch, a gastronomic London landmark to which many a Jewish family would regularly flock to.

Now Lyons Corner House was the one restaurant that had class and panache written all over it. I think I'd be right in saying that Lyons Corner House was one of our finest and most well-appointed eateries. Lyons Corner House catered for those who just loved their food and plenty of it. It was glamorous and a magnet for the stars.

It was a restaurant for the elite and discerning, for those with a bob or two in their pocket and a voracious appetite. I'd go so far as to say that Dukes, Duchesses, Earls and Lords would eat at Lyons Corner House. You can imagine the celebrities of the day popping in for a snack at lunchtime.

It had a certain style and cachet about it that very few restaurants could boast at the time. In fact I'm surprised they didn't ask for your passport before entering!

Anyway, the point is the Lyons Corner House was my childhood on a Sunday afternoon. Both my parents and I would open the doors, gently stroll over to the reception area and join the queue.

Now let me tell you that this queue was utterly unlike any queue you're ever likely to see. It was the longest queue in recorded history. In fact, I'm sure we ought to have brought a tape measure with us just to find out if it was. The Guinness Book of Records would have been completely intrigued.

Even now, I can remember those splendid lights hanging majestically from the ceiling. As we inched along the passageway, these bright lights would shine theatrically from on high. There was a glorious sense of anticipation as my parents and their son would gradually move along to the food section.

Then we would arrive at the Lyons Corner House banqueting suite, replete with fabulous sweet cakes and any meal of your choosing. My mum, a noted epicurean, would grab her favourite dessert, a rumbaba, and move our trays along the brightly lit counter.

Now I kid you not, Lyons Corner House was, to a child's eye, a veritable food palace. The chairs and tables reminded you of some Victorian dining room. But I'll never forget how immaculate and tidy everything looked. Chairs were neatly tucked under the table, cutlery and crockery just sparkled and the waitresses were called Nippies.

The Nippies of course were those busy, hard-working ladies who seemed to spend most of their working day running delightfully in and out of the kitchen. From morning to early evening, they would perform miracles of balance and dexterity. With both hands, they would pick up huge piles of wobbling plates and then smile politely.

For me this was the age of neatness, order and utter formality. Everything about Lyons Corner House smacked of class and an almost Victorian grandeur. There was about the restaurant a tangible sense of regal elegance. Everything was polished, correct and proper. I'm sure the Lyons Corner House took hygiene and cleanliness to another level.

Even now, I can remember being ushered into this high class West End eatery like a member of royalty or the aristocracy. At the reception area, my parents handed their coats over to a member of staff and we would casually stroll over to the long and winding queue.

We are often told that the Sixties were all about outlandish fashions and memorably groovy music but I'd like to think of it as a gentle age of childhood innocence. It was a time when neighbours would chat to you and milkmen would give you the cheeriest wave.

I must have spent more or less every day of my school summer holidays on my wonderful lime coloured bike, hurtling around the back roads with boyish enthusiasm. My memory may not be as good as it used to be but very few people were murdered, threatened or seriously hurt.

Perhaps I may be looking at life through rose tinted glasses but the Sixties seemed to have its own dress code, a very distinctive personality, a sense of liberation from the pain and suffering of the Second World War.

My parents would think nothing of taking me to the local park and just giving me the freedom to run around and have fun. I can still see the playground with its two slides and the obligatory roundabout. The age of high tech gadgetry was still some two decades away but, although a very shy, reserved kid, I'm sure my childhood was idyllic.

We may not have had clever computers, or iPads that could play any game in the world but we still had Sunday Night at the London Palladium. We had two telly channels, the Light Programme on the radio, Charlie Chester on Radio 2 followed by the incomparable Sunday evening shipping forecast.

As a kid, I was naturally inundated with all the familiar toys and games of the time. There was Etch a Sketch, an enchanting gadget that was probably the nearest equivalent to today's iPad or Tablet.

I think the best description I can find for an Etch a Sketch is a small, drawing mechanism on which you could literally use the full extent of your artistic talents. I used to draw houses that turned into small communities and, in my childish imagination, people's faces resembling nobody in particular.

Then there was Lego and Meccano, two marvellous boxes of plastic, coloured bricks that built my boyhood Empire. If you were interested in architecture or engineering in later life, then Lego or Meccano was your initiation into that world.

But I don't think I'll ever forget the Hornby train set that my parents bought me for a very early birthday. I can still see myself sprawled out on my mum and dad's carpet, setting up long pieces of railway track and then just immersing myself in imaginary train journeys. I'm sure the whole of the living room looked like the early morning rush hour at Euston station: a huge amalgam of signal boxes and bustling commuters.

I'm sure we all look back on the birthdays of our youth with a wistful lump in the throat. There is a lot to be said for those special occasions throughout our life when time seems to fly and the seasons pass in a nostalgic haze.

I can still remember my mum and dad taking me out to the West End in my dad's grey Ford Cortina car and just strolling down Regent or Oxford Street without a care in the world.

Life is beautiful and sweet. It's a warm family gathering, a day out with friends by the seaside, glorying in the sight of nature, breathing in the air and admiring the scenery around us.

I'm sure I was never spoilt as a child and for this reason, my appreciation of life has been heightened. I was always content with my station in life and never demanded anything that my mum and dad couldn't afford.

I may have been a withdrawn, introverted child but that didn't stop me from enjoying my own company or playing with my classroom friends at school. I've a vivid recollection of those hilarious playground games. The boys would play their stereotypical football matches and the girls would indulge in one continuous sequence of skipping and tennis ball throwing.

Thinking back, we also had conkers shortly after returning from our summer holidays. Now there was an odd spectacle. Every September all of the school children would come back refreshed and reinvigorated from their summer break with brown conkers in their coat pockets.

Now this was a yearly ritual I could never quite understand at first. But gradually I began to see that there was indeed a point and purpose to it all. You would pick up as many of these conkers as you could find on the autumnal ground and just thrash the living daylights out of your friend's conker.

From what I can remember, the conker had to be thoroughly soaked in vinegar to be effective. Still, it was an enormously enjoyable pastime and many was the occasion when this conker attached to a piece of string was either chopped to pieces or simply got tangled up with your friend's.

The boy's football matches were invariably preceded by the team picking ceremony, a very male and masculine act that only the boys could do best. I'm sure that some of the boys had favourite friends and they would be the ones who were always picked before you. I'm sure there was a kind of pecking order, a hierarchy if you like. Brian always bought Frank sweets and therefore was always chosen first in playground football matches.

For the girls, there was the traditional game of Kiss Chase, hop scotch or comparing notes about the boys they fancied. It was a harmless, gentle and inoffensive time when playtimes seemed to go on forever and the bell only rang intermittently.

Some of the school teachers also occupy a snug place in my memory. There was Mrs Wilson, a lady of height and stature who everybody thought highly of. Mrs Wilson was a tall, commanding teacher who wore the most remarkable stiletto shoes you're every likely to see.

You always knew when Mrs Wilson was about by the military clip clop of her high heels. She, or so it seemed, would always march down the corridor with the most authoritative stride, cheerfully exchanging frivolous jokes with her pupils. She was simply the most charming of all primary teachers and taught me everything I know about English grammar and the joys of the English language.

Then of course there was the inimitable Mr Aston or Ken Aston as I would discover in later life. Mr. Aston was the most extraordinary headmaster any primary school child could ever have wished for. I will never forget Mr Aston and to this day his impact on my life and that of my family will never be erased from my mind.

Quite simply, Ken Aston was, apart from my late and wonderful dad, the loveliest, warmest gentleman it has ever been my privilege to know. Mr Aston was a tall, majestic and highly approachable man, a man of substance and honour. Ken Aston never had a bad word to say about anybody or anything. Mr Aston seemed to rise above any crisis with a commendable dignity.

At lunchtimes in particular, he would make his towering presence felt. In the assembly school hall, Mr Aston would set up what would become known as a thriving chess club. Now this chess club was one of the most popular of school diversions. I did try to master the finer points of chess but never progressed any further than pawn to queen four.

There was of course the outstanding chess player who seemed to beat every child he was faced with. I seem to remember though, yours truly once holding this chess champion to a draw. I should have beaten him of course but we still shook hands with each other at the end of the game. How gracious of me.

Then of course there was the school assembly before the beginning of the lessons. For as long as I live, school assemblies were always beautifully observed. Every day, the pupils would dutifully stand to attention in neat lines. We would all wait for our music teacher to tinkle the ivories on her piano and Jerusalem would ring out from a hundred angelic voices.

That yellowing hymn sheet had a religious resonance for all of us and I can still see those wonderfully evocative words on the sheet. For the Jewish children, a special Jewish room was created and I did finish off school work in there from time to time. Somehow, adolescence and teenage years seemed like another country. Life would become, for me, a wondrous discovery, rather like a child opening up their birthday presents.

Before school, I used to pop into a family further along the road from my mum and dad. Here I would become friendly with their son and I can still see him tucking into his breakfast and packing his school satchel with all the relevant books, rulers, pens and pencils.

I think the best days at primary school were spent on our playing fields next to the school. Here we passed many a noisy playtime, playing without inhibition and full of the joys of the season. There were the endless games of football, cricket and for those in the infants school, a large sand-pit.

10

But the big day for most of my classmates was quite definitely Sports Day on the playing fields. Now Sports Day was rather like the most entertaining act at a comedy club. It was the signature event of the year, a magnificent tour de force of a day when everything seemed to go right.

You must recall your Sports Day. It was a day when eight or nine year olds would climb into a sack, hold an egg and spoon or just abandon themselves to outrageous silliness. It was when your doting mum and dad would shout at you incessantly, "Come on Joe". If you don't win the egg and spoon race, you can go to your room without dinner.

I seem to remember there were also athletic events such as the 1500 metres for the nine year olds and the 100 metre sprint. I think they added the shot put and javelin when I reached my secondary school.

In my mind's eye, I can still see the buildings around our playing fields. At the far end, there was a huge building that looked like some ancient factory. When I got to secondary school, I soon became acquainted with the inside of the building. This was the metalwork and woodwork block, a vast monolithic structure with no character. Even the windows looked as though they'd seen better days.

But these childhood, misty eyed recollections put the present day into some perspective. You look back to the old days and simply wallow in what might seem to be acres of nostalgia. It was a time when my whole young world was filled with the simple pleasures of life.

There was the jolly, tinkling sound of Rossi's ice cream van as it drove its way gently into our road. This was the cue for hundreds of excited children and considerate parents with purses by the ready. It was a scene that was constantly repeated every other day of the week. Mum would stride out of the house, reprimand little Johnny for running too quickly and then lovingly oblige her offspring with a 99 ice cream, cone and flake.

Ice creams, funnily enough, remind me of our unforgettable Sunday excursions to Westcliff, which is Southend's next door neighbour. Every so often, my parents and grandparents would jump onto a train at Barking station for one of our regular seaside pilgrimages.

My lovely grandparents (my mum's parents) would take a shopping bag that was literally groaning with hundreds of egg and cucumber sandwiches. This is a complete exaggeration of course but I'd like to think that there were. My grandparents loved their food and as soon as we settled on the Westcliff sea front, my grand-ma would dip into her bag, plucking out several bags of egg and cucumber sandwiches for eager consumption.

We would all then walk slowly back to the famous Rossi's restaurant, which to this day remains a Westcliff favourite. In fact, it's part of the Westcliff landscape. After a day of intensive sun bathing in the deckchairs, we would all have tea at Rossi's. For some reason, I would always plump for a bag of Ice Gems, a delectable mixture of tiny flavoured bite sized biscuits.

Which brings me to the present day. How very fortunate I am to have a wonderfully loving and supportive wife, and two beautiful children. My family are my rock and inspiration, a driving force behind everything I do.

I've now reached 50 and when I think back to those sun drenched, summer days, it is with a fond glance over the shoulder. I'm a very humble, unassuming man with no grandiose ambitions and dreams. Life is for the living, the here and now, taking every day as it comes and just luxuriating in the glow of the moment.

All I want now is to see our wonderful children happy and healthy. They've already given both my wife and I so much to be proud of. I've always thought of myself as an affectionate and caring husband, a man who wants to give as much emotional support and love to his gorgeous family.

May I now go back to my grandfather and another classic childhood anecdote? This story goes back to the hazy, crazy days of the 1970s. Now my grandparents had never set foot outside England and holidays were something that only the wealthy could afford. True they did accompany my parents and I to places such as Westcliff by the sea and a hotel in Kent called Windsor Hall, if memory serves me correctly.

But a holiday abroad for my parents came as a complete and unexpected surprise. Anyway the news was broken to my grandparents that they were about to join my parents and I on the trip of a lifetime.

Spain had just become the new tourist destination for English holidaymakers. It would be the start of what would become the packaged holiday boom, a purple period for the tourist industry.

Anyway, the holiday was organised, the flight paid for and my grandparents were about to embark on a holiday of Spanish siestas, natty sombreros, and long days by the swimming pool. This was truly a revelation for my grand-pa and grand-ma for whom this was indeed paradise.

What you have to remember is that both of my grandparents had endured the full horrors of the Second World War. I'm sure they must have thought that Spain was the fulfilment of every dream they'd ever had. Now they too would be members of the Costa Blanca set.

One day though will always remain with me for as long as I live. My grand-pa, dad and I were innocently relaxing at the shallow end of the swimming pool when the funniest of all incidents suddenly and quite literally erupted.

Mid- way through the afternoon, with the sun dipping over the hotel roof, my grand-pa, dad and I took ourselves off to the pool for a bracing dip. Then, out of the blue, my grand-pa let out the loudest sneeze you've ever heard. I kid you not this was the heartiest sneeze in the history of Western civilisation.

Now I've no idea what the rest of the holidaymakers must have thought but my dad and I roared with laughter. What made this occurrence so riotously amusing was the way in which my grand-pa sneezed. You or I would have hygienically put our hands over our face. Not my dear grand-pa. He quite unashamedly sprayed everybody with the contents of his nose. I'll leave the rest to your imagination.

Part 4:
Anyway, let me return to some more childhood reminiscences.

Childhood, for me, was a time of exploration, curiosity and a sense of eternal optimism. I had no idea what the future would hold but I knew that adolescence was just around the corner. The teenage years were a dot on the horizon, an age of opportunity and endlessly fascinating school days. It was five years of study, academia and contemplation. A time for learning and a good education.

I'll always remember the huge brown brick building in the primary school playground. The story is that my secondary school premises shared their playground with my primary school.

So inside the building, there was housed the headmaster's office, the secretary and all the administration staff. As you entered this building, you were reminded of all the images and memories that were somehow the essence of your youth.

In one passageway, there was a drinks' machine and the boys' shower-room, a place of steam and teenage testosterone. Most of the boys would quickly shower after a gruelling PE session, urgently throw on their clothes and then converge on the drinks' machine.

I was always a hot chocolate boy, that lovely concoction of smooth drinking chocolate and hot water. I think a cup of tea, coffee or chocolate would set us back the princely sum of roughly 10p or 20p. But I do believe it was the most refreshing drink of all.

In the school hall, the boys would gradually assemble for the morning assembly and a marvellously humorous headmaster, who I'm sure was an after dinner raconteur. He would tell some of the most heart-warming stories and jokes ever told. Before him, we had another headmaster who always wore a bow tie and adored Jazz music.

Then there was our deputy headmaster, a strict and upright man who always barked out orders to ill-disciplined boys. He would sternly chastise you if you ran down one of the corridors or had forgotten to wear your tie and jacket. He used to occupy an office in the hall where he would busily work away, only emerging with a badminton racket for a game of shuttlecock. Most significantly, I can always recall him wearing a brown jacket with three buttons.

Then there was that incredible afternoon when everything quite literally blew all of the pupils away. How we managed to keep a straight face I'll never know but I'm sure there was much hilarity and merriment.

One afternoon, we had chemistry in the science lab. Nothing out of the ordinary you might think. But this was to be an afternoon never to be forgotten. It was one of those golden days when everybody in our class simply laughed out loud for the best part of a delirious half an hour.

When our regular chemistry teacher cried off sick, our maths teacher was summoned to the breach as a replacement. Mid-way through a late afternoon our maths teacher set up, an elaborate experiment that will live on in my mind. Firstly, a screen was placed around a set of Bunsen burners and test tubes were mixed with what seemed to be the appropriate chemicals.

Little did we boys know what was to follow. Suddenly after much mixing and matching of chemicals there was a huge explosion and bang. A couple of seconds later, all the boys instinctively looked up to the ceiling and gazed up in stunned amazement. There was a big black mark on the ceiling and what can only be described as smoke everywhere. How we laughed and chuckled. I think sodium chloride got slightly confused with nitric acid. Suffice it to say, the boys were in hysterics.

Now here's a memory that still induces a private giggle. Behind the car park at my now secondary and primary school, there was a large hut that stretched the length of the car park. This is what became known as the dinner hut, a lunchtime retreat that was rather like a food palace. Hot meals were served to ravenous groups of boys and appetites were more than satisfied.

The food of course had to be seen to believed, a delightful selection of mashed potato and cholesterol. I have to say my wife's cooking is far tastier but I think you get my drift. Frustratingly, I always seemed to find myself on one of the last tables for food. We would all converge on the first table as if our life depended on it, rushing into the hut and then frantically finding the best seat in the hut.

I'll always remember one of the puddings. On some Fridays, we were invariably served honey cake with apple strudel. This was undoubtedly one of the most delicious sweets ever to enter my mouth while at school. Most of the puddings used to be accompanied with custard and I have to say they were simply a culinary masterpiece.

I may have been a solitary and introverted teenager but I did like to take part in the boys' games of football. As I remember it, we all had our own set of friends and nobody really felt excluded. You know what it's like. Some kids will become your best friend while others will simply ignore you.

I don't think I ever felt any real sense of alienation because there were kids at my secondary school who I could easily get on with. Some of the kids were Jewish and I did have an affinity with them. I think it must have been the lokshen pudding and chicken soup we were occasionally plied with. Come to think of it though, they were never on the menu. But we did enjoy each other's company immensely and for that I'll always be grateful.

Another very striking recollection from Gearies Secondary School was what was known as the house teams. At the beginning of a new school term, all of the boys were placed in different teams. Everything was very structured and regimented at my secondary school and this was the school's way of identifying you.

All of the house teams were royal palaces and yours truly was in the yellow team of Windsor. There was also the blue of Buckingham, the red of Balmoral and the green of Sandringham. I've always been a monarchist and to have a royal palace as your school house still resonates with me. I have to say I felt quite honoured.

There are one or two comments about the school which I'd like to make. I will never know for instance why certain subjects were forced upon you. It was as if there was a conspiracy against you and these were compulsory lessons. Whether you liked them or not.

For instance, in my first year at secondary school we had to do Drama and Music. Now for reasons beyond me, Drama and Music were part of the school curriculum. For those boys who wanted to be eminent actors or melodious musicians these were ideal classes.

But I'm sorry, I've never wanted to tread the boards at the National nor have I ever harboured any ambition to be part of a famous orchestra. I'm no critic of the education system in this country but Drama and Music were by far my worst school subjects at school. In fact they were a complete waste of time.

I know you should look back on your school days as some of the happiest of your life but the utter futility of Drama and Music does leave you with a bitter taste in your mouth. For one Drama lesson, we had to jump about in the dark. This continued for what seemed like an age and to this day I don't think I'll ever know why. Suffice it to say I felt like a complete fool.

Then there was Music, a stimulating experience you might think. But once again, I found it be both boring and incomprehensible. For some lessons, you were expected to write perfectly formed musical notes in your exercise books. My book was one sequence of crotchets and quavers, those cute little symbols that make up the famous classical pieces.

The other academic nightmares were Woodwork and Metalwork, two of the most ghastly creations on the school syllabus. Naturally, if you wanted to be a carpenter or a metal sheet worker, this would have been exactly what you were looking for. But for me, Metal and Woodwork represented everything that was bad about school. It took me the whole year to produce a miniature sized book case and even longer to fashion a shoe horn in Metalwork. Both subjects seemed to me to be pointless.

For me though, English and French were some of the most satisfying subjects in the five years I spent at Gearies. I loved English because it gave me the opportunity to use the full range of my burgeoning vocabulary. English, of course, was the language of Charles Dickens, Thomas Hardy and William Shakespeare. I could never understand or even begin to fathom Shakespeare but Hardy and Dickens gave me a solid grammatical foundation.

I'm sure we read The Lord of the Flies and Shakespeare's Macbeth for our CSE literature exam but I can honestly say that neither of the books really held my attention. Still, I did look forward to English with much anticipation and having read most of Hardy and Dickens, I have to admit that both authors have left me with a warm glow of achievement.

French had to be the only subject that none of my school mates liked. I think they must have had the misleading image of beret wearing Frenchman carrying bags of onions on their backs. Or the Eiffel Tower and the Parisian boulevards. Still I always enjoyed French and found the subject a constant source of fascination.

For French, we had a teacher by the name of Mr. Winters. Nothing unusual about that you might say. But Mr Winters was by far the most unique teacher at Gearies. With his greying hair and thick beard, Mr Winters had an unconventional approach to teaching. There will never be another like him.

During the lesson, he would attach great emphasis to French verbs and tenses. He would then pick out unsuspecting boys in our class for a full rendition of je suis, tu es, il est, nous sommes, vous etes and ils sont. The bemused lad would painstakingly repeat the same verbs and tenses.

But Mr Winters was different you see. Come lunchtime, he would have no hesitation in digging out his reel to reel tape recorder. I kid you not when I say that this reel to reel tape recorder was something nobody had ever seen. True cassette recorders were still in fashion but this machine was like nothing I'd ever set eyes on.

The whole point of the reel to reel tape recorder would become abundantly clear. Mr Winters was an avid opera fan, a man of high culture, a man who believed that Tosca was the greatest contribution to the world of classical singing. I have no reason to think that there was anything strange or odd about Mr Winters behaviour but personally speaking, listening to lunchtime opera never appealed to my teenage ears. As they say opera, for me, was an acquired taste.

Sport was seasonal and enormous fun. I can't remember whether it was my primary or secondary school but I do recall those exciting and frenetic games of rounders. Rounders was the kind of game anybody could take part in. I can still see it now. Children with wooden rounders bats, anxiously waiting their turn before cracking the ball as far as they could. Occasionally, there were hilarious collisions in the field as two kids crashed into each other apparently going for the same ball.

They often say that school is the ultimate preparation for life in the big world of employment. School, they told us, would give us the building blocks for a glittering career in finance, commerce or an apprenticeship in the building trade. We too could make the seamless transition to engineering, catering, sport or the rarefied world of management or recruitment.

It all sounded so impressive and appealing but I would always retain my love of the English language. English was the language of poetry, rhythm, beauty and expression. It was the language that would always be your constant companion, the most loyal of friends, while those around me lost their heads in a crisis.

For many years, I would devour books with the hungriest relish. Literature would leave its permanent legacy on my mind. It was the subject that would accompany me throughout the Eighties, neither judging nor criticising, posing or posturing. English literature would enlighten, educate and enthral me in all its pleasurable splendour.

When I think back to those formative years of my childhood, I can clearly see just how happy, carefree and precious those days were. I don't think we can ever begin to appreciate just how lucky and privileged we were as kids. Sadly our parents had to endure the sheer grotesque experience that was the Second World War. They were the people who witnessed the appalling tragedy. They were privy to the screaming bombs, the nights in the underground, air- raid sirens that never seemed to stop, and death and destruction on the most appalling scale.

I was born 17 years after the Second World War, the loss of millions of lives still raw in our parents' minds. But childhood for me was idyllic. I could still run out into my parents' garden and indulge myself in fantasy worlds. I can remember thrillingly kicking footballs against pebble dashed walls, chucking countless tennis balls against the wall with rapture in my heart.

For some reason, the whole image of the garden is beginning to appear in my mind rather like some splendid fairy tale. I can still see the rather large and imposing shed at the bottom of my parents' garden. For years, it stood there defiantly and stoutly as if categorically refusing to succumb to its age. I think it must have remained rooted to that one spot for years and years. My parents always kept the usual garden furniture in there. There was the trusty lawn mower, which my dad would lovingly heave about, huge forks, shears for the cutting of my mum's roses and a countless variety of chairs for sunbathing.

I'll never forget one end of my parent's garden. It was indescribably higgledy piggledly and totally intriguing. At the very far end there was what could only be described as a miniature forest. Here was the most magnificent profusion of bushes, green leaves and tree branches. It was the most chaotic tangle of flora and fauna that you're ever likely to come across.

But for me, this fabulous piece of horticulture was an adventure like no other. Through the dense foliage, I somehow managed to find a clearing or pathway. Surrounded by hundreds of leaves and branches, I discovered steps which led to nowhere in particular. Still it did represent another world for me, a world where wondrous nature met a childish imagination.

There was also the incinerator. Now the incinerator for me just looked like the most incredible mess. I could never figure out why my parents allowed it to just rot there for year after year but rot it did. How can I describe it? Well what we had was a rusting, decomposing heap of mud and what appeared to be burnt cinders.

Then there was the rather incongruous tree stump. It's hard to describe but this tree stump was like nothing you've ever seen. This was a thick tree stump which looked as if it had been cut down to size and just neglected. It reminded me of some proud wooden statue or the painstaking work of some dedicated tree surgeon.

At one point during the Seventies, my mum had another brilliant idea. One morning, she decided to potter down to a garden centre. My mum, ever the forward thinking parent, decided that she wanted a hammock for the garden. So after careful assembly a hammock materialised before us.

This extraordinary piece of garden furniture was quite the most exotic looking structure designed for both complete comfort and luxury. For hours on end, we would all swing on this most comfortable padded seat oblivious to the outside world.

Then there was our lovely neighbour's fence. On either side of my parents, we had two of the loveliest neighbours in the world. They were both elderly and both possessed of a unique generosity of spirit. Mr and Mrs Webb were the most approachable and obliging neighbours you could ever wish for.

Mr and Mrs Webb would spend interminable amounts of time in their garden. Now Mr and Mrs Webb loved their garden with an almost endearing affection. From morning to late evening they would mow their grass to the point of perfection. Beautiful red and white roses would gently sway in the breeze while magnolias and tulips nodded graciously in their direction. It was a garden that resembled Paradise.

Anyway, this fence seemed to have a mind of its own. For ages it would droop down into our garden in a kind of drunken stupor. I always felt deeply sorry for the fence because it would never buckle under the weight of its own decay. For years, it would rot and crumble away relentlessly and inexorably.

Then there were my golden days at my cheder classes, a place of religious calm and learned rabbis. Here, we were taught the finer rudiments of Hebrew and all of the most compelling tales of Jewish history. After digesting the Aleph Bet (Hebrew Alphabet) and its entire letters, we would embark on the great defining moment of a Jewish teenager's life-the Bar mitzvah.

Now my Bar mitzvah always reminds of me of my Jewish teacher. His name was Mr Kaiser and Mr Kaiser was by far the most erudite scholar I've ever been taught by. Every Tuesday and Thursday, I would bring in my classic tape recorder and we would form that innate bond that can only be established by pupil and teacher.

Mr Kaiser was one of those teachers who always looked as if they'd read a hundred Hebrew books after their supper. He would speak a combination of thick German and a smattering of English for good measure. For the whole year, we would sit attentively in his classroom, waiting patiently to be called up by Mr Kaiser. Every word, syllable and sentence was meticulously pronounced.

Now my Hebrew synagogue was one of the most magnificent buildings in the whole of Essex. Situated near a parade of shops, the religious classes were held every Sunday, Tuesday, Thursday, an oasis of Jewish academia and contemplation.

The one image though that will always stay with me though is the outside of the building. I have to tell you that the curtains were quite the shabbiest curtains I've ever seen. I don't know whether the synagogue had a laundry or washing machine on the premises but these curtains looked as though they hadn't been washed since 1948. They hung on the windows looking for all the world, grey and forlorn.

I could never be sure whether they were ever cleaned again but I do know that tourists from every corner of the world would flock in their hundreds and thousands to take pictures of this remarkable landmark. Surely it was a figment of my imagination. Personally, I think that these curtains were a throwback to another age. Or maybe they simply couldn't be bothered.

Still, it was a constant source of amusement and every time I passed the cheder building for the next year or two, I still felt slightly nostalgic and connected. The mystery though is that nobody appeared to care. If you bumped into one of the cheder teachers, they would give you a long and despairing look of indifference, totally unconcerned and, I suspect, bewildered.

Anyway, I always looked forward to Sunday. Sundays were somehow more relaxed and altogether more absorbing. On Sundays, we used to learn Hebrew songs and recite the Hebrew alphabet to Yankee Doodle Dandy. I often wondered how James Cagney would have reacted had he lived in this very agreeable Gants Hill retreat. Then again, Mr Cagney, my dad's all time hero, was always on top of the world.

At break time, all of the cheder pupils would suddenly descend on the sweet shop or the tuck shop as some of us would jokingly refer to it. I don't know why I can remember it so clearly but I can still see the whole row of shops next to the Hebrew classes. I think the brain and mind are quite the most formidable of our faculties. They can take you to places that you might have thought had long since vanished into the distance.

In a sense, they probably had but you can still see vague outlines, like contours on a map that never fade into oblivion. They are like those sweet photographs our parents used to take, still visible and prominent all those years later.

Before I move away from the point, there was a television store and a supermarket on the corner of the street. This supermarket stocked all the traditional wares but it did have one significant feature. On the top of the supermarket roof was a clock. Now I'm sure that this clock stopped working before the outbreak of the Second World War. I suspect that Churchill was the last person to check the time.

Moving away from this moment in time in my life, I now take you to my local park, Valentines Park. Now Valentines Park was by far the prettiest and most scenic of parks in Essex. I say this with the broadest of bias but somehow Valentines Park remains a symbolic reminder of my childhood.

There was the picturesque boating lake with its sleepy Weeping Willow, bathing languidly in the water. It was almost as if nature had found perfect contentment. I'm not sure whether I ever ventured out onto the boating lake but there was something about it that reminded me of a Constable painting. Truly this was a rural idyll.

Next to the boating lake, there were more nods to the Essex countryside. There was what can only be described as a wishing well. Now I don't think anybody will ever know how many coins were at the bottom of the well but a top City financier must have been employed to find out.

Then there was the Valentines Park cricket ground, a picture postcard in the middle of Essex and home to Essex cricket club. Valentines Park was undoubtedly one of the loveliest and most ravishing parks in the whole of England. I suppose I would say that having lived there for over 45 years.

Whenever I think about the cricket ground, I'm always reminded of something the great cricket writer John Arlott once said. Valentines Park, Arlott said, was one of his favourite cricket grounds and very few would argue the point. The ground, I think, has an almost poetic beauty and serene stillness that only a cricket ground seems to have.

As you move away from the cricket ground, you find the most exquisite of bowling greens. The bowling green is more or less next to the cricket ground and has been for many a decade. There, you find England in all its splendour and finery. The green looks like the most decorative piece of embroidery. It is almost as if a groundsman had spent hours, weeks and months, delicately stitching together every blade of grass.

I can remember one summer when Essex were playing at Valentines Park. In the first or second week of June, Essex play a whole week at Valentines. To this day, I can still see myself peering through the hedges and the immaculate bowling green. Essex had a fast bowler called John Lever who became a legend at the club and I gazed almost admiringly at the slanting Lever run up to the wicket.

Essex had a good side in those days and boasted a huge galaxy of star names. There was Graham Gooch, all bushy moustache and buccaneering batsman. Gooch's bat was rather like a magic wand and he once scored over 333 runs, I believe, against India. Gooch was a cavalier rather than a roundhead and English cricket will always be indebted to him. Gooch would throw the bat at anything loose or short and when he came out to bat at Lord's, the supporters knew exactly what to expect. It was reckless abandon all the way.

There was another batsman who would simply adorn many an Essex performance. Ken McEwen was the boldest and most dashing of Australian batsmen. McEwen was a kind, obliging man who would do everything he possibly could for the club. He was an exemplary opening bat who would score centuries for fun. Essex cricket would always have a soft spot for their courageous Australian hero.

Then there was that permanently reliable and loyal of cricketers by the name of Keith Fletcher, a man who embraced life and one of its authentic organisers. I think Fletcher must have been responsible for some of the royal garden parties. But the fact remains that Keith Fletcher was one of the finest of Essex captains. Fletcher was the leader of the pack, a spontaneous joker and commander in chief.

I mustn't forget Ray East, an Essex spinner, who immediately won the hearts of Essex with his easy going and breezy nature. East was one of those cheerful characters who had Essex blood running through his veins and arteries.

On the subject of cricket, I thought I'd give you another illuminating childhood account. This one takes me back to my school summer holidays. How we longed for those seven weeks of unmitigated fun, enjoyment and recreation.

I'm sure I must have spent every morning during the holiday transfixed to the TV rather like a train spotter at Paddington. But the main incentive for getting up in the morning was the classic BBC Test card. Now the Test Card was rather like one of those daily news bulletins that the Beeb were internationally renowned for.

Shortly after breakfast, the BBC would roll out one of their proudest creations. The Test Card, I believe, defies any rational explanation. It somehow belongs in a category of its own. To this day, I have no idea how it came into existence and why it was there. What I do know is that it occupied that strangely uneventful period before the Test Match cricket.

For no particular reason, a little girl with a cheesy smile would suddenly appear on the screen. Nothing unusual in that I hear you cry. But this girl with the cheesy smile was unlike any girl you were ever likely to see. You see this girl was accompanied by perhaps the weirdest looking puppet in the world. I think only the BBC could tell you why but both the puppet and little girl seemed to form the most bizarre double act.

I'm sure this was the BBC's surrealist and experimental period. Well this was the Sixties and Britain seemed to be a heady cocktail of sheer indulgence. But the story of the girl and the weird puppet will remain a mystery. I don't suppose I'll ever know how a girl and a puppet came to be playing a game of noughts and crosses. Not any ordinary game of noughts and crosses but a game on a blackboard. I always try to reassure myself that the game of noughts and crosses did produce a winner. Then, I think they both retired to the BBC bar for a couple of swift brandies. I think the puppet got a full time job as a Blue Peter presenter and the little girl is now a high flier in marketing. Or even as one of the regular contributors on Radio 4's Woman's Hour. But this is pure guesswork and sheer presumption. I'm sure they're both very creative and, above all, happy, which is all that matters.

Throughout my childhood, there were always train journeys, excursions that would take us to the back of beyond. These were the kind of journeys that stick vividly in the mind for posterity. They were the youthful pilgrimages that flicker happily in my subconscious because they were part of the very fabric of my early life. Some people recall the toys and games of their youth but I cherish the train journeys.

For instance, there was the Sunday trip to see my grand-ma, my dad's mum. Every so often, we would take ourselves off to Gants Hill station for intermittent travels to see my grand-ma. Now my grand-ma was quite the most amazing woman. In fact, I'd say she was a phenomenon. In the entire London suburb of Shepherds Bush, there was simply nobody like my grand-ma Dora.

I'm sure that Dora was quite the most strong- willed, resilient and indestructible of women. My grand-ma Dora was of Russian stock and had the most indomitable spirit which sustained her for roughly 90 years. We were never quite sure how old she was because her birth certificate was lost during the Second World War. But what I do know is that despite breaking almost every bone in her body, she lived to a ripe old age.

While I was growing up Dora was a very thin, frail and elderly. She had, from what I can remember, this very wiry, greying hair and although undaunted by any setback, always looked very vulnerable. To my childish eye, walking and general mobility always seemed to present a problem for her.

I'll never forget her visits to our house in Ilford. What you have to remember is here was an 80 year old woman who could barely stroll, let alone walk. To this day, it is one of my fondest of recollections. Somehow, it's just indelibly imprinted in my grey matter.

Shortly before lunchtime, my lovely dad – bless him- would ask me whether I'd like to go down to the local bus stop to pick up my grand-ma. Here was an 80- year- old lady who had just travelled from one end of West London to the other side of East London, a truly astounding feat of stamina and endurance. How she managed it beggars belief.

But Dora was one of life's fighters, a woman who survived numerous hip replacements, fires in her Shepherds Bush flat and goodness knows what else. Even now, I can see my dad and I slowly walking down our road with a woman who refused to accept that anything was impossible.

With her walking stick in one hand, she gently strolled her way back to our house. It may have taken us quite a while to do this but I think my grand-ma must have enjoyed every single moment of this journey of all journeys. I have to tell you that grandparents are quite the most extraordinary of people.

Anyway, trips to the mighty and impregnable grand-ma Dora were trips into wonderland. We would get onto the Central Line train at Gants Hill on a Sunday morning and wend our way to the lush green pastures of Shepherds Bush.

Now I'm not sure why but the whole venture seemed to be one long and continuous revelation. In fact there were times when I genuinely thought our train would never reach Shepherds Bush. From Gants Hill, we plunged into the mysterious world of tunnels and more tunnels. These were the longest and darkest tunnels you could imagine and they just seemed to go on forever.

Then you would suddenly arrive at platforms like Redbridge, Wanstead and Leytonstone stations with their own distinctive personality. The train itself would creak and clatter its way from one station to the next. I don't know why but the train seemed to have its own rhythm and narrative, rattling, wheezing, whining and groaning to its inevitable destination. It seemed to be conveying some kind of message to my parents and I. Or perhaps it was simply expressing its emotions.

To this day, waiting for the train at Gants Hill was rather like listening to an orchestra tuning up. Deep in the tunnel, all you could hear was a faint whistling sound and the kind of weird noises you normally hear in the Chamber of Horrors. They were short, sharp bursts but they were, it has to be said, haunting.

The train then rumbled and thundered its way into Gants Hill station. Now for some reason, I can still see the Nestle chocolate bar machine on the platform wall. In those days, you could buy any bar of chocolate for a couple of shillings or so. These machines were almost permanent fixtures on Tube platforms.

Anyway, onto the grey train we would go and so the excitement would begin. I would stare at the Tube map with a mixture of sheer wonderment in my eyes and increasing admiration. So this was the famous London Underground map with its squiggly lines and splendid sounding stations.

I don't know why but Wanstead station used to have the most fragrant smell on the whole of the Tube network. I can only describe the smell as that of smoky diesel and whenever the train pulled into the station, it was rather like sniffing the sweetest perfume for the first time.

Then there was the arrival at, I think, either Leyton or Leytonstone. For some reason, London Underground had decided, in its infinite wisdom, to stop the train at one of these stations for a 20 minute tea break. For what seemed an eternity, this grey wonder of engineering would grind to a halt. Some believe that one of those grey trains is still at Leytonstone and the train driver is half way through War and Peace.

Liverpool Street was always the station where huge crowds of people would either get onto the train or disembark. Needless to say, it always seemed one of the more popular and populous of stations. Liverpool Street was the station where all the bowler hatted City types would slide into the carriage and open up their Daily Telegraph.

On Sunday though, the carriages were more or less empty and you could always be guaranteed a seat. So the doors shut at Liverpool Street and off we would head into the strange and mystical world of The Tunnel. For the best part of 10 or 15 minutes, this lovely old train would bend and twist its way through an interminably dark chasm. It was rather like one of those Ghost Trains you used to go on at the fairground or the dingiest basement where all you can see is dripping water.

So my parents and I would get out at Shepherds Bush station and yours truly would accompany them to my grand-ma's flat nearby. On arriving at the flat, we would then open the door and find ourselves in complete darkness again. My grand-ma lived on the top floor and for whatever reason, the light would only come on after a couple of minutes. We would stagger up to the first floor, reach for the light switch in almost comical fashion, before finally arriving at the flat.

My grand-ma lived with a lodger who cared and tended to her every need and whim. On the dining room table were endless cups of half-drunk tea and packets of dates. My grand-ma loved dates and would immediately offer my parents and I dates. She would also think nothing of devouring kippers for tea and Welsh rarebit, a kind of an omelette that looked moderately mouth watering

One visit to my grand-ma will always painfully stay with me for quite some time. As a kid, I was always the playful and adventurous one. On one afternoon though, I'm afraid I paid for my curiosity. Wandering out onto the balcony and trying to lean over the top, I must have stumbled over something and fallen awkwardly. Before I knew it, my forehead was a mass of blood and panic set in.

Now I'm not sure whether my grand-ma was ever at the cutting edge of medical science but she did come up with one of the most ingenious of cures.

Not for her the conventional bandage. She was convinced that butter would stem this cascade of blood.

At this point, my mum and dad were positively frantic and almost desperate. But my grand-ma insisted that a dab of Flora would be the antidote for a cut head gushing with blood. I've a very vague recall of what happened next but I can only assume that accident and emergency dealt with the whole crisis in a very professional manner. What I do know is that you can still see a faint stitch mark on my forehead, the legacy of the incident.

I think it's amazing how kids think nothing of taking enormous risks from a very early age. Somehow, we all think we're invincible and no harm will ever come to us. I frequently kicked my football into thorny rose bushes or our lovely neighbour's garden without a thought for the consequences.

Quite fearlessly, I would plunge into the prickly bushes and somehow disentangle the ball from the sharp thorns. This was a world where danger simply didn't exist and pain was something you didn't experience. I think I must have felt somehow immune to any disease or ailment.

This takes me right back to a very early age. As kids in our road, most of us had bikes and most of us knew all of those familiar street games that our predecessors must have played. Back in the 1950s and shortly after the War, I'm sure the kids of that generation bounded out into their streets, threw down their coats into the road and joyfully played hop scotch or football. In those days, I suspect we must have been out for hours on end until darkness set in. Or until our concerned parents would order us back in to the house and insist we eat our supper.

Days on our bikes were days of energetic high jinks and reckless tomfoolery. I'm not sure whether any of us really cared what time it was. All we knew was that life was one long and continuous ride on the fairground carousel. How we abandoned ourselves to the simple joys of life.

It never ceases to amaze me how I can still hark back to those specific moments or incidents in life. I'm sure our minds are wired up so efficiently that all we have to do is simply pick out any at random. There is, I feel sure, a special mechanism in the brain that enables us to remember.

For instance, although I didn't come from a big family as such, my parents still had their small group of friends or neighbours in the road. Some of them were very friendly while others would just keep to themselves. I'm sure they weren't at all secretive or afraid of us in some way. I think they were all very private people who preferred the quiet life.

When we first moved into our house in Ilford, my mum tells me that I flew up the stairs and couldn't wait to find out what was up there. The bathroom and toilets were obvious for all to see. My bedroom, until the day I moved out, would become my second home, a place to study and reflect and a place to read and listen to music. It was a hideaway, the place I retired to when school homework had to be completed or games of darts were played out.

I don't know why but I always craved peace and solitude. I was never the sociable party animal with loads of friends and to be honest I don't have any real regrets. Sure my parents and I knew the family across the road from us and there were times when we simply lived in each other's houses.

But for me, there was a kind of detachment from the rest of the world. This is not to say I deliberately chose to be lonely and isolated, just an acknowledgement on my part that I couldn't mix with other kids of my age. I have to say that, even on reflection, I feel no resentment or any sense of remorse. I've rationalised with myself, happily accepted who I am and feel enormously grateful for everything in life.

In our teenage years, we all make mistakes and the wrong decisions but now that I've reached this age, I can confidently say that I've got all a man could possibly wish for. I've a beautiful wife and beautiful children, the loveliest father in law, brother in law and sister in law, mother, brother, their children and their grandfather. I have everything in life.

But above all, my late and wonderful dad still figures prominently in my childhood memories. There was another ritual which still leaves the broadest smile on my face. It was almost as if my dad knew it would amuse me, a conscious attempt to strengthen our flourishing relationship.

Shortly after our evening dinner, my dad would take himself upstairs and prepare for a shave. Now my dad's shaving had to be the most complete and thorough shave I've ever seen. This was my introduction into the world of male grooming and a clean shaven face.

Never before had I seen a man go through this strange procedure. I was only eight or nine and here was my dad doing something I'd never seen. He would take his shaving stick, slap thick cream all over his chin and neck, before gently removing the stubble. But this was no ordinary wash and shave. My dad simply caressed his chin as if it was the most important chin in the world.

What made this nightly act so eye catching was the fact that he wet shaved in quite the most remarkable fashion. Half way through, without a second thought, he would accidentally nick himself on every part of his face. He would never cut his face seriously but there were bloody spots on the affected areas. He then dabbed on pieces of paper to stem the flow of blood. This was both startling and slightly alarming to watch.

But my dad knew best. He reassuringly cuddled his bemused son and told me that this is what male adults had to do. Son, when you grow up, shaving will become the daily necessity. I must have been the most relieved child in Essex that night.

It was at this point that my dad did something that I'll never ever forget. My dad started singing to me while he was shaving. My father was treating me to the loveliest sea shanty ever heard. Suddenly, he broke into a stirring rendition of 'Michael Rode the Boat to Shore, Hallelujah'. That was followed by Zena Zena Zena, Can't You Hear the Music Playing in the Village Square, a deliciously catchy folk tune.

When I hark back to my early childhood, it's hard to believe that there could ever have been a more idyllic time. My mum would wake me up with a start and if it was the weekend, you would leap out of the bed and jump

25

unashamedly for joy. I knew that my parents had a mortgage to pay and bills to be paid but I was safe and protected. Of course, I empathised with my parents but bills were for a much later stage in life.

For me, childhood was rather like the prettiest woodland where everything seemed just perfect. Unfortunately, the payment of bills was my parents' responsibility and as a child, I suppose I must have felt that worrying was something that only adults experienced.

When it came to the summer school holidays, nothing ever bothered me. It was six weeks of no lessons, no bossy teachers and, for me, no Maths. You could be whoever you wanted, assume any persona and just revel in six weeks of freedom . It was just the most joyfully hedonistic fun any teenager could possibly have.

But I do remember that, naturally, the summer holiday had to come to end. There was a time when swimming by the Lido had to stop and the serious business of education would suddenly appear on the horizon.

I'm not sure why but the last day of the school summer holiday would fill me with dread. I know most of the kids of my generation must have felt exactly the same way but for me, the thought of going back to that grey, forbidding building just reduced me to a quivering wreck.

I would go to sleep the night before going back to primary school and cry myself uncontrollably to sleep. I can still see the tears rolling down my cheeks and soaking the pillow.

I'm not sure why but these seemed to be genuine tears of inconsolable sadness and desperation. I was never a nervous or anxious child but I'd like to think that these were the tears born of some inexplicable fear or anxiety. I think children find it impossible to articulate raw emotion but I was always very sensitive and terrified of the unknown.

Next to my bedroom table was the one feature I was to become completely dependent on for almost my entire childhood. It was one of those adorable children's alarm clocks. But this was my clock, my personality perhaps, and something I can still look back and think of as almost an integral part of my character.

This was one of those cute children's alarm clocks but at 8.00 there was the most easily identifiable of childhood figures. At 8.00, Noddy, complete with cap, would burst into life. I think the rest of the clock was also made up of household cartoon figures but Noddy was the chap who woke me up and probably sent me to sleep.

Then there was my very small but highly valued record player. To this day, my record player has a certain symbolism for me. I'm sure I must have regarded the record player as something of a luxury. Materialistic possessions have never meant anything to me so a record player was something to be cherished.

I can see it now. The player had four speeds: 16 rpm, 33, 45 and 78. Now in those days, some records could be played at the conventional speeds of 33 and 45 and, while I was growing up, also 78. By the time I'd reached four or five, 78s had been phased out and eventually disappeared. But the one speed that did baffle me was 16.

For some reason, the inventor of this music box had seen fit to include 16. To this day, I've no idea why 16 was included. 16 was the slowest speed for any record of that era. Some of the records my parents bought for me at that age were completely unsuitable for the 16 speed so I probably just scratched my head with bewilderment.

I can remember some of the very early records in my burgeoning collection. The first LP, I'm sure, was the musical score from that children's classic Jungle Book, the Rudyard Kipling novel. In later years, I would read quite a few of Kipling's novels but here was the soundtrack to Jungle Book, complete with Mowgli and friends.

Do you know something? I must have played Jungle Book so many times that it was almost a way of life. It became such a repetitive routine that eventually, the record became irreparably scratched. This meant that one day, the record would completely miss out large chunks of the song and perhaps ruin your enjoyment of the album. Still I don't think I cared at the time. It was my kind of music and I was the privileged listener.

Then there were those bright orange single records that were somehow designed solely for the listening pleasure of toddlers. These vinyl marvels were the most splendid creations of all time. To this day, I'm not sure where they came from but I do know they occupied most of my leisure time.

If memory serves me correctly, they were traditional nursery rhymes that were probably recorded just for our generation. There was the marvellous Three Blind Mice, a strong contender for the Number 1 spot in April 1965. I think the Beatles and the Stones were deeply concerned at the time although this has never been confirmed. Then there was the toe tapping classic, Ring a Ring a Roses, a classic masterpiece that never quite made it to the hit parade.

Childhood days were like precious pieces of porcelain. They were our childhood, our streets, our roads, our alleyways, our Lidos, our sprawling parks, our park cafes and our ice cream vans. Nobody could ever claim them as theirs because we were the ones who lived through that era and we were the ones who experienced those halcyon days.

I can now look back with unadulterated affection on those hazy, crazy days because most of us look back at the past with rose tinted spectacles. They tell us that everybody opened their back doors, everybody spoke to their neighbours and nobody felt threatened. It may sound like the most idyllic existence but I have no reason to doubt that this was so.

If I go right back to my first days on the planet, I have the most uncanny recollection of me as a baby. I don't know whether this is a figment of my imagination but I'm sure it happened. I've often told people about this story and they still find it hard to believe me.

My mum and I always paid regular visits to see my grandparents on a Friday. Nothing unusual about that you may think. We would jump onto a train at Barking station and then travel to my grandparents' home in Upton Park. I can always remember the haunting Fleetwood Mac record, Albatross, as the soundtrack to my life at the time. There was that other late Sixties chart topper, Robert Knight's rhythmical Everlasting Love. Somehow these records were synonymous with that time in my life. They were my pieces of music and my songs.

I can still recall walking into the kitchen of my grandparents' home to find my lovely grand-ma cooking up the most delicious soup. She would patiently stand by the pressure cooker with steam pouring out of the top. My grand-ma was the most affectionate and tactile grand-ma you could ever wish for. She lavished me with everything: love, attention, care and the utmost consideration. Nothing was ever too much trouble for her grandson. She adored and worshipped the ground I walked on.

Anyway, the point is that having boarded the 86 bus back to our Ilford home, here is the memory that comes flooding back to me. My mum, with baby in her hands, slowly climbed the steps to the top deck of the Route Master bus. This is a bizarre confession but I can still remember how she carried me upstairs in a snow white blanket. I've no idea why I can remember that one specific incident but I'm almost certain that my mind is an accurate record of this event.

And so to the place where it all began. It's true to say that the town, city or village where you were brought up in, can often shape your whole outlook on life. Ilford was for me the beginning of the journey, the starting point if you like. It gave substance and meaning to my early years. When we're young, we never know where life will take us. Somehow, we are guided instinctively by the people around us and the decisions they make.

Whether I liked it or not, I knew that I had to go to school, that at some vitally important juncture in my life, I would have to learn all about life's rich tapestry. You had to read books, learn the ABC, and then count up to 10. It may have seemed the most complicated of worlds but you had to be part of it. You were the student and society was your teacher. It was time to grow up and look for some semblance of maturity.

Anyway, Ilford was my base, the place that gave me a solid grounding, my first perspective on life. True, I was born at the Royal London Hospital in the East End of London but now my anchor in life was Ilford, a rather pleasant Essex suburb. Ilford was the town where I discovered who I was and what I was supposed to be doing.

In the beginning, Ilford was the town that gave me an identity and structure. It introduced me to neighbours, families and friends. Ilford would become my community, my postal code and my address. Ilford gave me a very embryonic personality. It moulded me as a person, surprised, amused and occasionally baffled me.

Occasionally, Ilford would reduce me to tears and then wrap a comforting arm around my shoulder. Certainly Ilford exerted a powerful influence on me. Ilford had its very own atmosphere, its very own mood and character. Ilford would tell me exactly what it thought of me and then sigh with despair if I made a mistake. You could say that Ilford was the very first chapter of my life.

While I was growing up, I wasn't really aware of Ilford's everyday behaviour. I suppose every town and city has its own distinctive behaviour. It's safe to assume that Ilford had a very unique code of conduct, rules and regulations and a sense of pride in itself.

Ilford, I feel sure, had impeccable manners, an air of respectability and would never argue with you. Sometimes you would find it hard to understand Ilford or maybe you would ask it for directions.

Like any town, city or suburb throughout England, Ilford had all of its familiar landmarks and characteristics. There was the town hall, the pedestrianised shopping centre and above all the thunderous roar of the traffic. There were the Route Master buses, cars and lorries in an endless but orderly procession. And on the corner of Ilford High Street, there was the jokey and jovial market trader who was almost permanently happy.

This was the first sound system of my life, the backing track if you like. These were the acoustics of my infant years. From a young age, all I had to do was walk out of the door as a youngster and just listen. All I had to do was just watch and observe. Nobody told me about Ilford's great street theatre. You would simply know that people had to go to work and Ilford was just going about its daily business.

Ilford was my first glimpse of shop windows and traffic lights. Ilford was never dull or humdrum. It was a moving and living organism that changed from minute to minute. People would rush into their shop of choice and then rush out, slowing down at one moment and then speeding up the next. Ilford had its own pace and momentum.

There were the two major department stores, Marks and Spencer and British Home Stores, two giant emporiums of clothing, fashion and appliances for the home. Both stood there patiently waiting for the doors to open. Marks and BHS were never less than considerate and utterly welcoming.

I'd like to think that both of these impressive looking shops almost beckoned us into their magical exhibition hall. This is no exaggeration for both Marks and Spencer and British Home Stores were rather like huge art galleries or giant cathedrals. They were the kind of shops who just wanted you to feel at home. They had no airs and graces about them and always seemed to ease with life. You would never hear any complaints or grievances from their customers because both were truly respectable.

Whenever I accompanied my mum to Marks and BHS, you always felt like a fascinated tourist on holiday. Women would quite happily rummage amongst piles of clothes, determined to buy the bargain of a lifetime. All human life was there. There were babies in pushchairs quietly sleeping, mums gently rocking prams, and restless three year olds who refused to keep still. They were always running about and forever active. It seemed to me that all children had this endless supply of energy.

For me, I suppose Ilford was rather like a revelation or apparition. I couldn't quite believe what I was seeing and maybe this is how all shopping centres looked like: busy, bustling, humming and every so often purring with a strange satisfaction. Listen to those cash registers almost singing with pleasure. Listen to those Route Master buses rumbling and thundering their way to the bus stop. There was that constant tap-tapping of a thousand shoes on the pavement, men digging up the road and then that deafening, boisterous pneumatic drill. How that sound seemed to go on forever.

But Ilford was a town with its own pulse, its very own throbbing heartbeat, its own veins and arteries. You somehow felt at nine o'clock that somebody would flick on a switch and everything would work automatically. Ilford had never felt better. For Ilford, it was a good day to be alive, to stretch its arms and whistle a tune. Ilford was indeed flourishing and raring to go. But then for Ilford, every day was a good day.

While I was growing up in Ilford, though, I still felt this horrible sense of detachment from the hurly burly around me. My teenage years were sadly a no man's land where shyness and awkwardness would leave me on the margins of society. I never felt a part of the environment I'd found myself in.

This is not meant as a personal criticism because my childhood years were deliriously happy and carefree. It was just I felt that maturity was somehow alien to me. While the other kids were running into youth clubs, I was that lonely wanderer on the outside, forever gazing in through the window or door but never comfortable.

This was never meant to be deliberate or intentional because I knew I had no control over my emotions. When my lovely dad pleaded with me to go into a youth club, I knew that I was terrified. I think most of us can recognise the sensation of fear and anxiety. But for me, walking into a youth club was the most dreadful, stomach- churning experience of all. I just couldn't face those kids. The overpowering sense of the unknown simply swallowed me up.

Anyway, I mustn't become bitter or morose because now that I've reached my 50s, life has now taken on a beautiful complexion. I have my own gorgeous family who I deeply love and always want to be part of. I may be lacking in career or employment but to be honest, I just want to live for the day and just enjoy every single minute of it.

If I look back to those lonely teenage years, there were the everyday interests that I could still engage with. I could still find an alternative way of life, something that would hold my attention and absorb me throughout my adolescence.

Music for me represented another aspect of my life, a way of escaping from what might been considered to most people as self-imposed isolation. There was nothing wrong with being on your own perhaps but the fact was that I just didn't socialise with my peers. Children of my age were just distant strangers who led a completely different lifestyle.

Music throughout the 1970s had everything I could have hoped for. It was the kind of music that was right for me and highly appropriate. It was almost as if every record producer knew exactly what my taste in music would be. Perhaps they knew that it was music for my age and my generation. These music moguls, it has to be said, were very perceptive. And for that I thank them profusely.

Now let me see, there was Showaddywaddy, a lovable group from Leicester who literally took music back to the 1950s. Showaddywaddy somehow belonged to that golden era of rock and roll, coffee bars on every

Soho street corner and of course the juke boxes. They were the group who were determined to keep the spirit of rock and roll well and truly alive.

I think Showaddywaddy were heavily influenced by the past and never forgot those responsible for that past. Of course, they wanted to sing like Buddy Holly and Eddie Cochran but then you could hardly blame them. Somehow, Holly and Cochran were vitally important role models, standard bearers of rock and roll in its heyday.

On stage, I seem to remember that the lively lads from Leicester would swagger onto the Top of the Pops stage in their most perfectly ironed teddy boy suits. The haircuts had that easily identifiable 1950s quiff and the drainpipe trousers were utterly cool and vaguely reactionary. They told us that the teenagers of the day couldn't wait to get out of school and hang about languidly on street corners.

Then of course there was a pop combo who went by the name of Mud. Now you could have been forgiven for thinking that Mud were simply Showaddywaddy's brothers. Mud were classical rock and rollers, nostalgic throwbacks to the days of Hancock's half hour and the first episodes of The Archers.

Mud though gave 1970s music a slightly different slant on the entire concept of rock and roll. Mud offered us sentimental love songs, Elvis Presley impersonations and catchy numbers that always left you longing for more.

Sadly, I narrowly missed out on the legendary sound of the Beatles and the Stones but years later, the radio provided us with constant reminders of the extraordinary legacy that both bands had left behind them. Perhaps, both the Beatles and the Stones felt as if they owed an enormous debt of gratitude to both Buddy Holly and Eddie Cochran.

The point is that I had no specific reference point for either the Fab Four or the strutting Mick Jagger and company. I'd heard about them but by the time I reached my teens, the Beatles were no longer around and the Stones were allegedly equally as famous. I have to say the Stones never really appealed to me. True, they were the most fascinating, intriguing, most gossiped and discussed pop group in the world. But why did they behave in such a bizarre and outlandish fashion? I'm not sure why but perhaps they'll tell us one day.

But I'm afraid they didn't quite tick all the right boxes for me. They were never rude or disagreeable but there was something about their general appearance on stage that I found slightly disconcerting. I could never really understand why Mick would insist on stomping around the stage with microphone in hand. Theirs was an unnerving and ever so slightly unsettling presence.

I could always hum the infectious Hey Jude or the reflective Strawberry Fields but Jumping Jack Flash to my ears sounded like a noisy if well-crafted rock song. I preferred the more whimsical Sergeant Peppers and for me the highly underrated but exceptional A Day in the Life.

I have to say that A Day in the Life had an almost poetic sensibility about it. It had a rich lyricism that was almost perfect and, dare I say it, symmetry. But 1970s music seemed to mean so much more even if the Sixties still had something constructive and profound to say. Not so much Bob Dylan as Bob Segar, although Dylan's songs are rather like stunning landscapes or memorable short stories, always fondly remembered and never forgotten.

The 1970s music was rather like the decade: outrageously funny, wildly unpredictable, deeply angry and politically savage. I'm sure Johnny Rotten was a very decent family man but The Sex Pistols seemed to me to be permanently discontented. I'd like to think that music was meant to be life affirming and informative. Music had to convey a very real story line, almost a definitive message, maybe even the sound track to your life.

As far as I was concerned, the Sex Pistols were always raging against the Establishment and challenging the system. I wanted happy go lucky, carefree music that made you smile. You could say I was being optimistic. Surely it was a quality to be admired. In my teenage world, I had to listen to music that I felt was pleasant, sensible, entertaining and enlightening. Punk music to my ears had nothing positive to say for itself but then we're all entitled to our opinions.

I think my musical ear was far more readily suited to the kind of sounds that I found much more attuned to my ears, far more understandable and sweetly plangent. It was the music that I felt comfortable with, music that was almost welcoming and accommodating. I think it was the kind of music that I wanted to relax to, feel good about and never feel threatened by.

I think I probably felt punk music was just too aggressive and perhaps intimidating. This is not to say that bands like the Pistols, the Jam, the Clash or the Boomtown Rats sent shivers down my spine. It was just that I felt uncomfortable in their presence. Punk may well have been some political statement but it was one I could never believe in.

No, for me music was all about American soul, disco, suave and sophisticated jazz, everything that was somehow thought provoking and significant in my life. I wanted my ears to be caressed and soothed by music that played with my senses. Soul music, for me, was rather like the most perfect bath, the sweetest box of chocolates or indeed the most uplifting book you can never put down.

My heroes were groups such as the Bee Gees, Tavares, the Stylistics, the Detroit Spinners from Motown, the Four Tops, the Whispers, Herbie Hancock and that splendid crooner Al Jarreau. These were the artistes who had that indefinable quality we all look for in music. They were my teenage friends, acquaintances perhaps at times but nonetheless people I would have been quite happy to spend an evening with. Dinner party guests perhaps.

Soul for me had an almost sensual and tropical feel about. It had a style and sensitivity that punk music, I felt, completely lacked. There was something very carefree and joyous about soul music that always left you wanting more. Apart from its smooth dance routines and contagious rhythms, soul music, throughout my teenage years, was simple and unaffected. It would never make any personal demands or exploit me in any way.

I always felt I knew where I stood with soul music. There was never an underlying danger about it and always the hope that today and tomorrow were just very special. It's a cliché but life, whatever it may bring, has to be enjoyed and appreciated. I think groups such as the Bee Gees were the answer to my questions, a band which oozed togetherness and cohesion, a family unit with sense and intelligence.

During the mid-Seventies, the Bee Gees appeared in one of the most outstanding and momentous of films. Saturday Night Fever, I'm sure, must have been the most popular box office film of the decade, a defining moment in our cinematic lives.

It was a film that simply exploded onto the screen and for a while, just refused to go away, a cinematic landmark. It pushed back boundaries and gave me nothing but personal gratification. It was the film that simply delighted and amused. Saturday Night Fever was never awkward or argumentative. It was just very easy on the eye and never less than obliging. I'm sure it was just glad to see me and determined to be entertaining.

I thought it was just straightforward fun, the loveliest trip down memory lane. It was cheesy, frothy, frivolous and, at times facetious. I don't think John Travolta ever quite knew what Saturday Night Fever was all about. I think somebody gave him a script and simply told him to have the time of his life.

I was one of the many privileged to see Saturday Night Fever and, to this day, will never forget the monumental impact it had on the regular cinema goer. It was the one film that made you glad to be alive, had humour and wit in abundance and songs that permanently resonated in the mind. Above all, it had a feeling of genuine happiness and euphoria in every scene. It was, I believe, a teenage Nirvana.

When John Travolta first appeared, he was the kind of character most of my generation could only watch with open mouths. There was never a likelihood that any of us could be the British version of Travolta. None of us could ever pull on a leather jacket. None of us could ever comb our hair in the style of Travolta. And most of us had about as much sex appeal as Steptoe and Son. None of us had his animal magnetism and we could never fool ourselves into believing this was so. Still Travolta was the very epitome of cool and that's all that mattered.

Anyway, I still felt part of the Seventies even though I had nobody to accompany me or confide in. I had no friends, nobody to share jokes and everyday observations with. I simply couldn't relate to kids of my own age. Perhaps it was a fear of the unknown or perhaps I was just petrified. The fact was I could never relate to my peer group no matter how hard I tried. It remains one of the mysteries of life. Call it shyness or just immaturity but I simply found myself on my own.

The irony was though that I still had an extremely small circle of childhood friends. When I was small, my parents became very friendly with two families. One was a family who lived across the road from us and another from just around the corner.

One of the families had a son and daughter while the other had two daughters and a son. For some inexplicable reason, I had no trouble in forming friendships with any of their children.

I would think nothing of knocking on their door and asking whether they wanted to play. I had no inhibitions whatsoever. It just seemed to come naturally. We would all jump onto our bikes and charge off into the distance. It was almost as if the world had somehow presented us with all manner of exciting opportunities. The world, I must have thought, was, quite literally, our oyster. We were indeed the privileged ones.

In hindsight though, I think my peer group always knew that one day, we too could make our way in the world. There were never any restrictions and no limits to our ambitions. Sure we'd have problems and setbacks but maybe one day we too could reach out for the stars. Perhaps we too could enjoy the simple everyday things of life. Possibly, quite possibly, we too could pass our school exams, meet new friends and expand our intellectual horizons.

Of course, there would be bumps and disappointments, a realisation that nothing would ever run smoothly for us. But that was how life worked, the mechanism which made it tick. Sometimes, the batteries would run out and sometimes not. Life was one long continuous sequence of triumphs and disasters. There were the moments when everything in the garden was rosy and not so the next. I just had to be the creator of my world and use the tools that were available.

My teenage years, through no fault of mine or anybody else's, were both complicated and turbulent. Life, now of course, is deliciously sweet and I have the greatest family of all but all I can say that when I was about 12 or 13, my natural lack of confidence and utter immaturity did hold me back.

It was about the time of the Winter of Discontent during the Seventies that I suddenly began to drift away from everybody and everything. I don't think I was aware of this sense of dislocation but while all around me were having the time of our lives, I was this remote island in the sea. I was disconnected, detached and not ready for the adult world that lay ahead of me.

During that period of my life, Britain was a country of deep industrial crisis and general turmoil. It was a time of divisions, miners strikes and power cuts. All I can remember is that this was the country that was very ill at ease with itself, that everything that could go wrong did. We were in the most horrible state of unhappiness and disenchantment.

Maybe it was self-inflicted and perhaps, as usual, it was all the politicians' fault. The fact is that the electricity had been turned off and the lights had gone out. Most of us would keep bumping into each other and nobody had a clue what was going on. We all knew that our house lights were temporarily out of order and my family were reduced to candles in our kitchen.

This was undoubtedly a time of disagreement, friction and fracture. Politicians had ruined our lives, the Prime Minister should have been thoroughly ashamed of himself and nothing would ever be right. I suppose, as a nation, we've always blamed Prime Ministers when the truth was that only we could repair the damage.

Personally, I was still that lonely, introspective teenager who was rapidly in danger of vanishing into the emptiest of voids. Throughout society, there were disturbances and disruptions wherever you looked. Why on earth did we, as a nation, have to pay for the incompetence and ineptitude of others? Edward Heath, bless his cotton socks, did as much as he could but that hearty laugh and his passionate interest in boats did nothing to make us feel any better.

Our Edward did nothing to comfort us or alleviate our insecurities. Britain was torn in half, trapped in the muddiest quagmire and all Edward could do was shrug his shoulders and chuckle. Or so we perhaps felt. I was growing up and totally unaware of the country's trials and tribulations. I couldn't help so Ted Heath had better knuckle down and just get on with it.

Anyway, life continued and we just had to find our own source of motivation. If you couldn't help yourself, then that was something you had to sort out for yourself. For me, life without electricity was ever so slightly baffling and totally incomprehensible. As a family, all we could do was eat our dinner in the dark and listen to the radio.

But as a family, we did find all the relevant coping mechanisms; there were ways of dealing with emergencies and contingency plans. The candles were, quite metaphorically, our light on the world. They guided us and illuminated our path to recovery. It was a time when hope was a distant rumour and nationwide celebration the loveliest dream. But although a cliché, it was true that all things came good to those who waited.

I still had the whole of the 1970s to face up to and everything that it entailed. None of us knew why the miners were on the strike. But we simply got on with living and pretended that normal service would be resumed sooner rather than later. The electricians would go back to work eventually. Or so we hoped. These power cuts were just a confounded nuisance, just a temporary inconvenience. Ted, though, would sort it out, no sweat.

If Mr Heath could somehow negotiate a deal with the unions, then we could all get back to our everyday lives. But for most of that winter, everybody and everything seemed to grind to a halt. It was just as well that my parents had a gas oven otherwise my family and I would have had to starve. To this day, I'm not sure how we survived because there was no TV and presumably no heating. So it was that we had to be resourceful and we had to be strong. There were ways of coping and this was the time to be collectively united.

But life did return to something like normality and we did manage. Although painfully shy, I could still find important cultural interests in life. There was the world of art, the aforementioned cinema and, the all-consuming TV. I think I must have found all three of these a constant source of intrigue. They didn't impact on my life as such but you were subconsciously aware that Britain was undergoing a radical change.

Wherever you went in London, the landscape had suddenly altered, that somehow Britain was moving in another direction. There was a significant time shift and all of us would have to be more adaptable. Even our streets and roads were trying to tell us something, something revolutionary.

During most of the 1970s, there was one event that seemed to lodge firmly in our consciousness. On reflection, it was just a personal observation but it did catch my eye. It seemed to be part of the everyday news agenda and for years it was just there.

Nobody knew why but George Davis was innocent. On more or less every wall or building, George Davis was the best thing since sliced bread and the flavour of the month. People were convinced that George Davis had been wrongfully convicted of a crime he didn't commit. Let George out of prison. It was a case of mistaken identity. George must be allowed to walk the streets.

I had no real opinion on the subject but it dominated the news agenda for ages. I had to admit that some of the graffiti on London's walls did catch my eye. In big, bold colours, you would see the immortal words. It was, I feel sure, a plea for mercy. GEORGE DAVIS IS INNOCENT, it would proclaim. Even now, I can still see the message scrawled garishly at Stratford flyover. Most of London was protesting his innocence. I have to say I was just indifferent.

Anyway, back at home, I was finding ways and means of filling in time on my own. If I had nobody to talk to as a kid, there would have to be some kind of consolation. School homework was of course compulsory and I did find that I could spend a couple of hours busily swotting away at French, History and Geography.

I think I must have privately accepted the fact that none of this homework would lead to anything concrete or positive. For me, secondary school never seemed exam oriented, so in a way I just had to get on with revising for nothing. Still, it did occupy my time and maybe it was doing some good. There were French verbs to learn and almost fiendishly complex Maths. What, I asked, were logarithms and algebra about. As for Pythagoras Theorem, well that simply sounded like some Greek Prime Minister from the 18th century.

Anyway, I retreated into my cosy sanctuary, completely cut off from society. I didn't really know what I was missing out on, so therefore this world was somehow safe. I locked myself in my bedroom in much the way that all reclusive people do. I opened up my school books, started scribbling away, almost dutifully, and switched on Radio 2.

Now this was the world that had its very own magical properties. Radio 2 used to broadcast live coverage of all the big European Cup football matches. For me, Wednesday evening during the football season was the night of all nights. There was the very polished and professional Peter Jones, the sweetly poetic Bryon Butler and a gentleman by the name of Maurice Edelston, a former Reading player, who brought a very special lyricism to the radio.

Throughout the evening, Liverpool were involved in some of the best European Cup games ever played and these were the commentators who brought the game to spritely life. It was rather like listening to the sound of gently lapping waves by the seaside. It was soft and soothing to the soul. Never hurried and permanently calm. Bryon Butler would seem to whisper his words in a very measured fashion and Peter Jones would emphasise the letter R as if it was some kind of some new grammatical device.

But it was the quality of sound on Radio 2 that I could never figure out. Here was an English radio station broadcasting from London and yet something was missing. Radio 2 always sounded like some off shore pirate radio station in the middle of the Atlantic. All I could hear was an incessant crackling and whistling, which made listening, at times, almost impossible and infuriating.

Still despite the remoteness of Radio 2, I could still hear its sister station Radio 1, a marvellous banquet of cheesy pop music and catchy jingles. Radio 1 was essential listening for kids of my age. You had to find out the latest developments in the charts and you had to watch Top of the Pops.

Then there was Radio 1, the bright, young energetic new kid on the block. Radio 1 was designed for teenagers, the youngsters, those who liked their music to be up to date, modern, lively and above all catchy. It was music that was cool, hip and mainstream. Radio 1 mirrored all of the latest trends and fashions and followed the latest bands and singers on their journey to the top of the pop charts.

In the early days, I suppose Radio 1 might have been regarded as too loud, brash and reactionary. Radio 1 was ever so slightly naughty, rebellious and subversive. Radio 1 was a very plausible response to the pirate shop stations at sea. Up until then, Radio Caroline had crackled its way into our transistor radios and always seemed to offer something that Radio 1 could never deliver.

Radio Caroline was bold and daring, forever challenging the status quo and permanently at odds with the British Government. They knew in their heart of hearts that what they were doing was wrong but that sense of illegality never seemed to bother them. They continued to play their album tracks carelessly and blithely and remained where they were, somehow untouchable, and every so often were punished for their misdemeanours. They were raided out at sea, taken off the air and the Establishment breathed a sigh of relief.

But Radio 1 was the new kid on the block and nobody could stop them. They were that disruptive kid at the back of the class forever flicking elastic bands at the teacher while they weren't looking. They were that moody, disagreeable teenager who refused to listen in English and was then sent to the headmaster or headmistress. Throughout the lessons they were always talking, whispering, up to no good.

By the same token though, Radio 1 was both experimental and pioneering. They changed the direction in which BBC radio was heading. Radio 2 had been quite content to play big band War time music by the likes of Glen Miller, Joe Loss, Syd Lawrence and Duke Ellington. But now it had the ultimate opposition in Radio 1. Whereas Radio 2 had given us smooth, easy listening and relaxing music, Radio 2 were now breaking down what must have seemed like stubbornly conservative barriers.

Radio 1 had become dynamic, adventurous, always catching the mood of the nation at the moment, always, quite literally, with its finger on the pulse. Radio 1 dared to play the Rolling Stones, the Beatles, the Who, Manfred Mann, Status Quo, Led Zeppelin, Black Sabbath and many more. These were the bands that were radically different, revolutionary, the noisiest of neighbours and refreshingly imaginative.

They were everything that Radio 2 must have, at first, snootily disapproved of and then fiercely resented. Somebody had to tell them that Radio 1 was just morally unacceptable, a pain in the neck. Why couldn't they turn the volume down? They were getting on Radio 2's nerves. All of that deafening, boisterous nonsense would give them recurring headaches. There had to be a compromise and yet there was none. No apologies, no remorse. If you didn't like Radio 1 then that was too bad.

From September 1967 until the present day, Radio 1 has stuck to its guns and taste in music. It's music of the now and present day. It's music with an edge, a hint of anarchy and non-conformity, a station that tries to cater for everybody. Sometimes it gets it wrong and sometimes it gets it gloriously right. Disc jockeys have come and gone, rules have been irretrievably broken. But Radio 1, for all its faults and strengths, comfortably survived my childhood and long may it reign.

I've one particularly fond memory of Radio 1 in its early 1967 incarnation that gives me a warm glow. Before leaving to go to my primary school in Ilford, I would pop into a family who used to live down the road to me. Here, the son, with whom I was friendly, and I would set off to school.

I don't know why but I would always wait patiently for my friend Lawrence to get ready for school. But in the background, I could hear the Radio 1 breakfast show introduced by Tony Blackburn. Every morning Lawrence and I would prepare for our day of education, learning and academia.

Frantically, Lawrence would stuff all of his books, pens, pencils and rulers into his satchel while I listened to Radio 1 in all its late Sixties glory. Tony Blackburn, rather like Radio 1, was a by-product of the pirate ships and brought his own infectious personality to the station.

Suddenly, you would hear ground-breaking radio jingles, a dog called Arnold and a whole variety of silly but funny innovations. There was never any pretension or pomposity about Radio 1 and I, for one, believed in them. There was an air of trustworthiness and sincerity about them that other stations perhaps lacked. Radio 4 was always newsworthy, serious and responsible and Radio 3 always played some of the most rousing classical music. But Radio 1 seemed to have an entirely different music agenda. It was fresh, vital, ambitious, of the present day, possibly controversial and contentious but always in the forefront and never languishing behind. And that's why I liked Radio 1.

And now I find myself making genuine comparisons with the music that I was brought up with and the music of my teenage years. I've always been reluctant to draw parallels with the past but I think it only fair to point out that any exercise in nostalgia can be both interesting and thought provoking. When we dwell on the past, it would be easy to assume that in the old days, everything was much better, healthier and safer.

Everybody knows the Beatles and the Rolling Stones were two of the most consistent and influential bands in the history of modern music. They wrote some of the most distinctive and unforgettable lyrics ever written. The Beatles and Rolling Stones were immensely gifted musicians, prodigious song writers and, quite often, humorous. The Beatles and the Stones were legendary, magical and impulsive. Nothing seemed to be staged and there was nothing false or contrived about them. What you saw with them was what you got.

The Beatles, for their part, were just sensationally creative, constantly looking for angles and perspectives that nobody had ever thought possible. When Paul McCartney and John Lennon formed their seemingly inseparable song writing partnership, nothing could stop that endless flow and fertility.

Every day, Abbey Road, the Beatles second home and recording studio, would witness four men from Liverpool with a positive statement to make about their generation. They would pluck their guitars, beat their drums and firmly push back the musical boundaries. They created sounds where none had previously existed, harmonies that made for compulsive listening and lyrics that had both style and craftsmanship. They had a completeness and finesse about them that most of the Sixties bands could only envy.

The Beatles, above all, were likable, charming, cheeky, charismatic and the finished product. They always dressed smartly because that was what their fans had come to expect, privately recognising that one day, their fans would no longer be there. So they had to give us Hey Jude, Yesterday, Sergeant Pepper's Lonely Hearts Club, Strawberry Fields and many more. Otherwise nobody would ever remember them and they'd just be a historical footnote.

But the Beatles had a unique professionalism that had to be worked on and developed. It couldn't just be dragged out of an old cupboard and cobbled together on the spot. So they toiled tirelessly in Abbey Road, ceaselessly trying new methods and techniques until eventually they found something that was ingenious and completely unexpected. There was a visual sumptuousness about the Beatles. They dressed with style and produced music that was several decades ahead of any other band of the time.

Maybe the Rolling Stones could also find the same kind of production values, the same ingenuity, the same presence on stage. But I have to say the Rolling Stones were never my cup of tea or flavour of any month. For me, the Stones were ever so slightly overwhelming and unmanageable, out of control perhaps and maybe too energetic. There was something frenzied and frenetic about the Stones that didn't seem to make any sense to me.

Admittedly, Mick Jagger, Bill Wyman and co were loud and strident but then that was the way they wanted their music to be, their mouthpiece. But I never thought of the Rolling Stones as important or formidable and there were times when I simply ignored them. I feel duty bound to apologise to Mick Jagger but it certainly isn't personal. Sorry Mick, the Stones were not my musical heroes.

Back at my parents' home, the Beatles and Stones were very much of the golden period of the Sixties when everybody partied excessively, drank profusely and shamefully dabbled with illicit drugs. Woodstock though had been and disappeared, hippies were still protesting at Trafalgar Square and reality TV was some far off distant dream.

Then there was the Electric Light Orchestra, a Seventies band of sheer, unadulterated brilliance and imagination. The Electric Light Orchestra, overnight, transformed the mood of the time, crashing into our living rooms like a meteorite from space. ELO were quite the most astonishing models of creativity and experimentation. They were purposeful, pioneering and masters of re-invention.

The ELO were years and years ahead of any pop group of that era. Whereas pop music had been dominated by disco divas like Donna Summer, Gloria Gaynor and the Motown influenced Diana Ross, the ELO were a radical departure from the norm. The Electric Light Orchestra were startling, brave and adventurous, simply remarkable.

Nobody in music would ever have thought the fusion of sweeping violins and electronic sound effects could ever work effectively. But work they did. It was the most successful musical project. It was clever, full of delightful improvisation and ingenuity. It was a music of flashing lights, hypnotic colours and sensual shapes.

But I was fascinated by the ELO because they introduced us to a new musical project, full of glorious imagery, wondrous scenery and amazing stagecraft. Whenever they appeared on the stage, you somehow knew that this was a band at the very height of their powers, a band of completeness and craftsmanship, always willing to take risks, never afraid to be different and original. They were professional and polished, at the very cutting edge, bold and daring, full of vim and verve, epic grandeur.

On the other side of the Atlantic, another band had come into my focus. The Eagles were one of the most visible and prominent of American bands. The Eagles were the ultimate stylists, easy listening, memorable story tellers, lyrical to their fingertips, exploring new areas and regions of popular music.

I always liked the Eagles because their music was never loud or brash, political or outrageous. There was never any arrogance, self-righteousness or strong arm militancy about them. The Eagles were never outspoken activists or bombastic trouble makers. They never fought against the system or revolted against the do-gooders.

The Eagles were just plain, simple, affected American Apple Pie Boys with a Hotel in California. Hotel California was almost symptomatic of where American music was during the 1970s. It was an elegantly designed piece of easy listening music with a smooth melody, logical lyrics and a beautifully constructed story line. It was the loveliest of narratives, wonderfully descriptive, genuinely moving and somehow decorative.

Music though was just a background accompaniment for me. It came to me when I needed it most. Now I began to think about the passing seasons, the temporary months, the yawning, stretching years that simply dragged. Life, at the time, must have seemed like the most monotonous of cracked records and winter, spring, summer and autumn must have been rather like some theatrical backdrop with the dullest of curtains.

Spring of course was a season of renewal, regeneration and renaissance. It was the time of year when hope and optimism shook hands with everything that was healthy and invigorating. But spring meant so many other things to so many other people. For me, it was that glorious moment when winter handed over the baton to Spring.

But spring though was suspicious, nervous, rather uneasy and understandably so. Winter seemed to be permanently dark, secretive, mysterious, a season with a hidden agenda. In my lonely teenage innocence, spring was something to be looked forward to with enormous anticipation rather than being regretted.

Spring was that wonderful revelation, laden with promise, overflowing with optimism, overcome by the sudden realisation that everything was possible. Most of the seasons seemed to collide into each other and I didn't take a great deal of notice of the changing moods of the British climate.

There was something though about spring that made you feel that life was something to be enjoyed and savoured. There were the buds on the trees in Valentines Park, the blissful emergence of the tulips, those delicious tulips abundant with yellow. The birds were about to come out of their winter hibernation and quite suddenly, nature had presented me with an altogether more melodious soundtrack.

No longer could I hear the melancholy sighs of winter, the conspiratorial whispers of December, January and February, the mournful laments of those whistling winds, the sheer darkness and emptiness of it all.

Spring, though, was far more open and extrovert, serenading you endlessly with the inevitable cuckoo, chanting the sweetest of anthems. Spring had a healthier complexion, a rosier outlook, a pleasing pallor and disposition. My personal journey through spring was singularly uneventful and almost totally devoid of anything in the way of exciting incident.

I think I'd resigned myself to whatever spring would bring me, a realistic acceptance of whatever the future had in store for me. Spring though had a different tone, a more stirring narrative, a song and a dance, no more hidden agendas. Spring could do whatever it liked and promptly did. I could, quite literally, see the wood from the trees.

At long last though, I could now see my parents' garden. Suddenly everything had come out to play, stretching and yawning, shrugging off the aching limbs of winter with an almost palpable sense of relief. Thank goodness everything looked greener, happier, newer, utterly brilliant and shiningly iridescent.

Spring represented gradual transformation, a welcome re-adjustment to new circumstances. Spring was the handsome knight in shining armour, the boats on Valentines Park lake were about to come out of their winter hideaways. Spring was open for business, confident, convincing, no longer that shy stranger who refused to smile.

I used to think that all the trees during spring knew exactly what I was going through and grudgingly acknowledged my existence. Or maybe not. I was just feeling sorry, wallowing in self-pity. Why should the seasons care about us as individuals? People were starving in Africa, rubbing their hands together for warmth on lonely street corners. Poverty was rife, everywhere, the world was in a permanent mess, nobody really cared about each other and here was I dwelling on my apparent misfortune. You couldn't make it up.

But nature was kind and compassionate, it did offer a shoulder to cry on when everything seemed lost. The trees and branches waved at me sympathetically, the leaves slowly and tentatively peeking through the misty gloom of winter. They nodded at me, shuffling and scuttling across the ground, swirling, twisting, dancing, perhaps offering me consolation and redemption, an escape from what must have seemed the hollow echoes of winter.

And then there was summer, the very summit and pinnacle of the year, a time of blossom and brilliance, radiance and sheer gorgeousness. Everybody came out to play, the gardens in my parents' home in Cranley Road in Ilford positively bursting into life, a glorious collision of sounds, colours and shapes. Children, hidden and frustrated during the winter, bounded out onto the green grass, grateful and overjoyed, screaming and screeching with inexhaustible joy and elation.

Summer had finally come out to joyous play, a time for family barbecues, families, priceless togetherness and sunbathing almost incessantly until eventually that yellow globe in the sky dipped its deferential cap in the handsome blue sky. For make no mistake, summer wore by far the prettiest of dresses, its fluffy, feathery clouds hovering and floating, waiting for nothing in particular but fondly observing events below.

But although I spent most of my summer holidays in Valentines Park lido, days by the swimming pool, summer still felt horribly and socially awkward. I was still trapped in a world of solitary seclusion with no friends and very little prospect of finding any or making any.

Of course mothers and wives still hung out their washing on their eternally waving washing lines and of course fathers would dig out their lawnmowers for their yearly attack on the grass. Mothers and wives, pegs firmly clenched between their teeth, would chatter endlessly to their neighbours over the garden fence, sheets and shirts flapping and flopping over their heads, obstinately refusing to do what they were told.

But summer had richness, ceremony, celebration, pomp and ceremony, vitality and vivacity, wholesomeness, dizziness and giddiness. And yet for me, the shy, lonely petunia, summer inexplicably meant nothing. Yes, I did try to blend in with the rest of my generation and yet it didn't quite work out in the way I'd hoped it would.

True there were the immaculately pruned beds of yellow and red roses at one end of Valentines Park but metaphorically there was no beginning, middle or end for me. Summer, during most of my teenage years, was, without my being aware of it, completely unrewarding, a time of wasted opportunities when there was nothing to gloat or boast about.

Here was summer in all its colour and pageantry, pleading with me to make new friends, to run about wildly and freely until deep into the evening. This should have been the happiest time of my life but here was I in retreat, hiding away, covering my face, refusing to participate, frozen with fear, petrified, alone and never quite knowing why.

I don't think I was deliberately lazy and indifferent to summer's alluring charms, just lost in the concrete jungle, afraid to find out if life could potentially offer me something else. Here I was blinking in the summer sunlight, running frantically through a forest that led to nowhere. A forest that must have been choking and strangling me, a forest with no open spaces, no clearing and no clarity. Just frightened youth and inescapable terror.

But summer did offer its blessed compensations and individual satisfactions. I can remember walking through Valentines Park, staring up into a sky of heavenly sunshine and warmth, feeling that life was still good. I still had my faculties about me, I could still smell the flowers and acknowledge the simple pleasures of rustling, whispering trees, kids playing football with all the unhampered freedom that somehow came naturally to them.

I don't think I ever felt their summer was just a hopeless cause, more of a wasteland with no end product and nobody to share these precious times with. I must have been so wretched, sad, totally adrift, cast into the coldest corner of sorrow and dejection. A world that never ever looked as if it would look or feel any better for me.

And yet summer for me was still that permanently enthusiastic and restless kid with boundless energy. Around me, the kids were still playing hop scotch at the end of their roads, girls were skipping until they dropped and the boys. Well, the boys were splendidly mischievous and devious, full of impishness and impudence, constantly pushing their luck and boundaries. All of the kids were determinedly rebellious, unaccountably non-conformist and never home by ten. It must have been heavenly and divine.

I always got the impression that most boys of my age were experiencing all of the feelings that adolescence had made available to them. For me though, this was just one long bewildering, dispiriting alleyway. I must have felt that quite subconsciously, I'd locked myself in some damp, dark prison cell and the voices in the distance were just muffled and totally incoherent.

Still Valentines Park did offer me its café, a café that had been there for almost as long as I could remember. I can still see those long summer queues outside the café, stretching their way around the back of the café, like some bizarre tropical snake. Here were small huddles of young kids racing back to the park's outdoor swimming pools, 99 ice creams and flakes dribbling furiously from their lips, lollies rippling in their mouth, a rainbow of colours on the necks. What rip roaring indefinite fun.

But then there was the harsh reality that was my life, the sudden realisation that throughout all of the seasons, I was still essentially unconnected with everything around me. There was a sense that for life in all its pastel shades, dreariness, drabness and uniformity, contained nothing that would propel my life into the stratosphere. I had nothing to look forward to and nothing to look back on.

I could still look back on specific incidents in my life such as my Bar mitzvah, with all its attendant ceremony, formality, pride and celebration but that seemed a lifetime ago. I can still see my parents' living room decked out with all the furniture of the time. The images are indelibly marked in history's cosy little corner.

There was the round glass topped rectangular shaped table, a 1970s must have fashion accessory, the orange curtains drooping listlessly from an empty ceiling, the Bar mitzvah photo of yours truly, angelic and baby faced, cherubic smile lighting up my face.

Then there were the ornaments. Some very striking, some very pretty and ornate. There was the onyx cigarette lighter with its turquoise finish, the Capa Di Monte ornament depicting a sad and scruffy tramp on a park bench, a man without hope and desolate. There he was sprawled across the bench, dirty, dishevelled, nowhere to go, surrendering to inevitable fate and trapped in his inadequacy. I'm sure that any inferiority complex he must have felt on the park bench was completely unintentional.

And so for the rest of the living room. On the wall, there was the most incredible painting which to this day my mum still holds a very soft spot for. I think my parents must have bought the picture when we first moved in because I can remember it being there as a young child.

The painting shows a stunning landscape, with birds flying into the evening sky, the sun shining romantically, the sea rolling incomparably into the distance, a golden destination where all was right and serene. There were breathless browns, yellows, subtle orange, spilling and overlapping into the smooth lines and contours of the picture.

Then there was the living room carpet, thick and unyielding, comforting and consoling, quiet and civilised, never a murmur nor grumble. It was dark, undeniably soft and very satisfied with its lot. I can still remember playing some strange, improvised game of cricket in the living room with my brother.

But I knew in my heart of hearts that this was just unnatural, a young teenager playing some silly game with his brother in his parents' living room. I should have been out there, playing table tennis and badminton with kids of my own age, drinking deliriously into the early summer evening. Bottles of Tizer and lemonade pop you understand. Nothing alcoholic or illegal.

In my mind's eye, I knew that I should have been copying the antics of my young contemporaries. I knew I should have been playing five a side football with boys of my own age. And yet there was some kind of invisible barrier, some unconquerable emotion in my mind that refused to come to terms with whom I was and who I might become.

I was now in some uninhabited wasteland, a desert of desolation, an overwhelming sense of numbness and repetition, of greyness and gloom. Every day had that same recurring theme, the same paragraphs, the same order and that same soullessness. There was no life in me, very little desire, no rampant ambition and no drive. Just the same creaking, groaning machinery, clanking and squeaking discordantly.

But then the day arrived, the day of reckoning, the day of judgment, the day when everything that had gone completely wrong was now about to be absolutely right. Little did I know that in the first week of January 1983. To be honest, the year itself, on the news front, was something of a blur but for me personally, the year was about to flourish like the proverbial bed of roses.

So let me see. In 1983 punk music still had a persistent hold on the public's consciousness but it was the New Romantic sound that had suddenly hijacked our attention as well. It was a smooth, well produced sound that veered from the sublime to the ridiculous.

There were groups such as the Human League, ABC and Spandau Ballet. The solo singers were varied and musically versatile. Paul Young had that very soulful and seductive sound, a singer with heartfelt lyrics and a powerful voice. Young was indeed young, reaching out to an audience who wanted to be moved and feeling the way that they were feeling.

The Human League were one of the many groups of the early Eighties whose appearance and presence invited comment. Their hair was spiky and provocative, their lyrics bold and adventurous but touching. Everything about the Human League suggested that the nation was completely at ease with himself, untroubled, totally cool and yet still capable of protesting.

Likewise, ABC had all the slickness and assurance of a band who knew where they were going in life, who didn't need to be told that theirs was a statement that had to be recognised. ABC were not only the beginning of the alphabet, they were the rest of the alphabet. They were well dressed, well-tailored, everything had to be precise and presentable and nothing was ever left to chance.

Then there was Spandau Ballet, perhaps the best of them all. Spandau Ballet were outstanding, effortless, full of confidence, oozing wit and bravado. Their music was quite literally a breath of fresh air, full of confidence and to some people inspirational. They were never likely to be the new Beatles or Stones but they did write songs that were instantly identifiable.

Anyway, back in that far off distant day at the beginning of 1983, my life was about to undergo the most magnificent transformation. It was the day when everything I'd always hoped for became a marvellous reality. It was that defining day, the day when you wake up in the morning and suddenly discover that the personality you had now became dramatically re- tuned, re- calibrated, tweaked and tampered with for all the right reasons. You had suddenly been re-assembled and re-furbished, ready for show, display and the finest of performances.

Ilford B'nai Brith are one of the most influential Jewish charitable organisations in the world. Their influence spreads far and wide with a very real presence in all that was humanitarian and philanthropic. They raised money at all times of crisis, chronic poverty and distress. They were a force for good and now I'd found B'nai Brith in all her shimmering colour and glory.

I can remember that night vividly. It was a dark, Sunday evening in January and not everything looked promising or auspicious. I think I must have felt that I'd never be accepted but here was a group that needed me and felt I was essential to their future, almost indispensable. It was the most fantastic and exhilarating feeling. Oh how thrilled I must have felt at the end of the evening. From now on everything would begin to flow and surge, forge ahead and make everything seem just right.

Part 5:
How life must have been for my grandparents' family in the early 20th century.

This is my very imaginary account of what life must have been for my grandparents' family in the very early part of the 20th century.

I'd always been curious to know where I came from and why things panned out in that way for their family and their children. There can be nothing but guesswork and hypothesis on my part but I hope you'll gain just a very personal insight into a world long since forgotten but in its way, affectionately remembered. A time when life was utterly different and completely unrelated to events that followed in the 21st century.

Both of my grandparents' family-on my mum's side-came from Warsaw in Poland so it's hard to imagine what life must have been like. Presumably, they experienced all of the stresses and strains, hardships and deprivations but for all those seemingly interminable setbacks, maybe life in Poland did offer a life that was both peaceful, tolerable and satisfying.

What did my grandparents' family do for a living and what exactly were their lives like? I've always thought of them as very decent and hard-working, determined to make the most of what must have been a very difficult time. I believe they came from a very respectable family where the work ethic was utterly predominant.

Maybe they were silk weavers, tailors who worked in very trying conditions, constantly sewing buttons onto coats and shirts, toiling and sweating for hours on end, dedicated and yet by the end of the day totally drained. Theirs was a life of work, more work and hardnosed drudgery.

Perhaps they worked in factories with their constant undertone of humming and murmuring machinery. Every so often, you would hear the clumping thud of the hammer and chisel or the discordant sound of drilling and sawing.

I can only presume that my grandparents' family were at the very heart of the manufacturing industry, valued members of a society that made and created everything that was essential. I can see them now, men and women, hard and indomitable figures who clocked on at unearthly hours of the morning and very rarely saw daylight.

My grandparents' family probably dressed accordingly for a day at the factory, mill or shop floor, forever wiping the sweat from their fevered brow. How demanding and demoralising the day must have seemed. From early morning, it would be one long hard grind, gruelling and relentless with little in the way of reward or pleasure.

But this was the existence that provided them with their livelihood, metal crashing down on metal, grease and grime on their overalls, dirty, filthy hands and fingers pleading for respite. Hour after hour they laboured meticulously, checking and re-checking their work, thoroughness and accuracy their ultimate objective.

And yet this was how life was meant to be for them. It was harshly, unfairly and remorselessly back breaking work. By the end of the day, which had now turned into early evening, they must have been completely shattered, worn out and maybe totally disheartened. It was the factory shift from hell; there were no redeeming features about their day. True, they might have stopped for the briefest of lunches, two 10 minute tea breaks but not a great deal else.

I can see them now, heaving and lifting, sighing and despairing, groaning under the impossibly cumbersome weight of it all. Their days, months, weeks and years would be the same, distressingly repetitive and yet burdened by the knowledge that today could be their last factory day. It was the most cruel and unforgiving of existences, an existence that hung by a thread, uncertain and precarious. They must have known full well that they too could be sacked because nobody was indispensable. Redundancy must have been the last and dreaded word. And yet they survived because that was all you could do. You had to take every day as it came and they did. How wonderfully admirable.

And yet their powers of survival, when the odds were fiercely stacked against them, can only be whole-heartedly admired. How easy it would have been to slump over the cotton loom, grim faced with utter exhaustion, totally devoid of all hope for the future. Because, quite clearly, factory work was hard and unrelenting with little time for small talk. It was a spartan existence and livelihood with little in the way of light heartedness or relief.

In the early days of the 20th century, the mills and factories of Northern England must have been at their most productive and prolific. But what exactly did the hands of my grandparents' family look like at the end of the day? Were they thick with dirt and grime, twisted, grubby and aching from the sheer unforgiving exertion of it all?

The question on my mind is, where were they living at the time? I have to assume that it must have been somewhere in Eastern Europe. Russia or Poland perhaps? My grandparents-on my mum's side-were born in Warsaw, Poland so I would think it had to be in either of these two countries.

Of course, I could be completely wrong, labouring under the misapprehension that theirs was the hardest and most gruelling of lives. Perhaps they were fairly wealthy and well connected. Perhaps they were financially comfortable, or even well to do and not short of a bob or two.

Perhaps they worked in banks, perhaps they were renowned businessmen or women, affluent jewellers or owners of big shops and department stores. Perhaps they were town hall councillors or civic dignitaries. Perhaps they were talented artists, highly respected musicians, classical singers, film producers or directors. I would think this is not very likely but still there is food for thought and I would like to think that perhaps they were.

Still, at the end of a typically hard day, it is easy to imagine them trudging wearily through dark and misty evening streets, factory chimney stacks blowing fitful puffs of smoke into the air, gentlemen in flat caps treading on their cigarette ends sadly and resignedly.

It is hard to know what went through their minds as they dawdled down narrow cobbled streets, deep in animated discussion and wondering what their children must have been thinking. Would their lives be any easier, more endurable and tolerable? Could they too make for themselves a life which would be far less tiring, far less awkward, far less bothersome and, in a way, less cruel.

Sadly, though, my grandparents were never to experience the joys and simplicities of domestic bliss. Their worlds would be irreparably scarred, crushed and trampled upon by the dire ravages of the Second World War and all its ghastly repercussions. I think my grandparents' family must have felt mortally wounded and tragically traumatised by the entire bloody legacy left behind in the First World War. But there had to be something to cling onto.

Maybe, though, there were tiny, cosy corners of consolation for my grandparents' family. The First World War must have been equally as horrific and harrowing, slicing as it did through whole neighbourhoods and communities, punching lethal holes into their brick walled homes of warmth and stability.

But they must have enjoyed some good times. Perhaps they too could gather around their dining room table, playing cards, singing songs around the piano, playing endless games of chess, reading, and smoking to their hearts content. It would be comfortingly convivial, precious family time as the bombs rained down and the guns boomed resoundingly.

I maintain that they privately prayed that my grandparents would never have to suffer in the way that their parents had to. As the gas fuelled lanterns and candles were blown out before bed, my grandparents rested with heavy hearts and yet fervently believing that their lives would never be torn or disrupted in the way their family had.

So what happened on the day the First World War broke out. Where exactly were my grandparents' family. Were they gripped by panic, fear, terror, the whole terrifying unexpectedness that the next four years would bring? Did they go down on their hands and knees, knowing full well that something ominous and dreadful was about to visit them?

As the bullets and bombs peppered the day time peace, did they hide and cower away in dark cellars, tremble almost uncontrollably, white ashen faced figures, their bodies shaking uncontrollably, minds numb and frozen? Was it quite clearly a case of rampant anti- Semitism, why the Jews, why couldn't they leave my lovely great grandparents and my mum alone?

Why, they must have felt were they were also the persecuted ones, why the filthy, utterly deplorable racial discrimination? Here were my poor great grandparents, lives ripped and devastated, broken and convulsed. And all because several European nations just couldn't stand each other and then let out their murderous intentions in no uncertain terms.

The questions keep arising. From my very distant 21st century view, speaking as a great grandson, it almost seems too unimaginably horrid? Did they hold hands together in their own bomb shelters, their own sanctuaries, huddling together in close-knit groups, crouching down in defiant solidarity, eyes permanently tired, weary and blinking? How long would they have to be subjected to this evil dictatorship, this grinding tyranny?

But come the end of the First World War, here were my great grandparents, alive, triumphantly alive, unbeaten, undeterred, if anything stronger than they'd ever thought possible. There is something about the human spirit that refuses to give in, refuses to concede that whatever obstacle or hindrance it may encounter, you have to believe that deep within that tortured soul, there is something deeply miraculous and jubilant.

So the final thud and crash of the First World War was silenced and the world returned to something like normality. Some semblance of business as usual. I believe this was a time of great decision making for my grandparents' family. Did they leave Poland or Russia or did they take the calculated gamble of travelling somewhere else?

I can only assume that all their thoughts and plans had already been formed for them, that the destiny of their lives would be well and truly coloured by the four years that had gone before. For the time being, they would keep their belongings in Warsaw, settle themselves down and try to re-construct their battered homes.

My mum would often tell me of the food that was the family speciality. They would sit down together and out would come the hot warming soup. It was Russian borscht, a purple coloured soup that must have tasted like heaven. The Borscht was a thick, ravishing soup that was presumably accompanied by huge chunks of black Polish bread.

After years of heavy lifting, toiling inexorably on sweaty factory floors, running for their lives, scampering and scheming, now would be the time for dignity to be restored, for body and soul to be revived and revitalised. This was that vital period after the World War, that heaven-sent period of safety and painstaking re-building. How good that must have felt.

But how many sacrifices and concessions they must have made just to keep their children in the clothes they were standing in, the food and drink that must have been so scarce in those long forgotten days of the 1920s and 30s. How divided and polarised their society must have been.

While my great grandparents would scrimp, save and struggle for every zloty, the rest of Polish high society, I suspect, was probably having the time of their lives, waltzing, doing the Charleston, drinking Schnapps, vodka, smoking the most expensive cigars and cigarettes, arguing, laughing uproariously, arguing, blustering, heckling, ridiculing and posturing.

I'm not sure whether my great grandparents ever knew what was happening on that distant planet known as high aristocracy and the upper classes. All they could see were huge groups of people dripping with outlandish jewellery, full of their own puffed up superiority and pomposity, showing off outrageously, displaying their full range of gaudiness and garishness, roaring, possibly boring and boorish, crying with laughter and convinced that the upper classes knew far more about life than my great grandparents would ever know.

And yet, this was the backdrop against which my great grandparents lived their lives for better and for worse. It was, I suspect, very grim, gruesome, dispiriting and too pessimistic for any further detailed description and let's face it, they were the battle hardened survivors. They were my family and I think it only right and fitting to pay tribute to their remarkable courage, guts, tenacity, hardihood, gritty fortitude and, above all, devotion to family. And yet the First World War had been won.

It was the grandest of all victories, when the blood and pain of the First World War, Passchendale, Sommes and Ypres would become a far distant memory. It was time to open several bottles of vodkas, a time of painstaking re-construction and yet a period when they could safely hand over to future generations, knowing that they had done their utmost to ensure a peaceful co-existence. A time of comfort, making up for years of lost time and reconciliation.

Meanwhile, here was I roughly 90 years later glancing over my shoulder and observing the whole and vast panorama as it was now. Why, I must have thought, had everything been so desperate, tragic, shabby, dirty, poverty stricken, totally without any light or redemption? Why had everything been so scarred, scattered, torn and wrenched apart savagely and seemingly irredeemably. Why because of things they'd had to endure had their lives been marked by want, deprivation, hurt and struggle, a sense that in the end things would never be right?

But although my teenage years had been dominated by the coldest air of sadness and sombreness, I still had people I could look up to without feeling that I'd totally missed out. There were my pop idols, the weird and wonderful characters from the world of TV, music maestros, eccentrics and their eccentricities, the ones who had their very own personal or hidden agenda, the ones who jumped out of boxes and surprised you, fooled you, scared you at times but then apologised for their silliness and misdemeanours. And then there were my musical heroes.

For as long as I could remember, Stevie Wonder had always been by far and away the most outstanding and fabulous musician I'd ever seen. He was the living embodiment of a child prodigy and genius at its most illuminating. From the moment Stevie Wonder was born, he was blessed with some of nature's handsome gifts. He was gifted, he could sing like an angel and he could play the harmonica in a way that very few of his contemporaries could.

I'm convinced that had he so chosen, Wonder could have become the most accomplished lawyer, doctor, engineer or surgeon in the world. Not only was he a capable instrumentalist but he could be multi skilled, versatile, humorous and a model of consummate professionalism. He could write lyrics which were both affectionate, sentimental, elegantly melodious and evocative.

There was one album by Stevie Wonder that swept all comers, that overtook and transcended everything that had come before it. It was the album that, once heard, would never ever fade away into some dark corner of your mind. It would glisten, glow and glitter like the most translucent ruby or emerald.

The album was Songs in the Key of Life, a vast and beautiful masterwork, not so much a record, more a gloriously designed tapestry with every stitch in the right place. There was the masterful Sir Duke, a tribute to the great Duke Ellington, superbly crafted, polished to perfection, logical, a piece of music that was smoothly symmetrical without ever descending into soppy sentimentality. It had balance and versatility.

Then there was Isn't She Lovely, Stevie Wonder's unashamed song for his new born child. Isn't She Lovely has all of Sir Duke's qualities and many more. It is Motown at its finest and most well varnished. Isn't She Lovely is not only witty and playful, it's also Wonder at his most musically refined and resourceful. The harmonica blends perfectly into the broad structure of the song.

On future albums, he would give us songs that were profound, richly imaginative and instantly recognisable. I'd played most of Stevie's albums repeatedly and consistently but Do I Do was just sensational. Half way through Do I Do, Wonder would pay the most flattering homage to Dizzy Gillespie, surely one of the greatest trumpeters of all time. This was the Stevie Wonder I'd always respected, enjoyed and loved. Do I Do was quite the most exceptional of all musical journeys, vital and visionary, technically perfect, a reverential nod to one of Wonder's all time heroes.

But above all, there was and is something deeply humanitarian and charitable about Stevie Wonder that confirms him in my Hall of Fame of all-time favourites. He remains a passionate campaigner, committed to stamping out repulsive injustice, admirably fighting racism and tireless in his search of peace.

And then there were the other performers who somehow made up for everything I felt I'd somehow lost sight of. They were brilliant, terrific, resounding and resonant lyric writers and just a joy to hear at all times. They had that very definite something, some exquisite quality, some insight into the future, a premonition that life could only get sweeter and more soulful.

George Benson, rather like Stevie Wonder, must have come into this world with a song book in his cot. Benson wrote and still writes with an almost effortless command of the language of love. Benson writes love songs, jazz at its richest and most varied and has that rare talent for reducing his female audience to helpless adoration and idolatry.

I've seen George Benson twice and was somehow lost in admiration. Here was a grown man in the most stunning white jacket, playing the most gorgeous piano and looking for all the world like somebody who knew exactly where his life was going. Perhaps it was time for me to follow in his hallowed footsteps. Benson was nerveless, cultured, a model of sultry sophistication, well-mannered and a man with an unwavering loyalty to the fans who had followed him around the world.

This is not to suggest that I was somehow obsessed or besotted with the magnificent George Benson. I knew that I'd never be able to write songs with Benson's perfectly modulated harmonies, his splendid love ballads, the oozing and flowing jazz and American soul with beautifully executed hooks, riffs and late night mellowness. Benson appealed to soul and the spirit. That was all that mattered to me at that most delicate time of my life.

It would be remiss of me to forget the likes of Nat King Cole, Tony Bennett, Dean Martin, Ray Charles and all those performers who glided and floated through their singing repertoire as if it were some gentle cruise down the Mississippi. I would have loved to have been a fly on the wall at their recording sessions. Can you imagine the atmosphere in the studio as the likes of Nat, Tony, Dean and Ray combined to flex their well-oiled vocal chords, carefully handling every note of the songs as if they were precious pieces of porcelain.

Both Cole and Bennett had already carved out major and high profile careers at the very height of their gifts. They were cool crooners, relaxed to the point of complete relaxation, softly caressing and manipulating their songs with the practised air of experienced maestros. America had never seen anything like this, the golden and purple days of Sinatra and all who had followed him. Nat King Cole had Unforgettable, a song of warmth and heartfelt sincerity while Bennett left his Heart in San Francisco, which for some might have been regrettable but for others may just have been the most romantic statement they'd ever heard.

I suspect I must have felt a slight twinge of envy at the way Nat King Cole, Tony Bennett and Ray Charles captured hearts. How did they manage to come out in front of an enraptured American TV audience and make it look so easy? How did Nat sit down at a piano, place his glass of brandy next to him, light up a cigarette and then just lightly brush those elegant fingers across the keyboard as if it was something he'd been doing for all of his life. I was convinced that, had he shut his eyes, he would still have known every word, every lyric.

What drove and propelled these giants of show business and song birds to the point where nobody could ever hope to match or equal them? There had to be some formula, some method, some supernatural force. They couldn't have been born with a microphone in their hands and a song sheet to memorise. That would have been far too easy and yet time after time, they delivered their performances with all the ease of a butterfly flitting onto another leaf. It was that simple and yet in a way, I suspect ever so slightly nerve racking.

I think there was a part of me that longed to possess the confidence and self-possession of a Nat King Cole or Tony Bennett. Surely it couldn't have been that difficult to walk out of my childhood home in Cranley Road, strutting and swaggering from side to side, totally composed and never even remotely concerned about anything at all. All I had to do was to straighten my tie and collar, pull up my collar, flick a comb through my hair and walk that almost nonchalant walk.

The only difference was that unlike Cole, Bennett or Martin, I didn't have a prime time show on a CBS or NBC show in the United States. I didn't have a recording contract, I didn't have hysterical fans pleading for my autographs and I didn't have a successful singing career. I had none of those Las Vegas connections or that magnetic stage presence. I had none of the influence or appeal of either Sinatra, Cole or Bennett but I did have me, so maybe there was something to be said for being Joe Morris.

Mind you, all four of the above did have the kind of qualities for which I could rightly admire. Of course, I could throw a hat onto a hat stand in the way that Sinatra did, of course I could play the piano as instinctively as Nat King Cole, and of course I could sing with the impeccable conviction of a Tony Bennett. They were acts of stunning simplicity but maybe in a metaphorical sense as well.

I used to look at my dad, Manny, listening to Frank Sinatra and wonder if he'd been transported to that recording studio where Sinatra and Bennett were shaping and sculpting their masterwork. Perhaps they'd given him a free pass into their studio, perhaps he was actually sitting in some smoky bar in Las Vegas and just drinking in the magnificence of it all.

Perhaps my dad had been given a privileged glimpse into a world that none of us would ever be privy to. I'd like to think that in front of my dad was a long, cool glass of shandy lager, low, moody but soft red lighting and above all Sinatra, just there in some heavenly pose, cigarette hanging from his lips, grey coat over his shoulder and just the smallest hint of alcohol in his glass.

***

This was the stage my dad had always longed to be in, the one moment where peace and contentment would shine its spotlight. Then, both my dad and Sinatra would slowly wander over to an American pool table, pick up wooden sticks and then click click their way around the table.

Then both my dad, Sinatra, Bennett and Cole would hang out in some cosy and private jazz club where Duke Ellington and Count Basie would be ready to unveil their gorgeous range of trumpet skills, blowing and puffing vigorously, then letting their fingers loose on a piano that had versatility written all over it. It was an evening that my dad would never ever forget.

My dad loved to be surrounded by flashing coloured bright lights and being the life and soul of the party. He adored those Hollywood celebrities, those men and women who lit up his life and made him feel like a million dollars. According to my dad, this was the case and I have no reason whatsoever to doubt him for a moment. These were the stylists, these were the people with genuine star quality, they were the ones who would never ever be forgotten and whose worldwide appeal would always span the decades and centuries.

In 100 years' time, my dad would say you could walk into any pub, wine bar or shop and you could still hear Sinatra in all of his understated majesty, booming out My Way and I've Got You Under My Skin. There was a timeless quality about his music and its meaning could almost be reached out for and touched.

Then my dad would slip into the largest American Cadillac, or outlandish limousine, with both Sinatra and Bennett for the most honorary company. They would slide into their appointed seat at the back of the car, turn on the radio and then embrace the sounds of Basie and Ellington as if the moment had somehow been fated to happen.

They would all then jump out of the car, strut purposefully towards the Las

Vegas gambling casinos, light the most expensive cigars, before embarking on hour upon hour of cut and thrust roulette and poker at its most competitive. Let me say straight away that my dad would never have dreamt of gambling but it was the esteemed company he was in. My dad was never a betting or gambling man but I'd like to think that if he had Tony Bennett or Frank Sinatra for company, then the world would, quite literally, be his oyster. Something that brought life, unashamed happiness and vibrancy to the way my dad wanted life to be.

Because there was undoubtedly a very artistic and thoughtful side to my dad that may have been bursting to break free, bristling and seething under the surface. Had it not been for the Second World War, I feel sure that my dad would have happily pursued a career in either music or art.

After his retirement, there was an almost creative restlessness about my dad that just had to find expression. It was as if my dad had been keeping all of those drawing and musical inclinations deeply hidden away. How my dad's generation would have loved to have been top fashion designers, thrusting advertising executives or talented record producers. How would they have given anything to write memorable pop songs or draw breath-taking landscapes? Some of my dad's peers probably did achieve their ambitions but maybe my dad felt horribly deprived and thwarted. But he could always dream and besides, my dad was never one to hold grudges or claim sour grapes.

Quite suddenly, I noticed my dad quite happily putting pencil to paper, busily fleshing out cartoons from the daily paper or a magazine he just happened to stumble across. Here was something that had finally given my dad complete pleasure and freedom. Here was a man lovingly reproducing his favourite film stars and fulfilling all of his private aspirations. What sweetness. What a discovery.

I don't think my dad ever saw himself as a professional cartoonist or caricaturist but he loved to be in control of an ordinary pencil and try to bring something special to life. I think my dad's generation must have been frustrated at the wasted opportunities that the War had done its utmost to kill off once and for all.

My mum used to get a weekly TV listings magazine called TV Times. My dad, by his own admission, was never a reader but he did like to casually flick through the magazine in the hope that he'd find something that stimulate his imagination, releasing him from the dull, mundane routine of work. There had to be something that would open up new channels, pathways and frontiers in his mind. There had to be something that he could wholly concentrate on, distract and occupy a mind that hankered for artistry; that longed for liberation.

Nothing gave my dad more pleasure than idle, innocent drawing, sketching, scribbling, outlining and pencilling in eyes, ears and hair with an almost affectionate attention to detail. Of course, to the outsider, these were not works of art but in my eyes they were works of art, something that brought him the most guilty satisfaction. And in a way, that's all that mattered. My dad was at peace with himself, his family and those who adored him. He was my dad, by far and away the best.

Whenever my dad took me, my brother and my mum to his beloved West End, we used to pass that artists' quarter near Piccadilly. Every so often, we would wander pleasurably past all of those handsome paintings and it is only now that I try to imagine how my dad would have felt had one of his creations been displayed on that pavement. How immensely proud he would have been because I feel sure that art was my dad's calling in life.

Meanwhile, Sunday mornings were still providing my dad with the kind of outlet he needed. They were his Sunday mornings, his indulgences, his fantasies and his personal moments. Time for reflection, appreciation and re-appraisal of everything that had happened that week.

And yet for my dad, life was far more about Sinatra, Bennett and Nat King Cole. There was the wartime Forces sweetheart Vera Lynn, the girl who provided salvation and redemption when all around my dad's world was crumbling, fading and finally vanishing.

Vera Lynn had melted the hearts of thousands of young soldiers for whom the booming guns of War had now become the harshest reality. In a way, Vera Lynn was the one woman who stood out from the rest, who soothed the fevered brows and made everybody feel so much better about themselves.

She was the girl who applied the most perfect bandage to thousands of wounded men, who revived the spirits of those who must have thought that everything had been lost. And she was the one who made my dad's life complete. My mum always joked about our Vera but dad insisted that she was the one figure during the War who had never ever let the nation down. She was the medicine for all ills, the antidote to a thousand hurts, injuries and pains.

And then there was Ella. Ella, the voice of Ella Fitzgerald, a tremendously powerful, authoritative and all conquering singer. Ella Fitzgerald was the most magnificent voice my dad had ever heard. She had the ultimate delivery and projection, the most stupendous of singing voices, a voice that could be heard in every corner of the universe, a voice that travelled, carried and finally reached its most glorious destination.

Ella Fitzgerald could do jazz in a way that very few of her contemporaries had done, punching out her songs firmly, forcefully, clearly and articulately. It was rather like listening to one of those rousing political speeches from an American President. It was like the loudest of all messages, a cry from the depths of her heart, loud, positive and stirringly strident.

And once again I find myself in complete awe of Ella Fitzgerald. Had I been born with her female talents and faculties, I feel sure that Ella would have been exactly the singer who I would have modelled myself on. She had the strongest, most effective and most influential of all voices. Her voice was the most formidable of all instruments, a huge, substantial proclamation, a vast advertisement, a hugely convincing musical promotion, a ringing endorsement for all the good in her industry. Just unmistakable and in one fantastic TV advert, the voice that broke a glass. It was remarkable and unique.

I will never be able to thank Sinatra, Bennett, Vera Lynn, Ella Fitzgerald or the hundreds of others who illuminated my dad's life on a Sunday morning. Because quite undoubtedly they were the ones who took my dad to far and away places, who mentally transported to him to smoky jazz clubs, to recording studios in downtown LA and may just have been persuaded him into believing that Sunday mornings at home with the family were the best place to be.

And then there were the Hollywood icons who decorated my dad's all time Hall of Fame, the men and woman my dad idolised, worshipped, respected, elevated to the highest pinnacle. They were the movie legends who entered into my dad's life almost without effort and any notice at all.

Jimmy Cagney was the cocksure, snarling, sneering gangster who lived life on the edge and didn't much care for niceties or formality. He was a gun toting, fast living rebel, a mean, moody maverick, never obeying the laws, always ready to put his life on the line. My dad loved Cagney because he was cool, menacing, dangerous, resentful and argumentative.

Shortly before he passed away, my dad was given a copy of Yankee Doodle Dandy, one of Cagney's most highly acclaimed films. Now in my dad's estimation, Yankee Doodle Dandy represented everything that was so superlatively brilliant about Cagney. Here was a man who had conquered all the obstacles that life had put in his way. Cagney was the one who towered above the rest and now, he hoped, was top of the world. Cagney was the rowdy renegade who finally came good. In a way, I think my dad had seen something in Cagney that he could identify with. In a sense Cagney was everything my dad would ever strive towards and ultimately achieve.

For the best part of several years towards the end of his life, my mum would tell me that my dad had watched Yankee Doodle Dandy for the 750th time. Over and over again, he would memorise the song, absorb it like a sponge and reproduce in his mind all of those wonderful songs, numbers and the familiar Cagney mannerisms.

I think my dad had subconsciously taken in every twinkle footed Cagney dance, the cheeky grin, the sheer disregard for any of the movie conventions, the determination to be a hugely regarded movie star, the yearning for more and more recognition and publicity, the stubborn belief that nobody could ever stop him from being the greatest of all movie stars. Those were the qualities my dad admired and always would.

And then there was that unforgettable and supremely gifted Al Jolson. Now Jolson was Jewish, an unashamed exhibitionist and fiercely protective of his Jewish background and identity. Jolson was the one who shocked all sensibilities by overnight blacking up on screen, at the time one of the most provocative acts in the whole of Hollywood history. And yet it wasn't provocative because Larry Parks took on a role that he knew would arouse comment and reaction. I suspect Al Jolson was the cleverest creation Hollywood had ever seen. He broke down religious, racial and cultural boundaries in a way that none of us could ever have anticipated.

The irony is that the Jazz Singer, the film that would propel the character of Jolson to worldwide attention, received its first showing in 1927, the year of my dad's birth. Jolson had style, daring, chutzpah, brashness, boldness, sheer impertinence. Jolson was the character who wanted to live the ultimate life, a life of glamour, independence, a thousand record deals, top billing at every movie theatre, his name in sheer incandescent and sparkling lights, forever associated with Hollywood stardom and greatness, printed and published for ever more in posterity and Variety magazine.

For this is the world my dad was desperate to inhabit. Jolson was quite undoubtedly the singer my dad always wanted to be. My dad wanted to be that big time Hollywood movie star, belting Mammy out with understated vigour and relish. He craved and desired to be the next Jolson and yet there was a gracious acceptance on my dad's part that maybe this would never come to pass. And yet the showman in Jolson was something my dad would have loved to emulate.

But I have no doubt in my mind that Al Jolson in the Jazz Singer was the living embodiment of style and grace, of a time and place in America where everything seemed to be happening or was about to happen. It was a time of Prohibition, the first talking movie, coincidentally the Jazz Singer, the Wall Street Crash, the horrible Depression and yet here was my dad's hero Al Jolson quite literally tearing up the record book and just singing with the most fervent passion.

When Jolson fluttered his hands and smiled broadly the whole of America fell in love, became besotted with an image and character who just wanted to perform for ever more. It was gutsy, forceful, irresistible, out there, the strongest of pronouncements against all of the odds, campaigning on behalf of Jolson and rallying the nation together in its darkest hour.

And then my dad returned to Jimmy Cagney and Edward G. Robinson because they were the men who showed ruggedness, doggedness, persistence and masculinity. Cagney and Robinson were never afraid to take risks, never afraid to make that jump into the unknown, get their hands dirty, roughly aggressive but smoulderingly cool.

My dad knew Cagney and Robinson would never accept defeat, never throw in the towel, never ever surrender in the face of adversity. Cagney and Robinson fought and battled, defended their corner, slammed their opponents into the wall and demanded justice and retribution. Revenge was a dish best served cold.

Whenever my dad settled down to watch a Cagney or Robinson film, he knew that good would always triumph against evil, that the villains would always get their comeuppance, the baddies would always end up with blood and egg on their face. They strutted, swaggered across the silver screens, completely unaware of ever the slightest hint of danger to their lives and oblivious to pain and discomfort. These were the confident and purposeful figures who provided the backdrop of his heavenly life, the family he so lovingly cherished for ever more. Dad you were the greatest.

My dad always knew greatness when he saw it because he was by far the most knowledgeable of all critics. He was a man with a keen appreciation of the stylish, masterful and the cream of the crop. Nobody ever escaped the notice and attention of my quick witted and sharp thinking dad.

Singers like the great Nat King Cole, Barbara Streisand and Lena Horne belonged in the highest sphere, classical artists with voices that were made to measure and beautifully tuned. They had balanced, vocally complete voices that had never been tampered with or ruined by anything that could ever be described as ruinous or detrimental.

In fact, although the 1960s did have its drug pushers, experimenters and alcoholic reprobates, there was a good part of that decade when all the star names and celebrities did turn up for work sober and rational. I think they must have known that had any illicit substances passed their lips, then the consequences might have been fatal.

One name in particular stands out as the perfect example of somebody who became swallowed up and consumed by his own fame and notoriety. He was the one man who simply couldn't climb out of the black hole that his life had now sucked him into without any kind of explanation as to why.

Jim Morrison was the lead singer of the 1960s band The Doors, a brilliant on stage performer on stage but off it, utterly tortured by sleazy temptations and horribly bad influences. Morrison never recovered from drugs, alcohol and so much more that was unhealthy and repulsive. Morrison just surrendered to life on the edge and then fell off it because life had now become intolerable.

He can hardly be blamed for doing so but my dad could never understand the groups who were growing up in my generation because none of them seemed to make any sense. He did once tell me though that when Tom Jones first appeared on the Top of the Pops during the Sixties, he knew that the boy was destined for the top. I think though that he did that find hip shaking sexuality just a little distracting but the Jones voice had power and vitality. My dad knew what he was talking about.

But when the Who, the Beatles, the Stones and Pink Floyd arrived towards the end of the 1960s, I think my dad must have regarded them as a terrifying culture shock, quite literally a shock to his system. Look at those long haired, scruffy drummers and guitarists. What on earth were they singing about and nobody could hear a word they were singing about. It was all very loud, muffled and discordant?

I think my lovely dad must have made allowances for the Beatles because they were nice, tidy and vaguely presentable. Some of the Beatles, my dad must have privately admitted, were indeed coherent, intelligent and thrillingly lyrical. But as for the rest of that wacky mob, it had to be said that they were just one hit wonders with no method in their madness and beyond description. According to my dad, they were just long haired louts who couldn't string a sentence together let alone craft a moving love song.

No, my dad admired the kind of singers who everybody could hear quite clearly and who were trained and coached by the finest. It was the generation when my dad's music became firmly rooted in his way of life. Vera Lynn, Cleo Laine and Johnny Dankworth now found the most comfortable place in my dad's life. Vera Lynn had the most triumphant voice while Cleo Laine and Johnny Dankworth were a husband and wife team who were jazz personified, laid back, contented and permanently mellow. They were the ultimate embodiment of late night radio listening, professional to their fingertips;

smoothly cultivated and, according to my dad, just what the doctor ordered.

So this was the musical soundtrack to my life, fully formed and neatly constructed. It was the music that made my dad feel so good and the music that stirred and stimulated me. Of course, Shakespeare had always believed that music was the food of love and both my dad and I knew exactly what the necessary ingredients were for that perfect marriage of taste and satisfaction.

As the 1980s dawned, I knew that the music I'd already been exposed to would have to make way for a new and refreshing sound, a sound that a completely different shape, format, style and method. By now the likes of Led Zeppelin, Black Sabbath and Pink Floyd were still situated at one end of the musical spectrum while at the other, The Osmond's, David Cassidy, David Bowie and David Essex occupied a platform that was altogether different. In fact the contrast could hardly have been greater.

Led Zeppelin, Black Sabbath and Pink Floyd were heavy rock at its loudest, hard driving, pounding and battering the ears and senses for all they were worth. This is not to suggest that it was any less worthy or intelligent as some of the music of that time, because quite clearly it was music that was fashioned and designed for heavy rock aficionados. It was music that had to blast out at full volume in your bedroom so that walls shook and trembled, ceilings and carpets shivering with fear, utterly petrified. This was not my musical environment though and heavy rock was totally at odds with the way I wanted music to be played.

There was a part of me that harked back to those wonderful Herb Alpert days by Spanish swimming pools where everything in life was permanently laid back and easy going. There were those lazy, almost lethargic trumpets drifting out from my parents' tape recorder, lovely, lingering and sensuously entrancing. There was a hint of sultry salsa, playful jazz, something rich and enormously satisfying. It had a clarity, fluency and delicious fragrance to it that had me hooked. I could almost roll it around my tongue like a vintage bottle of red wine.

And so it was that the 1980s brought with it something that sounded like a direct descendant of the 1970s. It was American soul, funky, danceable and infectiously energetic. Now they came hurtling off the music conveyor belt like well packaged products. They all had a gleaming freshness and originality about them that had an unmistakable quality.

There was Shalamar, Shakatak, Level 42, the Whispers, Al Jarreau, all of those high tech masters of funk and soul that made you want dance from dawn to dusk. This was the kind of music that I felt made complete sense out of the chaos, that sent the warmest of sensations through me. It was music that had an easy to follow grammar and eloquence that spoke all languages.

It is now though that I'd like to take you back to my grandparents (my mum's parents), the two people who made admirable decisions at the right time and the right place. Their influence, it was, that gave me the opportunity to paint a picture of my life, the two people who made everything blissfully possible while those around them were doing their utmost to stop them from doing so.

Right at the beginning of my journey, I told you about my grand-pa's first job in the heart of London's East End. I told you about this strong willed barber who had used all of those formidable skills, cutting the hair of the great and good without a single protesting voice.

I told you how the spine of England's 1966 World Cup team had happily sat in my grand-pa's barber chair, willingly offering their hair for a short back and sides. Bobby Moore, Geoff Hurst and Martin Peters had all been groomed, shaven perhaps but always treated with whole hearted and consummate hospitality.

What I may have forgotten – and I have this on the best authority – is that my grand-pa also cut the hair of yet another celebrated and well decorated footballer. This was an England centre forward who typified the football that the Seventies had no shame in presenting to its supporters.

His name is Kevin Keegan, a bundle of English dynamite, full of bullish aggression, darting, dashing brilliance, a busybody, tireless, indefatigable and just a nuisance to opposition defenders. Keegan was always on the move, restless, a workaholic, full of bravery, daring and goals galore.

Keegan carried the 1970s along like one of those well illustrated banners on Liverpool's fanatical Kop. Keegan was a player of his time, hustling, bustling around the pitch, hunting and foraging for space, jostling for a convenient chance in the penalty area, never afraid to make his presence felt.

But I can now proudly tell the world that Kevin Keegan had his hair cut by my grand-pa. Yes that Kevin Keegan. This is no mean achievement, a feather in his cap but how good that must have felt for him. It was an accolade that had been bestowed on my grand-pa and was something I think he must have taken enormous pride in at the time.

Throughout the Seventies and Eighties, Keegan's hair had undergone a whole variety of styles. There was the curly look of the Seventies and then there followed the afro and the bubble perm of the Eighties. Keegan always seemed to be completely in tune with all the latest fads and fashions but back in the 1960s, his flowing locks were the subject of my grand-pa's splendid scissors.

On the subject of my grandparents, I couldn't help but recall their Saturday nights. Once they'd settled down in the cosy domesticity of Vaughan Gardens in Gants Hill, they returned to the one routine that had somehow become familiar and fundamental to the way of life.

Quite regularly, they would be hosts of a regular card school. Card games are as much a part of our social fabric as baked beans on toast or roast beef and Yorkshire pudding. There's the childlike Snap, Pontoon, Kalooky, Black Jack and of course Poker. But my grandparents knew all of the tricks of the trade, chief exponents of the five card trick.

Now I'm not suggesting that my grandparents were hardened gamblers who spent all of their hard earned money on the casinos or the horses. But they did like to have their friends around for a night of Black Jack and Kalooky. Quietly ,they would gather around their immaculately lace cloth dining room table and a respectful hush would descend on Vaughan Gardens.

The games would start, cards swiftly slapped down in the most orderly fashion and strategies cunningly formulated. Jack and Rachel, my doting grandparents, would religiously conduct affairs with all the wisdom and enlightenment of experienced card players. Suddenly old pennies, shillings and ha'pennies would appear on the table, loosely sprinkled for all to see. It was all very civilised and part of my grandparent's weekly leisure time.

It is now time to slowly wander my way towards the end of the first part of My Life Story. It has been part of a journey that encompasses so many other varied aspects of my life. My whole story is far from complete but there are so many components of that life story that give it full expression and colour.

From that first day in Ilford in 1965 and right back to the Second World War, it was a life that was loaded with possibilities and yet haunted by the ever present sense of danger. As a child, I'd not the remotest idea of what had happened 20 years earlier. To a youngster growing up in the 1960s, the Second World War was rather like some creepy, sinister and ghostly shadow that had occasionally tapped us on our shoulders.

And yet, although my parents had reluctantly volunteered details of the Second World War, there could have been no recognition of why, how and if. I think the War had left my parents just cold, bemused and indifferent. As far as my parents were concerned, the War was something that had happened a long time ago and would now be condemned to some dark and dingy basement of the past, a single light bulb hanging from the ceiling and the drip drip of water from the leakiest pipe.

Rather like most parents from my present generation, the War was the most impossible of subjects to talk about. It was painful, sensitive, hurtful, tragic and horrific. I don't think they ever went into denial but the images were burnt into their minds and this meant that any reference to War or full confession of what had happened was somehow locked away, never to be revealed.

I don't think my parents ever tried to hide anything away from me. There was never a sense that they were refusing to open up about the War, protecting me with a shield. I think they must have felt that if they did give me chapter and verse on the Nazis, then perhaps we'd dwell on that past and ask the kind of questions they could never ask.

I now take you back to one or two favourite sports writers, writers who have fed and nurtured my love of sports writing. Sport has always been brief, temporary, fleeting and flirtatious. Sport is deeply emotional, tribal, petty and yet critical. Sport can give you a complex, irritate and frustrate, puzzle and confuse. It can almost leave you on the top of the world, delighted, enthralled, questioning and investigating. Sport takes you to the highest of highs and lowest of lows.

Sometimes, sport quite literally leaves you breathless and lost for words, gasping for verbs, superlatives, adjectives, at a total loss for words, moved to tears, clutching at straws, gaping at thin air, utterly devastated and utterly inconsolable. And then there were the sports writers, the carvers and sculptors of words, elegant paragraphs, the men and women who transform the dullest and most mundane of prose into works of art.

David Foot remains one of the best and most distinguished of all cricket writers. He is now enjoying a well-earned and honeyed retirement but for several decades he was one of the Guardian's foremost of writers, a man who brought to the sedate world of cricket writing a masterful command of language and syntax. His prose was as sweet as sugar, by turns both decorative and picturesque. When this humble West Country man sat in his Somerset press box, the images would leap eloquently to life.

He was wonderfully descriptive, delicately illustrating cricket's characters and historical landmarks with the most tender loving care. The dreamy, drowsy but delightful summer game of cricket was David Foot's most cherished domain. Bowlers were always regally tall and totally dominant, white flannelled and hungry for wickets, while batsmen were rather like composers of an orchestra or conscientious country farmers ploughing their land from dawn to dusk.

For David Foot, cricket was always the game played by gentlemen and played, devoted to their craft. Cricket was always played against a princely backdrop of English meadows, sheep dotting the hillside and wise, contemplative churches. David Foot always drank in the very pretty scenery of a Sunday afternoon cricket match and transported us to another world, a world that was far removed from the noise and commotion of the City as it was possible to be.

For the best part of six decades, he persuaded us into believing that cricket was by far the simplest game in the world, that the gentle crack of ball against willow was similar to the cuckoo in spring time. His world was that of the village green where the vicars would summon the flock to evening service, the church bells were always punctual and the local summer fete would always offer the sweetest of homemade jams. This was the wholesome cricketing world of my favourite cricket writer David Foot.

And then there is Patrick Collins, surely one of the accomplished of sports writers, a man with a beautiful turn of phrase and witty observations on all sport. Since his early days at the old Evening News in London, he has cornered the market in sharp, perceptive prose neatly seasoned with all of the most linguistic relish.

I can remember being mesmerised by Collins when I first set eyes on his work at the Evening News. His pearls of wisdom on the 1980 Olympic Games in Moscow took my breath away. Some of his opening paragraphs were just majestic works of description and throughout those Olympics and many more literary dispatches, I would make a point of looking out for him.

When Pat Collins joined the new Mail on Sunday in 1982, it almost seemed a logical progression. Collins had established a regular spot in my Sunday newspaper reading. I've now been reading his well informed and descriptive match reports and columns for 32 years and that mellow, cleverly written delivery is as good now as it was back in 1982.

On an equally literary scale, both Hugh Macilvanney and Brian Glanville continue to provide writing of vintage quality and prose that has the loveliest texture and lustre. These are two of our most distinguished of sports writers, combining as they do the very best elements that make sports writing the most riveting to read.

Hugh Macilvanney, for the best part of 50 years, has been firstly one of the Express's finest of writers and latterly a consistently brilliant sports columnist for the Sunday Times. This seems highly appropriate because the Sunday Times remains one of our most highly esteemed of all Sunday papers.

Macilvanney is, I think, unlike any sports writer you're ever likely to feast your eyes on. This is because Macilvanney takes sports writing into the elevated world of poetry. His sentences and paragraphs remind you of some classical 20th century novelist. There are impeccably detailed and deeply literate sentences that leave you gasping for superlatives. To the impartial observer, he could be seen as too clever, too elaborate and just a bit of a show off. But this is because he regards sport as the highest of art forms. I have read Macilvanney but not quite as much as perhaps I should have done.

Brian Glanville is another football writer who I haven't quite read at any great length but I know enough about the man and his works. Glanville is beautifully articulate, precise, concise and enormously readable.

And finally there were Richard Williams and Michael Hart, who in their very different ways projected themselves in both clear and incisive sports writing. Their styles are contrasting but never less than intelligent and intelligible. Both have been at the coal face of sports writing, conveying both a hardnosed enthusiasm and whole hearted passion for sport.

For the best part of 40 years, Michael Hart was the daily voice of football at the Evening Standard. Hart, I suspect knew everything there was to know about London in football. He was the official campaigner on behalf of football as it affected all of the London teams in the old First Division.

I always had the highest regard for Hart because he would write very simply, crisply and accurately on London teams and footballers. There was something very well balanced, honest and unpretentious about his writing. Hart was never blunt or insulting and will always tell it the way it is rather than the way it should be.

Sadly he has now retired from that very lofty footballing pinnacle. The world of football literature is markedly poorer for his departure. Undoubtedly, his regular appearances on the back pages of the London Evening Standard will be much missed but in my eyes his descriptions of London Footballers of the Month will remain matchless. There was a smooth and conversational style that flowed from his typewriter like the finest syrup.

Richard Williams was another writer who ticks all of the correct literary boxes. Williams used to be one of the most hugely knowledgeable music writers this country has ever produced. Williams seemed to know everything there was to know about groups, singers, song writers, bands and record labels.

He seemed to have an almost encyclopaedic knowledge of everything from Motown to middle of the road late Sixties and Seventies rock. If memory serves me correctly, I think he used to own one or two record labels and also had a very emotional investment in some of the greatest names in the business. As editor of Melody Maker, he should have pursued a career in music writing with unashamed zest. But then sport gripped him and he then became hooked on its romance, its drama, its melodrama, tragedy and its palpitating heartbeat.

For quite some time, Richard Williams has become something of a mouthpiece for sport. He remains one of the Guardian's most elegant and analytical of sports writers, combining piercing wit, lush craftsmanship and penetrating comments. He is both hard hitting, investigative, thorough and extremely insightful.

Williams also gets to the heart of the matter and gets to know all of the people he knows without becoming too intrusive. He exposes corruption in sport in a way that leaves nobody in doubt that there has to be something dodgy and unsavoury, rotten to the core about it. He describes the legends and the unknown with a towering majesty and formidable style. From Hendrix to Bowie, Beckham to Lewis Hamilton, I've always felt Richard Williams knows both the good, great and the lesser known without ever allowing standards to decline.

I once had the honour of sitting next to Richard Williams when he was the chief sports writer at the Independent and while I never quite made it to the same illustrious level of this very literary man, I still believe that it was the most fruitful of all life's experiences.

And now I take you to the pleasures of the palate-food, drink and all those associations that satisfy our appetites.

In a sense, I suppose we all take the food and drink that passes our lips for granted and I now look back to my childhood meals that were neither good, bad nor indifferent. Eating and drinking are two of the most natural of functions and without them, it's safe to assume that none of us would be here to tell the tale.

My eating and drinking experiences can be placed into very specific categories, time frames and very different environments. They were very rewarding experiences and in a way utterly typical of the era they took place in. The first one that readily springs to mind was the whole procedure that went with school dinners.

Back in our Gearies Secondary School hut, we were all lined up outside in a very military and regimented way. With tickets in our hand, we would all politely march into what can only be described as a Nissan hut. Once inside the hut, we would then scramble furiously for the best possible table or seat. It was very comical and slightly absurd but, on reflection, invigorating. I think it was the most physical challenges to all of the boys, a way of finding what exactly made the boys tick.

Once at our respective tables, we would each be called up by the head dinner lady, a Mrs Butler, strict but very fair-minded. She was never bossy, prissy or domineering, simply a calm head above the general noise and commotion. The food was quite simply a hotch potch of good, hot and well-made meals that were heart-warming and utterly fatty. I remain convinced that my waistline had expanded way beyond way any reasonable level. And yet it was well cooked, hearty and exceptionally tasty.

The meals varied from bangers, mash and peas on every Friday with gallons of gravy to the traditional meat, two scoops of potato and vegetables throughout the rest of the week. It was all very standard and ordinary food with little in the way of variation but you knew you'd been adequately fed. The food was invariably served by three very maternal ladies with huge, billowing aprons and demure, tightly knotted hats. They always reminded me of those mother earth figures who always smile very broadly and understandingly at you as they dolloped another pile of mash onto your plate.

Then there followed two of the most painful and agonising of all school eating experiences. There was the ghastly dessert. On frequent occasions, dessert seemed to be tacked on almost apologetically to the main meal. Now those poor Gearies boys were about to suffer the very worst of all catering nightmares.

At least two or three times a week, we would be confronted with what can only be described as something looked revoltingly sickening. It was supposed to be semolina and rice pudding but any resemblance to either would have been a complete understatement. It was slopped onto your plate rather like the worst kind of punishment. I'm not sure how any of the boys ever avoided food poisoning but miraculously did.

Meanwhile, back at home in Ilford, my mum was doing her utmost to satisfy my infant appetites. The meals were honest to goodness, filling and always eaten in the kitchen. I'm not sure why but as a family, my parents, brother and I always ate in the kitchen. I feel sure that a vast majority ate in their living rooms but I think my mum wanted to bring a different dimension to eating times.

One meal does though stand out for me. Wednesday nights, for whatever reason, were always spaghetti evenings. My mum boasted this rather impressively long tube of spaghetti, tightly packed together. Over the next couple of years, I would develop an increasingly ravenous love of spaghetti with the most delicious mince.

Then there were the Sunday family gatherings, an hour or so devoted to reflection and a discussion of the weekly domestic events. What had school been like? Could anybody explain why there was a neglected shopping trolley in the nearby Cranley Road alleyway? Did the morning milk float ever disturb any of our neighbour's tranquillity? It rattled loudly and clanked but never really bothered us as such.

Anyway, meal times at Sunday lunchtime always consisted of beef, lamb, roast potatoes and the inevitable Brussel sprouts. We were invariably given cabbage or lettuce but the lingering smell of Brussel sprouts is something to be savoured. The sprouts were hot, smelt good and were out of this world. Quite the most pleasurable of taste sensations.

There was a lovely intimacy about those Sunday lunchtimes that, on reflection, seem like an idyllic moment in time. Had I been able to call on any real friends then, perhaps I'd have eaten very amiably at a friend's house. But this was never the case so there can be no way of second guessing what might have been.

Then of course there were the yearly Jewish feasts. Now this was quite unlike any meal I would ever encounter throughout the year. To this day, this is the one meal that has to be the tastiest and most well-earned of all dinners. It is the one meal of the year that is eagerly anticipated and in a way rightly celebrated.

In the Jewish religion, Yom Kippur is the Day of the Atonement, the yearly Fast. For 25 hours, all Jewish families must go without food, drink or any conceivable pleasure. For 25 hours, we must devote ourselves to worship, prayer, forgiveness for our sins, repentance and above all no food, complete abstinence.

While I was growing up, I would complain and moan to my parents. Who in their sane minds could possibly starve themselves without questioning why? I'm sure there was a perfectly plausible explanation but nobody ever gave me one.

But every year at roughly the end of September, all of my family and friends would undergo this very steadfast ritual. My mum would always insist that if you deprived yourselves of any kind of sustenance, it certainly wouldn't hurt you. And so we all went home at roughly lunchtime from Beehive Lane Synagogue, whiling away the remaining hours of hunger and starvation in varying states of discomfort and disenchantment. Why did we have to put ourselves through torture every year?

Food occupies a very prominent place in the Jewish heart. Food dictates most of our emotions, shapes our outlook on our lives and defines who we are and where we come from. There can be no psychological reason for this natural function but eating is something that is ingrained in the Jewish psyche. And long may it be.

At the end of Yom Kippur, my mum would always have a bountiful banquet ready for my dad Manny, my brother Mark and I. We would all retire to the kitchen where huge plates of fried fish would mingle with delightful salmon cutlets and glorious potato salad. Then there was my personal favourite, coleslaw, and the abundance of varied salads.

But above all, there was my mum's speciality. The central feature of the Yom Kippur fast was my mum's milky coffee, a frothy but stunning libation that fizzed and bubbled in your mouth. Naturally it had loads of sugar and would give you the most wonderful feel-good factor.

Drink though never really figured on the Morris menu. I'd never been a seasoned pub drinker so lager and beer were somehow seen as forbidden. But as a kid, I can still see my parents' very modest drinks cabinet. As you opened it up, a light would automatically go on and there you would find a more or less alcohol free zone.

Every New Year's Eve, my parents would always go out with a couple of friends but if they did see in the New Year at home, they would always partake of a slight tipple. It was either a Tia Maria or a Snowball. But neither of my parents were hardened drinkers and would only occasionally indulge in something akin to a celebratory New Year drink.

And now I approach another very revealing part of My Life Story. I'd like to think that this is also the part of the same journey that most of us have been through. There were the dark rooms, the empty roads, the teenage turbulences, the storms that never seemed to relent, the happy, triumphant days when it all went right for those precious hours.

I'd like to look back over both of my shoulders and find literary consolations. There went Mr Thomas Hardy, that grandest and greatest of all literary authors, breathtakingly descriptive and the most contented of Dorset country souls. There would be Hardy, standing reflectively on a distant hill, weathered hands bunched tightly in his coat pockets, wisps of greying hair fluttering in the gentle breeze, Tess and Far From the Madding Crowd wildly spinning around in a crowded but fertile mind.

Then Hardy would move forward, pointing delightedly at the wheeling seagulls and then slowly shuffling forward with that distinctive leisurely air. He would dig his country walking stick purposefully into the Dorset earth, spot a brooding mountain in the distance and the ageing eyes would weep with emotional joy. So this is how it was meant to be and how it always should be. Every day of our lives, every waking hour, every sleeping hour, long winding country lanes with joyous, yellowing sunsets.

Perhaps, along the way, I might bump into Charles Dickens who by now had just spotted us in a low timber beamed pub in Dorset. Or perhaps it was just some gossipy coffee house in Piccadilly. I can see Dickens quite clearly because he still has that distinctively well-trimmed beard, a slight moustache and that very quintessentially London air about him.

He waves at me with in that very wise and worldly fashion. Dickens always looks tidy and distinguished, clean cut and gentlemanly. I think he's just finished the last page of Nicholas Nickleby because he looks so relieved. Dickens always has time for his legions of his admirers because gracious 19th century authors are never rude or offensive.

Then Dickens and I would meet up with Thomas Hardy on some misty moorland, where everything is still and, for a moment, very melodramatic. Together we would march forward, sniffing the invigorating country air, grateful and satisfied. Hardy with his wiry grey hair and Dickens with that gently graceful bearing would give me a beautiful analysis of 19th century literature.

The rumour, of course, was that both Dickens and Hardy never saw eye to eye with each other but on this occasion, I think they must have come to some amicable agreement. Their eyes are sparkling and there is an intellectual alertness about them. They both acknowledge their strengths and weaknesses but can never tell me why they are at loggerheads with each other.

Both men sip their coffees with an almost Victorian lightness of touch, laughing at the inadequacies of the English upper class and then poking fun at their alleged wealth. Dickens would briefly take off his pince nez glasses, polish them ever so slightly, dab them with his handkerchief and then take out his well-appointed diary.

Dickens always looks very organised and methodical. I feel sure that he knows exactly what his list of engagements because it's all written down in clear and legible writing. For all his fame and celebrity, Dickens does look ever so slightly surprised at the adulation. I can well imagine him being completely unfazed by frequent returns to his Portsmouth birthplace.

But I feel sure that his ego must have been considerably boosted by all of those gushing newspaper headlines and rave magazine reviews. Dickens smiles at me knowingly, coughing almost modestly, and then gingerly pecking at a slice of chocolate cake. This has to be his one of his final meetings of the day and I have to tell you it has been a rare honour.

It's hard to tell what Dickens must be feeling at this moment. I can only tell you, at first hand observation, that he looks very tired and emotional. The hair looks very ruffled, the tied cravat on shirt now ever so slightly adrift and there is a general weariness about him that I hadn't spotted before.

He did tell me that while he was writing Nicholas Nickleby, he did feel ever so slightly under the weather. But I'm inclined to think that this was the time of the year or maybe some irritating cold. He's taken all the necessary medication and his doctor has administered all of the right tablets so there can't be a great deal wrong with him. I have to tell you that I'm neither bothered nor concerned about Dickens welfare.

And then after a hearty lunch and tea, Dickens and I go to our respective homes and find that the whole day has been richly enjoyable and rewarding. I did notice one or two unusual mannerisms. When Dickens eats or drinks, he does so very delicately. There is a caution about him that I can't quite understand. He seems to pick at his food, nervously shifting his vegetables about his plate and then briefly closing his eyes. It's almost as if he's become very self-conscious and can't tell me why.

In contrast, Thomas Hardy, who has no more than a grudging admiration for his great literary rival, is a model of confidence. Hardy has just finished Tess and Far From the Madding Crowd and when I meet him in the most gorgeous of Dorset taverns, I find a man of wisdom and enlightenment.

I don't think I'll never know why Dickens and Hardy are, in a literary sense, poles apart, diametrically opposed to each other. I feel sure that this has everything to do with their diverse backgrounds and their very unique approaches to writing. Hardy, Dickens once told me, was very dark, dramatic and pessimistic. There was a brooding quality to Hardy's work-or so Dickens told me. I didn't agree with him but then we're all entitled to our opinion.

But whenever I met up with Hardy, I always knew that he would confide in me, trusting that I would never blurt out any of his secrets and intimacies. There was a comfortable country air about Hardy that I always found enchanting. In his slightly crumpled grey jacket, thinning grey hair and grey moustache, he looked every inch the Dorset farmer with just a hint of world weary disillusionment about him.

Hardy always gave me the impression that there was unfinished business in his life, that he hadn't quite figured out why there was so much bitterness and cynicism eating away at him. He would lean over towards me in the most confidential way and whisper something very private. Hardy, I think, was never troubled by the daily chores of life just never entirely sure of his place in society.

But then he would nervously fidget and fret about nothing in particular, staring at the beer mat on the table, tapping the tea spoon against his cup and then looking at the well varnished walls with a very solemn gaze. Hardy was never entirely regretful about the past and in a sense he was never really burdened by it.

During our conversation, Hardy took out a comb, brushed that thinning grey hair ever so precisely and then sneezed almost apologetically. In the top pocket of his jacket, there was a demure handkerchief ever so discreetly folded. Like Dickens, Hardy looks very sad and despondent. He asked me for re-assurance. Were any of his novels tragic and turbulent? Did I think he'd truly let down his reading public in any way.

Hardy then flicked through his diary, lit up a very clandestine cigar from his cigar box and then seemed to sit up very straight up in his chair. I thought Hardy was totally misunderstood and slightly downtrodden. Of course, his novels were highly regarded by the public but the critics were like savage beasts. What did they know about Tess and the Return of the Native?

Thomas Hardy wrote from the heart very sensitively and truthfully. All of his characters spoke in very measured and honest tones. Hardy told me that he was a man of loyalty and integrity. He could never let anybody down. And so we said our goodbyes. Out of the corner of my eye, I could see emotional tears trickling down his cheek. It was the loveliest and most poignant moment. Once again Hardy had been moved to tears, crying perhaps but crying with happiness. That was the man.

And then onward we tread along well-trodden pathways, neatly trotting very respectfully past neatly arranged cornfields, smelling, the summer fragrances of passing flowers; the exquisite buttercups, the sweetest smelling mimosa, the now fading odours of August and September. For me, this has been the most unforgettable encounters, a scintillating experience, a time of the year when all of the suggestions of spring have now given way to the crowning glory of summer.

Hardy and Dickens have been quite remarkable companions, men I've come to know, fully understand, sympathise with at times and then admire enormously. They've given me a revealing insight into, not only their world, but the whole panorama of the 19th century: its peculiarities, its idiosyncrasies, its eccentricities, its mannerisms, its class divisions, its irritations, its extravagances and its inexplicable mysteries.

And so I would now like to take you down to another chapter of my journey towards that concluding chapter of childhood. Along the way, I've tried to give you a much clearer picture of my childhood and the way a very troubled adolescence became a much more stable and happier time.

I can never begin to thank both Hardy and Dickens because they were responsible for smoothing my way forward, easing my way into a better world. As two remarkable literary authors wave me a fond farewell with their walking sticks, I begin to see that life has been metaphorically very good to me.

Life is indeed that beautiful chocolate box cottage in the country, with red roses and wisteria, twisting and winding their way around picture postcard windows. Life is that quaint village green with its own post office, its own butcher, its own baker, its own blacksmith and its own compassionate doctor.

Life is that lighthouse out at sea, winking its recognition of me; life is that windswept valley, that well embroidered landscape with everything in just the right place and proportion. Life is a magnificent tapestry. Life is that roaring log fire in a pub, that cheerful vicar on a bicycle, an ordered and harmonious society.

There can be no doubt life is a pure white snowdrop on a winter's day, weekends spent on golden sands by the seaside, lively street festivals festooned with pretty flags, secretive second-hand bookshops overflowing with old first editions. It is about village summer fetes of timeless magnificence where nothing ever changes, children playing on street corners, frolicking happily in fields and parks, dancing and cavorting seagulls, swooping and darting.

I can now see what life has all been about. Of course, there were times when it all seemed too overpowering and overbearing. On many days and weeks, it didn't seem to make any kind of sense to me. It was as if somebody had given me the most complex jigsaw puzzle and had left me the unenviable job of finishing it off.

Then it all became abundantly clear, the clarity, the majesty of our lives, the splendour of it all, just how it should be. Finally, my childhood in riotous Technicolor, extraordinary clarity and in the sharpest definition, the full silver screen, a life of supreme accomplishment and richly textured sumptuousness.

And now the day draws to an end and everything melts and fades into the distance. Hardy, Dickens, loyal lunchtime acquaintances, the local village cricket teams with their neatly peaked caps and fluttering shirts. There they go, the fishermen by the gently rocking harbour rolling in their nets, the sheep and cows deep in thought on the hillside, contentedly chewing their grass and perhaps considering the humanity around them. It is all very calm, all very settled, all utterly peaceful and not a hint of urgency for miles around.

This indeed is my very unique perception and imagery of my life. It is that very sedate tea shop with the strongest cup of tea in delicate bone china. Tea is served daintily with small, triangular shaped cheese and cucumber sandwiches, scones with butter and jam and all the old fashioned courtesies you could possibly wish for.

And then there are lengthening shadows of evening over the village green, the cricketers clattering into the pavilion for their final draught of ale, the jackdaws and the crows jumping almost playfully across the cricket strip. Over there, I see a group of farmers busily discussing the latest crops, the length of the wheat or maybe the agricultural industry. It is all very still and the way it should be, undisturbed, unruffled and serene.

I think this is the way I'd always like it to be. There is another hushed silence, the farmer's tractor parked outside the sweet shop, that lovely tea shop called Mario's in Ongar, with its pretty fish pond outside, full of charm and humility. The sun is dropping romantically and idyllically into its nightly hiding place, laying its head on the softest of pillows.

It is here that I here that I take leave of my childhood. Finally there is this deeply green land of ours, fairy tale cottages, terraced houses, flats, tall, towering council estates, the urban sprawl, electricity pylons marching in stately procession, policemen pounding the pavements, rows and rows of houses, streets, flickering TV screens, the thunderous rumble of vans, lorries and cars down below, a lonely tramp in a state of permanent regret but maybe privately optimistic.

Now it's time to focus on the present day . Time to tuck away all of the remnants of my childhood, savouring perhaps those last gleaming jewels now safely stored in a comfortable cupboard. It is time to heartily embrace the way life is now rather than the way it was. It is time to believe that life does have poetry, smooth surfaces, shimmering tranquillity, mellow sunsets and breath-taking scenery. This is the way that life should be and could be in the future. It is the way this very humble man would like it to remain. Stunning, absolutely stunning.

Part 6: Norway –
A European jewel in the crown –My first cruise with my family.

Norway is one of those countries that seems to hide away in the most discreet of corners. I'm convinced that Norway is too modest and assuming for its own good. Perhaps somebody should tell this sleepy Scandinavian outpost that it does indeed have a timeless beauty.

For my lovely family and I, a holiday in Norway was just what the doctor ordered. In fact, it was one of life's sweetest experiences. Most of us long for the sun-kissed beaches of the Mediterranean and two weeks in sultry, sweltering Viva España. But for my family and I, this was a holiday that would leave a permanent imprint on my mind. It was the most joyous and joyful holiday any father could have.

I have to admit that when my wife mentioned that we were going on a cruise along the Norwegian coast, I did have my reservations. Sorry I couldn't resist the pun. But this was the holiday that would leave us all with the warmest of glows for some time. It was a radical departure from the norm. Norway was different, magical and stunningly spectacular.

We all look through the holiday brochures, endlessly searching for that holiday of a lifetime. When I was about 11, I was lucky enough to be taken on a 10-day jaunt to Spain. During the school half-term holidays at the beginning of June, I was whisked away to the Costa Brava plain. I'm not sure whether I was old enough to appreciate it but the land of the flamenco dancer and the bullfighter seemed like a startling revelation. It was quite the most astonishing of spectacles.

Anyway, the fact is that my family and I had seen the Med on numerous occasions and Norway represented something new, something refreshing and delightfully pretty. Norway seemed to have everything that Spain, Italy or Greece could never properly match. Norway had scenery and more scenery. The kind of scenery that the great 19th century authors would have waxed lyrical about for ever more.

Our trip started at the historic Kent port of Dover. Now we all know that Dover was immortalised during the Second World War by Dame Vera Lynn. Dame Vera was, of course, the Forces sweetheart who lifted the spirits of the nation with the classic White Cliffs of Dover. For my family and I, there could hardly have been a more uplifting song to see us off on our way. It seemed like the most proper musical accompaniment as the ship set sail.

Now I have to say I've never been the sea going sailor but life on the ocean wave did convert me. I thought I'd be sharing jolly sea shanties with the Captain. Or shouting Land Ahoy Cap'n and Splice the Mainbrace but this was far more thrilling. But this was one nautical adventure with the most beautiful of differences. I had my family around me and I felt like the most important dignitary in the world. I could hardly have asked for more special company.

So it was that our suitcases were taken to our cabin and we settled down to 10 days of sheer bliss on board a ship called the Braemar. Built in Scotland, the Braemar did have all of the traditional tartan fixtures and fittings. I seemed to recall that there were quite a few tartan reminders although nobody wore a kilt.

For me, the world of cruising always seemed the ultimate in luxury and elegance. Cruising, I assumed, was something that retired couples did when the kids had grown up. This may have been a myth but my family and I couldn't help but notice that this was true.

Still, we all had the kind of holiday that would have been the envy of many. We came down for breakfast at the appointed hour and simply indulged ourselves. You could eat and drink to your heart's content for as long as you wanted. We had kippers, croissants, scrambled eggs, salmon, tinned fruit and more fruit. There were the obligatory fruit juices and hundreds of cups of tea and coffee. Oh, I mustn't forget the Corn Flakes, essential breakfast fare on any holiday and of course the toast.

But I'd been told that food was the central feature on any cruise, that food was somehow the main selling point on any cruise. They told us that you had to sample the huge abundance of food on board. True, we all ate and drank heartily throughout the holiday and we did consume far more than we knew was good for us.

The fact was, though, that mealtimes were never medieval banquets and you always felt you'd had enough. I think that all of us enjoyed both the morning and afternoon teas. The afternoon tea in particular was a very English gastronomic feast consisting of tea, scones, mouth-watering cakes and yummy sandwiches.

Of course, we stopped off at a number of Norwegian ports on a daily basis. Now I think I speak for my family when I tell you that most of these Norwegian towns were roughly the size of a postcard. Of course they were lovely and picturesque, rather like chocolate boxes with ribbons around them. You could almost spend all day painting them.

There was our first port of call, Bergen, a quiet Norwegian haven simply minding its own business. It nestled by what looked like the most contented of fishing harbours. Nobody ever bothered or troubled the good citizens of Bergen. Personally, I'll never forget the two gentlemen playing the concertina as we walked into Bergen. Well done chaps.

Then there were other unforgettable high points of our wonderful holiday. On one day, we travelled up to the glaciers. Here were some of the most majestic of all Norwegian jewels in the crown. It was a landscape of epic proportions and we were all speechless at the vastness and grandeur of it all.

What unfolded before me were some of the most flamboyant waterfalls it has ever been my privilege to see. It seemed to me that the water seemed to dance its way to the bottom of the fjords.

What I hadn't bargained on was a sight that simply left me open-mouthed with amazement. Strolling over towards one of the deck windows my eyes were taken aback by something truly wonderful. It was an extraordinary phenomenon the like of which I'd never seen.

At roughly 11.30 in the evening, Norway was still bathed in daylight, a truly fascinating panorama to behold and never to be forgotten. It was without a doubt nature at its most romantic and mystical. By the end of the evening, with midnight approaching, I could have sworn that I was imagining this natural wonder. My body clock, I'm sure, must have taken an age to re-adjust.

Then there were the impeccably presented dinners and the charming waiters whose lavish hospitality will live me with forever. Most of the catering staff and waiters came from the Philippines, oozing both kindness and infectious happiness. How we'll remember their birthday celebrations invariably accompanied by tambourines and castanets. You got the impression that this was one long party and we were the most welcome of guests.

The dinner of course was followed by the evening's entertainment. Now when I tell you that the standard of entertainment on board a cruise ship was like nothing else on earth, I think you'd have to believe me.

Truly the entertainment was absolutely outstanding and the acts surely reached the most soaring heights of excellence. They had quality written all over them. This was the kind of all singing, all dancing cabaret that most of us were privately hoping for. We were treated to five star comedians, two hilarious magicians and the Braemar Company, a fantastically harmonious group of singers and dancers.

But the holiday memories will shine for ever like the stars in the sky. There were the nightly cocktails, the splendidly amusing quizzes during the day and the games of bingo which always left us with the broadest of smile on our faces.

They tell us that travelling aboard gives us a different outlook on life and broadens our horizons. I've no doubt that most of us will always be intrigued by the world and all the challenges that await us but for 10 days, my family and I had the most fabulous holiday in a gentle country called Norway.

When we look back on our lives, there are moments that simply stand head and shoulders over all of the others that have preceded it. These, I feel sure, are those golden moments when everything fell into place and the world was a good and safe place to be in.

Part 7:
How it all came good, my wonderful wife, children, Michael Caine, Delia Smith and my London.

But on one magical evening in July 1991, I experienced one life changing moment that would transform my entire outlook on life. It would, quite literally, turn my whole world upside down and inside out. It was the definitive day, quite simply the definitive morning, afternoon and then evening.

For most of the 1980s, I had spent most of my life aimlessly traipsing the streets and heading for nowhere. I was unemployed, unqualified and, when all is said and done, completely lost. I felt useless, confused, cynical and disenchanted. True, I'd held down one or two insignificant jobs in warehouses but nothing of any meaningful value. And besides, which employer would even consider taking me on without any qualifications.

So it was on one balmy summer evening at the beginning of the Nineties that one woman would change my life completely and dramatically. Up until then, it did seem that nobody could save me from a life of complete failure and embarrassing mediocrity.

I was destined to be a pathetic nobody and when I look back, I'm convinced that had it not been for that one evening, I would surely have ended up on a permanent park bench or some youth hostel.

Up and until then, I'd been used to the same daily repetitive routine. I would wake up at some unearthly hour–usually 11.00 or certainly lunchtime on occasions, wash almost dutifully, walk downstairs almost reluctantly, before staggering into the kitchen for breakfast. At roughly 12.00, I hasten to add. It sounds bad and, to be honest, I can think of no other adjective. Shameful and disgraceful could be alternative descriptions but sadly it happened.

I then shuffled out of my parents' home with the weary tread of some prisoner simply resigned to his fate. I hadn't committed any terrible crime but it probably felt that way. I then strolled through the park, admired the boating lake and trees around me and then bowed my head shamefacedly.

Having arrived in the main shopping centre, I pottered around for a bit, popped into the library for a while and the rest is rather like some sad historical episode of my life. Thankfully 1991would bring with it one of those delicious moments that would forever be engraved on my mind- rather like some wonderful birthday present. The girl I would meet at a friend's birthday Chinese meal would become the loveliest wife in the world. It would be the making of me. Very special and very cherish able.

It's another week and time to dwell on the absurdities and mysteries of life.

I refer of course to the celebrity culture, that curious phenomenon that leaves us totally baffled. From the moment we wolf down our first bowl of corn flakes to the late night beverage with just a hint of caffeine, all life spreads out in front of us like the neatest of table cloths.

We open our red top newspapers, switch on and gasp with astonishment at the outrageous antics of our dear friends from the world of celebrity. They come in all forms and guises: ranting politicians who speak from the moral high ground, frothy soap opera actors and actresses, the Shakespearian community and those West End theatre types with a book or play to publicise.

Spotted at Liverpool on Saturday was Mike Myers, that lovable Canadian film star who seems to have captured the hearts of everybody. Myers was that comical figure who pretended to be James Bond but never quite made the grade. It made you think about those other celebrities from yesteryear who also attached themselves to English soccer teams.

At one point during the Sixties, film stars were literally queuing up as supporters of teams. There was Max Bygraves, Sir Michael Caine, Kenny Lynch, Sir Richard Attenborough and a whole host of the great and good.

What is about football that lured these TV luminaries to the various directors' boxes at West Ham and Chelsea. Perhaps they were attracted by the pungent smell of hot dogs and hamburgers. Perhaps it was the irresistible fragrance of the Beautiful Game. For fragrance it is. Football has always oozed this quite remarkable aroma and when the thousands squeeze through the turnstiles on a Saturday afternoon, we are seduced by its charms, whether we like it or not.

Why else would celebrated cook Delia Smith wrap herself in the colours of Norwich City? In fact, what is the connection between cooking, catering and football? Throughout the season, Delia Smith sits very comfortably in her plush directors' box seat, smiles rather knowingly and then bellows out her encouragement. It is a sight that warms the heart and restores your faith in human nature.

A couple of seasons ago, our Delia made the most extraordinary rallying speech ever heard in footballing circles. It was never Churchillian, nor did it belong in the repertoire of one Martin Luther King, but it did stop everybody in their tracks. On that evening, you felt sure that our Delia had something very pressing on her mind.

Quite unexpectedly, our Delia grabbed hold of a half time microphone at Carrow Road and shouted out the most mind-blowing of all statements. If it had been made at a Labour or Conservative party conference you would never have blinked twice. But because it was in the setting of a Premier League football match you had to wonder if perhaps she thought she was a politician; "Let's be having you". Somehow you knew she meant it.

Let's be Having You, sounds rather like a plea from the heart, a heartfelt yearning that was almost too sweet and touching for words. According to Delia, Norwich needed a kick up the backside and Let's Be Having You was inspirational, a cry from deep within. Norwich just weren't responding to her powerful exhortations. If Norwich City really cared, they'd score three quick goals and put the game to bed. Three points in the bag. No problems.

Until recently, there was Mohammed Al Fayed, chairman of Fulham and a master of the one liner. Al Fayed never really said anything questionable or dubious but you didn't quite understand his motives. True, he was just trying to whip up his devoted fans but there were times when Al Fayed wasn't entirely convincing. Perhaps he was just misunderstood.

Recently, Al Fayed unveiled the most magnificent statue of Michael Jackson outside Craven Cottage. To murmurings of disbelief at the Cottage, Al Fayed had presented us with what seemed to be a curiosity. Yes, of course you could have statues of footballers but Michael Jackson was just completely off the wall and utterly out of context. It was baffling and incongruous. There had to be an explanation but Al Fayed never gave us one.

To those on the outside, the relationship between football and the world of celebrity is at best distant and platonic. You'd hardly expect the likes of Delia Smith to be yelling out instructions from the managerial dug out. Admittedly that half-time announcement did border on the passionate but until our Delia dons a track suit and tells Robert Snodgrass to drop back into midfield, it is safe to assume that the world of football chairmanship is in safe hands.

A couple of decades ago, football and politics again shook the friendliest of hands. One Michael Foot, Labour Party leader and a man of undoubted principles, quite clearly expressed his footballing loyalties. Foot always looked like one of those elderly geography teachers: quiet, thoughtful and scholarly. Never flustered, always in control.

Foot was, quite unashamedly, a Plymouth Argyle supporter. Now if you support a team like Plymouth, you have to be open to the most merciless ridicule. Unfortunately, Plymouth, rather like most other Football League clubs, have never won a thing and the suspicion is that they'll never win anything. I do hope I'm wrong but my suspicion is clubs of Plymouth's station in life are destined to remain in the wilderness. Perhaps they'll surprise me one day and win The FA Cup. I hope that day will be sooner rather than later.

Still, you had to admire the likes of Michael Foot. Throughout the many seasons, he made himself at home in the directors' box at Plymouth and believed in the impossible. Perhaps he felt that constant exposure to the House of Commons would drive him over the edge. Football, he must have felt, was his medicine, a way of releasing tensions and difficulties. It must have been that green and white or maybe that very matey atmosphere at Home Park.

Then there's Michael Palin, that worldly, well-travelled comedian and shrewdest of observers. Palin has pinned his colours to Sheffield Wednesday, one of those Football League clubs who never quite scaled the heights. Wednesday did enjoy the briefest flirtation with the old First Division (now The Premier League) but never quite made it to the top table. Perhaps they used the wrong knife and fork.

Wednesday did reach an FA Cup Final in 1993 but were just outclassed by an Arsenal side who seemed to be at their peak. But Palin, although a proud Wednesday fan will always be known for his travel programmes and that magisterial comedy team known as Monty Python's Flying Circus.

It could be that most celebrities are rather like the rest of us. They cheer loudly when things go wrong and curse wretchedly when our teams lose. They are, after all, as human and vulnerable as the rest of us. Nobody likes to see their team beaten or indeed relegated so maybe it's understandable their disappointment and regret is our disappointment and regret. It is not a cause for unspeakable grief but perhaps they feel the way we do.

Alistair Campbell is one of the nation's most influential of political voices. Campbell was one of the great driving forces behind Tony Blair's Labour government. Campbell lifted the morale of his party when things were wrong and then made it abundantly clear that he was a Burnley supporter.

When Alistair Campbell told us that his football club was Burnley, most of us thought of cotton mills and Lancashire hot pot. Some of us even remembered Bob Lord, the 1960s chairman who never quite saw eye to eye with the big wigs or the FA hierarchy. Lord was a butcher by trade and it may be true that some of his cuts of meat weren't quite as appetising as they could have been.

Still, I feel sure that Alistair Campbell was never bothered by reputations or egos. Campbell is now an after dinner speaker, author and at times piercing wit. In recent years, Campbell has been extremely honest about his private life but Burnley and Turf Moor, you feel, will always be close to his heart.

Michael Parkinson, one of the most refreshing and entertaining of TV faces, makes no secret of his fondness for Barnsley. Since the early 1970s, Parkinson has interviewed and frequently caught out some of the brightest stars of stage and screen. From James Stewart to the hugely popular Billy Connolly, Parkinson has been the amusing inquisitor, fascinated listener and ruthless task master.

You remember the occasion when he reduced Robert Mitchum to almost total silence, when beautifully constructed questions about Mitchum's private life were met with an icy stare. Parkinson, you felt sure, was probably more concerned about his beloved Barnsley. Still Mitchum did mutter 'Yep' to Parkinson, so he must have heard the question.

But it was Barnsley for our Michael. Barnsley was the team he supported, a no-nonsense, hard tackling Yorkshire side who never quite made it to football's top table. Barnsley were firm yet fair, well organised and always disciplined. I think Michael Parkinson supported Barnsley because they were down to earth and logical rather than over-elaborate and outlandish.

Parky always favoured the practicalities of life rather than the so called fancy dan theories that Barcelona advocated. Barnsley were never pretentious and pompous, just straight down the line and no questions asked. I suppose Parkinson felt Barnsley were your next door neighbours, polite to strangers and simply intent on minding their own business. But of course they were still Barnsley, honest, straightforward and no airs or graces.

In fact, I've always wondered if you could do a considered analysis of the whole of The Football League. Perhaps you could give them all the relevant characteristics. So let's do that.

Arsenal, of course, need no introduction. Arsenal are those strolling, swaggering 19th century aristocrats who live in grand country houses. Arsenal were never snobbish or patronising but at the moment their football is both richly rewarding and scientific. Perhaps their football reminded me of their French manager Arsene Wenger, members of the Parisian café society, carefree boulevardiers, sophisticated, connoisseurs of the finest red wine, smoked salmon and caviar for tea.

Manchester United, a side steeped in history, legend, immense popularity, pillars of society, internationally known, highly regarded, gentlemen and scholars. Manchester United were footballing soul mates, exemplary role models, impeccably dressed, well mannered, tasteful and discerning, permanently hungry and ambitious. Perhaps they rubbed shoulders with the highly knowledgeable students of Oxford University.

Liverpool were the club who reminded you of those priceless landscape paintings, a side of pedigree, beauty and perfect posture. Liverpool had a certain social status, breeding, poise and an air of complete assurance. Liverpool received the best education, always listened to their teachers and always dressed immaculately for dinner. They were a side of politeness and propriety, a side who graduated with flying colours. Liverpool had footballers who played football, passed the ball rather than abused it, won League titles. Liverpool were neat and tidy, prim and proper. Kevin Keegan, John Toshack, Ian Callaghan, Steve Heighway, Ian St John, Ron Yeats and Peter Thompson. Top of the class, never flustered.

Chelsea were members of London's nightclub fraternity, a side who burnt the candle at both ends, partied the night away into the wee small hours of the morning. Chelsea mixed with the celebrities, schmoozed with the shakers and movers, completely disregarded convention, did whatever they felt like doing. Chelsea could roll in to work at their leisure. Chelsea just wanted to be noticed, remain in the spotlight forever, make unsavoury headlines, attention seekers. Blissfully arrogant, full of themselves at times almost bordering on the contemptuous. They turned up their noses at the rest, felt that others were beneath them. Charlie Cooke, Alan Hudson, Ian Hutchinson, the long throw and Peter Osgood, goals galore.

Tottenham were also night-time revellers, party animals who lived life on the edge. But Tottenham were essentially London, carelessly and nonchalantly London, smoothly London, a vital cog in the machinery. They were Arsenal's London neighbours but neighbours, snooty and disapproving neighbours. Spurs had better fans, better terraces, better everything. So there! Spurs had reliability, tradition, more class and streetwise know-how. Spurs, or so they believed, just had that indefinable quality, an unquestionable something. Just superior and supercilious. We look down on our North London neighbours. That's official. Spurs had Danny Blanchflower, midfield general, Terry Dyson, Bobby Smith, John White, Ralph Coates and Alan Gilzean. Spurs had one of the most natural goal-scorers ever to wear the white shirt-one Jimmy Greaves. Poor Jimmy was broken hearted when the World Cup Final of 66 shirt went to Sir Geoff Hurst. Totally inconsolable. Mind you he was injured so that softened the blow.

Aston Villa were rather like one of those old fashioned department stores, firm, dependable and well established. You could always find the right clothes and the right food at Villa Park. Nothing was ever overpriced. It was reasonable, respectable, never posh and always good value for money. Aston Villa were like that quiet cat that curls up snugly by a roaring log fire. Villa are one of the oldest clubs in The Premier League but there is a timelessness about them that invites admiration. Villa are sturdy, steady, content with their station in life. After what must have seemed like an eternity in the old Third Division Villa, in their mellow claret and blue, are now socialising with The Premier League toffs and snobs, the gloating gadabouts. Those money makers in The Premier League have never, you suspect, ever impressed Villa.

Everton, rather like Villa, seemed to have been around for more than more a century or two. In the kindest possible way, Everton are rather like a well-polished mahogany table or the most stunning cabinet. Everton are a well preserved cutlery set, knives and forks gleaming, a crystal decanter with brandy. Everton smoke the best cigars, complete The Times crossword, make pleasant small talk, reminisce on the good old days. Everton had Alan Ball, Colin Harvey, Howard Kendall, Duncan McKenzie, Graham Sharp, Bob Latchford, Brian Labone and Harry Catterick, footballing men but men who were designed for Everton, men with an impeccable footballing grammar.

Manchester City were another example of a team who never slouched over the dinner table. They would always have their soup with the right spoon and never talk while they were eating. City had excellent manners and perfect etiquette. Until their recent Premier League triumph though, City were all music hall, farce and slamming doors. During the Eighties, City fell flat on their face and tumbled down the divisions like rocks on a cliff top. It was almost as if somebody had deliberately knocked over a set of dominoes. City were always pleasing to the eye and good for the purists but when City were in the old Third Division, it was rather like waving farewell to an old steam train. You knew where they were going but you feared that you'd never see them again. The days of Colin Bell, Rodney Marsh, Mike Summerbee and Francis Lee were like a throwback to the days when back doors were open and kids played on the streets. Giddy, heady days when the bells at Maine Road always rang.

Then there was a team called Wolverhampton Wanderers, football's very own Greek tragedy. To those who have carefully monitored the progress of Wolves over the years Wolves, were the side who once topped the bill at the Palladium and many decades later rather sorrowfully ended up at a Birmingham working men's club. You sympathised with Wolves plight but knew in your heart of hearts that things would one day improve. The wounds and scars would inevitably heal. But for Wolves, there were the lean times, that horrible period, those years of humiliation when nothing seemed to go right. One minute you're on the top of the world and the next you're cleaning the boots of the apprentices. Wolves fell from grace in the most embarrassing fashion. For years they were rubbing shoulders with the bigwigs of the old First Division.

Then they tumbled down the Leagues like some politician who'd fallen on the hardest times. One minute you're on the Commons front bench and the next you're on some sleazy and notorious park bench. During the Seventiesj Wolves could quite happily boast players who were sent from heaven. John Richards, bold and fearless, Kenny Hibbitt, tigerish and tenacious, Derek Dougan, tall, imposing and utterly dominant in the air, Mike Bailey, at the back, stern and totally uncompromising. It would have been hard for a bus to get past Bailey. Bailey was unforgiving, no-nonsense and unrepentant. No way through for opposition defences.

For part of the Seventies and Eighties, Ipswich Town appeared on the footballing radar rather like some shining star that shine but then vanished when circumstances intervened. For many of us, Ipswich Town played some of the most attractive and exciting football of the time. It would be easy to put Ipswich in some cosy stereotype but since Ipswich come from the Suffolk countryside, the temptation is just irresistible. Ipswich were rather like that friendly country uncle who always lavished you with kindness and sweets. Ipswich never forgot your birthday or your name. Ipswich were warm, thoughtful and sincere. Ipswich had principles and honourable intentions. Ipswich were good to their family, never disappointing, always there for you, inviting and accommodating. Their manager was one Sir Bobby Robson. Robson was the man who restored Ipswich, brought them back to life, put them back on the footballing map. In one breath-taking season at the beginning of the Sixties, Ipswich won the League Championship. The man who guided the Tractor Boys was a certain gentleman by the name of Sir Alf Ramsey. Ipswich had players like Leadbetter, Phillips and Ray Crawford, players of silk and chiffon, foot loose and fancy free. Just over a decade before Sir Bobby Robson grabbed Ipswich by the shirt collar, shook off all the restraints and allowed Ipswich to express themselves. During the late Seventies and early Eighties, Ipswich were the proverbial children in a toy shop. There was Eric Gates, Trevor Wymark, Clive Woods, Roger Osbourne, John Wark, David Geddes and Paul Mariner, quite literally a giant among centre forwards. Ipswich just moved through the gears, put their foot down on the accelerator and flowed across Portman Road. It was rather like watching a peacock unfurling its plumage. Somehow, you knew you were in the most elevated company. Ipswich were a cut above the rest but never quite the finished article. Ipswich had completeness about them but could never hit the right notes. Ipswich were genuinely classical but always frustrating runners-up. One day they'll step over the threshold and win something with flair and flourish.

I always had time for Leeds United. I know that people criticised and unfairly condemned them but I thought Leeds were a force for good rather than evil. The popular assumption was that Leeds were as hard as nails, hard tackling and totally misunderstood by those who didn't like them. When Leeds were in the best of attacking moods, they were gracious and dignified. They played the kind of football that had timing, texture and excessive class. There was a velvety richness about their football that spanned the generations. There was Johnny Giles, a midfield technician and playmaker supreme, Billy

Bremner, tireless and fiercely ambitious but, to all outward appearances, permanently seeking perfection, dissatisfied with imperfection, always striving for that magical moment. I don't think Bremner was ever deliberately hot headed and temperamental but throughout the Leeds side under Don Revie, there was a lovely thread running through them. Leeds had an underlying purity and clarity about them that spoke volumes. There were never any ulterior motives at Elland Road. Peter Lorimer had the most powerful shot ever seen on a football pitch, frightening missiles delivered with merciless ferocity. Mick Jones was forceful, ever present and always assertive. Jones perfectly weighted cross was met with Alan Clarke's dramatic diving header. That was Leeds in a nutshell. Neat, well-proportioned and streamlined. It always seemed a shame that nobody gave them the credit where it was due.

Part 8:
And now for a summary about London-a potted history if you like from my perspective.

It is true that I was brought up in the leafy shires of Ilford, Essex and to some extent this is the place that shaped my outlook and gave me the equipment for everything else that took place in my life in later years. It formed me, moulded me, influenced me, affected me and made me the person I am today. How could I not be grateful to Ilford? But there was somewhere else in my life that I had yet to discover, another location, another geographical landmark that must have existed.

London is the capital city, the seething metropolis, the bustling, noisy, fast, frantic, lovable yet vulnerable city that I came to know. I was brought up roughly five or ten minutes away from the Central Line tube railway system and this was the most direct way you could get to London from my parents' house. But it was accessible and you somehow felt that London was a distant but kindly neighbour just waiting for you, very obliging and always helpful. Perhaps London would offer me a cup of tea and a biscuit. It was but a fond hope.

The fact is that London remained slightly out of my vision until I was about five or six. London was that energetic, excitable and totally unpredictable character who refused to sit still for a moment. London was vibrant and throbbing, flashing and flickering, temporary and permanent. You had to watch where you were going in London; you needed eyes in the back of your head.

In London, you had to be careful, wary, vigilant and ever so slightly concerned. Of course London was everything: the little arcades and alleyways were surprising. They were surprising, endearing and beautifully historic. London is always moving, talking and walking. London is changing by the day, subconsciously perhaps, but always buzzing, drilling and hammering.

From a very early age, it was Piccadilly Circus that held my attention. My late and wonderful dad always believed that Piccadilly Circus was the centre of the world and to some extent it probably was. Piccadilly Circus was quite the brightest, most vivid and colourful place I'd ever seen.

Until then, from a very young viewpoint, Ilford had seemed extremely drab and dreary, grey and soul-less. Little did I know that London was about to offer me a brand new set of colours. The darkness and indistinctness was about to be replaced by a rousing riot of reds, stirring yellows and oranges and enthusiastic greens. Not forgetting the boisterous blues. London had burst into my consciousness rather like an unexpected guest at a party.

Piccadilly Circus, though, was my introduction to the capital city. It was an invitation that I just had to accept. Piccadilly Circus was just the most incredible place I'd ever seen, a hive of activity, jumping, jiving and pulsating. Piccadilly was a walking, talking advertisement for the greatest city I'd ever seen. It hummed, purred, mumbled and muttered. Sometimes it could be sarcastic and very hurtful, but then again it could also be sad and poetic. But nobody could hold Piccadilly back. It was just charismatic, relentless, pleased to see you.

My dad always felt a very emotional almost spiritual connection with Piccadilly Circus. Piccadilly was a blaze of light, constantly flashing, flickering and occasionally flirting. Piccadilly surrounded you, hit you between the eyes and startled you. It was outrageous, outlandish, excessively exuberant and utterly beyond belief.

There was something about Piccadilly Circus that convinced you that everything would turn out for the best. I think my dad felt that the West End was the place where all that was good in life could be found. Piccadilly had value, significance, a very real sense of theatre, fame, celebrity, worth its weight in gold. My dad always felt that Piccadilly made him feel important and this was undeniably true.

There were the shops, shop windows forever advertising winter, summer and spring sales. There were the cosy cafes with their very intimate atmosphere. There was the Quality Inn restaurant with its soft lighting, the still very prominent Aberdeen Steak House, Lyons Corner House and the Cumberland Palace Hotel in Marble Arch. There was a very cultural air about the whole of the West End which will always exist.

You always felt that the West End had unexplored passageways, narrow alleyways, haunting arcades, a place that was both mysterious and obvious. There were always signs pointing one way and clear indications pointing the other. Of course, the West End had its museums, art galleries and theatres. My dad had always told me about them.

But there was something indefinably alluring about the West End. It had a wondrous variety, vividness and a spellbinding sorcery. It was endlessly diverse, constantly changing and evolving, incredibly unpredictable; never less than surprising. But for all its fancy clothing and mischievous flamboyance, the West End did have an unmistakable shyness about it.

The West End that my dad showed me had a lovely intimacy about it. Away from the bright lights, the West End could also be very quiet and secretive. I always felt as if the West End still had something to hide. There was something it wasn't telling me. London had always been a very loud, brash and confident capital city but there was something deep within the cracks of its pavements that I could never see.

In between all of the big department stores such as Selfridges and C & A, there was something that must have been very unsettling and nerve racking. There was a chilling intensity about the West End. On dark winter evenings, I always felt there was something inexplicable and unfathomable about it. London had a genuine nervousness, an irrational fear of the unknown, a sense that nothing could ever be resolved or reconciled. London could be wildly optimistic one moment and then utterly heartbroken and defeated five minutes later.

I never got around to visiting the museums and art galleries but my dad loved everything about the West End. There were the seductive tea and coffee shops, there was a dizziness and giddiness about the place. It had constant movement, vigour and vivacity. The West End was always on the go, never pausing for a second, rushed off its feet. But then you'd have hardly expected anything else.

Throughout the West End, there was a feeling of restlessness which has always been there. London, for me, always felt as if it was trying to prove something to me. If Shakespeare had still been alive, you somehow suspected that London during the Sixties and Seventies would have made the perfect subject matter.

I felt that there were elements of the West End that would have moved Shakespeare to all of those heartfelt emotions. There was the tragedy of the homeless and poverty stricken, the drunks and tramps who were almost permanent fixtures in draughty doorways and yet there was, in complete contrast, a sense of ever present hope. There were the glitzy five star hotels, the magically opulent dance halls, Lyons Corner House and unforgettable musicals at the theatres. London had the lot: choice, diversity, quality and complete confidence. That could never ever be questioned. London had guts, energy, gallantry and gusto. London would always accept your hat and coat most politely. London was that kind of city. Or so it seemed to me. But then London always did.

Then of course there was Trafalgar Square, London's most historic landmark. Trafalgar Square had the most distinctive of personalities. During my early years, Trafalgar Square was just the most remarkable place I'd ever seen. It was fun, enormously popular, touristy, quirky and sociable.

On our way home from the West End, my dad would always make a point of driving around Trafalgar Square. I think he must have felt a deep affection and affinity for it because the Square had a certain magnetism about it. There was something very striking and commanding about Trafalgar Square that always made you feel good.

I seem to remember spending some of my Sunday afternoons feeding the famous pigeons, mingling with the other kids, their families and of course the thousands of tourists. You felt at one with the world in Trafalgar Square. For a young child, it was a good to place to be. There was a constant excitement and frenzy about the Square that made you feel that nothing else mattered.

Of course, the central feature of Trafalgar Square was Nelson's Column, that soaring monument that towered over the West End skyline. As a kid, Nelson's Column was just about the most astonishing of all sights. Even now, it still has a significance and permanence about it that takes the breath away.

The Square also had something else going for it. Pigeons flew in from the remotest corners of the universe. Pigeons seemed to take up full time residence in the West End. In fact, once they'd settled in Trafalgar Square, it was hard to budge them. They'd taken out a mortgage on the place or perhaps they were just lease-holders. No point in asking them for the rent. Still they did bring a smile to this innocent five year olds face.

I suppose the only reason why so many of our feathered friends gathered in their multitudes was food. For years and years, day after day, grey breasted pigeons would flutter in gracefully from far and wide. But the one underlying reason for their presence, there was bird seed and more bird seed. They were undeniably spoilt and at times, it seemed, over fed.

I can remember my parents wandering into the Square and buying the cheapest bird seed in town. I was suddenly surrounded by hordes of tourists and children, bursting with uncontrollable enthusiasm. Hundreds of pigeons would swirl and twirl in some almost ritualistic dance. They would then circle around us, ceaselessly nibbling at a carpet of seed. It was one of London's most unique of spectacles. Nothing ever challenged it.

But London, I felt, always had a very distinguished appearance about it. As soon as you arrived in the City or the West End, you were immediately made to feel hugely important, utterly dignified. Places such as Piccadilly Circus, Chinatown in Leicester Square, Trafalgar Square and the House of Commons in Westminster, had very distinctive characteristics; never pompous because that would have implied that it felt superior to you. Westminster was that well-read university student who knew everything but never boasted about it. Westminster was just very worldly, possibly stuffy but historically accurate. Westminster was very official and officious, a political nerve centre, a legal minefield, intolerant from time to time but, when the mood took it, comical and let's face it silly.

On our frequent Sunday afternoon journeys to the West End, my eyes would always be drawn to the captivating bridges. There were the advertising hoardings, revealing and culturally suggestive. You always felt that those huge advert boards were trying to sell you something while you were in the car. Old Spice after shave lotion, Coca Cola, boxes of eggs, milk, a Mars a day helps you work, rest and play. They were tempting offers, very persuasive, sometimes misleading but guaranteed to make you laugh.

Ah yes, there were the bridges, quite a number of them. There was London Bridge, Tower Bridge, Hammersmith Bridge and Vauxhall Bridge. The one though that captured my attention was the one on the Embankment. I'll always remember my dad pulling up to the traffic lights on the Embankment and being wide eyed with wonder.

This was the River Thames, that flowing, fluent and graceful stretch of water that never ever lost its temper. The Thames was soothing to the soul, relaxing and unperturbed by all the noises coming from the House of Commons. I would always see hundreds of tourists milling around the Embankment, waiting patiently for the next trip to Hampton Court.

In front of you was Big Ben, towering, sturdy, steadfast, upright, always in charge. Big Ben was one of the most punctual clocks in the whole of London. Most of us without a watch would always be reliably informed that Big Ben was always on time and never late.

As my dad's car approached Big Ben, I would instinctively know that I was in the presence of something very unique. I think I knew that Big Ben had always been part of my childhood because you were always conscious and aware of it. TV gave it a certain relevance but to see it up close and personal was something entirely different. It was tall, impressive and to some extent too majestic for words.

Big Ben had charm and a real sense of permanence. I felt that Big Ben would always be there, that it was very much a part of my history and your history. You'd read about in school history books, you'd seen it on the telly, you'd seen on it postcards. It was a souvenir, an essential part of the London landscape.

There was something about Big Ben that you felt deeply connected to. The clock itself had been there of course for many centuries but it gave you the impression that Big Ben would be there for eternity, immaculate, very professional, appreciative of the tourists around it but indifferent to the thunderous London traffic. Big Ben always looked well turned out, never scruffy or dishevelled. It combed its hair and straightened its tie.

Then there were trips back home that I think my dad always loved. It was via Trafalgar Square before veering off to the City of London. There was that splendid contrast of the brightly lit and dazzling West End and the City of London which always seemed very dull, dark and somewhat sombre to me. Still, I think it was for that reason alone that my dad was stunned and mesmerised by it all.

The City of London on a Sunday afternoon was a complete ghost town. The streets had a rather chilling emptiness about them, an unmistakable sadness that suddenly hit you between the eyes. The silence was somehow aching, an overwhelming sense that London had shut down for the day. London had an almost lingering air of hurt and desertion. The City of London, in my eyes, felt very wounded, isolated and alienated.

I used to think that the City on a Sunday was the one place in the world that felt very lonely, deeply upset by the gossip and speculation. Perhaps the City felt unwanted, cheap and sleazy, used and abused. Perhaps the City was one place that was simply taken for granted, ripe for exploitation. The City on a Sunday afternoon though, had no personality, no jokes, no laughs and no light. It was heartbroken, devastated and inconsolable.

Wherever you looked in the City, the buildings had that very real air of helplessness and solemnity. The big City banks were now cloaked in complete darkness, the Bank of England itself looked both grey and haunted, pale and weather beaten in the fading light of a winter's afternoon. The City itself always looked in need of a good holiday but never thought of popping into a travel agency. Mind you, there was always Monday morning to look forward to and all of those thousands of pin stripe suits and bowler hats.

But as we travelled through the City and all its financial powerhouses, I suddenly became aware of a very noticeable change of mood. Whereas the West End had been this explosion of flashing lights, now the City was nervously hiding away from public view, retreating into its shell. London wanted its privacy, London wanted to be mysterious and London had an air of entitlement. It was Sunday after all and of course London could kick off its shoes and enjoy itself. When all was said and done, it was the weekend. Undeniably so.

On a Sunday afternoon, the City and the West End were strangers to each other. If you'd told the City that it was going to be desolate, I suspect that the West End would have never believed this to be the case. You had to convince the City that the only reason it was so lifeless over the weekend was because the West End had robbed them of their flamboyance. It may have been cruel but this was how the system worked.

Not that the City ever looked as if it was ever interested in anything. Admittedly, it came alive during the week with its thousands of bankers and financial masterminds. But I always got the impression that the City, on a Sunday afternoon, just wanted to sleep. No hectic running after Route Master buses with an umbrella to hand, no sense of urgency or emergency, no rushing for Tube trains or the incessant clatter of feet. Everything was quiet, everything and everybody felt calm and composed. Just the way it should be.

London did like the quiet and there was a solitude about the capital that almost made your heart weep. When the street lamps went out and night fell, you somehow believed that London was on its own. The buses still hummed and the lorries still rumbled but there was an ever present sense that London had nobody to turn to. You held out your sympathetic hand but winter had that enveloping darkness that may have been too much for some.

During the winter though, London still had an irresistible magnetism about it. Long after the tourists had gone, the theatre signs were still very much in evidence: flashing and flickering hypnotically, flirting with us outrageously, luring us with those beckoning fingers, enticing us mischievously, giggling and laughing almost constantly. London could still be the centre of the universe. It had something that was simply indefinable, witty and frivolous. It would always leave you rolling about with happiness in the aisles.

But for all its showiness and flashiness, London was still appealing, good looking and adorably becoming. There was something you couldn't quite put your finger on when the subject of London cropped up. It was all very well intentioned and never disappointing, always the flavour of the month and never short of a good word.

And then there was Soho, London's favourite cousin, that slightly eccentric uncle that nestled comfortably next to the West End. Soho was that ever so slightly naughty kid, impudent and permanently artistic. Years ago, Soho might have been regarded with nothing but suspicion. There was, quite possibly, an air of seediness and shallowness about it that none of us could quite understand.

During the Fifties, Soho had classical coffee bars, jumping and jiving juke boxes and most of London's show business community: pop singers, Elvis impersonators, songwriters of some renown and Sir Cliff Richard in all his pomp. There were artists, painters, drinkers and every cultural icon you could think of.

But for me, Soho always seemed to have the sleaziest of reputations, an air of cheapness, shiftiness and superficiality. Soho, I felt, was the home of illicit sex, peep shows, nudge nudge wink wink, dubious women of the night. For much of the Seventies, Soho might have been regarded as distasteful, shameful and totally repulsive. Or so it seemed.

Soho though did change her image. In years to come, she became far more acceptable and nicer to all. When it finally shed its shabby, shop-soiled image, Soho re-discovered an altogether healthier alternative, something more invigorating and salubrious. There was a much cleaner air about Soho. Soho had now cleaned up its act and now looked fitter than ever. Somehow, Soho had quite literally re-invented itself, smartened itself up and felt good about itself. Finally it had found art and literature, a new found culture and eloquence.

Now the people who used to sneak their way into the peep shows quite shame-facedly, suddenly found that it was much easier to sit down in cafes and read. Now they could throw back their cappuccinos, safe in the knowledge that vulgarity was a thing of the past. Now they too could be wise, knowledgeable and learned. They were the well-read and well-informed members of society. They were the ones who went to the latest art exhibitions and jazz clubs. Soho had found its music and its soul.

Then of course there was Covent Garden. Covent Garden is by far the most attractive part of London. Covent Garden is one of those London landmarks that I would never tire of visiting and revisiting. Even as a child, it seemed to have that lovely air of old fashioned grandeur. Covent Garden was pleasing to the eye and utterly presentable.

But it's still essentially Victorian and, for all the right reasons, utterly charming. There are the delightful street performers, the piazza, a sprawling open air square with hundreds and thousands of tourists. There is a feeling that all in the world is well and that London can joke and smile.

Then there are of course the restaurants and cafes, bristling with chit chat, roaring laughter and cheerful banter. Both the restaurants and cafes seem to spread right across the length and breadth, sweeping out onto two floors and invariably busy. There is a distinct Dickensian feel about Covent Garden with its narrow passageways and quaintly designed shop windows.

I'm sure my parents must have taken me to Covent Garden but alas the memories are now fading and vanishing. The old markets have now long since gone but I suspect you can, if you listen carefully, still hear the voices of the barrow boys, the market traders in full cry.

Day after day, season after season the fruit and veg sellers would stand there rubbing their tired hands, adjusting the apples and oranges and yelling out their infectious chants. These are the people who were an essential part of the London furniture. Without them, I suspect London would, quite possibly, feel lost and disenchanted.

The people who ran those stalls wouldn't have dreamt of judging you, merely impartial observers who just wanted to be your friend. Covent Garden never left you feeling that you owed something to them. They would never leave you with a guilty conscience and nothing was too much trouble. Covent Garden was a living and breathing theatre. There were the people in silver and bronze who never moved, the jugglers or acrobats, the daredevil stuntmen and women, the musicians who played endlessly and blissfully for a penny in their caps.

Of course, London had its faults and foibles. It could drive you crazy, leave you speechless and dumbfounded and occasionally throw you off the trail. London went forwards, backwards, revelled in the moment and then collapsed with exhaustion. I believe London was always on the move, tireless and indefatigable. But then again, London could be irritating and unreliable, occasionally late for its appointment.

Most of the heavy traffic in the West End seemed to be confined to Oxford Street, Marble Arch and Piccadilly Circus. How could I ever forget the stately procession of double decker Route Master red buses. They stopped and started, paused and pondered, vehicles with a very real air of superiority about them. They gave London a very real air of nobility. They were hugely respected and respectable. In many ways, they gave London a distinctive character, a golden hallmark of quality.

There was about Oxford Street a pulsating energy, throbbing intensity, the sense that something thrilling and important was about to happen. London was always a hive of activity, its shops were alive with wandering and admiring customers. There were the huge department stores, its windows a glorious tribute to London in all her commercial pomp. You almost felt that London couldn't stand still for a moment, winding and twisting around sharp bends, then sprinting and accelerating from the traffic lights at some ridiculous speed.

But Oxford Street and Marble Arch always seemed to be clogged up with buses, cars and lorries, choked and strangled by those repulsive exhaust fumes. There was about the West End a rich air of constancy and regularity, a feeling that this is the way it had always been and always would be.

Selfridges was that stunning department store that seemed to dominate Oxford Street. Everybody shopped at Selfridges, everybody pushed and jostled their way into the winter and summer sales. It was London at its most chaotic, London at its greediest and breathlessly frantic. There was no reason for all the madness and mayhem. Surely that new sofa or coffee table could wait for a while but it had to be now.

London was just grabbing and grasping, impatient and materialistic. There was no need to be so uptight and inconsiderate. Surely London could just slow down, have a breather, think of others and politely ask for help from an assistant. Why did London have to be so demanding and, at times unreasonably aggressive?

Eventually, London would be served and there would never be a reason to panic. Why did London have to be so edgy and agitated? Why was everything so urgent and critical? London had to buy all of the latest gadgets and electrical appliances. London had to be in the front of the queue, desperate to possess, acquisitive, must have it immediately. No time to waste. Besides, the neighbours had it so why shouldn't we. You had to keep up with the latest trends otherwise you'd be left behind and that would never do. It was all about appearances and nothing else.

But I think we all embraced London like a long lost relative. We would rush up to London and hug it with a tenderness that only we could feel. Other people had a very unique way of showing how glad they were to see London. I think most people thought of London as the centre of their universe. London was rather like the best birthday present, a classic childhood toy, a golden treasure that never lost its sheen.

On the subject of childhood toys, London also had Hamley's, possibly the most famous toy shop in the world. I may have been taken to Hamley's on a few occasions but my parents never believed in spoiling me so I think they must have believed that Hamley's was just another fleeting visit.

Now Hamley's was that toy and game gold mine in Regent Street. I seem to remember walking down Regent Street as a child and never realising just how dignified looking it was. It was the kind of street that commanded an almost instant respect as soon as you set eyes on it.

Regent Street has that very distinctive bend and curve that seems to give it character and identification. I don't know why but Regent Street reminds me of some very pompous Dickensian figures who think they know everything. There's something very upper crust and haughty about Regent Street that never ceases to amaze me. But there can be nothing wrong with pomposity.

I can remember both my parents and I slowly wandering, admiring, and then pointing at all manner of clothing and ornaments. There were shop windows that were permanently posh and garishly ostentatious. They were the shops that were undeniably stylish, wonderfully picturesque and utterly decorous. Your breath was taken away, your senses suspended, your eyes illuminated. London in its finest colours, its shining light.

I suppose I must have felt that the West End was too glamorous for its own good and that maybe I was just too spoilt. Perhaps I'd seen London through rose tinted spectacles and refused to see its darker and dingier side. Of course it had its faults and foibles. You had to acknowledge that not everything in the garden was green. Of course, London had its prickly thorns, its sharp edges and grey, dubious side-streets.

London had those windy, draughty back alleyways in both the City and the West End. It had hidden, secretive passages, never seen during the day but quite clearly visible at night. The West End and the City, although business-like and commanding during the day, would always fade into anonymity at night.

London, I suppose, did have an air of cheapness and shallowness at night. For years, some might have believed that Soho made sure of that. Late at night, the mascara on Soho's face would look smeared and smudged but perhaps that was part of its inescapable charm.

Anyway, there were times when London seemed to put on the most outrageous mask or maybe it wanted to disguise itself so nobody would recognise it. I'm sure that for all its boldness and bravado, there remains an air of very real fragility. It seems to be nervously looking over its shoulder, wary and cautious. Occasionally London gets very moody and broody, particularly during the winter months.

To my untutored eye, those lovely theatres and fountains in Trafalgar Square somehow look very demoralised and dejected. I get the feeling that during November, December and January, London looks as though it has lost some bloody battle: broken, defeated and utterly dispirited.

Admittedly, its Aberdeen Steak Houses, Prêt A Mangers, Costas and Wetherspoons are still thriving businesses but the lights in other shop windows look dimmer. London seems to lose its focus and bearings. It almost feels as though somebody has, quite deliberately, thrown a blanket over the whole of the West End and City.

But during the summer, the West End throws off its stifling coats and pullovers before springing into action. Covent Garden is one enormous street theatre, Trafalgar Square becomes the People's square, a mass of humanity, democracy at its best, tourists, campaigning and rallying activists, a political platform, worldly and utterly cosmopolitan.

In contrast to the winter months when London becomes very sad, regretful, reflective and introspective, summer is one spectacularly colourful festival. Wherever you go in the West End and City, everybody seems to feel better about themselves. No more aches and pains, stifled hopes or general pessimism. But when summer arrives we always feel free, healthier, released, liberated, nothing else matters. It is an ecstasy we're all capable of feeling but are too reluctant to show during the winter.

You can now walk down Oxford Street, Regent Street through Hyde Park and Green Park without a single twinge of discomfort and self-consciousness. In fact, you can walk through any park and feel comfortable about yourself, deeply appreciative of the huge beech trees towering over you, suddenly aware of the lush, lighter green grass, skateboarders weaving all manner of intricate patterns, people licking endless supplies of ice cream. London is around you, in front of you and behind you, grinning, giggling, shouting, yelling, laughing, posing and strutting.

London was, and remains, richly intoxicating, wistfully yearning for long, hot summer days, simply breath-taking and beautiful. London tells us that it's always been good to be alive. There was a very real feeling of light and shade. Summertime in London reinforced your sense of well-being, illustrated the finer things in life, broadened your outlook, convinced you quite categorically that there was never anything to worry about.

London undoubtedly and rightly boasts some of the prettiest, divinely stunning and idyllic parks I'd ever seen. Both Hyde and Regents are huge, sprawling, all-encompassing and magnificently green. They remain London's healthiest lungs, its virile veins, active arteries and fully functioning blood vessels. I always felt that all the roses, tulips and lakes had something of a royal and aristocratic look about them. There was something serenely undisturbed about those endless avenues of trees. They seemed to have a timeless beauty, something of the countryside, rightly poetic, wonderfully lyrical.

92

So this is the London I'd always dreamt about, longed for, fondly imagined, constantly questioned and never doubted. I'd always believed that London art galleries were cultural goldmines where knowledgeable and erudite people stand in complete adoration. Some might have thought of them as pretentious and perhaps too clever for their own good.

I've never been to the National Portrait Gallery but it is easy to imagine groups of tourists gazing admiringly at some of the finest historical characters who ever lived. Art galleries and museums gave London an almost enviable status and prestige. They were very real centres of education, engaging the mind from all angles. Not only were they thought provoking but they also took you on the most absorbing intellectual journey you'd ever been on.

When I was a kid, we were always taken on those occasional days out to museums and art galleries. It was invariably the Science Museum or the Natural History Museum but you were always guaranteed a good day out. My mum would pack me egg and onion sandwiches for lunch and a bag of crisps. But for reasons that were beyond me, I think you had pay for your own can of Coke as well. Still it was refreshing and nourishing.

Museums also attracted the interested and fascinated, the know-alls, the cognoscenti perhaps. Most can see them and some will form very definite opinions of them. They stand around together, deep in concentration, glasses hanging around the neck, pondering, analysing and considering. Every so often, they'll point at the paintings, scratch their chins and whisper something very learned to their friends. Then they'll move very quietly to another position, all the while staring and examining, instantly making new judgments and observations.

Art galleries are peaceful, thoughtful places and London I feel sure has always had a soft spot for its art and literature. As a kid, you dismissed museums and art galleries because you probably felt that at no stage in later life would you ever need to know anything about Degas, Constable or Turner.

So what were museums like? The Science Museum did give you an intriguing insight into the world of weird and wonderful objects. Wherever I looked, I could see cogs, wheels, strange mechanical creations, levers, pulleys, boxes with electrical currents and things that may well have gone bump in the night.

The Science Museum, though, somehow seemed irrelevant and insignificant. Admittedly, it was interesting and really gave you some mental stimulus. But as a youngster, you somehow felt that the Science Museum would never lead you into the promised land of riches and prosperity.

It was all well and good if you wanted to be a chemist or a physics teacher but to my very immature and impressionable mind, it was just an excuse to compare Pannini football stickers with my mates.

Then there was the Natural History Museum, a vast and towering structure that had everything you could possibly want. It had huge prehistoric dinosaurs, glass cases with all manner of plant life from another time. The Natural History Museum was the place to visit, a maze of corridors and amazing exhibits.

Then there was Madame Tussauds, a very distinguished looking building that looked as good on the outside as it did on the inside. Madame Tussauds was popular, touristy, always fashionable, never dated and somehow architecturally correct. Madame Tussauds had that wonderful air of solidity and superiority. It left you with the impression that nobody could match it. Madame Tussauds was in complete charge.

One of the most notable features of Tussauds was that brilliant green dome, strikingly dominant and well proportioned. For as long as I can remember, that green dome came to represent everything that is essentially traditional about London. That green dome seems to have spanned the decades and centuries without as much as one complaint. I don't think I ever heard a restless sigh or a muffled grumble.

But Tussauds will always be famous for those monumental queues, those queues that went on forever and ever more. Madame Tussauds, I feel sure, was wholly responsible for the whole concept of queuing. The only other London tourist attraction that comes anywhere remotely as the queuing capital of the world is the Hard Rock Cafe in Piccadilly.

But those queues for Tussauds were something else. For as long as I can remember, Baker Street has always attracted the great and good in their hundreds and thousands. They swarmed around Madame Tussauds like the proverbial bees around a honey pot. They were the magnificent multitudes, snaking around the building and then slowly drifting towards the entrance in a steady and stately procession.

I seem to remember that you were spell bound by the sheer size of the crowds and the babble of voices increasing in volume. From all corners of the universe, the tourists with hats, without hats, with cameras and without cameras, money purses permanently by their side. English, French, Germans, Italians, Spanish, South Africans, South Americans, Australians, Chinese, Japanese and Russians. They would flock together, huge families, close friends, intrigued by-standers, obvious admirers. They were all there waiting patiently, mumbling, muttering, murmuring, giggling and guffawing. Sometimes clear but, from time to time, totally incoherent.

Are these the normal sounds that I've always heard in London or is there a distinct pitch in their voices I've never heard? Are there times when London spends most of the day whispering or does London acquire a different personality as the day progresses?

We all know about the market traders in Oxford Street, the souvenir sellers with their Union Jack patriotism, a rich tapestry of everybody and everything. London had and still has that inclusive, warm-hearted air about it. Because of its history and its tradition, you felt under obligation to be kind to London. Besides London has never done anybody any harm and you had to show your appreciation.

There was never anything deceitful or devious about London. You never felt London there was anything suspect or underhand about the capital city. It would lay its cards on the table and make its very brave pronouncements. In Trafalgar Square, the pigeons have gone and during the summer, London becomes expressive and opinionated, vocal and vociferous, righteously standing up for its rights and never less than confident.

London always had the guts to try something new and was always ground breaking. London wanted to be in the forefront, leading the way, creating, inventing, carving and chipping. London was proud of everything it had turned its hand to and succeeded. London could never stand still, it had to be experimental and pioneering, it had to be the best and never the worst. London had to put its hand on the accelerator, follow the rest of the world, keep up with technology, speed up and forge ahead. Of course London had considerable influence but it wasn't so much a case of what you knew, more who you knew.

As a kid, I'll always remember Nelson's Column in Trafalgar Square and remember being astonished by it. It confirmed everything I'd ever been told about London. Nelson's Column gave the West End height and stature. I would gaze spellbound and awe-struck as Nelson proudly surveyed his West End, his people. There were the inimitable theatre goers in Shaftesbury Avenue, hurrying and scurrying, pausing and stopping, sometimes reflective but always on the go.

Then of course we had England's national treasures, the places that are always associated with England, frequently mentioned at dinner parties, freely discussed at all manner of social gatherings. They were the familiar locations of our childhood, those celebrated events that we all know. All you had to was open up on the subject and you'd know exactly you were in the right company.

There was Lord's Cricket Ground in St John's Wood, one of London's most enduring and most revered of all sporting grounds. Lord's was English cricket's headquarters, an immense cricketing bastion with a secure place in cricketing folklore. Everybody had heard of Lord's, Bradman's magisterial batting displays, Fred Truman steaming in from the pavilion end like a locomotive train, Jim Laker, sleeves dutifully rolled up, trundling in with his mischievous spin.

I don't think London could ever be frozen in time because there is a sense that everything has to move forward quickly and purposefully. London must undergo transformation, there has to be development and evolution otherwise London would become very dated, static and antiquated. London would become very lifeless, set in its own ways, stuck in a rut and just utterly complacent.

Some things though should remain as they are and not the way we'd like them to be. For instance, London should never ever lose the Hare Krishna religious sect. For years and years, these lovable characters have marched up and down Oxford Street, happily oblivious to the outside world and happily harmonising all the way up to Marble Arch.

Hare Krishna was part and parcel of the West End scenery, men and women in silky robes, gently tapping their tambourines and dancing to the folksy sounding beat. There is an almost hypnotic intensity about their act that has to be remarked upon. It is consistently London.

Then there was the Sandwich Board Man, a delightful chap who would walk around the streets of London cheerfully acknowledging passers-by. He was the man with the humorous spiel and a message to convey.. The Sandwich Board Man made the West End tick, a much understated man with understated ways.

So what about London on the day of the 1966 World Cup Final? It was the day England finally got to show off its fanciest clothing, the day it all came right, the day we were recognised and honoured by the great and good. It was the day we discovered just how good it feels to be triumphant and victorious. Nobody could argue that at long last, we too could win things and shout about it afterwards.

So what were we doing that unforgettable day? What were you doing? Why did that day feel just right? What was so promising and auspicious about it? Why did the day mean so much to England? Of course we were the centre of attention and of course we'd win. It was in the stars, the red top papers had said it and you had to believe it. It was fated to be England's finest sporting hour.

London, of course, was still buzzing and still consumed with itself. There were the thousands of fluttering pigeons in Trafalgar Square, gentlemen with long coats feeding those pigeons, husbands and wives with their children. The fountains were gushing and spraying with effervescent fervour. There was a naturalness and spontaneity about it all. There was something just electric and truly magical about London. Nothing was forced and so fitting and deserving too. It was about time.

During the Sixties, London and its suburbs were somehow the transport capital of the world. There were clattering, rattling trams and trolley buses. I've no personal recollection of the trams and trolley buses but I do know that this was what they did for a living. They would slide along wires suspended but firmly attached, hurtling around corners and quite literally sparking.

Then there were the Route Masters, those marvellous red buses that dominated the London landscape. The Route Masters were those magnificent feats of engineering, smooth moving vehicles that eased their way around the West End and the London suburbs. You had to be pretty sharp and brave to catch one of those buses because if you didn't, they would simply fly away into the distance, leaving you gasping for breath.

But the roads of London during the 1960s just seemed so much emptier and quieter. The black cabs, an essential part of the London scenery, were huge and very distinctive, winding and weaving in and out of the West End traffic. The cars, of course were fashionably big or dinky and small.

Around the streets, women, wearing those long dresses, would happily stroll around the West End with black handbags faithfully by their side. Most of the ladies of that era had the same hair as the pop icon Helen Shapiro, smartly combed with scarves on their head.

But what about London with its flashing Piccadilly Circus neon lights, the brazen advertisements for Coca Cola, Timex, Bolivar, Timex, Wrigley's Spearmint Gum and Schweppes, constantly playing with our imaginations, on and off. London had the Talk of the Town, quite the most handsome centre of show business and cabaret. London felt absolutely brilliant, in the rudest of health.

So what about London on the day of the 1966 World Cup Final, England against West Germany. What did you do that scintillating Saturday? You must have woken up early because everybody else did. You must have gone downstairs in your clean shirt and well ironed trousers wearing, quite possibly, braces. Those men who worked in the City during the week must have deliberately dressed down over the weekend.

Then I suspect you settled down for breakfast in your kitchen. Now at the time, there was a wonderful telly advert singing the praises of eggs. Tony Hancock, that comic genius but troubled soul, would happily tap his spoon on his egg encouraging the masses to eat runny eggs.

Then we would munch our Corn Flakes, study the form at the Sandown races before finishing the crossword in that new paper called the Sun. In those days, the football pools were remarkably popular and most of us loved to scribble in our 8 draws. Maybe it would be our week to clean up the thousands of pounds in prize money. Besides, Viv Nicholson had done it so why couldn't we?

We would then take the dog for a walk around the local park, excitedly discuss the World Cup Final with our neighbours and then hope against hope that this would be the day when England would be appointed as World Football Champions.

Outside, the family Ford Anglia car, which looked like one of those Dinky Toys that my mum bought for me, would gleam in the watery sunshine. Then, the postman would merrily whistle his way along the roads and the Unigate milk float would clink its bottles with the most musical melodies.

I think most dads of the Sixties had their tried and tested routines. Walk the dog, pop into the bookmakers for a bet or two and sneak into the pub for a swift pint or two. It was all very customary and inevitable. It was rather like the act of sleeping and breathing.

Then there was Mum, immaculate, neat, hard-working and industrious. There she was, washing up the breakfast tables, scrubbing the plates and cups, dedicated to the family unit. Mums, of course, with very few exceptions, were never really interested in sport or football so would listen to their husbands and sons kindly and indulgently. Mums would never complain about the amount of sport on TV but it wasn't something they could get excited about.

Then dad would return from the bookies, walk into the kitchen, wolf down a couple of cheese and pickle sandwiches and then down that cup of tea, a cup made from the finest bone china. This was a Saturday unlike any Saturday. This was not a day for rummaging around in the garden shed or sorting out the fishing gear. This was a day for righteous patriotism, supporting the national side, digging out the red, white and blue scarf and cleaning the rattle. It was the best of all days for those who were there in 1966.

What happened next? The shoes would be lovingly polished, the hair, a lustrous slick black or blonde. Everything had to be done correctly and properly because this would be the day of all days. I'm not suggesting that the whole of England threw celebratory street parties but I think England must have known that this was a day quite apart from any other. We would all go crazy, become ecstatic and jump around with complete abandonment.

So father and son would set out in the Anglia car or the grey Tube train, perhaps the Route Master bus. I think we must have been privately confident about victory that day but all the same, ever so nervy just in case the unthinkable happened and we lost. The Germans would gloat unashamedly, knock back their innumerable beers and taunt us mercilessly about the Kaiser, the Emperor Franz Beckenbauer, the obviously stylish central defender who would conquer the world and the English.

Dad would treat his son to the conventional beef burger or hot dog and chips for the princely sum of a couple of shillings. Then they wandered around the famous Wembley Stadium, sniffing the Saturday afternoon air, surrounded by masses and masses of England fans, bright eyed and bushy tailed, breezy, happy go lucky and buoyant.

Suddenly there was the heartiest of cheering, a Hoorah and Come on England from the permanently enthusiastic teenagers. Flags and banners would flap and ripple in the gentle summer wind listlessly. Rattles could be heard far and wide punctuated by those wonderfully timeless klaxon horns. It sounded like a rehearsal for the Last Night at The Proms.

Then dad would sidle up to the programme stall, the most prized souvenir. Now these were the days when everything and anything would set you back a mere couple of shillings or old pennies. The days of millions and billions were a far off galaxy in the 21st century.

Everything was cheap, available for a bargain price, a mere pittance. Clothes were just incredibly attractive, toys and games were just too good to be true, food could be bought in huge quantities. Tesco's was now a flourishing concern, Sainsbury's was now becoming a household and renowned name and everything seemed to be expanding.

But a programme for the 1966 World Cup Final must have been particularly special. Remember, England had achieved nothing for as long as anybody could remember. So a World Cup Final programme would be something to boast about proudly to our grandchildren and their children. Oh what a day, what a location, what a post code, what a month, the penultimate day of July was bathed in endless sunshine and radiant warmth.

And so we would enter the old Wembley Stadium with its domed towers and marvellous sound system, those great acoustics. How the dads, sons, uncles and cousins all came together in one big united family, one harmonious collective unit. That day was like the punctuation mark of our lives, our dad's life, the comma in between, the semi colon and full stop. Victory would be ours, the utter certainty.

Everything boiled down to that one stupendous 4-2 victory against the West Germans in the World Cup Final. It was the greatest of wish fulfilments, that thunderous crescendo, that moment when the waves crashed onto the beach, when Beethoven was in his pomp and Churchill gave his two fingered salute to the nation. It was the biggest result in our lives, the culmination, a labour of love. Glory Glory England would be that male and macho chant. Glory indeed.

And so they emerged from the tunnel. Sir Geoff Hurst, Martin Peters, Nobby Stiles, Bobby Moore, the immaculately tidy and clean living captain, Roger Hunt, Alan Ball, tough tackling, tenacious terrier, Jack Charlton, tall, absolutely assured, positively and unequivocally domineering. Jack never stood for any nonsense, no holds barred and was ferociously combative. George Cohen, honest, obliging and co-operative at full back. Gordon Banks, a goalkeeper with the safest hands in the business was agile and flexible.

So these were the men who were responsible for July 30, the men who gave dads and sons a reason to feel that everything would turn out for the best. Nothing could possibly go wrong. I think there was a widely held belief that this day would be the ultimate in rags to riches stories, fruitful, positive and moderately profitable but then very few of the players were money grabbing mercenaries. You played the game because you loved it.

Anyway, back in the tunnel, father and son waited patiently for the kick off, flicking eagerly through the match programme and then discussing how unfortunate Jimmy Greaves had been. Greaves, of course, was the unlucky one that day. Poor Jimmy had been injured on that day of all days and was left out of the final eleven. Jimmy had to kick his heels and was therefore deprived of his place in the sun. Of course he would receive his World Cup winner's medal but not playing in the Final was tantamount to failure. It just wasn't' the same. Still this was England's day. It wouldn't hurt to be ever so slightly smug and nationalistic. Everybody else was.

And so father would turn to son in his Union Jack cap and scarf, father and son on the same wavelength, both communicating on the same level, both united in their love of football, a perfect understanding and the most remarkable rapport. It was almost as if they could read each other's minds, anticipate each other's sentences and punctuate each other's conversation.

What exactly would father and son been talking about in 1966. Dad would probably have mentioned the latest exploits of Elsie Tanner and Ena Sharples, a fleeting word about Len Fairclough and Ray Langton. When all was said and done, Fairclough and Langton, rather like dad, were essentially working class with working class attitudes and values. They were both hard-working builders who laboured tirelessly to support their families. They were never driven, arrogant or idealistic. Just happy to earn a bob or two.

Rather like Fairclough and Langton, dad probably drank in the same kind of pub as they did. In the days before Sky TV, it's easy to imagine dad and his work colleagues deeply absorbed in a game of dominoes or shove ha'penny. Perhaps he'd order a pint of Watney's beer or maybe Truman's best. Then he would dig out his Daily Herald or the Daily Sketch, complete the crossword and shuffle wearily into the loving arms of his adoring family.

And so to the stunning spectacle that was the 1966 World Cup Final between England and West Germany. Dad would rattle his rattle, the one he'd bought in a souvenir shop in the West End for a couple of shillings. Then he would smile knowingly at his son and wink briefly, hungrily devouring a burger and neatly downing a cup of tea or two.

Then the whistle began and then there we were England, the England of William the Conqueror, Henry the Eighth, Queen Victoria, Queen Elizabeth, Harold Wilson, the Beatles, red post boxes, sleepy villages, winding, meandering streams, the whistling postman, Dickens, Hardy and literary greatness. England, the land of Eton, Cambridge and Oxford University, of imposing cathedrals, country estates, dreaming spires and poetic valleys. It was the England of public schools, snobbery and class distinctions. The England that dad had always told his son about.

Dad would try to explain to his son just why the Germans were still slightly despised and reviled by some. It had something to do with the War but the explanation didn't quite have the required impact. Maybe the Germans would always be vilified by those who found it hard to forgive. It was admittedly only a football match but those Germans had to be taught a severe lesson.

Half way through the first half, the Germans committed the ultimate sin by scoring the opening goal. How dare they? This was never in the script. It was somehow intolerable and almost sacrosanct. According to the Charles Buchan football annual, dad had always thought the Germans were arrogant, disrespectful, never as good as they thought they were. Dad and son were convinced though that this was just an urban myth. It just couldn't be true. It was just a rumour, just propaganda. Nobody believed that the Germans were unbeatable and invincible.

So it would prove. Bobby Moore's beautifully rehearsed free kick floated precisely to the criminally unmarked Geoff Hurst and the header flew almost effortlessly into the net. 1-1 and the game was on a level playing field. It was in the most delicious of melting pots. What could possibly happen next? Who could forecast the outcome? Even the bookmakers were biting their fingernails

But there was a kind of happy ever spontaneity about the whole day that could never be reproduced. Everything seemed destined to go right for England, everything fell into place. There was never any indication at any point that something would go desperately wrong for the English football team.

Besides the morning had started perfectly for us. Dad would find everything in the kitchen just right. The tea-pot, freshly brewed, had its gorgeously knitted cosy and two slices of toast with butter almost waiting to be eaten. Then there was the bowl of Corn Flakes eaten with an almost rapturous relish.

When Martin Peters slammed the ball into the net for England's second goal, there was almost an air of sweet revenge and vengeance about it. Peters meant it quite categorically and ruthlessly. There was never any hesitation or doubt about the manner of the goal. The goal had virility and vehemence stamped all over it. Martin Peters quite clearly took an almost sadistic pleasure in that second goal.

Then the final seconds of the game. England were clinging onto the slenderest of leads, clinging on to it by their well chewed fingernails. You could almost hear the church bells ringing, the vicar singing, dad and son waving their match programme in the air and willing England to victory.

But maybe the game hadn't quite finished. The game was still tilting in the balance, nothing was safe yet and there was uncertainty, a sense that those final few seconds were deliberately played in slow motion. We were unsure, there was an element of danger, something in the air. It was all too nerve racking and precarious for both father and son.

And then the dreaded incident took place. With quite literally the final kick of the game the Germans committed the unpardonable. They brought the score back to 2-2 with a last gasp equaliser. Time had quite seriously stood still. Father and son froze, son dropped his Bovril and dad's face turned a Whiter Shade of Pale. Dad turned around and Wembley looked stunned, grey and haggard. Nobody for a couple of minutes moved or reacted. It was almost as if the whole stadium had been permanently silenced and rooted to the spot.

Then there was extra time. By this time father, was beginning to wonder whether he'd be home in time for Dixon of Dock Green or Dr Who with Patrick Troughton. Dad had to be in time for the Black and White Minstrel Show, that was a must. Dad had to do all of the customary things that he'd normally do on a Saturday evening. There were the football pools to be thoroughly checked, the Saturday evening meal of scrambled eggs on toast and a pint of Watney's for good measure. Then dad would fill his pipe with tobacco and smoke contentedly for the rest of the evening. But this would be no pipe and slippers evening. This was the World Cup Final evening and when the final whistle went and England had won, dad and son raced out onto the pavements and declared deliriously that this moment in their lives would, quite possibly, never be repeated. And so they cheered and they cheered and they cheered. It would always work out this way. Somehow it was fated.

Then dad and son would pat each other on the back and celebrate with the heartiest of all celebrations. During the Sixties, there was an almost unwritten agreement that you could be whoever you wanted to be. Dad must have told his son about all the good and positive things you could do in life. There would be none of the Fifties severities or restraints. Everything was now in colour rather than black and white. London was finally convinced that there was potential and talent would blossom. Everything that had seemed so dull, dusty, dirty and mundane now assumed the most colourful of shades.

From that fantastic afternoon at the end of July, everything would literally come up for roses. Dad had that wonderful job in the City, employment had been restored to its proper level, the economy was supposedly thriving and there were jobs to be had in their thousands. All you had to do was walk across the road, make yourself available and shillings would turn into pounds, hundreds and thousands of pounds.

But Dad, although secure and happy with his lot, must have felt that there was something more than he could offer. That golden, halcyon day when England won the World Cup was a victory not only for the nation but a victory for perseverance. How the country had been longing for the World Cup, something to tell their mates on the factory floor or the accounts department. Finally, that Monday morning had arrived and not before time.

So what happened to father and son after the 1966 World Cup. They must have grown even closer to each other than they already were. There must have been a rugged masculinity about that whole period. Boys and fathers would know instinctively that Saturday afternoons were something to look forward to. Football was something they could relate to and always find common ground on. Something they could bond together with and never be parted from.

Of course Mum had her vitally important role to fulfil. Mum was the tender, maternal, caring and nurturing one who held everything together. Mum paid the bills, organised the finances meticulously and, above all cooked the meals, ironed the clothes and washed the dirty clothes. Mum was Superwoman.

I wonder though if Dad ever felt horribly undervalued or undermined, perhaps threatened by something he could never explain. Football, fishing and everything that had a male trademark, was his property and his patch of land. Football gave dad a stamp of approval, an obvious recognition within his society. Football had the capacity to be his friend, to guide and follow him, to be his supportive influence when United were hammered at home quite embarrassingly.

Dad always felt that if only he could have twice as much as his neighbours, then everything would be perfect, that if only he could show a little more ambition and drive then he too could have two cars, two TVs and two washing machines. But what about two cookers and two ovens, two sinks, two kitchens and two of absolutely everything?

Dad had noticed that in his neighbour's gardens, that the children were playing on swings while his son had to be content with a solitary leather laced football. It was a travesty of justice, deeply unfair. The neighbours had just taken possession of the most handsome looking boat anybody had ever seen. There it was in the neighbour's garage, glamorous, gleaming and utterly desirable.

But father and son never really envied their neighbours because their family were very closely knit, tightly bound as a drum. Who cared about those toffy-nosed neighbours with all their fancy ornaments and stupid boats? Father and son had something different, something unique and something that could never be equalled and replaced. They had each other, friendship, fish and chips after the game, a lovely sense of equality, positive communication, something that was mutually exclusive and never stolen or damaged.

In those final years of the 1960s, father and son finally found a kinship, a passionate belief that things would indeed get better and better. Of course, there was that glistening July day when everything and everybody felt that nothing could possibly go wrong. We were growing as a nation, developing as a nation, rightly revered by other nations as a force for good. It was only a matter of time before father and son would plant their flag at the top of the mountain.

By the end of the Sixties, dad had found just the job he'd been looking for and his son had moved through his teenage years, through university and then into the fiercely competitive world of employment and career. It was as if both father and son had successfully accomplished everything they'd ever striven for. Everything was now complete.

There must have been times of course when dad must have deeply frustrated, rejected, misunderstood, always denied, thwarted, never really appreciated. The boss he'd taken orders from during his City years had made dad's life a living hell, agony, purgatory, unbearable.

Dad had always done his best, never been late, a valuable asset to the company. Dad was responsible, dedicated, hard-working and permanently productive. Dad was never lazy or lethargic, sloppy or messy. Dad just got on with the business in hand, never complaining or dissatisfied. He would go over to his desk, chat amiably to his colleagues and then concentrate on the tasks and assignments of the day

I'm sure dad was happier than he'd ever been before. His colleagues were civil, the workload was never demanding and there was a sense that he'd found a job without any stresses or strains. Finally there was no pressure, no turmoil and turbulence in his life and nobody breathing down his neck. Nobody to tell him that if he didn't finish what he was doing in five minutes, he would immediately get the sack. There were no more whispers, malicious gossip, no more hidden agendas or ulterior motives. No more spiteful remarks, a deliberate attempt to humiliate and destabilise dad. Dad had found definition and confirmation in his life. Everything was just perfect, smooth running, assured. There were no more disruptions and disturbances. If people would only allow dad to function as a working man with an adoring family, then nobody would upset the flow and equilibrium of his life. He would enjoy his son, watch his son graduate at university, embrace his grandchildren and ultimately the roses in his metaphorical garden would always bloom.

I'm sure his son was a resounding success, a high achiever because back on that fateful World Cup winning day in 1966, dad had promised his son that everything would turn out for the best. Dad had given his son every encouragement, inspired him, enthused for him and absolutely convinced him that nothing could ever get in his way. Undoubtedly, he could be that driven stockbroker in the City, the wise economist, the enterprising businessman, that high flying lawyer. It was a world with no limits, no restraints, no constraints and no insurmountable obstacles. Of course he could be the man his dad always knew he'd be.

Part 9:
And now for my considered analysis of Words and Literature.

I've always had the strongest relationship with words. Words were the inanimate objects we were taught when we were young. Words gave birth to ideas in our mind, powerful sentences and moving paragraphs. Words explained all of life's mysteries and possibly confused and annoyed us. Words were the flesh and bones, the spine, the missing link, the solution to all of the absurdities that had left us baffled.

Maybe there were words which simply drove us to the point of despair, enriched our soul and uplifted us when things seemed to be dark and forlorn. Words, quite literally, gave our lives punctuation points and underlined quite emphatically the point we were trying to make. They were our pulsating heartbeat, our driving force, our motivation, our reason to move forward rather than backwards.

I believe words had the capacity to do whatever we asked them to do. Of course, words were emotional, almost unreasonably unpredictable, perhaps too upsetting but always loyal. Words would always make you feel better, improve your mind, comfort you in grief, share your sense of well-being and rejoicing.

Words, I believe, are our constant companions, gently guiding you to the point of salvation and redemption. Words would pull you back from the brink, avoid any unnecessary confrontations, will you on, coaxing and cajoling, always on your side.

Words needed no introduction, adapted themselves to all circumstances and always worked in your favour. I knew that words had a proper function, a real honesty. When all was said and done, words were our most refreshing cup of tea, our favourite television programme, the 19th century composer we'd always admired, that Tuesday steak and kidney pie, the friend you'd known for as long as you could remember, the day you played with your children on the swings and slides, the stunningly romantic sunset, those riotous reds and yellows, flirting with you and then sinking reluctantly into the night sky. Words could do that to you unconditionally.

I don't think I was ever shocked or dismayed by the power of the written words or their hold they could exert over you. I always believed that words would have a decisive impact on me, flatter me, criticise me, play games with me and believe in me whole heartedly.

I knew words would shape my future, be the architect of my destiny, colour the outlook on my life, cheer me on, support me positively when the going became too tough. Words wrapped a comforting arm around my shoulder, never gave up on me and confided in me in any predicament or moment of trouble. And for that I will always be grateful.

Wherever I was in the world, words would pat me on the back sincerely, join forces with me on the great voyage of life. How could I possibly throw in the towel, crumble, capitulate feebly when all the odds were heavily stacked against me. I couldn't just give in and accept failure and inadequacy. I had to be stronger than that.

I had to keep going for words had given me a head start, another opportunity, a second wind, an unbending faith in me. I had to persevere, I had to show some backbone. There would no point in just resigning myself to my fate. Words had taught me that there would be choices, very plausible reasons for the way things should be or could be.

Words gave me the reason and excuse to fight for my rights, reach out for the impossible, question the status quo, aim for the stars, to be in contention for the star prize. I had to be persistent even when, in all probability, I could go no further. I had to make the effort for the sake of words. It was the least I could do.

During that very empty and hollow period of my life, when nothing seemed to be going right for me and nothing was available, I began to discover books, library books, the captivating but mysterious world of classical literature. Books were richly varied, enlightening, gloriously informative, infectiously enjoyable, deeply instructive and extremely beneficial in later life.

I'd always been drawn to the written word, those mighty bastions of 18th and 19th century classical literature, those exquisite practitioners of the English language in all its purity and fluency. Books had always been my guilty pleasure, a chance to expand my intellectual horizons, satisfy my literary curiosity.

And so it was that on dark winter evenings, I would take myself off to Ilford library, situated next to the local town hall. Here I would avail myself of everything Ilford library could provide me with. There were row upon row of the great and the good, challenging and ravishing hard back books by all of those authors from a misty yesteryear.

There was Charles Dickens, HG Wells, Joseph Conrad, DH Lawrence, George Eliot, CS Forrester, Anthony Trollope, Marcel Proust, Leo Tolstoy, Feyedor Doysteyefsky, Thomas Mann, the Bronte sisters, Jane Austen, Sir Walter Scott, Franz Kafka, Ernest Hemingway, Henry James, William Faulkner, John Galsworthy, Rudyard Kipling and countless others who's names now escape me.

I'll always remember walking down the town hall corridors to get to the library. There was the most repulsive smell of stale food and suddenly you were trapped. This smell would follow me all the way down the corridor, a horrible, rancid mustiness that was barely tolerable. I'm sure there was some kind of conspiracy against the residents of Ilford and I don't think I was the only one who one who was just reviled by that nasty odour.

The one author who had the most profound effect on me though had to be Thomas Hardy. At school, we read most of Hardy's poems and love poems, beautiful and sentimental pieces of verse that touched the heart and tugged at its strings. I was instantly struck, transfixed by the language, stirred by the stanzas, revitalised by his verse and just speechless with admiration.

Thomas Hardy was by far the greatest author I'd ever read. I had bought a huge volume of some of his most lyrical work. Tess of the D'Urbervilles, Far From the Madding Crowd, Under the Greenwood Tree and Jude the Obscure, remained firmly lodged and lovingly preserved in my mind.

Hardy wrote some of the most sweetly flavoured prose I'd ever seen. True, it was very richly detailed and possibly complex but it was literature that sung and danced in front of my eyes, caressed my soul and mind; literature that had its own music, rhythm and cadence. Hardy was the very embodiment of literary precision and artistry, a free, wild and uninhibited spirit with an uncanny knowledge of the Dorset countryside.

When you read anything by Hardy, you were transported to a time when everything was gentle, leisurely, reflective and philosophical. Of course, there were tragedies and dramas in Hardy's novels. Of course, there were conflicting emotions and raging passions but I knew exactly what was going through his mind. He was speaking from the depths of his tender heart. Hardy, though, was essentially good and virtuous, warm and compassionate. The characters in his novels were always well rounded and convincing, troubled perhaps but always triumphant. Hardy was the finest of all story tellers.

And then there was Charles Dickens, the most natural story teller in history, the literary governor, the towering colossus, a man who carved out the mightiest of reputations, the most polished wordsmith of all. Dickens, overnight, revolutionised the English language, brought a newly minted expression and eloquence to it. When Dickens roamed the London streets looking for inspiration, he found exactly what he was looking for.

Dickens found that the market traders and costermongers in Convent Garden were somehow tailor made for his novels. He found that the bricks in those Victorian buildings were full of hidden secrets and untold stories. He knew that the pavements, streets and roads were just desperate to express themselves. If they listened to Dickens, then David Copperfield, Oliver Twist and Nicholas Nickleby were sure to follow. It was writing of the very highest quality, magnificently and stunningly lifelike and realistic.

Then there was Henry James, an American born author but an almost adopted Englishman who wrote with the most decorative of flourishes. James, I felt, almost lived inside the characters he wrote about. He was a very real inhabitant and participant of the people he'd given flesh and bones to. I can just see him carefully observing and analysing the ladies and gentlemen who were his creations. I can see him standing at the top of those palatial, sweeping staircases and balustrades, magnificent chandeliers hanging languidly from the ceiling.

James, I think, had an almost intuitive grasp of the English language, knowing exactly what his characters were thinking about and eloquently painting all manner of word pictures. James knew everything there was to know about the upper classes and English aristocracy. He knew what they had for breakfast, what books and newspapers they'd read, their likes and dislikes, their affections and disaffections, their manners and mannerisms, their thoughts and tastes, inclinations and intentions.

Henry James wrote Daisy Miller, Washington Square and the Aspen Papers, novels of classical beauty and extraordinary scholarliness. It goes without saying that James was elegant to his very fingertips in bot his choice of words and the way he conducted himself in the public domain. James had an enormous wit and perception, acutely aware of the changing times and eagerly devouring every word, gesture, paragraph and sentence. James had a lovely self-awareness, an instinctive knowledge of society's pecking order and a full note book of gossip and innuendo. I'd like to think that James swallowed up and totally absorbed the whole of his very exclusive world. A world that was both intimate and private but at the same time very open and extrovert.

And so I move onto Joseph Conrad, a Polish born novelist who became hugely skilled in the arts and crafts of the English language. In fact Conrad, I felt, executed his story lines in a style that was richly traditional and very vivid. By nature, Conrad was brilliantly descriptive, superbly illustrative and magically capable of conjuring the perfect setting.

Conrad wrote about the high seas, big, bold and expansive novels, stories of salty adventures and captains of troubled boats. Conrad wrote as he saw it: an objective on looker, totally impartial but very sympathetic. I think he must have felt a very strong emotional attachment to his characters because this was the environment that he wanted to be a part of. When Conrad described those 'boiling seas and mountainous waves', I almost felt that he was, quite literally, fulfilling his boyhood fantasies.

George Eliot was a quintessentially Victorian woman who clothed all of her characters in the most lavish costumes. In Middlemarch and Mill on the Floss, Eliot describes a world long since forgotten but in a sense fondly remembered. There was nothing over the top or extravagant about Eliot. Mary Lou Evans. George Eliot, as she was known, brought both a simplicity and sincerity to all of her very English novels.

One of my early attempts at reading the classics would find me at George Orwell. Orwell covered most of the literary genres. He was an essayist of the highest order, the most capable and accomplished of novelists, a man with a huge intellectual curiosity with his finger on the pulse of the nation. There was a very real sense that Orwell had reached some very profound conclusions about life and society. He was a political activist, deep thinker, powerful speaker and controversially outspoken. During the War, Orwell made those opinions quite categorically clear in front of a BBC microphone. He'd also become almost unavoidably involved in the Spanish Civil War. But Orwell was honest, passionate and forthright. 1984, Burmese Days, Keep the Aspidistra Flying, Animal Farm, were all written from a very fertile mind, a mind that never stopped questioning and probing.

I could hardly miss out those other literary greats, Proust and Tolstoy, because both men satisfied my hunger for the written word in remarkable detail. Both Proust and Tolstoy wrote books of completeness, greatness and sheer immensity. In fact, there were times when I didn't think I'd ever finish both War and Peace and Remembrance of Things Past.

War and Peace was an epic, a stunning and fabulous project consisting of well over 1,500 pages, a masterpiece of description and storytelling. It was the fruition of everything that Tolstoy had ever dreamt about, a labour of love and a sheerly magnificent tour de force. War and Peace was a rich tapestry of words and feelings. War and Peace was deeply dramatic and tragic, both moving and touching, brutal and bloodthirsty.

But in its last 400 pages or so, Tolstoy, or so it seemed, unintentionally got lost, missed the road he was looking for and wrote about something that was completely unconnected to the rest of War and Peace. Am I the only one who thought the first 1,000 pages had no tangible connection to the final 500 pages? Still, War and Peace encompassed a huge slice of Russian history and maybe that was the author's intention.

Finally, there was Marcel Proust, an early 20th century writer who was determined to write one of the longest books in the history of literature and succeeded admirably. Proust achieved his lifelong mission and gave us one of the most revealing portraits of French society of that time. It was a rigorous examination of French life and French lifestyles.

In the end, Remembrance of Things Past was a huge canvas. Over 4,000 pages divided up into three volumes. Proust highlighted and emphasised everything and everybody in French life. I'm not sure how he managed it because it must have been the most daunting of tasks. The fact is that here was a book that accurately portrayed all of France's most distinctive characteristics, its scandals and sorrows, its successes and failures.

I took great pleasure in Remembrance of Things Past because it conveyed to me everything I wanted to know in a novel. There was an underlying sense that everybody in Paris spent most of the early 20th century at breath-taking society parties, dancing and waltzing into the early hours of the morning. It was a world of winking, sparkling jewellery, wealthy financiers with an utter contempt for those around them and chandeliers dripping with light. It was a world of champagne and caviar, majesty and opulence, dining salons with an abundance of food and drink, card games that seemed to go on forever, gambling almost constantly, and incessant conversations about class. The inescapable fact was though that France had class and loads of it.

But above all there was me. Why, in all honesty, what possessed me to read the kind of books that perhaps I shouldn't have been reading. Perhaps I should have felt extremely guilty about what I was doing. Books were just stories, novels, the written word. How could I hope to reap any benefit anything from reading the great Classics of literature?

Books were rather like consoling and comforting uncles who you confided in. Books reminded me that my mind was still working and fully functioning, that there was an inquiring and receptive mind that wanted to learn much more about life. The likes of George Orwell, Henry James, Thomas Hardy and Charles Dickens had the feel-good factor that stirred and provoked you, enthused and excited you, gripped and captured you, conveyed something to you, confirmed everything you'd ever believed in and, above all, electrified your imagination. They crossed continents, conquered new lands and challenged you. It was a world I had to explore.

It would have been hard to forget Anthony Trollope because Trollope wrote at considerable length and at times seemed to be unstoppably prodigious. Trollope wrote with the kind of purposeful intensity that by the end of his life must have left him exhausted. I'm sure that his study must have been a veritable off licence of drink, goblets of whisky, brandy, soda, quill pens gently nestling on a wonderfully clean and tidy desk. How Trollope must have wrestled with his Victorian conscience on a whole variety of subjects.

Trollope was, above all, a political novelist first and foremost, a man who passionately held forth on the Tories, the Conservative Party, then known as the Whigs. Trollope faced the full onslaught of the House of Commons in all its outspoken magnificence. Trollope tackled all of those delicate political issues that others refused to handle.

In his celebrated Barsetshire novels, Trollope tackled all of the thorniest of political issues head on. Trollope dared to poke fun at all of those British institutions, the daft, the pretentious and the susceptible. Labour and Conservative parties would actively engage in the bloodiest of all verbal battles while the Liberals just looked on with helpless detachment. Trollope exposed, ridiculed and held to account everybody and anybody. He was shameless, merciless, fiercely dismissive and clinically ruthless. In the world of politics, nothing was off limits and everything was up for debate.

How I must have thought that now I'd found a very proper and constructive hobby, one that would stretch and ask all the most pertinent questions that history had posed. Not for me though those worthy and well intentioned books on the First World War, the Second World War or heavy tomes on science or art.

No, for me the great literary masterworks of the 18th, 19th and 20th century filled the most inviting gaps in my devastated education. From the groaning library shelves, I pulled out all manner of heavyweight literature. This was classical prose, golden nuggets of wisdom and enlightenment. They were stories of matchless construction, splendidly designed, created, built and, had it been a chair or table, beautifully upholstered.

Back at home, I was still surrounded by all of the cultural reference points that had been an integral part of my life, perhaps too vital and essential because there was nothing else. There were still those wonderfully charismatic TV celebrities and programmes that occupied most of our evenings.

The comics were there in all of their guises and disguises. The Seventies was almost too good to be true. There was Tommy Cooper, Bob Monkhouse, Dave Allen, Norman Wisdom, Max Wall, Max Bygraves, Jasper Carrott, Billy Connolly and two comedians of the sweetest vintage who left the most extraordinary impression.

Back in the early 20th century, comedy had been all about the old musical hall, an endless variety of cheeky chappies, strange acrobats, fire eaters, mickey taking, parody and pastiche. Max Miller somehow embodied everything that reflected the Second World War. At the beginning of his act, he'd offered us two alternatives: the blue or the white book: vulgarity or harmless tomfoolery.

Now though, four men gave my comedy landscape something that would never be forgotten. It was well crafted, polished to perfection, furnished and burnished. It was the kind of humour that I didn't think for one moment would ever quite have the immediate effect that they did.

Morecambe and Wise had already established themselves as two of the funniest men I'd ever heard or seen. Their act was firmly rooted in early 20th century musical hall. Morecambe and Wise were consistently and thrillingly hilarious, discreetly clean and extended members of your family.

Here were two men who had found the correct comedy formula. Their Christmas shows were like momentous conclusions to the year, perfectly tuned, tweaked and fashioned to perfection. They had star guests like Shirley Bassey, Glenda Jackson, Angela Rippon, Tom Jones and, certainly the most best and consummate of them all, Andre Previn. On reflection, all of the above mentioned reduced me to hysterical and constant laughter.

But Morecambe and Wise seemed to have that most enviable chemistry. They would come onto the stage rather like the oldest of friends. Their relationship and dialogue had an almost telepathic feel to it. Theirs was a partnership that was bound by a lasting trust, complete understanding and an almost wondrous compatibility. They were like two twins who knew exactly what the other would say. One would crack the inevitable gag and the other would respond with that perfectly timed response. At times they seemed to quite literally read each other's minds. It was uncanny but superbly entertaining to watch.

Then there were that other classical comic double acts the Two Ronnies. The Two Ronnies, Ronnie Barker and Corbett, gelled together like bread and butter, two men who seemed to read each other without any script. Their sketches were both artistic and supremely articulate. Ronnie Barker had worked for a bank before hitting the big time. But Ronnie B seemed to have this lifelong affection for the English language and it was amply reflected in some of his delicately sculpted work. His plays on words and language were the stuff of legend.

But it was the Two Ronnies together who really took comedy to another level. The famous Fork Handles sketch, featuring Ronnie Barker as a country yokel and Corbett as the downtrodden shop assistant will never, it is safe to assume, ever be equalled or surpassed. They had glorious timing, a rich comic technique and the most compatible of friendships. A friendship that would last for as long as anybody could remember.

Then there was the fantastically incomparable Billy Connolly, one of the most naturally talented comedians I'd ever seen. Connolly was, or so we were led to believe, rude, crude, brash, deeply offensive, horribly obnoxious and a complete outrage. He was the one from whom children should have been protected, high maintenance, somebody who should have been issued with a government health warning.

Connolly seemed to be excessive, wild and wanton, over the top, constantly trying the establishment's patience, pushing, prodding and provoking, angry and at times anarchic. He first came to our notice on Michael Parkinson's regular Saturday night chat show and from that golden Seventies night, Connolly, with that wispy beard and broad Scottish accent, would delight and enthral audiences far and wide.

At times, I always believed that much of his humour was just intentionally brilliant but then you suddenly noticed that there was something much more than met the eye. He didn't crack the jokes that his counterparts were telling. He was being deliberately disobedient, shockingly irreverent and a master of the observational gag.

He is also a very physical comedian who was both restless and tireless. It was hard to believe that this was the man who provided the instrumental backing on Gerry Rafferty's instantly familiar story of Baker Street. Connolly briefly flirted with the world of folk music but then decided to pursue a career in comedy that endures to the present day.

The Irish comedian, Dave Allen, was one of my dad's favourite comedians and he also made a very distinct impression if not quite to the same extent as Morecambe and Wise. Allen also had that inborn gift for storytelling. I always found Dave Allen confessional, ever so slightly edgy and endearingly provocative, a man who grabbed hold of a religious stereotype and tore it to pieces.

He would sit in that high chair, fag tenderly held between his fingers and a glass of whisky faithfully oiling his vocal chords. Dave Allen told the kind of stories that for the world of TV, no comedian would dare try his hand at. All religions and classes were mercilessly exposed and held up for scrutiny. Allen was fiercely controversial, perhaps upsetting those who were too sensitive and then meekly apologising for anybody who took immediate offence.

And then there was one of my all-time funny men. Norman Wisdom was the ultimate in comic excellence. Wisdom was silly, clumsy, childish, vulnerable but brilliantly comical. He was genuine and maybe a tad irresponsible. Perhaps there were things that he shouldn't have done and others, when it seemed deliciously right and proper.

Norman Wisdom was, I believe, just adorable and harmless. That tight fitting jacket and cap somehow gave him the look of the medieval court jester. Wisdom never jumped onto tables or entertained Henry the Eighth but he did warm the hearts of generations of children who were just waiting for somebody like him. The well-rehearsed tripping over, the silly pratfalls and butter wouldn't melt in his mouth face, was somehow destined to be my lasting comedy memory.

For me, Bob Monkhouse was one of the most intelligent and smartest of all comedians. When Monkhouse came out onto the stage, you knew you were in for a night of tightly and intellectually delivered comedy. His appearance, all black dinner jacket and bow tie, was something to behold. He was clever, always well-informed, a complete wordsmith and the most professional of joke tellers. He was an exceptional story teller and had professionalism personified.

No stones were ever left unturned and he almost seemed to glide through his act. Nothing was ever forced or false and all who associated with him felt immensely honoured.

And so we move back to my childhood again. A world where time seemed to be irrelevant and events moved with almost graceful sensuality. I'd like to think of the age when nothing really mattered and everything paled into insignificance. Who cared if you missed school for no reason in particular when of course there was a reason? Why worry about things when there was nothing to be concerned about. My dad went to work, my mum stayed at home dutifully and loyally and the rest would take care of itself.

Then there were the sweets of my childhood, those exquisite moments when the end of a day seemed like the most amazing treasure chest. Suddenly, I was presented with what seemed to be innumerable riches. There were sweets galore, chocolates in abundance, crisps that were utterly addictive, ice creams and lollipops that were too good to be true. So here they are in all their sugary splendour.

Mars was one of those gorgeous and mouth wateringly palatable chocolate bars that you could eat and enjoy over again. If a chocolate bar could be said to possess a gender, then Mars would be male. Mars had a rugged masculinity and machismo that very few chocolate bars could rightly claim to. It was strong, muscular, marvellously satisfying, a treat for the senses.

In those far off days, Mars used to be unforgivably expensive, costing 8d as opposed to Milky Way which was 6d, something that I found to be deeply unfair. But Mars was smooth, honest, uncomplaining and consistently edible. Mars, or so the advertising slogan told us, repeatedly helped you to work, rest and play. Perhaps it had both variety and versatility without being aware of it.

On the other hand, Milky Way was light, frothy, fun filled and frivolous. Milky Way seemed to be smaller and yet compact, not exactly nervous or apprehensive but somehow very brief and temporary. A Milky Way, rather like Mars, had a soft, chewy taste but never really hung around to find out whether you'd enjoyed it or not. It was like a ship passing in the night, something that was completely harmless and inoffensive.

Who could ever forget Milky Bar, Rollo, Marathon (now Snickers), Fry's Turkish Delight and my personal favourite, Bourneville, a truly aristocratic bar of dark chocolate. It was undoubtedly chocolate of the highest class or rank. A chocolate that deserved to be knighted, recognised by those in the know, the highest of high?

Packets of Rollo were to be feasted on with enormous relish. One after the other were closely packed together like some very private community. Rollos were small round chocolates, squeezed intimately into the most confined of spaces but never a source of disappointment. I can almost see them now, deep in discussion in the packet, debating the issues such as the Three Day Week, finding fault with Ted Heath and chuckling at the State of the Nation.

But the sweet that will remain with me are Ice Gems, delectable bite sized chocolates that melted in the mouth and made you feel good. Ice Gems were quite literally guilty pleasures, sweets that were so sweet that they should have been banned and forbidden.

Who am I to forget Fruit Pastilles, Opal Fruits, fruit flavoured chews, Spangles, Jelly Tots, Refreshers and a whole host of others? Some that had an almost regal and palatial air about them, some you looked up to with the deepest reverence, some you detested and some you couldn't help but love.

Fruit Pastilles and Opal Fruits had a far away, tropical flavour that was somehow indefinable but a marvellous authenticity. You somehow knew that both Fruit Pastilles and Opal Fruits were very much part of your childhood. Fruit Pastilles were sugar coated, compulsive, obsessive, fundamentally you and those very early years.

Fruit Pastilles were playful, flirtatious, amusing and yet indescribable. I don't think I could ever find out why but Fruit Pastilles would invariably follow a hard day at the coal face known as school. You would open up one packet and then start eating one after the other. It was just predictable and ritualistic. Part of your existence and upbringing.

Opal Fruits were valuable allies, chums and colleagues to the bitter end, devoted to you, always smiling, cheerful, bright and breezy, a carnival in your mouth. A packet of Opal Fruits would always last several weeks and months, possibly a lifetime had you let them. They were very sociable childhood companions, tantalisingly tempting, moreish, continuous and seemingly indefinite.

I think I must have been roughly 13 when it suddenly occurred to me that journalism was the career path I wanted to pursue. I'd always written tentatively and I'd always been interested in the written word. From a very early age, I would eagerly scan all of the red top tabloid newspapers hungry for sports stories and everything that related to sport. I don't think it ever became an obsession but I did lap up all of the latest journalistic contributions from writers who were at the very height of their powers.

Every time I went around to my grandparents, I would invariably pick up a copy of one of their well-preserved, if slightly yellowing Daily Mirrors. They would be carefully stacked up in the corner of their kitchen seats. The Mirror was, and still is, one of the most popular and accessible of daily papers. I've no idea why my grand-pa chose the Mirror but all I was concerned about were the football match reports the previous night.

Journalism seemed the most attractive of all professions. There was something thrilling and fiercely competitive about journalism. Perhaps it had something to do with my enduring love of words, the hectic deadlines, the sheer cut and thrust of it all. I just loved the whole atmosphere about a news room, the bustling ferocity and urgency.

The image I had was coated with romanticism. There were the American films featuring men in trilby hats and a pen in their coat pocket, furiously rushing and scuttling around in hot pursuit of the big, breaking news story. American newspapermen always looked as though they were to ready to dash out into the street with coffee and a half eaten doughnut in their hand.

But it was the noise in a newsroom that really did capture my imagination.

There was the constant clattering and rattling of the typewriters, the muttering and mumbling undertone of journalists in full story mode. There was irritation, impatience, fury and an explosive annoyance about the story that had got away. You could almost the smell the testosterone, the energy, the dynamism and electricity.

Then there were the phones, the phones that never ever stopped ringing. There was an insistence and persistence about those phones that just held me dumbfounded with admiration. There were editors, news editors, feature writers, feature editors, sports writers, sports editors, sub-editors, arts writers, theatre critics, writers on architecture, showbiz gossip and human interest writers, writers of all beliefs and prejudices. In other words, columnists with an opinion on their mind.

It was hard to put a finger on why journalism was the only career I wanted to be a part of but I knew that my slowly developing grammar and vocabulary would fit in perfectly into that hustle bustle world of panic and pandemonium. Newspapers were fast moving, constantly chasing, hounding, pestering, badgering, no time to stop. Must get that celebrity story before the Sun gets there first. It was cold, critical and clinical.

For me, the Daily Mirror introduced me to my first sports journalists. Men who could capture, quite exquisitely, the very heart and soul of a football match in short, sharp sentences, crisp references to the goal-scorers and even the names of the ball boys if they felt the story needed it.

Ken Jones was the Voice of Sport on the Mirror's sports desk. Jones was an integral member of the Jones football family. Jones was one of the greatest and most resonant football writers I'd ever read. When he was in full flight, Jones prose was meaty, punchy, easy to read, full of the spice and seasoning of a typical old First Division match. You could almost imagine him in the Press box, pounding away on his typewriter relentlessly but conclusively. Then he would clamp the old black phone tightly to his ear, forever chattering, smoking and pouring out lively words back to the Mirror's office. It was all very feverish, frenetic and somehow miraculous. It was quite the most astonishing balancing act.

Then there was his colleague Frank McGee, another sharp and perceptive operator, full of sparkling wit and mischief. McGee was the Mirror's boxing correspondent, a man who knew everything there was to know about that bloody and brutal sport. I could swear that he knew the leg measurements of Ali and Foreman, Frazier and Norton. It was easy to imagine that he was also on first name terms with the legendary Rocky Marciano and Henry Cooper. McGee was boxing.

Meanwhile at the Daily Mail, two men came to dominate and define the world of sports journalism. Men of integrity and credibility, men who covered sport in all its resplendent beauty and at times gruesome brutality. They were accurate, honest, insightful and admirably clear.

Jeff Powell was the Daily Mail's chief football correspondent and knew about all of the Beautiful Game's characters, subtleties and strategies. Powell got to the very heart of the matter, dug out all of football's essential mysteries:

the dodgy, duplicitous figures, the men who made the game breathe and tick. Powell explored most of the hard-hitting, pertinent issues. He was the man who knew Bertie Mee at Arsenal, Bill Nicholson at Tottenham, Sir Matt Busby at Manchester United, Ron Greenwood at West Ham, Bill McGarry at Wolves, Gordon Lee at Everton and Joe Harvey at Newcastle. He didn't know them intimately but he did know that all of these men loved the game that he did.

Powell was deeply acquainted with much of the game's enduring mystique and magic, the chairman who sat proudly in the directors' box surveying their Empire and their club. Powell described a football match with peachy little phrases, considered sentences and well-constructed paragraphs. He could capture in just a couple of words the very essence of a game. Goal scorers were rightly applauded, goal-keepers praised to the skies and managers were both keenly monitored and assessed. It was all part of football's rich fabric.

Then there was Ian Wooldridge. In the deeply emotional world of sports journalism, here was a man who lived life to the full and drank from its foaming glass. Indeed, Wooldridge came from sport's finest stock, a writer of the most vintage of all years, a man who encompassed every sport in all its different moods and faces.

Wooldridge interviewed all of sport's quirkiest, lovable and eccentric characters, men and women from all manner of classes and backgrounds. He seemed to embrace those who were ever so slightly fragile and vulnerable, those who'd reached the very summit and those who had unavoidably fallen from grace.

Wooldridge wrote lovingly of the good and bad, the sincere and the corrupt, the young and the old, the dashing and the devilish, the genius and the utterly flawed. Wooldridge always felt at home with cricket and wrote about it in much the way pen friends happily corresponded. It was heartfelt, confessional, humorous, supremely skilful and gloriously articulate. Of course he could be biting and sarcastic, he could be waspish and acerbic but then that was the writer who was Ian Wooldridge.

All of these men were of the highest intellect, men who happily acknowledged each other's gifts and enormously appreciative of each other's skills. They diligently worked at their trade, tried to rectify sport's deficiencies, highlighted its good times and shortcomings, and illustrated all its highs and lows, its roughest edges and smoothest surfaces.

Nothing brought greater pleasure to Wooldridge then cricket, both village cricket and Test cricket, rugby union and, grudgingly at times, football. Wooldridge had no time for the money mad footballers, the greedy agents, the chancers, the opportunists, the match fixers, the rebels and rogues. He could barely tolerate those shifty, grubby and shadowy figures, the ones who hid behind the pillars and giggled at misfortune.

For Ian Wooldridge, sport was all about pure, unadulterated sport, clinking champagne with the rich and the shamelessly well to do. Wooldridge loved his horse racing, cricket in all its manifestations, rugby union in all its muddy physicality, Wimbledon with its constant Pimms and above all sailing, the yearly yachting joust between the Americans and the British.

Wooldridge would simply soak up the very clubby atmosphere that only the America's Cup can generate. Here he would find all of those hilarious sailing anecdotes, the riotous parties that seemed to go on until the wee small hours of the morning.

Wooldridge loved to feel that he was very much a part of the elite, the social climbers, the arty and the aspirational. Journalism for him was the thrilling last jump at the National, the dainty drop shot winner at Wimbledon and Gareth Edwards diving valiantly over for the winning try at the Arms Park. Wooldridge always felt a deep sentimental attachment to sport. It was almost as if he felt enormously privileged to be a neutral spectator rather than take sides. Everybody in sport, he felt, mattered.

Then there was Frank Keating. Ah Frank Keating! Now there was a name to conjure with. I always felt that in some way Keating was related to Ian Wooldridge. Perhaps he was that very close cousin or the brother he'd always adored. Keating was the sparkling after dinner speaker, the raconteur with a compelling story to tell or witty badinage.

Keating was one of the finest and open of all orators, a man who could play to the gallery and leave that gallery falling about with hysterics. He was a brilliant wit, an instinctive comedian, frustrated actor and a vigorous gossip. Keating could quite happily and unhesitatingly tell you his life story, polishing off the evening with a toast to his beloved rugby and cricket.

I think Keating simply lived life to the full, drinking fully and enjoyably from a glass that was never empty. Keating lived, experienced and confronted life in all its forms, faces and guises. He was a rousing roustabout, bon vivant, the most faithful of all friends in a crisis, always available for weddings and bar mitzvahs, a man of his word and honour.

Then there were the sporting figures on the outside of sport, the commentators, the presenters, broadcasters, the men who brought the Olympics, World Cup, rugby union, tennis, cliff diving, football and cricket directly into our living rooms. The men on the other side of the desk, singing the praises of the underdog and rhapsodising about their gifts. They gave us the relevant and critical information that mattered, on the spot and live from Trent Bridge. There were the latest scores and graphic descriptions of goals and goal scorers.

ITV on a Saturday afternoon was the place to be. Without physically being there, you too could join in with live horse racing at Sandown, cliff diving from Mexico, darts from Alexander Palace, snooker from within the hushed confines of a Sheffield leisure centre and the incomprehensible wrestling.

World of Sport, a sports programme on London Weekend Television, was presented by Dickie Davies. Davies, once an amiable ship's entertainments officer on board the big cruise liners, introduced one of the most fantastic sports TV shows I'd ever seen.

Every Saturday afternoon, Davies, ever smiling and genial, would explain away the knotty intricacies of real tennis or American pool. Davies always looked as if everything was completely under his control. Not for a minute did we ever think that he would say anything outrageous because there were families and children out there who would never tolerate bad language.

Shortly, the smartly dressed and avuncular Davies would launch into his familiar patter, always in command and never even remotely flustered or ruffled, crumpled or rumpled. Davies was immaculate, rather like one of those models in a John Collier menswear shop window.

Then they would follow each other like Route Master buses in Oxford Street. There was On the Ball introduced by Brian Moore, a lively football magazine type show. International Sports Special, an astonishing pageant of sports from all over the world. There was cliff diving, men throwing themselves off cliff sides from an almost impossible height.

Then there was the ITV 7, a horse racing extravaganza from some of the leading race courses in Britain. Above all there were the ITV 7 presenters, men who must have known what the jockeys had for breakfast. They were warm, kindly figures with trustworthy faces and an air of jolly joviality about them.

There was the marvellous John Rickman, a man who was somehow destined to be a telly racing pundit. When Rickman took hold of the microphone, you almost felt that Saturday afternoons were good and virtuous, no worries or concerns. You put your feet up, relaxed with a pie and tea, opened up the Racing Post and Rickman immediately put you at your ease. There was that lovely moment when Rickman's trilby hat would be politely taken off by way of a greeting.

Rickman was accompanied by Lord Oakesy, a formidable racing figure, a man who used to be a jockey but had now been appointed as one of racing's notable experts, an aficionado with all the facts, figures and Pat Eddery's phone number on him. Or so it seemed. But Oakesy was one of those father like figures, somebody you could always look up to and believe in. He was a father like figure, a real patrician of the noblest kind.

What followed next was pure TV gold. It was an afternoon slot in the World of Sport schedule that had to be seen to be believed. Suddenly our senses were heightened and then stimulated beyond belief. It was a section known as an International Sports Special and suddenly you were subjected to the most bizarre and unheard of sports ever to be broadcast on mainstream TV.

Apart from the cliff diving from Mexico, there was stock car racing from somewhere, truck driving from what seemed to be America's deep south, ridiculous and totally baffling. You half expected to see a chunky bar of Yorkie dropping off the dashboard and then feeling disappointed because nothing of any note had happened.

Then there was the extraordinary spectacle of caber tossing, huge logs that were lifted off the ground and then hurled spectacularly into outer space. Men with shoulders the size of bungalows and muscles made from steel would, quite inexplicably, heave these remarkable missiles deep into another country, barking out the most vocal and vociferous of cries all the while. Their faces were twisted with pain, relief, real intent and utter conviction.

And then there was the ultimate of all sporting displays. At roughly tea time, Dickie Davies would hand over to the very capable voice of Kent

Walton. Walton had spent most of his career as a radio disc jockey at Radio Luxembourg but was now in charge of what looked like one of the daftest sports I'd ever seen.

It was called professional wrestling and quite how it had sneaked its way almost unobtrusively onto our TV screens is quite beyond me. Professional wrestling, or so some thought, made a mockery of sport, a passing joke or whim that would quickly pass, never to re-surface again.

But wrestling was no party game or charade. Wrestling was properly organised with real wrestlers and real wrestling rings. Wrestling also had characters but characters that always looked as if they were simply paid to entertain rather than compete for a Cup. What we saw and what we got defied description; men in leotards, huge, hulking gentlemen who kicked, punched, gouged and bit each other with unreasonable violence. Suddenly, otherwise sane gentlemen threw each other high up into the air, and then tossed them into the audience quite casually and arbitrarily. Rather like the lightest feather you'd ever seen.

And so World of Sport would enter its classified football results and those moments when all of the breaking sports news would be tied up into one whole and consummate bundle or package. Behind Dickie Davies, the ladies who'd been vigorously tapping away at the typewriters finally began to wind down. It almost looked like the most complicated military operation had just been carried out, quickly, stylishly and most efficiently. But of course there was the BBC and Grandstand, a well-established BBC sporting institution, long standing favourite and the sturdiest of broadcasting edifices. Nobody could possibly huff and puff their house down.

Since 1958 until very recently, Grandstand was that clean-living, civilised and respectable uncle who always made a fuss of you. Grandstand was pure, puritanical, prim and proper, the Establishment. At the beginning, Peter Dimmock, posh and quintessentially English, presented the weekly roundup of sport from around the world.

Dimmock was, or so it seemed, upright and upstanding and never dropped any Hs or Ts. There were times when it looked as if he'd just rushed from the Garrick gentleman's club after downing several brandies. Dimmock belonged to the elite, the cream of the crop, the dinner jacket and bow tie brigade. Utterly charming.

Then Grandstand gave us David Coleman, briefly a local club runner, but then beckoned into the warm bosom of the BBC family. Coleman followed all of the rigid policies that the BBC had set down quite unquestioningly. He became the right face for BBC sport, the man for the occasion, a probing journalist who never sold his audience short.

For years on end, Coleman combined athletics and football with an almost effortless authority. You always felt that Coleman was in the right place at the right time, thick coat warmly wrapped around him, a jaunty hat on his head and the toughest questions on his lips.

I was brought up with his football commentaries, confident and forthright deliveries delivered with a consummate style. When teams scored the opening goal or the winning goal Coleman would pronounce the inevitable 1-0 or something similarly momentous. Coleman told us that Liverpool were going through their party pieces in the 1974 FA Cup Final against Newcastle. He was quite obviously and evidently right.

Coleman also did athletics, having sampled all of its richest flavours before Grandstand. Coleman covered innumerable Olympic Games and on one tragic occasion conveyed all of the harrowing horrors that an Olympic Games could descend to.

In the Munich Games of 1972, Coleman presented quite the most moving and poignant news bulletin anybody had ever seen. You could have made a very correct comparison to the Walter Cronchite broadcast on the Kennedy assassination but Coleman's delivery was hauntingly dramatic, a masterpiece in every sense.

But Coleman could turn his hand to any sport and his appearances at the Grand National were yearly treats. Wearing just the right coat and hat, Coleman became the live link, the punter with twenty quid on Red Rum, deeply involved and connected with the National's pure and untainted atmosphere.

In later year,s Frank Bough and Des Lynam fitted into the BBC's family home like the proverbial gloves. Bough was also precise, thorough and fastidious with a wonderful sense of occasion. Like Dimmock, Bough could capture a big sporting occasion with concise descriptions and a lovely emphasis on every word.

Des Lynam had just joined Grandstand after a long and successful stint on Radio 2, now adapting to the rigorous demands of TV. It was a seamless transition, because Lynam had natural presentational skills and a strong grounding in sports journalism. Lynam had a flair for using the right comment at the right time. He was an avid Brighton and Hove Albion football supporter but there was never any bias in his football commentaries.

Part 10:
And so we move back to my early years as a child.

My parents had just moved to Ilford when I was three, a mere spring chicken, young enough and small enough not to know anything about life, the present, past and the future. Cranley Road was my first window on life, my first atmosphere, environment and neighbourhood.

When we first walked into the family home in Cranley Road, my mum told me exactly what happened when we first moved on. I've no recollection at all but if we look back to our enchanted childhood, it's possible to believe that these were the days that should be prized and fondly recalled. Rather like time and nostalgia I suppose.

My mum told me that I rushed upstairs to the bedrooms and bathrooms with all the excitement that you would expect to find in a three year old. Now I can only assume that the house itself had nothing of any consequence or value in it. It was ragged, very basic and, dare I say, very primitive.

I can see the house now, completely unfurnished, bare, damp walls, creaking floorboards and nothing of any substance inside. But here was I, a mere three year old, wide eyed with astonishment and completely taken aback by it all. I think I must have believed that eventually, the house would indeed have its own settee, chairs, tables, carpet, kitchen utensils, fixtures and fittings.

Rather like the 1960s, everything in my life would have a logical pattern and events would have their progression. Life would present my parents and I with very real opportunities, possibilities and a sense of order.

It's hard to imagine what life must have been like for my parents and I but I'd like to think that although there were obstacles and challenges that they could face, I was still very young, innocent and unaware. There was an unspoken belief that once they'd settled into their new home in Cranley Road in Ilford, then Cranley Road would help them to settle down and then make new friends with new neighbours.

I'm sure that one day they could sit down on their reflective sofas and bask in the satisfaction of a job well done. And yet of course things would be difficult and of course there would be problems and complications but surely everything would just fall into place.

When my parents and I moved in to our new home in 1965, the living room bore an uncanny resemblance to a small cardboard box. To say it was cramped and claustrophobic would be an understatement but to be perfectly honest, I'm sure my parents didn't really care one way or the other. It was cosy, compact and more than adequate. It served a very real purpose and nobody ever quibbled or moaned.

I can also remember the fire-place. Ah the fire-place, how could I possibly forget the fire place? It wasn't a proper roaring fire place, simply one of those electric fires with imitation logs and flames. Still this was our home, the home my parents always felt they deserved after years of testing times, trauma, trials and tribulations.

Of course the bathrooms, kitchen and living room were achingly lacking in all of the basic amenities but then there was time and plenty of it. Rome, of course, was never built in a day and with patient industry and endeavour, everything and everybody would take shape. My parents were convinced that the family they'd always wanted would fulfil its potential, because there were potentialities, horizons with red sunsets, good people and good relationships. Of that there could be no doubt.

So what of Cranley Road, its families, friends, neighbours and passing strangers? From a distance, it was a road rather like in any other pleasant and polite Essex suburb, the straight backed terraced houses that had a sense of permanence and indefiniteness about them. They stood there rather like Buckingham Palace guards, stern, unbending and correct.

Every house would look much like the next. The living room windows were always clean and the curtains had a showroom quality about them. Both the bathroom, toilet and spare-room windows were just as attractive and architecturally right.

I'm not sure whether this applied to all the houses in Cranley Road but most of the houses had that pebble dashed look on the outside of their houses. I do remember the pebble dash at the back of the house because here was the place where for hours on end, as a kid, I would chuck a tennis ball against that pebble dashed wall, oblivious to the time and the repercussions of my childish actions.

Cranley Road, rather like the rest of the nation's houses and properties, had its very distinctive appearance, its own individuality, its own rules and regulations. Cranley Road had its own chimney stacks, it's very vocal children, impromptu games of hop scotch and bikes parked breathlessly outside their houses.

But then Cranley Road had its irregularities, the things that didn't quite seem to match or blend in with the rest of the neighbourhood. Why was there a supermarket trolley in a nearby alleyway? Why did we play in that alleyway when there was nothing down there? Could it hold the key to some hidden treasure trove or was there a short cut to some distant land of milk and honey?

For me, those early years in Cranley Road were marked by some very special moments. I'm not sure why but it was the one occasion when I felt I knew so much more about my parents than any other kid in the road. I knew exactly what their very specific roles were and how they operated as they did.

My dad had been in menswear for quite a few years now and everything seemed to be running very smoothly. He got up every morning for his daily bus to Stamford Hill in North London and nobody knew what fate would befall him in later years. But in those very early far off days of his life, everything would be hunky dory, happy and rewarding.

It was roughly dinner time in Ilford, quiet, uneventful and normal. At roughly 6 or 6.30, I would run out onto the pavement outside the house and wait. I would wait for my dad to come home from work and it was a rational act. There was nothing unusual about what I was doing, nothing that was a radical departure from the norm. Beside he was my dad, the man I'd grown up with, the man who I thought the world of, his first son, who doted on me, applauded and recognised me, never failed me as a father and always believed that nothing would ever be too much.

But the fact remained that every day I would patiently and excitedly await his arrival home from work, the child who adored and never stopped adoring his dad. For all his personal troubles in later life, he was still the man who made every dinner time the most meaningful of events.

Suddenly he would appear on the corner of Cranley Road, cigarette tightly clenched between his fingers, grey jacket, Rael Brook shirt, tie perfectly knotted, handkerchief in his breast pocket and to all outward appearances without a care in the world. But little did my family know at the time that inwardly, my poor dad was suffering, gritting his teeth and enduring his very personal nightmare.

Still, through thick and thin, I would run outside our house and when he appeared at the bottom of the road, I would race over to him, hugging him deeply, affectionately and passionately rather like a wife welcoming her husband home from the Second World War.

It was at this point that I realised just how much my dad meant to me. He was the breadwinner, the man who earned the money to feed and clothe me, the man who made extraordinary sacrifices, who went beyond the call of duty, who pushed himself to the limits, a man in tireless pursuit of the impossible and miraculous. A man who desperately tried to overcome his own demons, his own lack of self-worth and self-esteem but privately knew that his son deserved the very best in life. But at what cost? His mental health was about to decline and decline very rapidly. I felt absolutely helpless but loved him and would never stop loving him.

Part 11:
Let me now tell you more about Cranley Road and Ilford.

At the bottom of Cranley Road, there were several very prominent and notable local landmarks, landmarks with valuable associations to the neighbourhood. I used to pass these landmarks quite regularly and was always fascinated by their sturdiness and steadfastness. They served the most useful of purposes and were very much a part of everything Ilford stood for.

Here there was the timber merchant George E. Gray's with its vast array of wood, building materials, DIY gadgets, drills, hammers and screwdrivers. George E. Gray's was an Aladdin's cave of everything that mattered to men. But predominantly, there was wood and piles of wood wherever you looked. There was wood where you'd least expect to find it. It was the most practical of shops that catered for the most practical tasks at home. I'd always imagined that the shop's busiest time was Easter because that was the time when most families would venture out into the garden and men would be in their element cutting, sawing, hammering and drilling things.

On my way to school in Ley Street, I would pass what looked like an extension of George E. Gray's, chock full of long wood, wood shavings, huge fork lift trucks, bags of cement and anything that was related to DIY jobs around the garden. It always struck me as unusual. Maybe this was due to the fact that I'd never seen anything quite like it before. Still it did catch my eye.

A couple of yards further down Cranley Road, there was the place that would provide me with my first social introduction to the world. I must have been about two or three when I started at my local nursery. Now here was the place where it all started for me. The whole process of mental, emotional and intellectual development began at the little nursery at the bottom of Cranley Road.

The memories will never be vivid ones but the outlines of those memories can still be deciphered. There was something about this nursery that represented the opening sentence of a brand new book, that first smell of your parents' cooking, that first insight into a world that had been locked away, hidden from view and carefully concealed.

What I do remember were those new discoveries, those playthings, the fixtures and fittings of the nursery. Here I would find buckets, spades, water, weird looking sinks, tons of sand and aprons. I think the kids of my age were expected to use all of our motor skills, the skills that promoted good hand to eye co-ordination. There were coloured bricks, clay, plasticine and all manner of toys and games.

I'll always recall the loud and positive voices, the encouraging sounds of enjoyment, the yelling and screaming of happy and modest children just glad to be alive. There was never any structure to any of those golden nursery days but I think there was a lovely togetherness and solidarity about our group. We all mucked in together, playing, exploring, holding and feeling our most primitive childhood tools. We filled our buckets with water painstakingly and haphazardly with total disregard for the consequences.

The nursery then and still is that first meeting point when the children of our generation gathered together under the same roof and created our community. But there was something else about the nursery that only came to my attention in later years.

This nursery doubled as a church. I have to say this was possibly the smallest church I'd ever seen. But this was a church, with its weekly Sunday congregation, parishioners, a vicar whose sermons were always mesmerising and religious, and the choir never less than resoundingly clear. I'm inclined to believe that Cranley Road took a very civil pride in its Christian beliefs and doctrines.

I think religion was something that every community held precious and Cranley Road was no different. There was the tiniest of crosses on top of this very small corner of religious worship. I'm inclined to think that every Sunday morning the local residents would devote themselves whole heartedly to everything that was thoughtful and important in their lives.

And then there were the people in Cranley Road, passers-by, the travelling salesmen, the gossipy neighbours, the milk floats with their eternally clanking bottles, the families outside their houses, chatting, confiding, believing, disbelieving, belly laughing, cackling, housewives folding their arms, men pottering about with their dismantled cars, washing their cars so that they would shine romantically, children rushing, racing and then thundering past on their permanently gleaming bikes.

I often felt that Cranley Road was the place where everything seemed to happen and everything was constant and unstoppable. There were tiny ripples of activity which gradually fanned out into other roads. It was rather like watching a very placid lake that, once provoked by a stone, would suddenly shimmer and flutter, shake and tremble. The effect was automatic and natural. Everything seemed to expand, get bigger and bolder until we were all encouraged to join in.

There was the aforementioned hop scotch, which involved the simple and undemanding act of throwing a stone as far as you could and then quite literally hop, skip and jump in between the paving stones. It had a permanent peculiarity about it, a sense that perhaps that the game hadn't really been thought through properly.

But these were times of sensible simplicity where everything seemed to made up on the spur of the moment. There were the boys playing football out in the roads before grabbing the ball, cars suddenly hurtling down at top speed. It was all very rough and ready, totally improvised and hastily conducted.

The house doors though were always wide open and nobody really ever felt as if their privacy had been invaded. During the summer, most of the kids on my road knew that life could not have been safer, that there was a sense that we could play for as long as we liked. Nobody bothered us, there were never any unwelcome intruders and you had to be dragged back into the house for supper. It was football, skipping for girls, endless games of hide and seek and the amazing Space Hopper, very odd and orange.

I think Cranley Road was almost comfortingly ordinary, almost enclosed and sheltered from the rest of the world's problems. It was our outlet, my outlet, somewhere where you could release all of your pent up energies, the healthiest sanctuary, the chance to form lifelong alliances, friends with common interests.

We would swap football stickers, play marbles, throw pennies against the wall, race, chase each other, lose our inhibitions, forget about school and besides, who needed to think about school when there were six weeks to fill during July and August. Summertime in Cranley Road was probably one of the finest experiences of our lives.

I can still remember those very local pieces of street furniture. There were the red post boxes conveniently situated on the corners of roads, those tall and very august street lights with what looked like a hat on the top.

On dark winter nights, I would stare out of one of our bedroom windows and it was almost a sight to behold. Across the road, I could see the flickering black and white images from the TV. Every so often, the room would darken quite perceptibly and then a grey shaft of light would return almost mystically. It was both an eerie and sinister light but in a way, it never ceased to amaze.

I can also remember the name of the neighbour. His name was Bert and he was one of the friendliest neighbours you could wish for. Bert had worked for Ilford Town Hall but was always available as our family handy man. Whenever we wanted something to be fixed, built or repaired, Bert was the man for the job, never complaining, troublesome or loathsome. He was, I feel sure, our angel.

Many were the time when Bert would, and without hesitation, build a shelf for my parents or tighten up something that was loose. He would easily engage with both my mum and dad and nothing was a problem that he couldn't deal with. My mum would quite happily put the kettle on and indulge in small talk. I feel sure that, as well being a very able town hall worker, Bert was quite the most skilful odd job man in all civilisation.

When I look back, I can also remember another very indispensable tradesman in our house. There was-wait for it-a Mr Power, our electrician. He could hardly be anything else, I say amusingly. Mr Power quite literally lit up our house, ensuring that live plugs were safe and gently ensuring that all of the hall and kitchen lights were secure.

And then there were my family lodgers. Now here were a gallery of characters who, on reflection, brought nothing but fun and amusement into the family house. Each had their own very personal habits and eccentricities to what became an overflowing table. You had to be there to see it and believe it.

Way back in the mid Sixties, our parents invited in one Mr Chisholm. Now to say Mr Chisholm was one of the funniest men who ever stepped into our family home would be putting it mildly. He was quirky, very set in his ways, maybe too traditional. Mr Chisholm, though, had a novelty value about him, an air about him that didn't really much care for the new-fangled gadgets or inventions of the day. Mr Chisholm though was a gentle, kindly soul who never really got irritated or upset the established order, a man who knew his place and station in life and stuck to his guns, a decent man who loved his own company.

Then there was Mr Webb. Mr Webb was never a drinker in the alcoholic sense but he did like a drop of the hard stuff from time to time. Mr Webb was, you see, a wine drinker. Nothing wrong with that but he was partial to a drop of Beaujolais or a cheeky red from the vineyards. We knew that he was a very competent messenger for the BBC and that he possessed the most brilliant of bikes with pillion.

Every so often, he would traipse into our house with a large glass bowl of newly made wine. But this was no newly made wine because Mr Webb had quite obviously taken plenty of time to brew the wine and then allow it to mature overnight. My parents were never drinkers but Mr Webb did break down their tentative resistance.

This is not to say that both of my parents would polish off bottle after bottle of wine because this was not their preferred choice of wine. From what I can remember, Mr Webb had all of the equipment: tubes, pippets and probably glasses from which to drink. But Mr Webb did like his own company and would often retire to his room when there was nothing to do. He was solitary and yet chatty, gregarious company.

Now it's time to introduce you to Mr Webb's successor. His name was Mr Gosling, a very grey- haired, frail and, at times, baffling character. I could never be sure why he looked so troubled and torn but there was something of the sad, long distance traveller about him. He always looked very tired, lifeless and completely lacking in energy.

What I do remember is that he always carried around with him a shopping bag. He had the air of a man who didn't quite know what he was supposed to be doing. My parents and I knew he'd retired but there was a shuffling, hopeless and disgruntled look about Mr Gosling that never really left him.

It seemed to me that he was carrying the weight of the world's problems around with them and that life had delivered the cruellest of blows to him. He would come back to my parents' home and would almost apologetically shamble his way upstairs to his room, slowly, wearily and defeated by whatever he'd been defeated by that day.

Mr Gosling, though, looked as though he'd lost a thousand personal wars and had nobody to turn to when all hope had deserted him. He was untidy, unshaven and, dare I say it, very broken and very forlorn. For all the world, he looked homeless and yet here were my parents showing him comfort, hospitality, a sense of purpose, place, belonging and above all kindness.

Part 12:
And now for some very homespun stories about my dad's relations.

This is the story about the friends and relatives who peopled my dad's world. It is a story of small family gatherings, bitter uncles and cousins, neighbours and friends who lit up my dad's, at times, very private but from time to time extrovert world. It is about uproarious laughter, genuine happiness, alienation from the real world, the sad torment and suffering of illness and the ultimate triumph against the odds.

My dad always had time for people and people had time for him. I always felt that my dad was never happier than when he was in the company of people he liked, trusted and respected. There was never a time when my dad felt he'd been neglected by society because he always felt a deep and sentimental love for everybody. My dad loved life and we loved him deeply.

But there were people, on the other hand, who made his life achingly and unbearably uncomfortable, who told him what to do, dictated to him in a way that was deeply unfair and totally unnecessary. I think it might have been due to the fact that he was an only child. But there was nothing wrong with that.

When his dad passed away, my dad was left inconsolable, bereft, irreparably heartbroken and just nonplussed by the speed of events and the suddenness. There must have been a time at this point in his life when my dad must have thought that everything was worthless, pointless and hollow.

Still he did find my mum in 1960 and this was undoubtedly the moment that the relationship he'd been hankering after would eventually lead him to marriage. It was almost the most idyllic encounter and it would re-direct my dad's path in life onto its sweetest path.

Now let me introduce to you to my dad's cousin Harold. Harold used to take my dad to all of the West End's most fashionable night spots. I don't think he was a riotous party animal but I do know that he was there on the same night that my lovely dad met his wife to be.

Both dressed in their most elegant of all dinner jackets, shirt and tie, I can now see Harold and dad in full flirtation mode with similarly flirtatious ladies. Now my dad would notice, out of the corner of his eye, the most beautiful lady he'd ever seen. She wore the whitest and most divine of flowing dresses, eyes glittering, hair swept back and the prettiest of French buns in her hair. It seemed that my dad's prayers had been emphatically answered.

Shortly they were to be united, totally absorbed with each other, chatting like the oldest of friends. They talked and talked until deep into the evening, sharing the moonlight, an almost spiritual attachment to each other, a heavenly bliss.

It was the most romantic of unions, a lifelong and most warmly compatible friendship.

Soon they were going out with each other, intimate cups of coffee in low lit cafes, evening meals out in red lamped restaurants and the cinema. This was the place where all boy-friends and girl-friends would become spellbound by some mystical element at work. The cinema was one of those private and very secretive places where boys and girls would meet up after work and pretend that this was the only place where you could fall helplessly in love. There were no interruptions or interferences. Just the two of you together and nobody else, apart perhaps from the usherette, the torch and the tray of ice cream.

It's hard to imagine what must have been going through my dad's mind at the time. There was the sheer delight, the sheer ecstasy, a feeling that nothing would ever spoil, ruin or hold him back. For years, he'd been searching for the independence that always seemed to be elusive, hunting and foraging for that unique moment when everything felt just right.

And now for Harold, my dad's cousin and the man who just happened to be the man who was with my dad on that fateful night when my dad discovered the woman he wanted to spend the rest of his life with.

Harold always seemed a mysterious, unfathomable man who only allowed you into his world when he felt like it. He might have seemed very distant, aloof and stand offish and yet there was something captivating about his bachelor's lifestyle. I think he preferred to be alone so it couldn't have been out of choice.

I never did find out what Harold did for a living but he lived in Sydney Street in the heart of London's East End and had done so for as long as anybody could remember. I've no vivid recall of his parents but he had a brother who went by the name of Sid. They were the Goldberg brothers, Sid and Harold.

What I do remember vaguely were the occasional family gatherings in the Sydney Street home. I can still see the wooden chairs, steady but somehow rickety at the same time. There was the dining room table in the corner of the room with its lace table cloth and bowls of fruit.

I don't know why but I can still see Harold, Sid, his late parents and their close friends all huddling around the room, quietly then heatedly engaging in discussions, negotiations, small talk, genial gossip and relentless chit chat.

Then the afternoon would begin, the quickest of lunches consumed and then tea time would follow. Now when Sid, Harold and their parents threw a tea party, you knew that a good time was to be had by all. There was a low hum and babble of conversation, the tinkling of tea cups, more plates of salmon bagels, salmon and cream cheese bagels and the liveliest exchanges on everything and everything.

I can see the chairs, strategically strung around the edge of the room, rather like some surreal game of Musical Chairs but without the children and well wrapped presents. Every so often, elderly aunties, uncles and friends of the family would suddenly stand up and then swiftly sit down. You almost felt that eventually, some party political conference would unexpectedly break out.

I'd never seen anything like it before. Every so often, there was a veritable traffic jam of people, filing in and out, always seeking an unoccupied chair and then apologising for bumping into them. At times, it resembled the famous Whitehall farce, doors sternly shutting, then nervously creaking open almost grudgingly. There was nothing naughty, suggestive, rude or explicit about this scene. It was just the way my dad's relatives did things.

Then there were the little old ladies with their bone china tea cups and saucers. They would sit there, hour after hour, tenderly nursing their cup of tea and coffee. But then it happened. With the tiniest cakes and biscuits on their saucer, they would pick up their cup, blow on their hot, steaming cuppa and then pour some of their enticing beverage onto their saucer. It looked as if they'd rehearsed this routine a hundred times before leaving their house almost mechanically.

So this was afternoon by Sid, Harold and their parents' friends. An afternoon that had a very ordinary, very traditional feel to it. It was the way they had always done things in the East End in those days. I'm sure that all families had conducted themselves in this way for many a decade so maybe I shouldn't have been that surprised.

My wife always tells me about her cousins and uncles, aunts and friends all joining up for the most convivial of family parties. There were no holds barred, no taboos, nothing was off limits and all subjects were freely discussed. There were the friends from around the corner, those adorable children from No 20, Blooms, the delicatessen in Aldgate, the woman who used to work in Truman's brewery in Brick Lane, the very cosy intimacy among this closely knit neighbourhood.

As the years passed though, Harold and my dad unfortunately began to grow apart from each other, the result perhaps of some unspoken disagreement or just plain animosity. True they were still friends but for years, my parents and I had travelled down to Sydney Street to see both Sid and Harold and eventually the rift between my dad and Harold became painfully noticeable.

Anyway, the fact remains that on some Sundays, my mum, dad and I would pay the most fleeting of visits to Sydney Street. Harold would open the front door most amicably, smile at us and then ask my dad and I whether we'd like to come down into his toy warehouse- cum- children's grotto. Now here was something I hadn't expected, something completely out of the blue.

Walking down the hallway, we would then trot cautiously down some steps and into what looked like some shop basement. Now for reasons best known to nobody in particular, Harold would always ask me whether I wanted anything from his extensive selection of toys and games.

What I didn't know was that he'd also kept a large stock of well-preserved dusters. Yes dusters. But not any ordinary dusters. They were yellow dusters and cheap dusters. Hilariously though, I always seemed to pick up pens, pencils, writing pads or coloured pencils.

Then, of course, there were my dad's neighbours from Cranley Road. Across the road from where I used to live, we immediately became friendly with what had to be considered their young family. I think we bonded with them straight away because the parents also had very young children and my parents were just happy to be part of their lives.

Anyway, once the friendship had started to blossom, we would do the kind of things most neighbours would happily share. We would think of nothing of spending interminable hours in their house and we would gladly reciprocate the favour. I often think that they knew more about my parents and I than we knew about ourselves. There was a kind of mutual appreciation of each other's lives.

Some of the husbands were black cab drivers who had an almost chummy camaraderie among each other. But my dad used to get on with everybody, regardless of race, creed or colour. There were times when I was convinced that my dad knew complete strangers in nearby Redbridge.

I'll never forget the times when my dad came home from work with a neighbour at the other end of Cranley Road. Many was the winter's evening when both of them, Evening Standard tucked under their arm and warming gloves on their hands, would march down the road, rather like brothers who'd just come home from War.

Then there was the family who used to live roughly around the corner from where our parents lived. They were nice, easy going and permanent friends. I became friendly with their son. We were two kindred spirits with so much in common. We would eventually go to the same primary and secondary school; ours was an unbreakable friendship.

I'll never forget our very real partnership, the days spent whizzing around back streets on our bikes, games of darts in our houses, football on street corners, greying pavements, winding roads, and all the fun of the fair.

Then, after another day of supreme knockabout silliness, we would disappear into each other's houses. In my friend's house, they something called a Dansette, a wonderful record player with its own very startling talents. This was the most incredible invention I'd ever seen. You pulled out a small pile of your favourite 45rpm singles, piled them onto the top of the turntable and then watched in amazement as all of the records, one by one, plopped almost compliantly onto the turntable proper. It was rather like the unravelling of some great tapestry.

Part 13:

And now for another musical round up of the Britain, the music from the Sixties that caught my ear and much else.

Then all of the 60s classics boomed out of the smallest of speakers and your mission was complete. What followed next was the most glorious fruition of sound, sad and happy melodies, hopeful and hilarious, miserable and maudlin. There was Tom Jones, Manfred Mann, Fleetwood Mac, the Bachelors, the Tremeloes, Herman's Hermits, The Who, Eric Clapton, Stevie Wonder, Diana Ross and the Supremes, Smokey Robinson and the Miracles, everything that had a positive underlying message.

Tom Jones had magnetic sex appeal, Manfred Mann were all pounding, fluttering drums, tambourines, screeching, rousing guitars and an organ that had a mind of its own. Fleetwood Mac were one of the most inventive and original bands of the Sixties, combining a sound that was both haunting and brooding, dark and light. Albatross was mystical and thought provoking but pleasing on the ear.

The Bachelors, Tremeloes and Herman's Hermits were essentially and naturally British, tiny stitches in the rich fabric of British life, the writing in the seaside rock at Southend, Brighton and Bournemouth. They were as English as the rosiest of all English complexions, the Lake District, rolling green hills, the patchwork quilt that was the English countryside, wooded forests, the wheeling gulls and tea with the Queen.

The Bachelors were cheery, chirpy Irishmen who were clean cut and very humble. They sang songs that families used to sing in the days of the music hall or songs that had been passed down their family. It was all very jolly, jovial and jocular, songs that were easy to hum along to and ones that were catchy old sea shanties. In other words, they catered for the popular masses and pandered to the whims of all ages and tastes.

The Tremeloes were another from the school of good times, feel good and sing-along. Both the Tremeloes and Herman's Hermits also incorporated all of England's best qualities: its movements, its fashions, triumphs, disappointments and appointments. They were fun, crazy, ecstatic, and at times simply overjoyed. Herman's Hermits were one of those English 60s bands who didn't seem to mind anything. They were classless, carefree, bouncy and totally shameless. They rocked their guitars from side to side, moved in time with their very distinctive beat and enjoyed themselves vigorously. There was never anything brash or arrogant about them because they were essentially the boys from our neighbourhood. They were good, honest lads without a hint of pomposity in their guitars. It was beefy, muscular and utterly British.

There were also the individual artists who made everything seem worthwhile. Eric Clapton was very much of the Sixties and probably appeared on the music scene for that reason alone. Clapton was the ultimate rock star, thick long hair, wildly bearded, driven, committed and completely absorbed in his music. Clapton, for me, epitomised everything that rock music meant to him His overriding passion was his electric guitar and everybody who knew him must have acknowledged that here indeed was the most talented practitioner of his craft. Clapton threw himself whole heartedly into his songs and never held back. There was an unrestrained brilliance about Clapton, a force of nature, absolutely mesmerising and at times overwhelming, totally unrepentant. He made no apologies for what he was doing and his fans just lapped it up.

On the other side of the Atlantic, music had undergone several revolutions and the Sixties revealed and confirmed all of the stereotypes. America was a vast, epic and sweepingly spacious country, a country of many moods and complexities, contrasts and contradictions, excess and extravagance, at times too much of all. But it could also be the friendliest nation on earth, asking you repeatedly whether you'd had a good day and then offer you several doughnuts and a couple of burgers for good measure.

As a British observer, I could never quite understand what it was all about. What did I think of the Americans and what did the Americans think of us. My perception of the United States seemed to be the same as the rest. The Americans played baseball, American football, watched a million TV channels, consumed and devoured everything in sight, swallowed up their culture, breaking news, the dizzy world of celebrity and superstardom.

But for me, American music seemed to have its own signature, a different gloss and sheen, an unhindered style and sophistication, at times both sarcastic and deeply ironic. The critics believed that there was an undercurrent of aggression and hostility in their music. But then what do they know about American music.

America, as we all knew, is the land of the Free, brash, rash, brazenly vulgar or allegedly, overwhelmingly enthusiastic, passionate about everybody and everything. America was the place where it all happened and always would happen. America always did things on a monumental, gigantic scale. It never did anything by halves. What you got with America is what you saw.

I always felt that the Americans were simply generations ahead of the rest of the world. But there was something unmistakable large and at times unhealthy looking about the States. There were the soaring skyscrapers, New York in all its flashiness and bolshiness. New York had its yellow taxi cabs, its salt beef bagels, delis, formidable cops and above all, its furious pace. At times there was an air of intolerance about New Yorkers because nobody could keep up with them.

Then there were more skyscrapers, huge pavements and theme parks for both children and adults. Like the rest of the world, America also had poverty and wealth and, at times, uncomfortable neighbours. There were the Manhattan ghettoes, the luxury penthouse suites, the office blocks that tower over humanity, the sheer incessant restlessness, all mixing and blending in perfect and, from time to time, imperfect motion.

America, I always felt, was too fast and frenetic, very rarely stopping to pass considered judgments and somehow missing the point. I always felt that Americans were almost too friendly at times. Of course they were well intentioned and hospitable but it all felt just a bit too much at times. Yes, they were trying to make you feel at home but it somehow felt that they were going overboard. I think it was all just a bit forced and contrived. Why couldn't the Americans do things in moderation rather than indulge in over indulgence?

Why did the Americans have to eat and drink so much? Why were their lunchtime and dinnertime portions of food so large, so substantial, so incomprehensibly and obscenely too much? There was starvation and deprivation in Africa, the rest of the world was just stunned by what they felt was naked American greed.

True Americans knew how to enjoy themselves, knew how to life by the scruff of the neck and make the most of all their opportunities and advantages. Besides, America had 9,276 telly channels, 9,275 radio stations playing rock, country, classical, heavy rock and Motown soul. At times it seemed America was spoilt for choice.

America threw wild and lavish parties, celebrated all kinds of achievements, the joys of living, the very best that life could offer. There was bustling New York, chic Chicago, political Washington, open Ohio, fulsome Philadelphia, dozens and dozens of streets, roads, tree-lined avenues, coffee and doughnut cafes. America lived their lives to the full.

Americans live their life, quite literally in the fast lane. It is a country of amazing sights and people, noisy convulsions, constantly atmospheric and, from time to time, completely beyond anybody's understanding. We scratch our heads at the occasional sheer absurdity of the United States of America, the things that never really make any sense at all, those ever present mysteries and imponderables.

America had dashing chat show hosts with the gift of the gab. America was a land of seething creativity, spectacular Las Vegas shows and casinos, of pronounced light and shade, darkness and sadness, incurable drug pushers and aching alcoholics. But then that applied to the rest of the world anyway. America seemed to have two different personalities at times. There were the dodgy, dubious characters with just a hint of illegality about them. Then there were the high school college guys and girls who became famous lawyers and rich businessmen and business women.

These were my observations on the United States. From my very humble Ilford upbringing, America offered a completely different culture, mentality, atmosphere and way of life. It was a giddy, dizzy merry go round, a fairground that never stopped spinning, whirling, twisting and rolling. It had its own life force and it was obsessed with having a good time. America was and remains in the rudest of health.

From a personal distance, it always seemed to me that the Americans were in too much of a hurry, that if they'd slowed down for a minute and just took their time, then maybe they'd find a certainly clarity and a firm resolution to their problems. Perhaps if they'd stopped for just a minute and smelt their own coffee, then things wouldn't have been quite as complicated as they seemed.

I'd grown up with those inherently American cop programmes. There was Cannon, a Man called Ironside, Cagney and Lacey and Starsky and Hutch, all good, rip roaring, action packed series with a multitude of everything American. Bad guys sprinting away down dusty streets, police cars wailing and whining, Starsky and Hutch jumping acrobatically onto cars, cardboard boxes, hectically flying in the wind. It all looked very nonsensical and absurd, but perhaps it was America holding up a mirror to its own society.

But there was something else about America that did rankle with me. I'd grown up in England believing quite correctly that nobody should ever attack, hurt, or attempt to kill anybody without any provocation. I'd like to think that I was brought up with civilised values, that common courtesies should come before violent aggression and everybody should try to get along with each other at all times.

And then I discovered that in America, there was a rampant gun culture that had been enshrined in their Constitution for as long as anybody could remember. Now there was a living contradiction of everything I'd ever been taught. In America, guns were legal and firearms were perfectly acceptable. Meanwhile, in Britain, we resolved crimes with the long arm of the law, handcuffs, no guns and a lifetime in prison.

Why I asked? Surely somebody could tell me why an unreasonable legitimacy had been attached to something that could kill instantly. Now I would be surrounded by American cops who shot from all angles and without any questions asked. Guns and rifles were fired indiscriminately from the tallest buildings, the loud crack and bang bang of bullets thudding into the chests of evil, blood soaked villains before dropping to the ground in slow motion and clutching their jackets almost melodramatically.

Where did this obsession with guns come from? For years in Britain, we had been told quite categorically that guns could only be used as a last resort. But here were American cops with guns as part of their everyday livelihood. Guns had to be used to kill the baddies because the baddies had to be taught a lesson and be put in their place.

I'd always grown up believing that the Americans were just a gun firing, all guns blazing nation where reason and compromise simply didn't exist. You were perfectly entitled to keep a gun in your house in all eventualities. You had to be prepared to defend if the worst case scenario arose. But guns were used quite unhesitatingly whenever you felt threatened.

Guns were used in cowboy movies, guns were used in the assassination of American presidents, guns used under all circumstances, on every street corner, at all layers of American history. It was pow pow!, you're dead buddy, as the baddie slowly crumples to the ground, face contorted with pain all the time clutching their hearts.

Then there were the American car chases, Cadillac's, swerving, racing, weaving in and out of other cars, hurtling along at speed, breathless and then crashing into shop windows or traffic lights. If this was an accurate picture of what America was like, then I'm rather glad I had nothing to do with it.

It was all too very visually shocking and faintly disturbing. I'm not quite sure what it told me about the America I'd already seen, but the perceptions were set in stone. If you robbed, murdered, raped, looted and pillaged, you were destined to die the appropriate punishment, death in an instant bullet, end of story.

There was a cruel finality about America's stance on guns. If you were caught up in the heat of an unfortunate incident, then you had to suffer. It was the electric chair, Death Row or the most agonising prison cell for life. That was America, pitiless and remorseless, pointing the most accusing finger at those who had unforgivably violated. America was ruthless and didn't stand on ceremony. It stuck in the proverbial knife or peppered with you rat a tat bullets.

But, no, this was not the way they did things in Britain or for that matter London. We grabbed our criminals unceremoniously, tied their hands behind their backs forcefully and then dragged them into the back of another wailing police van. In Britain, we dealt with criminal misdemeanours in what I thought was a very civilised manner. We sat them down in a police cell, pulled up a chair and asked all the most penetrating questions.

Then, we would take them to court, charged with whatever the heinous crime had been, and then gave them a life sentence. It was all loaded with a very proper formality and a grave sense of British justice. The English judiciary had always done things in a very sensible and ordered fashion. Trials had been always been conducted at the right time and with all the incriminating evidence to hand. I'd always seen judges as important and eminent figures immensely learned, utterly in charge of proceedings.

But both America and Britain, certainly in my view, always had very distinct cultural habits and idiosyncrasies that set us apart but never kept us apart. The Americans had always drunk coffee and doughnuts, wolfed down burgers with an almost heartless relish and then polished off 50 pizzas into the bargain.

Why couldn't the American follow in our footsteps and drink genteel tea in the afternoon, serenaded by a tinkling piano. It was tea, cucumber sandwiches and scones with jam and cream. It was so very British, so restrained, so self-conscious, so nervously reticent, polite and to the point. Always wary in case you were offended.

Still the Americans were still streets ahead of us in other respects. America had enjoyed colour television since the very early 1960s, or so it seemed. In America, there were so many channels and public service channels that it was easy to believe that they were at least two decades ahead of the rest of the world. Then again, perhaps Britain was reluctant to move with the times, reluctant to embrace the new technologies. But Britain still had that capacity to do so when it felt the time was right.

And now for a journey into the world of my favourite sportsmen and those who had been successful from another age or decade.

The world had always given us sportsmen and women and teams who were destined to be talented and together. This is my journey into the past and the present, those who fell horribly and dramatically and those who simply excelled in their own right.

In the dramatic and tumultuous world of football, it's sometimes impossible to find a team or player who so easily stands out from the rest of the crowd. Often. football finds greatness and genius when least expected and then happily stumbles upon it by complete accident.

In the case of the 1970 World Cup, there could only be one team who surpassed themselves every time, who rose above the dull and mundane, and overnight transformed the game into the most refined art form.

Since the very first World Cup in 1930, Brazil have dominated world football in a way that very few other countries have done. Their football is a thing of breath-taking beauty, stunning simplicity, glorious co-ordination, geometry, angles, right angles, Pythagoras Theorem, a sense of ballet, theatre, bountiful, full of the joys of all seasons, consistently thoughtful.

It always felt that Brazil had somehow transcended football, belonged to another footballing plateau, a cut above the rest, close to perfection, mathematical precision, effortlessly strategic, champions of sporting excellence, noble in the cause, sparklingly brilliant.

But one player above all had already reached the very summit of his profession. One player had embraced inherent genius and everything that genius had bestowed upon him. Already, the 1970 World Cup had blessed us with Tostao, Rivelino, Jairzinho, Gerson and Carlos Alberto.

But there was one player who stood high on his own Olympic podium, medal gleaming in the shimmering heat. Here was an example of sport at its most accomplished, an athlete who had proudly walked sports golden Elysium fields. A man at complete ease with quality, that sense of complete accomplishment, the air of the magician, that feathery touch, arrogant nonchalance, total disregard for the rule book. His name was Pele.

Pele had come from nothing, unashamedly working class or so it seemed. His was the rags to riches story that almost belonged in the world of fairy tales. He came from the most ordinary of backgrounds and, quite literally, dragged himself up by the bootlaces. One would imagine that his parents were supportive and inspirational because when Pele was at his most gifted pomp, you could almost see the influence that mum and dad had exerted.

In Brazil, they honour and revere their footballing heroes. Several decades earlier, a fleet footed winger by the name of Garrincha had stolen the hearts of a captivated Brazilian nation. Garrincha had remarkable feet, bamboozling and infuriating defenders. Garrincha was the darling of Brazilian football, he could do no wrong in their very appreciative eyes. He was acclaimed as the man who had no cracks in his armour and no blemish. In other words a rare perfection.

Now Pele had arrived at just the right moment in Brazilian history and he too was acclaimed as the man who would revolutionise the game, take football into the most heavenly realms. In the 1958 World Cup Finals, the 17-year old Pele would become the youngest player in World Cup history to make the most superlative impression on any football tournament. He scored on the highest stage possible and then bestrode the game like the most indomitable Colossus.

Pele was just beautifully balanced, a perfect combination of instinct and impulse, a spark plug and catalyst who started, continued and concluded attacking movements with grace and cutting incisiveness. He developed a platonic relationship with the ball and yet there was something deeply romantic about his approach to football. When he had the ball, he was both cunning and deceitful, then the shoulder would drop, the dummy would be sold and the bemused defender would be left with egg on his face.

During the 1970 World Cup, Pele would have his greatest hour, moments that would be engraved on our minds. For instance, there was the outrageous, outlandish shot from the half way line when the Brazilians kicked off for the second half. It almost dropped into the net and no shot was more richly deserving of such audacity. Sadly, nothing materialised but how good it would have been had he scored.

Then there was that breathless moment when the Brazilian maestro seemed to shepherd the ball towards himself as if it was his only, dummied the opposing keeper, waltzed around him and then casually tried to stroke the ball into the net. Sadly, there was no end product but had Pele scored, I feel sure that the goal would have been hailed as one of the greatest goals ever scored. Suffice it to say that those who were there in Mexico City must have felt enormously privileged.

I might at this point include all of those footballing geniuses who gave so much to so many and never realised just how profound an effect they'd had on the game. They were football's greats, legendary personalities, football stickers at school you never wanted to be parted from and players who could attract supporters from all four points of football's expanding frontiers.

There was Sir Stanley Matthews, Stan Mortensen, Tommy Lawton, Sir Tom Finney, Len Shackleton, Dixie Dean, George Best, Bobby Charlton, Bobby Moore, Johan Cruyff, Maradona, Bobby Moore, players who made you gasp with astonishment, made you feel good to be alive, lifted you off your feet, brought light in adversity and rescued Saturday afternoons from obscurity. Moore had class and breeding, Best was suave, slinky, neat, well-proportioned and deliciously creative with left and right foot. Charlton had the most explosive shot in the game, Cruyff did extraordinary things with the ball, dragging back and stepping over at will, Dean scored 60 goals in one season for Everton, Matthews was the most subtle of wing wizards and Shackleton was vital and vibrant.

Then there was Maradona, an Argentinean with that stocky looking, bullish frame that ghosted past defenders and, from time to time, bundled and barged his way into opponents penalty areas. This is not to suggest that Maradona was some brutish thug or bully but I think he knew he was going to score every time he picked up the ball. But he also knew that if things had gone disastrously wrong in his private life-which they frequently did-then he'd have to suffer the consequences.

It became patently obvious, though, that rumours about his private life were indeed accurate. It must have been the most traumatic time in his life but the drugs which almost destroyed him and the wild nightlife debauchery which followed, must have left the most painful of mental scars. It is hard to imagine just how much more Maradona might have achieved without the sleazy distractions that must have haunted him.

Len Shackleton, Dixie Dean, Stan Mortensen, Tommy Lawton and Sir Tom Finney were all idolised by their respective clubs for reasons which became obvious. They were all players who responded almost instantly to the big occasion, never demanding, greedy, acquisitive or in any way affected by their very private triumphs.

They all woke up on Saturday afternoons just glad, pleased and grateful to be an essential part of their team. Money was an important consideration but I don't think they ever felt that money was the be all and end all of everything. Money was a means of feeding and watering their families, paying the bills or snapping up a bargain in the sales.

All of the above players travelled on the same bus with their devoted fans, happily mingled with the supporters, laughed uproariously at the latest joke, swapping jokes and banter until the referee blew the whistle for the start of the match. It seemed from a distance that these were the players who gave you the perfect incentive to keep going back to your team every week.

The world of boxing had given us more than we could ever have hoped for. It brought Rocky Marciano, Joe Louis, Sugar Ray Robinson, Max Schmelling, George Foreman, Joe Frazier, Ken Norton, Joe Bugner, Henry Cooper, Ken Buchanan and above all one man who built his own very unique legend.

Muhammad Ali, by common consent, was arguably the most unforgettable boxer of all time. Of course there was Marciano, of course there was Louis and you could hardly forget Robinson. But Ali was skilful, charismatic, endlessly humorous, gentle and delightfully personable. When Ali was around you knew you'd been in the presence of the most engaging sportsman you'd ever seen. He would remain in your consciousness almost indefinitely.

Ali, of course, was the ultimate exhibitionist, smooth talking, persuasive both in and out of the ring, at times possibly tactless but then Ali just spoke from the hip and if you were offended then that was too bad. Ali was one of boxing's finest technicians, a man who had all of boxing's most relevant tools at his disposal. Ali seemed to hook, upper cut and jab with an almost repetitive authority.

He would dance, pose and posture his way into a Las Vegas ring, showboating and grandstanding, promising to knock down his opponents in a matter of seconds and then realising that boxing was no longer a sport but a hurtful, spiteful grudge match and a brutal punishment had to be administered.

Above all the brutality and savagery, Ali was essentially a nice guy, kind, good to his family, always thinking of others when the chips were down. Ali was open, extrovert, demonstrative, his very own travelling PR man, the most daring self-publicist and a man of the masses, a man of the people, somebody who simply wanted to be loved.

During those golden eyeball to eyeball confrontations with George Foreman and Joe Frazier, there was something of the pantomime about Ali. Ali, for all his genial joviality, was quite clearly a committed, hungry heavyweight. When Ali stepped into the ring, the general opinion was never divided. His fans were completely on his side, yelling approvingly at his every move, driving Ali on with all their vocal might. Come on Muhammad. This is your night. Foreman and Frazer were just bulky, apparently impenetrable barriers, giant fortresses that had to be smashed to smithereens. Ali could do that and more because he was the man who believed that anything was possible. All he could think of was sweet revenge, cold blooded vengeance and utter humiliation.

The Ali philosophy was simple and as clear as mud. If you come anywhere me, I'll take all my pent up frustration out on you and leave you flat on your back. And yet Ali was never vicious or bloody minded. He would torment his opponents, taunt them, demoralise them, dishearten them, make them look stupid. Ali was a master of boxing psychology and kidology, outthinking, outmanoeuvring and just outwitting you. Ali was always several steps ahead of his opponents. The dancing, skipping and teasing were just fashion accessories, something to carry around with him, tools of the trade, flashy boxing accoutrements.

Part 14:
And now for a review of my first introduction into the world of films.

My first introduction into the world of films and the cinema was rather like my first introduction into the world of fantasy, escapism, a world that was unreal and imaginary, but, in its way, very authentic and tangible at the same time. That may sound like a contradiction in terms but perhaps that's the way my young eyes saw everyday life.

One weekly event during my childhood more or less set the template for the rest of my life. It shaped my earliest perceptions of how people behaved in Hollywood and the lifestyles of the rich, famous, celebrated and notorious. It was that time of life which underlined and reinforced those first impressions.

Saturday morning pictures at Gants Hill Odeon had to be the most enjoyable period of time. To a child whose life had been framed by black and white TV pictures, this was the perfect chance to find out what happened on a huge Technicolor cinema screen.

Shortly, my young, untrained eyes would be bombarded by the sheer magnificence and bold personality of the silver screen. Suddenly I was confronted by Flash Gordon, a lovely throwback to the days when superheroes were superheroes. Flash Gordon was the macho, manly and straight backed character who saved the world. He was the epitome of science fiction, bold, unyielding and buccaneering, totally without fear or trepidation. He'd stepped out straight out of the comic books and conquered the universe.

Then there were the chirpy, cheeky and very suitably childish cartoons, one after the other in a kind of relentless sequence. There was Felix and Sylvester the Cat, Tweety Pie, Mickey and Minnie Mouse, Donald Duck, the cartoon version of the Pink Panther, Roy Rodgers on his fine looking horse. They were our characters, our cartoons and our entertainment.

Up until that mid 1960s point, my parents had always told me about the cinema's golden days. Back in the 1930s, 40s and 50s, films were big budget, glorious, sumptuous epics. In Hollywood's heyday, these were mighty, tumultuous productions with legendary actors and actresses.

Back in the very early days of cinema, the whole film industry must have been one fantastic dreamscape. Films were dynamic, challenging and provocative, confident and cavalier, never afraid to highlight the burning issues of the day. Films had the dashing verve of a Clark Gable or Errol Flynn, the sweeping beauty of Fred Astaire and Ginger Rodgers, fleet of foot and dancers extraordinaire, the dramatic poignancy of Gone with the Wind, tragic but compelling and then the Wizard of Oz, a film of great emotional intensity, following as it did the turbulent career of Judy Garland.

140

The Wizard of Oz was a film of huge imagination, initially black and white and then unmistakably colourful. It was a film of drama, clever imagery, tension and turmoil, triumph and an ever present sense that you were watching something vitally important, something that would give us a revealing insight into the way Hollywood was thinking. An immense film.

But my first entrance to the world of cinema had very honest echoes of the past. In a sense, the likes of Jimmy Stewart, John Wayne, Gregory Peck, James Cagney, Edward G. Robinson, Robert Mitchum, Deborah Kerr, Vivian Leigh, Katherine Hepburn, Robert Mitchum, Burt Lancaster were all still easily identifiable figures because they were characters whose acting skills had easily transferred to my generation.

Firstly, there were the Pink Panther films, brilliantly executed comedies that reduced me to uncontrollable hysterics. Peter Sellers had already established himself as one of Britain's most anarchic and irreverent of comics. The Goons was a ground-breaking radio comedy show from the 1950s that broke the mould and every tradition that the country had held so dear.

Along with fellow Goons, Spike Milligan, Harry Secombe and Michael Bentine, Sellers finally hit upon the kind of comic idea that would completely re-design the world of radio comedy. Sellers was the man with a hundred silly and ludicrous voices, flexing his vocal chords and reducing his audience to gales of universal laughter.

In the Pink Panther, Sellers would find the most idyllic comedy vehicle. Inspector Clouseau was the fumbling, bumbling, permanently accident prone French policeman who never seemed to get anything right. The Pink Panther series was possibly the funniest set of films I'd ever seen.

Throughout the Pink Panther, Sellers took us on a breathless journey of fantastically devised comic sketches showing Sellers in his all his variety and versatility. There was Sellers who tripped over chairs, set fire to curtains, fell backwards into ditches, broke priceless ornaments or generally messed up everything that he was assigned to do.

And then there was the classic Clouseau moment. Sellers, complete in Toulouse La Trec costume, shuffles into an antique shop legless and incapacitated. In his hands, he holds a hissing bomb that, at any given moment, would blow not only him to pieces, but the rest of the shop. It is the most exquisite piece of cinema gold.

Then there were the Clousseau conflicts with the martial arts expert Kato. Walking through the door of his apartment, Kato would attack Clouseau in slow motion and Sellers would respond with the most gorgeous retaliation. There were high kicks, flying legs and arms and moments that the Hollywood of the 20s must have thought had gone out of fashion with silent movies, Charlie Chaplin, Buster Keaton and all. The Pink Pinter was the most immaculately drawn and rounded character in the history of film. How fortunate I was to have seen it.

Then there was the cinematic phenomenon that was James Bond. James Bond lived the life that most of my generation could only have dreamt about.

Bond was suave, debonair, handsome, frighteningly intrepid, bold and swashbuckling. Bond was the realisation of our teenage fantasies. Suddenly, most of the lads of my age had suddenly discovered somebody who was the man we wanted to be but never could.

Bond was shrewd, calculating, fearless, a gentleman of the highest order, smooth as silk and utterly undaunted. Bond was the man who took on the baddies, avoided all manner of potential disasters and then dusted himself down when all seemed lost. Bond did everything, conquered everything and then smiled in adversity. What a man.

Sean Connery, George Lazenby, Roger Moore and all who followed fit the bill perfectly and turned Bond into the kind of silver screen figure we could all look up to. They fought off the evil characters with a courageous shrug of the shoulders, manfully clung onto the edge of cliffs in cliffhanging fashion, escaped near certain death on killing machines and raced across speeding trains as if this were part of their everyday itinerary.

Above all, though Bond had an almost unchallengeable masculinity and machismo that some of my peers could only envy from afar. Bond had an admirable individuality that none of us could ever aspire to. When Miss Moneypenny gave him his latest death defying assignment, you could almost hear the sighs from the cinema audience. He was tough as teak, battle hardened and persistent to the bitter end. Nobody could ever dislodge, remove or ultimately kill Mr Bond because Bond was indestructible, untouchable, immune from death, disaster and calamity.

But it is to my first ever venture into the cinema world that I now turn to. My first ever films as a kid were, in no particular order, Jungle Book and Bambi. Both of these films hold an almost tenacious grip on my memory. I'm not sure whether this had anything to do with the fact that they were my first movies.

Jungle Book and Bambi occupy this very special category because they were the films that opened my eyes to the true meaning of the cinema. They were lovely, life affirming movies that brought a real definition to my young and receptive mind.

Jungle Book was that magnificent adaptation of the Rudyard Kipling novel. It had now been turned into the most stunning cartoon I'd ever set eyes upon. Mowgli and Balou had suddenly emerged from a very mundane obscurity to the huge canvas that was the movie silver screen.

Jungle Book, to my young developing eyes, had a very lifelike feel to it, a moving and hypnotically riveting film that must have reduced every child to a hot stew of emotions. It was somehow realistic without being completely realistic, charming and simple, never snobbish or patronising. If you were a kid, then Jungle Book reinforced your childish perceptions and never for a moment did you feel threatened. Those cartoon bears, lions and monkeys were almost too good to be true, animals with feelings, humour and the most good-natured temperaments.

And yet, there was something else that also made visits to the Saturday morning pictures so worthwhile. In fact, it also applied to general cinema pilgrimages. Now of course, things are completely different but at the time, it was regarded as the norm, the way they did things at the time.

When the lights were dimmed and the atmosphere became feverishly expectant, there were the usherettes; dark and mystical figures who looked like shadowy silhouettes, distant and yet obvious characters. You somehow knew they were there because without making themselves look too conspicuous, they simply were.

The usherettes were humble, unassuming people, sellers of ice creams and little plastic cartons of orange juice called Kia Ora. But usherettes also had torches and led you to your seat gently but purposefully. I don't know why but I somehow felt that once you'd bought your tubs of popcorn and your orange juice, you were somehow richer for the experience.

Who could ever forget the adverts before the film? Now Pearl and Dean had already become well established as one of the foremost advertising agencies in the country. But before the beginning of a gripping thriller, romantic comedy or scintillating science fiction, there were the local advertisements.

In Gants Hill, there were a number of reputable shops that most of the local residents had grown accustomed to. There was Saunders, the menswear shop opposite Gants Hill cinema, a shop that oozed style and panache. In Saunders there were model mannequins, men dressed in formal shirts and ties.

But Saunders had now been thrust into the public eye, a cinema legend before James Bond. Saunders was to be found just outside Gants Hill station next to the café. It had to be the most amusing thing I'd ever seen on the cinema screen. Now gentlemen, you may be interested to know that Rael Brook shirts are still being sold for a bargain price but remember that Goldfinger is just minutes away.

Then, teenage males were suddenly confronted with life changing films, films that revolutionised our thinking and turned our young adolescent minds inside out. Up until then, our hormones had led a fairly sedate lifestyle but now there would follow two films that played havoc with our sexual urges. It was rather like being told that, overnight, you'd been told all about the facts of life without any manuals.

Saturday Night Fever and Grease were two of the most sexually charged and suggestive films I'd ever seen. Of course, we'd been taught Biology at secondary school but both Night Fever and Grease merely underlined all of the rumours. They were undoubtedly the most revelatory and celebratory films I'd ever seen.

In Saturday Night Fever, a very brash and vain John Travolta becomes the sole object of female attention and affection. Travolta quite clearly thinks he's the sexiest man on the planet, lusted after and desired by the whole of the American female population. Travolta thinks he's best thing since sliced bread, forever combing his hair almost religiously, looking at himself in the mirror and straightening the leather jacket. In short, he's the bees knees, completely self-confident and narcissistic.

Travolta wants to be everything we wanted to be. He was cool, good

143

looking, magnetic, charismatic and almost feline. In every restaurant, café or neighbourhood Travolta visited, he was the man who made everything look easy. And then there was that famous disco scene. Yes the one we'll always remember.

Suddenly, the dance floor conveniently cleared, the disco lights flashed a thousand colours and Travolta took centre stage. The white jacket had been repeatedly cleaned, now shining and sparkling before the man himself tripped the light fantastic. To the backing of another Bee Gees dance filler, Travolta glides onto the floor, whips off his white jacket almost unceremoniously and dances in a way nobody had ever seen the like before.

Travolta struts, slides, spins and carelessly throws away all of those dancing orthodoxies. I seem to remember there was a ball room dancing hall in the Romford Road, not far from where I used to live. For Travolta, the contrast between ball room dancing and his dancing could not have been greater.

Travolta looks supple, athletic, well co-ordinated and virilely vigorous. Staying Alive is given all of Travolta's best treatment. It was fast moving, feisty, sassy and electric. It was the soundtrack to our lives, the one we'd been waiting for. It had an almost unmistakable theatricality about it, a dizzying speed and natural rhythm.

Then, with an almost a splendid inevitability, there was the title of the film Saturday Night Fever. It was time for Travolta to cast aside all of his doubts and reservations. Suddenly, there was a whirl of arms, legs and feet, flinging himself across the floor with an almost absurd ease before ending the whole routine with an arm in the air and jacket perched nervously on his shoulder.

Now this was how we wanted to lead our lives. Well not quite. I think I'd have probably burnt myself out by the time I was in my twenties but I could fantasise. Saturday Night Fever became the film sensation of that year, showered with awards and internationally acclaimed. It had dance, it had funky disco music, boys falling in love and girls falling in love. It was constant, consistent, unstoppable, always taking the wildest of risks and clearly intent on making the boldest of statements. It was the film made during the Seventies that pointed cinema's compass in an entirely different direction.

I could hardly overlook my next choice of film. It was, quite literally, one of the most wholesomely enjoyable movies of the time. In many ways, the resemblance to Saturday Night Fever was almost uncanny. There could never have been any doubt that it would break all box office records and lift our hearts to its giddiest of heights. It ticked all of the right boxes, made all the right noises and left us spellbound and dumbfounded.

Grease was, quite definitely, the word. And without any shadow of doubt whatsoever, it had style, grace and rhythm. It was America turning the clock back to a time when everybody fell in love, everybody temporarily betrayed each other and then inevitably got back together again. There was an underlying theme of love, pettiness, approval and acceptance. There was sweetness and tenderness, pain and glory. There were high school romances, happy reunions, hurt, pain and rejection. But in the end, everybody kissed and made up, there could be reconciliation, compromise and agreement.

Grease had its two main leading stars. John Travolta and Olivia Newton John were cinematic bombshells. Travolta was a comparative unknown, American through and through and desperate to prove that he could be the one to steal our hearts. He was the one who would reduce young teenage girls to quivering adoration.

Throughout Grease, Travolta was the answer to every American teenager's prayers: he was tough, strong, confident, no-nonsense, ferociously rebellious and stubbornly non -conformist. Travolta must have modelled himself quite clearly on that other American rebel, James Dean. Travolta was determined to buck the system, he was assertive and he melted the hearts of the American girls. He was cool to the point of being lukewarm but frequently reasoning and warmly reasonable. As long as you broke the rules.

But Grease appealed to everything in the American psyche. It told the story which was as old as time itself. Boy meets girl, boy falls in love, girl very reluctantly but then willingly falls in love. Boy meets girl on the beach during the summer, both know that even a summertime romance was destined to flourish only to find that it didn't. It is America set in the 1950s when everything reflected that mood.

There was Travolta, all laid back, carefree and nonchalant. Travolta, with his black bomber jacket, combed back black hair and bolshy bravado. Nobody ever messed with Travolta because he had a unique way with the girls. No man could ever hope to compete with him because he was the unassailable one, the man who dictated the pace, the man who called the shots.

Of course there was Olivia Newton John. Olivia Newton John was the one that every male of our age wanted to have. How could they resist. The temptation was far too great. They'd have to write her letters, keep in touch, take her out for coffee, watch a weepy film with her, send her chocolates and flowers, wine and dine her, make her their girl, walk along the beach with her hand in hand. They'd fallen deeply in love with her, head over heels.

Olivia Newton John was sweet, cute, innocent, somehow protected from the wickedness's in society, cocooned and cloistered, just totally endearing. At the beginning of Grease, Newton John was a nervous, shy and inhibited soul, painfully unsure of herself, ill at ease and never at all confident. It was almost as if her whole personality had made up its mind to keep a respectful distance from boys. Boys could never be trusted, boys were too emotionally overpowering and boys communicated on a completely different wavelength.

Eventually, Olivia slowly began to unravel. The cutesy, winsome pig tails in her hair began to shake themselves loose, the apparently frumpy looking dress became less dowdy and eventually she began to understand that in order to catch the attention of John Travolta, she would have to change her whole attitude and approach.

There would be no point in hiding away from her male beau because nothing would be gained by being meek and submissive. She would have to get her act together, change her whole appearance and look as if she meant business.

And that indeed is what happened. Half way through the film, after repeated advances from Travolta, fleeting setbacks and tears, both Travolta and Newton John met on common ground, compatible, blissfully happy in each other's company and hopelessly devoted to each other.

But not before those heart tugging, mushy and sentimental moments. Not before they drove in to that Drive in Movie and watched a film out in a field. Not before Travolta teased and flirted with other women, stirring all the jealousy he could find in his female co-star. It was all very silly, tit for tat and revenge, reprisal and counter reprisal. Anything you could do I could do better.

When Grease came out towards the end of the late 1970s, I think it was widely felt that very few films had touched the minds and hearts of the nation, that no film had taken you on such a fun filled, emotional journey as Grease. No film had aroused such positive feelings in you, could convince that nothing could ever go wrong in your life, that despite everything, you too could be successful, affectionate, assertive, right and wrong at the same time but always ready to see the other person's point of view.

It is at this point that I cast my eyes at two of my other favourite films. At the time, they had a very profound and powerful impact on me, reaching out to me in a way that very few films had done before. There can be no reason why they made me think and think again. I believe they were films that spoke on the same level as me, never lectured or tried to prove anything to me.

West Side Story was an adaptation of the Shakespeare love story of Romeo and Juliet. It was the complete love story, bittersweet, heartfelt, tender and, most unfortunately, tragic. I'm not sure why I grew to like West Side Story but there was something about the film that affected all of my senses and sensitivities.

To be honest, I could never get to grips with Shakespeare at school and I don't think I'll ever understand Shakespeare, not now or ever. My English teacher at school did his utmost to explain what seemed to be the annoying complexities of Shakespeare's prose. But this was what he wrote and if that's how he delivered his stories, then I think you had to get the gist of what he was saying.

During our English lessons, we were all given our respective editions of Macbeth and the Merchant of Venice. They were very delicately bound, thin books that were slightly threadbare and the worse for wear. During the lessons, we were all encouraged to write translations of the Bard's language, noting in exact detail all the most salient points of the book.

West Side Story though was a superb love story, brilliantly told and immaculately photographed. It was the old, old story of boy meets girl, both fall deeply in love, gang warfare, gangs bullying and intimidating each other, Tony meets Maria and then they dance wildly on rooftops, buildings, around lampposts. It is America at its happiest, saddest, most rapturous, tense, soft, fluid and fluent. Everything that America held dear.

In 1968, or there or thereabouts, I was taken to see a film that reinforced everything I'd ever heard about Judaism. As a young Jewish lad growing up in Ilford, I'd been told everything I needed to know about my religion. On the Passover in early spring, Pesach, you were required to eat an unleavened bread called a Matzot and refrain from eating any bread for eight days. Then at the beginning of Autumn, I would observe the High Holy Days when the festival of the Jewish New Year and Yom Kippur would be rightly and resoundingly celebrated. In the interim period, I would share Purim, a fancy dress festival and Chanukah, a joyous fusion of doughnuts, latkes (potato cakes) and general festivity.

Judaism had been proudly instilled in me and now was the right time to discover much more about where exactly I'd come from. I was beautifully aware of my Jewish identity and the sense of independence that had given me. Of course, there was the whole moral code to be taken into account and you had to fast every Yom Kippur from your bar mitzvah onwards.

Now a film would appear on the silver screen which brought all of those wonderfully safe traditions and values to cinematic life. It was richly layered, richly textured, historically faithful to the plot and passionately proud of its spiritual roots. There was a religious warmth about it and something that was just beautifully uplifting.

Fiddler on the Roof was quite the most astonishing and intimately revealing film I'd ever seen. I was only six when my parents took me to see it but I can still remember the sense of wonder and awe I felt at the time. It was a film that took us on one of the loveliest journeys into the world of Jewish life. It was moving, touching, wistful, sad and very powerful. It tapped into all of those genuine hitherto dormant emotions that had now suddenly erupted into life on the cinema screen. It was a story about families, happy times, sad times, struggles, hardships, feuds and friction, betrayal and hurt. But ultimately, it was triumphant, happy ever after, singing riotously in the streets, dancing on farms, the glorious wedding, music, music and more music.

Fiddler on the Roof was a throwback to the days when although times may have been hard, families could still unite and harmonise, that if things ever went disastrously wrong, they could still smile and laugh. But there was something about the whole film that still resonates with me. It is the most personal of memories, so precious, special and meaningful.

I can still remember accompanying my mum and dad to the Leicester Square cinema in the West End. To this day, it remains one of the few cinemas which shows only one movie. I don't know but 1968 seemed to have a very distinctive feel to it. There was a hint of edgy protest and disillusionment in the air. Vietnam was very much on our minds, troubling and antagonising everybody, the Grosvenor Square riots outside the American embassy had just taken place and everybody must have felt very nervy, anxious and apprehensive.

There had been loads of political demonstrations and rallies in the past but why did I feel they were intruding on my visit to see Fiddler on the Roof. Surely they could find some other city or country to make a noise. Still it was the greatest of films and it confirmed me as the proudest member of the Jewish community.

At roughly the same time, there was another film that remains firmly imprinted on my mind. Once again my parents and I gathered outside Leicester

Square cinema. It was another classic interpretation of this time, one of Dickens best known and loved novels, Oliver Twist, a thigh slapping, jolly, stirring movie with lots of everything and much to comment upon.

Oliver Twist was absolutely outstanding, a soaring, towering blockbuster of a film, monumentally accomplished, beautifully executed, bubbling over with joy and exuberance. The film was called Oliver and for those who witnessed and experienced the sheer magnificence and magnitude of it, none will ever forget the legacy it left us.

Directed and composed by the great lyricist Lionel Bart and starring the wonderful Ron Moody, Oliver is the story of stories. It follows a young, impoverished child wandering the streets of London and seeking company. Suddenly he meets the villainous vagabond Bill Sykes, crafty, devious, wicked and scheming.

The story then turns to a whole portrait gallery of brilliantly drawn characters. There was the Artful Dodger played by Jack Wild, impish, mischief making, unpredictable but somehow lovable in a roguish way. Wild is full of dubious plots and underhand manoeuvrings. The Artful Dodger was the kid none of us wanted to be but privately felt the deepest sympathy for. It seemed to me that he got away with most things but not everything.

Then there was Fagin, played masterfully by Ron Moody. Moody was one of those very professional actors who could turn his hand to any role. But because he's Jewish and because he knew who the character was and what he sounded like, Moody gave the character of Fagin a very real force and personality.

Moody gave Fagin that superbly cultivated accent, that rich and rounded mannerism, a voice that was made in heaven and the inflexion in the voice that was simply divine. You've Got to Pick a Pocket or Two was Fagin's signature tune, a song written by the most gifted of songwriters. It would remain with me for many a decade.

And so I move in almost seamlessly back to the 1970s when films were just different, spellbinding and powerful. There are two more that readily spring to mind, films that had the stardust sprinkling of magic and enchantment. They were films that made me gasp with sheer disbelief, films that quite literally suspended my imagination, enthralling and dazzling in equal measure.

Star Wars was quite the most startling of all cinematic achievements. It had all of the attributes you could ask for in a film. It was a vast, overwhelming, years ahead of anything cinema had ever produced and hugely prophetic. Up until then, I hadn't taken a great deal of interest in anything related to science fiction. But Star Wars was like nothing I'd ever seen before.

Starring Harrison Ford, Star Wars was a visually spectacular movie that broke all box office records, a film that had a pomp and pageantry that blew away everybody who saw it. Star Wars looked into a very distant future that very few of us could ever have imagined.

Star Wars had exploding space crafts, spinning and whirling through space, odd looking animals that somehow defied description. There were strange voices, flashing lights, swords with laser beams, space age gadgetry, technical wizardry and stunning sorcery. It was one extraordinary roller coaster of a film, where the acting seemed to collide into the whole chaos and mayhem of the film. Still, it was the film to watch at the time and I'm convinced that even the most indifferent of movie goers must have spent a very pleasurable afternoon or evening with Star Wars as their accompaniment.

Part 15:
And now for some more classic childhood memories.

Most of my childhood memories can be traced back to the time when the whole world was never entirely at peace with itself. There always seemed to be something that was never quite right about society, an undercurrent of danger, edginess, volatility and dissatisfaction that never looked as though it could ever be healed.

I can remember my very early days at Newbury Park primary school staring blankly at the yellowing, crinkled hymn sheet and wondering what it all meant and whether we were to supposed to show any reaction to what we were singing about. It was a daily routine but I'm not sure whether any of my class mates knew anything about religion.

We sang Jerusalem with resounding vigour, listened obediently to a plinky plonky, discordant piano that hadn't been tuned for what seemed like decades. We stood together in childhood solidarity, bleary eyed and blinking from our morning stupor.

There were the regular PE lessons where boys and girls jumped and somersaulted the pommel horse with a reckless disregard for our welfare. But there were terrible and mortifying things going on around me which never really registered with me as a kid.

There was the above mentioned Vietnam, helicopters flying overhead, soldiers dodging the savage bullets and explosions, diplomats at the highest level trying desperately to bring everything to a peaceful resolution. It was all horrendous, unnecessary, futile and virulently violent. Even Mary Whitehouse would have looked away and shamefully bowed her head in despair.

All around me there was noisy commotion, furious flux and disruption at every level of society. Students always seemed to be protesting and hollering at each other, politicians permanently at each other's throats, tension thick in the air. There was hatred, venom and bile in their every word. There was outright anger in Whitehall and Trafalgar Square, seething, bubbling and boiling over at times. And just for good measure, we had street riots, scuffles, confrontations with the police and nothing was ever really solved.

I think things came to a head when poor Northern Ireland and the IRA came to bitter blows. For what seemed like a lifetime, London was held hostage by horribly naked terrorism. I think things got completely out of hand at the end of the 1960s and the beginning of the 70s.

I think England had just been humiliatingly driven out of the World Cup in Mexico City by the Germans and men started wearing short sleeved Fred Perry T-shirts. Anyway, the point is that all was not well back in Blighty, Edward

Heath seemed to be highly amused by everything from sailing boats to conducting orchestras while all around him seemed to be imploding and exploding.

Heath, on entering 10 Downing Street, had just signed up the nation to the Common Market, some all European agreement that entitled Britain to trade to its heart content with our European partners. But there were definite fault lines in the system, loopholes and discrepancies that could never be righted. The British economy was allegedly in tatters, Harold Wilson was a thorn in the Tory's side and Enoch Powell had said rather more than he should have.

Meanwhile back in Cranley Road, I was still that self-conscious seven or eight year old, valiantly coming to terms with school, the end of the summer holidays and returning at the beginning of the new term in September. I can remember being in floods of tears the day before that new school year. I cried into my pillow with little in the way of psychological comfort.

But Newbury Park primary school was the start of that first chapter in my life. I had one grey jumper and one shirt, the tie was a subtle shade of grey and red and the trousers were very short. Because I was Jewish, my mum insisted that I wear a clipped on Star of David to which I had no objection. But the kids at school would make fun of me, laughing and teasing me mercilessly, testing my emotional reflexes at a very early age.

However, the IRA had now started their murderous campaign of death and destruction on the British mainland. It was a bloody, tempestuous time when loyalties were irreparably divided and families were tortured, tormented and finally destroyed. It was a time when the Protestant and Catholic communities were bombed, blown to pieces and completely split down the middle. Previously harmonious Belfast neighbourhoods were now sworn enemies and were horribly caught up in the whole messy, fatal business.

Throughout the killing, stoning, looting and pillaging, Northern Ireland seemed to be at constant war with itself. I was just a teenager but I did get the impression that this was a conflict that nobody in their sane minds would have wanted. It suddenly occurred to me that here was a country that was just tearing itself apart.

When I came home from school, the TV news seemed to have only one dominant issue. All you were subjected to were endless images of bombs going off in the Falls Road, graffiti on the walls with screaming hatred and anarchic acrimony. And then there was the same scenario over and over again. All day and seemingly well into the evening and night.

There were soldiers with well-equipped guns, rumbling tanks with more ammunition and innocent kids on street corners lobbing stones at each other, or so it seemed. It was all very unsavoury and repugnant, a grotesque crime in broad daylight? How could two religious communities descend to this vile and vulgar level? It was premeditated murder and slaughter, an undermining of the very soul and heart of the Irish people, the most hideous and heinous crime against humanity, deplorable and unforgivable.

That the peace loving nation should now have to descend to the most despicable of all levels made no sense to me. I must have wondered how one nation could be overwhelmed with such loathing and revulsion of each other. It almost seemed inconceivable that at some point during the day, one man could plant a destructive bomb underneath their neighbour's car.

It just didn't seem possible that one nation could harbour such cruel and ultimately savage thoughts for no apparent reason. As the days, weeks, months and years passed, there was an almost appalling deterioration, a helpless weakening of the Irish spirit and soul. And here was I, a pained and shocked school lad learning my times table, tucking into the egg mayonnaise sandwiches my mum had made for my packed lunch and country dancing in the afternoon.

There didn't seem any rational explanation for any of it. Innocent soldiers and civilians were losing their lives, mothers were weeping inconsolably for their dead children, fathers and men just easy targets for these wicked and callous terrorists. It was all so immensely frightening, so inexplicable and, in a way, human nature at its very worst.

Day by day, you would watch the 10 o'clock news with its gruesome tales of bombing, bombing of churches, green grocers, grocers, post offices, sweet shops, village churches and of course the inevitable police stations. People of all ages were shot and viciously attacked, stern buildings demolished in seconds, age old resentments blowing up in each other's faces, crying, wailing, shrieking, pleading for help and salvation but never quite knowing when it would stop. And yet thankfully it did. What a wonderful day that was.

I don't think I was only the one who cheered vociferously when Mo Mowlam, eminent politician and lovely lady, came to the most amicable agreement with Sinn Fein and the people of Northern Ireland. The Good Friday agreement was probably the best day in the history of Northern Ireland. It was a victory for common sense, compromise and decency.

After years and years of violence, premeditated murder, loathing, hostility and bickering, the moment had arrived when brother met with brother, sister met with sister, mother with mother, father with father, friend with friend, and whole families shook hands agreeably and compliantly. The war was over, the bullets and bombs had been silenced, nobody would ever look unfavourably on each other.

I think there must have come a point when it all had become too much. There were bombs at Harrods, the bomb under a car which killed a politician. Throughout the troubles, there was an ever present sense of terror, paranoia and horrid uncertainty. When you woke in the morning, you were constantly reminded of just how easy it was to hate your fellow man. There was an air of almost neurotic nervousness, agitation, apprehension on every street corner and road. London seemed to be gripped by something that they simply couldn't handle, that was completely out of their control.

Both in the West End and particularly the City, Londoners crammed into their Tube trains fearful, worried for the own welfare and desperately concerned for those around them. There was an obvious siege mentality that almost strangled the very heart of London for years on end.

But the Good Friday agreement brought an end to all of the hurt, hell, confrontation, savage conflict and the monumental loss of innocent lives. So when Mo Mowlam dug her heels in, bashed heads together and bloody mindedly dragged the warring parties to a lasting peace deal, some of us jumped from the rooftops with unrestrained joy. It was a defining moment in Irish political history.

On the day after the Good Friday agreement, my wife Bev and I were shopping in a local Stoke Newington supermarket when, by sheer coincidence, we met the woman who'd made it all possible, that formidable woman who brought bitterness and intolerance to the most blissful of ends.

Mo Mowlam, on the day after the Good Friday agreement, was shopping in Stoke Newington, buying perhaps The Independent or Times. It was almost as if the moment was somehow fated to happen. It was pre-ordained to be, my wife and I bumping into the greatest political hero, disbelieving the evidence of our eyes but nonetheless grateful that normal life had been restored to the good people of Northern Ireland.

In many ways, I suppose, War had come to accompany my childhood. Not the serious, destructive business where the triggers were pulled and you were dead. But the evil, underhand and wicked kind where well timed grenades were planted under cars, next to schools, near churches, directly next to shops. It was all very cunning, all very secretive and all dreadfully unnecessary. But somehow, it had to happen but nobody really knew why.

What was the point of Vietnam, the Khmer Rouge, Pol Pot, Cambodia, the IRA, the horrendous dust ups which were to follow during the 1980s? Who were these tinpot dictatorships who deliberately, it seemed, were hell bent on gruesome genocide. How could one man harbour so much hatred in his heart?

I talk of one Idi Amin, the man Uganda came to dominate and command his troubled country before overthrowing them. Amin must have been one long and continuous nightmare, the most dreaded of all dictators and terrible tyrants. How long did the people of Uganda have to suffer his abominations, his sickening plots, that cruel and unforgiving face?

In Britain, I saw Idi Amin was one of those slightly odd but frightful of figures. He was always seen in military uniform, never remotely interested in peace and permanently on the warpath. Amin was fearsome, ferocious, brutally aggressive and yet, at first glance, butter wouldn't have melted in his mouth. Amin though was cold, calculating, shrewd and pitilessly harmful.

At the beginning of the 1980s, another news agenda suddenly erupted into the public domain. Once again the forces of war and conflict were to about to bring the whole of Britain to its knees. It was apparently without any plausible motive and without any provocation.

The Falklands War would become one of those bloody and barbaric of Wars that simply had no reason or foundation. Something that seemed so harmless and unaccountable. It was something to do with Argentina, land and territory. But none of us knew why and what for. But what I do know is that innocent British troops were blown to pieces and death darkened our corridors.

This is not to say that I was at war with myself because this was quite clearly not the case. I don't ever think I felt offended, bitter and upset.

Certainly, I never felt any festering grudges or sour grapes. I was never driven to unleashing my personal ammunition on the rest of the world or marching my armies into Europe. I would never flatten, destroy or obliterate Poland overnight. I was still the peace maker, the one who preferred order to chaos, sense rather than disaster.

As far as I was concerned, the governments of the world had to find a solution to apparently insoluble arguments. I was the one who supported Henry Kissinger, the man who just wanted the world to get on with each other. We are all here for an allotted time and war didn't seem to be the correct answer to any problem. I was convinced that there had to be a better way.

Throughout the70s, Kissinger was the one whose clever diplomacy and sharp judgments made everything seem right. When everybody lost their head and nobody could be pacified, Kissinger emerged from the anger and acrimony with his head held high. He was the one who believed that if you could only stop and see the heartache you were causing, then that was a good enough argument for eternal peace.

Which brings me back to the politicians who took up residence in my teenage years. I've mentioned Edward Heath and Harold Wilson but what about the others. There was Wilson's successor, James Callaghan, Barbara Castle, one of the first women I can ever recall in the Houses of Parliament, very much a mother earth figure, kind and maternal but also forceful and ruthlessly pragmatic. I don't think she took any nonsense. There was Jeremy Thorpe, never the most powerful or conspicuous of politicians. Thorpe, the leader of the Liberal party, always seemed to me to be very weak and ineffectual.

During the early 70s, the Labour party seemed to unintentionally attract scandal and controversy. There was that seedy Crossland news story, a man apparently with very few morals and oozing with corruption. Richard Crossland had apparently been involved in some very naughty jiggery pokery and sleazy skulduggery.

At the time, I'd always associated the Labour party with trade unions, working class ideology, beer and sandwiches. Harold Wilson was that safe pair of hands on what seemed to be a sinking ship. Wilson, with pipe in one hand and home-spun philosophy on the other, never looked fazed and had that most sympathetic bedside manner.

And then there was the Conservative party. Now the Tories, to my eye, simply invited mickey taking and parody. I'd always regarded the Tories as stuffy, snotty, snooty, privileged and pampered. The Tories had full time membership at the Garrick gentlemen's club, played polo during the summer and were quite obviously born with a silver spoon in their mouths.

Even before the Margaret Thatcher era, the Tories had Heath, Willie Whitelaw and a fresh, out of university, Michael Heseltine. Heseltine would later come to epitomise everything the Conservative Party stood for: rich, self-made, self-sufficient and totally without remorse. Heseltine got involved in that messy helicopter business but I always felt that Heseltine was somehow meant to be a Tory politician, very eloquent and thoughtful but only happy when things were going well for him.

I used to look forward to the party political conferences during the early autumn. Now I have to tell you that party political conferences were quite the funniest and most absurd spectacles. It was rather like watching the most farcical West End show you'd ever seen.

Suddenly, politicians from right across the spectrum were let loose on their devoted followers. It was time to bellow out their grievances and exhaust tiresome clichés. They would confidently stand on their platform and then indulge in some of the most peculiar body language; leaning languidly forward and then by turns wagging their fingers, pointing at nobody in particular, before shaking their fists indignantly and criticising the opposition's incompetence and spinelessness. It was definitely their fault that the country was in such dire straits. There was nobody else to blame.

The party political conference was rather like the most farcical comedy act you were ever likely to see. It was Punch and Judy, argument, counter argument, cut and thrust, mockery, sarcasm, facetiousness, we're far better than you're ever likely to be. They would insist that their party had got us into this trouble and unemployment would never come down under their leadership.

Meanwhile, back in the family home, TV seemed to have its own very regular and private agenda. My parents used to get the TV Times every week, an informative listings magazine which gave vastly detailed insights into the world of sitcoms, soap operas, glamorous celebrities, saucy kiss and tell stories, detective and period series, films and film stars.

The world of TV soap operas always seemed a mysterious and rather bizarre one, a world of gentle, humble characters with humorous names and volcanic tempers. My earliest recollections are now firmly imprinted in my mind. In 1960, a soap opera crept into our view very subtly and unobtrusively. It would assert itself into our minds, a constant source of fascination and a programme that would become a mighty social commentary on both 1960s, 70s, 80s, 90, 2000 and beyond. It would become our Monday and Wednesday highlight, our tasty gastronomic treat while mum was laying the dinner table.

Coronation Street, or Corrie, reflected, summarised perfectly, emphasised everything that Northern England was feeling at the time and still does. It was revealing, shocking, extremely alarming but absorbing and compulsively watchable. Coronation Street stunned, transfixed and took our breath away. Never before had we seen exactly what happened behind closed doors in Manchester even if it was fictitious.

Suddenly, we were allowed to see narrow cobbled back streets, well-trodden paving stones, chimneys belching out industrial smoke, cats curling up on rooftops and a pub called the Rovers Return. Oh yes, the Rovers Return, the pub where the whole of the community congregated, where all the local gossip was freely discussed.

Coronation Street was not so much a programme, more of a social documentary. It was rather like some psychological analysis of the human spirit. There were the tight, little back to back houses with chocolate box living rooms and vocally friendly neighbours. Tucked away behind their twitchy curtains, families would do all the things that come naturally to families.

Here was just a typical example of what life must have been like and I feel sure still does. It is a small microcosm of how we got on with each other, how we communicated, how we revelled in our neighbours good fortune when things went right and others further down our road wallowed rather unfairly in their misfortune if never spitefully. But never with our immediate neighbours in Cranley Road because they were the best.

The families were somehow handpicked from some heavenly corner of TV obscurity. There were the Ogdens, Stan and Hilda, adorable, brilliantly cast, always shouting, rowing, emotionally making up, reconciled and simply made for each other. The Ogdens were almost a central feature of Coronation Street.

I often got the impression that nobody could have designed a funnier or more touching set of characters in any TV soap operas in the whole history of soap operas. Stan and Hilda were the stereotype married couple. Everything was very strict and regimental and yet there was a sense that Hilda always wanted something better for both herself and Stan.

Hilda was a cleaner in the Rovers Return pub but always wanted to improve herself. She was, I feel sure, inordinately ambitious and aspirational but could never move to onto the next level. Perhaps she was frustrated by Stan and his lazy, rather lackadaisical approach to life. Stan was always in the betting shop or far more regularly in the Rovers Return downing a thousand pints.

But I was always intrigued by the dynamic of Hilda and Stan's relationship. They quite clearly adored each other but could never find the time to truly express their love. I don't think it was an assumed love but I got the feeling that perhaps there was a sense of presumptuousness rooted deep inside.

Still, Hilda and Stan did have several outstanding moments when their undying love for each other surfaced quite gloriously. There was that wonderful episode where Hilda had booked a hotel for their wedding anniversary. Now this was the stuff of sheer telly magic. It was just so breathtakingly simple and yet truly memorable.

In a moment of divine romance, Hilda pours a glass of champagne for her doting husband Stan and sips satisfyingly and longingly. Then would follow one of those golden soap opera moments. Hilda kisses Stan and lipstick would collide with a manly greying moustache. Hilda suddenly makes that scintillating remark. Stan, shocked and breathless, questions his wife and Hilda would remind him quite categorically that she was undoubtedly a woman. It was a marvellously executed and conceived piece of magic and summed up the soap operas I'd been brought up on.

Then of course there were the terraced house residents who always left us crying with laughter. There was the brash, brassy and boisterous Elsie Tanner, Ena Sharples, surely some Dickensian figure with hair net and a thick military coat. There was Len Fairclough, Ray Langton, Ken Barlow, Albert Tatlock, Maggie Clegg, Lucille Hewitt, Jack and Annie Walker, Billy Walker and of course the inimitable Ogdens. All long since largely forgotten figures but nonetheless essential to the whole narrative and structure of Coronation Street.

How could I ever forget the almost classic rivalry between Ena Sharples and Elsie Tanner. I always felt there was something deliberately confrontational about Ena and Elsie. I think they were just supposed to tolerate and then frequently hate each other. Why did they, for no apparent reason, find any excuse to fall out, to snigger, growl and groan before launching into the most explosive row. If Shakespeare had been around, I feel sure that both Elsie and Ena would have been top of the bill in a Stratford Upon Avon masterpiece. Nothing would give either Elsie or Ena greater pleasure than furious eyeballing or the icy stare.

Then there was the builder's yard inhabited by Ray Langton and Len Fairclough. Fairclough was that rather bullish, no-nonsense and aggressive hard man who loved a good scrap in the Rovers. Fairclough reminded me of one of those militant trade unionists who had been a shop steward for as long as he could remember. His partner Ray Langton would obey commands from Fairclough but still stand his ground when he thought he'd been undermined.

You would be hard pressed to ever forget Jack and Annie Walker, owners of the Rovers Return pub and somehow integral to the whole shape of Coronation Street. I often thought that both Jack and Annie had been land lord and lady since the days of Adam and Eve. They were well established publicans steeped in pub culture.

Annie Walker was that magnificently snobbish and pompous women who always felt that the ownership of a pub was somehow beneath her. Annie Walker was quite clearly full of her own wildly self-inflated sense of importance. She had snootiness written all over her, full of puffed up bombast and affectation.

I always felt that Annie just suffered and endured the antics of those who drank in her pub. She seemed to regard most of her punters with all the contempt normally reserved for lower class peasants. Annie was a superbly drawn character who you couldn't help but like. Annie would reluctantly engage Len Fairclough in small talk but was privately convinced that Fairclough was some pathetic commoner who had never read a book in his life.

And then there was Ken Barlow who married Val and then encountered every hard luck story known to mankind. Ken Barlow was Coronation Street's intellectual, a swot, deep thinker, an earnest academic, school teacher and the most profound of social observers. Ken always liked a drink but, in the eyes of Annie Walker, was the perfect gentleman, a man of breeding and substance, everything that Len Fairclough could never be no matter how hard he tried.

Then there was Albert Tatlock and Minnie Caldwell, two characters who must have been mentioned in some dusty Victorian novel or appeared on stage in some richly amusing West End comedy from the early 20th century. They were the kind of performers who lifted your heart and soul, brought a lasting smile to your face and just restored your faith in human nature. They were two charming old age pensioners who never ever bothered anybody and kept themselves to themselves.

Albert Tatlock was that elderly gentleman who, from as far back as I could remember, always looked old. Tatlock was a miserable, crotchety and cantankerous man who never seemed at ease with the rest of the Coronation Street. It seemed that, deep inside his head, the War had never really ended and that he was just destined to suffer forever more.

Tatlock was Uncle Tatlock to Ken Barlow and only ventured into the Rovers Return if there was a particularly stimulating game of dominoes or shove ha'penny to be played. He was a rather quiet and withdrawn figure who could never quite bring himself to take part in anything that was going on in the Street.

Then there was Minnie Caldwell, who must have been some old auntie in an Oscar Wilde play. I always felt that perhaps she was content to be in the company of those she knew. She was never demanding but always civil and courteous to familiar friends. But there was a kindness and soft hearted generosity about her that warmed your heart. There was something very delicate, frail looking, demure and utterly decorous about her, satisfied with her lot.

Many of us will never forget the three women who lived in the Corrie snug. There was Ena Sharples, Minnie Caldwell and until, the mid-Sixties, Martha Longhurst. These three women were formidable, robust and utterly redoubtable. When all gathered around the table in the Snug, it could be safely assumed that no subject was off limits and no resident in Coronation Street was spared their waspish tongue. It was character assassination on the grandest scale.

Then there were the accidents, disasters and tragedies in Coronation Street. Sometime during the 1960s, the Street would witness one of its first major disasters. My personal memory is a vague one but I do know there was quite the most horrendous train crash which literally seemed to crash into the Rovers with some ferocity. I do remember that most of the Street climbed into the smoking wreckage, desperately searching for the injured, helpless and critically ill.

Then there was the famous moment when Val Barlow, wife of the very studious Ken, made the most tragic exit from Corrie. Plugging her hair dryer into the plug socket, Val promptly electrocuted herself and vanished, until recently, without trace. Ken, suitably devastated and mortified, rushes home from the Rovers to find his wife on the floor. All very melodramatic and horrifically traumatic.

Then there were the fights, punch ups and general disorders in the Rovers Return. Poor Ken Barlow always seemed to be at odds with those he felt were inferior to him. Barlow's relationship with Len Fairclough was never the most amicable one so when Fairclough once said something to Barlow, it was almost as if a stick of dynamite had gone off. Suffice it to say that fists flew quite freely and insults were exchanged. It was as if the working class was determined to humiliate the middle class. It was the most unsavoury encounter as both Ken and Len tussled and wrestled each other to the floor of the Rovers. It was most unseemly and something that Annie and Jack Walker would never ever tolerate in their pub again.

I feel sure that most of the soap operas I'd suddenly been exposed to did their utmost to highlight all the class distinctions that were already were well entrenched in Sixties society. I think that it was nigh impossible for a humble dustman to rub shoulders with the wealthiest of businessman or lawyer. There was a very distinct coldness and distance between the factory floor and the stuffy, smoky boardroom. And, yet, maybe they could try to converse with each other because they had to. I suppose this became an unavoidable necessity since you could hardly avoid them in the Street. Or maybe not?

And so I move on to yet another Sixties soap opera. In a way, this soap opera seemed to be as far removed from the setting and atmosphere of Coronation Street as it was possible to be. Whereas Coronation Street had given us factories, cobbled streets and smoky chimneys this one gave us something that was altogether different, a soap opera that was situated in a hotel or motel rather than some very homely living room.

Crossroads came rather primly and properly to our attention towards the end of the 1960s. Nervous and unsure of itself at first and quietly making its mark, Crossroads was an everyday story of life in a very ordinary hotel where all the guests seemed to either hover around the reception and never really travelled that far.

Hotels, of course, accommodate people on holiday and yet, as far as I could see, most of the paying guests never really did anything. Most of Crossroads revolved around the kitchen, quiet conversations in the reception area and nothing that could really be described as a coherent story. Or maybe it was just me.

The manager of Crossroads was one Noel Gordon, a dignified and matronly woman who always ran her motel properly and efficiently. In the programme itself, Noel Gordon was Meg Richardson. Now Meg Richardson was the very model of tidiness and organisation, always on the phone, always concerned about the welfare of her staff and determined to keep everything in its right and proper place.

Although extremely popular to those who followed the soap, Crossroads didn't really excite or interest me in perhaps the way it should have. Coronation Street was unpredictable, controversial, questioning and challenging. Crossroads had something about it that always, from my point of view, struggled to emulate.

For instance, Crossroads had those now unforgettable opening credits. How laughably embarrassing and amateurish they must have been. Suddenly you were faced by directors and producers names that seemed to slide into view via a card. Then of course there was the notorious wobbly scenery in the programme itself. I have to admit I didn't really notice anything but maybe it was.

Still, for well over 25 years, tea times in Britain would be Crossroads time, an invitation into a very small Midlands bed and breakfast where the chefs always panicked, the phones always rang and Meg Richardson would hold it all together with admirable calm and restraint.

Meanwhile, back at home, I was still struggling and coming to terms with a life that was somehow lost in the most complex maze, a desolate wasteland, no friends to ring and make plans with on a Saturday night, and nothing to look forward to. It was almost as if I'd resigned myself to the worst case scenario, given up on everything and everybody, trapped by a stifling inferiority complex.

And yet while I sat in my rather reclusive bedroom, there were still things going on around me, a sense that the world had to get on with its life despite me and unaware of what I was doing. I think the rest of the kids of my age had no idea who I was and had no particular desire to find out why I was shy. It seemed a painfully cruel and unforgiving world and yet this was the harsh reality.

I used to look out of the bedroom window emptily and very vacantly. In the distance, I could see Ilford football club's floodlights standing tall and proud. Had I listened very carefully I could hear, very dull and low, the muffled sounds of the crowd. I'd always loved football and yet I could never bring myself to find out more about the club.

Life had now been silenced and subdued for me. It was almost as though somebody had turned the sound down on my life and made hearing almost impossible. I would shuffle listlessly down Ley Street in Ilford, head drooping, buried in thought and self-absorption. It was a life that had well and truly passed me by and would never ever make concessions for this lonely young kid. It was literally a hard world, no holds barred, no allowances made, very little sympathy. The quiet ones understandably had to make their own way in life.

I used to look at the petrol station around the corner from Cranley Road, the cars, lorries and vans gently pulling and then slowly but confidently driving away. I, in all my bewildered innocence, could never really get my ahead around it all. The kids I'd grown up with would soon be thinking about driving lessons and joining the adult world.

And yet here I was completely disinterested, indifferent and apathetic. I'd almost reached the end of my secondary school education and should have been in tune with the way kids of my age were thinking. Quite naturally, they wanted good jobs, a stable career and the ability to drive the fastest of sports cars.

Where was my self-motivation, enthusiasm, youthful exuberance, that vigour and vitality that my friends had in abundance. As soon as they finished school, they were off to the City for jobs in banking and insurance, post offices and estate agents. It was all planned. Perhaps they'd take a couple of months off with some bar work in Spain or simply travelling around Europe.

It was all in such complete contrast to what I had to look forward to. I walked out of Gearies secondary school with no social status, no employment, no academic course at a local college and seemingly no future. And yet here were my friends, fiercely ambitious, proactive, go-ahead with none of the debilitating shyness that simply swallowed me up and stopped me from functioning.

As I hung my head in what I felt was utter shame and distress, I began to

160

look back to those very young days as a child. I began to think of my Sunday evenings, carrying heavy loads of dirty washing to Ilford Laundry, being intrigued by the drinks machine in the corner of Ilford Laundry. For me, hot chocolate always seemed to be the most appealing of all options.

Back in the Seventies, of course, the cars of the time seemed to have strong associations with Ford. There was the Ford Capri, Cortina, Anglia and Fiesta. There was the Vauxhall Viva, Austin Allegro and Ford Granada. Cars had shape, sex appeal, virility and voluptuousness. If you had a car, you were somebody to be reckoned with and admired. You had your own empire, your own independence and your own identity.

And yet for me, cars just seemed to escape me, confuse and confound me. I had no way of telling just how important they must have been because nobody had said otherwise. It took me a number of years to realise that boys of my age had been driving for quite some time and I had just conveniently overlooked the whole experience. This apathy and indifference would leave me completely at a loss. But the reasons were I think understandable so I had no reason to reproach myself. It was time to look forward rather than back because had I continued to dwell on the past, I'd be sucked into a horrible black hole. I had to look to the 1990s for there I would find my lovely idyll.

So when all seemed to be lost and completely beyond repair, I arrived on a balmy evening at the end of July. Up until that point, I'd been muddling through life comforted by the knowledge that although things had moved along at a fairly leisurely pace, by now I'd established a small circle of friends. It was never going to be easy but I still had that re-assuring knowledge that I could ring up one of those friends and perhaps we could have a drink locally or go up to the West End.

What I couldn't have known on that one lovely time at the end of July 1991 was that everything that had gone before would now pale into insignificance. It was an occasion where, quite literally, time seemed to stand still. It was one of those moments in your life where you have to believe that fate does intervene and you simply don't question anything.

It was my friend Hugh's birthday and he'd asked all of his closest friends out to a Chinese restaurant in Ilford. I'm not sure what was going through my mind on that day because it had just felt like any ordinary Saturday evening. It had been quite the most beautifully hot summer's day at the end of July. I can remember sunbathing in my parents' garden and bathing in the glow of it all. My mum used to worship the summer warmth and would think nothing of lying back in her sun lounger, putting up her face to the yellow rays of sunlight and luxuriating in the luxury of it all.

But for some reason, I thought I'd take the opportunity to join her. That's what can only be described as the stunningly magical day I met my future wife. I used to take a book into the garden and if memory serves me correctly it was Don Quixote by Cervantes. It was the last word in gallantry and chivalry. It had been translated into English and was, as I seem to remember, very good and enlighteningly literate.

While I was growing up, the rest of the world was still spinning, revolving, giddily exhilarating, a joyously coloured and kaleidoscopic world. The Sixties, on reflection, was a thoroughly fascinating, eventful and breathlessly energetic decade. It had everything at your disposal. It had happy hippies, outlandish shirts, kipper ties and trousers, women with beehive hairstyles, pirate radio, the Beatles, mop tops, Sunday Night at the London Palladium with Bruce Forsyth, only two TV channels until 1967, Harold Wilson officially declaring the White Heat of Technology, illicit drugs, drug fuelled parties and last but not least Butlins.

During the 1960s, Britain suddenly discovered a rare capacity to enjoy itself, let itself go, took a break, a brief escape from the greyness of the 1950s, the grim reality of the late 1940s and the sheer relentless tedium as seen through the eyes of Tony Hancock on a Sunday afternoon.

Now Britain had Butlins. Throughout the 50s and 60s, Butlins became one of the most popular and fashionable holiday camps in the country. After all those years of depressing hardship and soul- destroying deprivation, a cuddly chap by the name of Billy Butlin revolutionised our recreational habits.

Suddenly, all over the country, people from all corners of the British compass descended on remote but totally accessible holiday retreats. The country had never seen anything like it. Overnight, the whole of our landscape had been changed. Wherever you looked, there were rows and rows of small chalets with their own kitchens, tiny living rooms, a telly and snug bathrooms and toilets.

Butlins then began to sprout up in every conceivable seaside resort you could think of. They were dotted around the country. They were spotted in Blackpool, Skegness, Margate, Camber Sands and the kind of places where only candy floss was consumed and buckets and spades could be easily acquired.

In many ways, Butlins was very much an extension of the holidays we used to get in previous generations. I'd been brought up on a regular diet of Southend and Westcliff on a Sunday but here was something that challenged the status quo and broke utterly with well entrenched traditions.

For my family and I, Butlins didn't really appear on their radar. My family and I instead preferred the equally as pleasurable and salubrious Windsor Hall in Margate. For somebody who'd been brought up with the idyllic charms of Westcliff, Windsor Hall was truly an eye-opener.

The Windsor Hall was a family run hotel in a leafy corner of Kent that was forever contented. It was peaceful, warm and inviting, rather like the bed and breakfast hotels around it, offering its guests everything they could possibly want. They were neat, compact, spacious with plenty of room for a young child to move around in and explore.

I don't know why but when my parents took me to Windsor Hall, it always felt special, a week or two weeks of winding down, relaxation, vitally important leisure time and an opportunity to see the world from a different perspective. Throughout the year, my dad had toiled industriously in his menswear shop and here was the chance to come up for air, to appreciate greener pastures, open up his lungs to what seemed like country air.

When you woke up in the morning at the Windsor Hall, you were confronted with what to me was something I'll never ever forget. Next to your bed was a small tray containing a pot of tea with cups and saucers. But this was no ordinary arrangement. I think it had something to do with the presentation or maybe I was being too observant. It had to be seen to be believed.

Every morning, I can only assume that the chambermaids must have been given specific instructions to do this. On the tray were two cups and saucers and on the saucer, two very cosy looking Tate and Lyle sugars. It was a daily event, customary and regular as clockwork.

A day at a Windsor Hall was more or less yours to do as you wished. I can remember the hill and slope outside the hotel. With bags in our hands, bucket and spade at my disposal, we sauntered down to the beach. I'm not sure how the day progressed but presumably I spent many an hour playing in the sand and filling up the bucket with overflowing supplies of sea water.

Then there was the evening entertainment. Now for somebody whose only previous encounter with music had been a vinyl orange single called Three Blind Mice, this was truly an eye-opener, a wondrous surprise.

In one of the main halls, chairs and tables had been strategically set up. I say strategically because there seemed to a method and order. I think they'd been set up in such a way that once you'd finished your evening meal, you could find an empty table and your evening was guaranteed to be truly enjoyable.

So it was finally that as a family, we would gather around for the Red Coat entertainers with their hilarious slapstick brand of impromptu fun. They would dance on stage in perfectly syncopated rhythm, sing heartily at the tops of their voices, perform intriguing magic tricks and then the rousing finale. Before it was time to go to bed, we would form a huge circle around the edge of the floor and do the Hokey Cokey, not so much a song, more a childhood game that brought the evening to a blissful conclusion. It may have been a conclusion to the day but I can still remember the feelings it left me with.

And then I move forward to the early Seventies. Technology was racing ahead and our attitude to holidays in this country had more or less remained very much the same as they'd always been. It was a week or two weeks by the seaside in Southend, Bournemouth, Brighton, Blackpool or Margate. It was a week or so of kiss me quick hats, long walks along the pier, biting into something called a sweet tasting Rock, struggling desperately with candy floss and just putting your feet up in a deckchair.

Most families from the late 1950s and 60s were just very contented with the simple pleasures of life. Dad, in his familiar trousers and braces, would slump back into his deckchair, tie a knotted handkerchief in his hair and then read his paper. From time to time, he would attend to his offspring's demands, plonking himself very deliberately onto the sand before painstakingly building sandcastles for his lovely children.

I don't know why but I have this wonderful image of dad bending down to help his children, crouching over awkwardly for a minute, but splendidly protective of his children. These were his and the children he'd worked for all year, just to spend quality time with them. Mum, of course, would be very logical and practical, lovingly wiping the sand from her children's eyes and making sure that their swimming trunks were pulled up and the adorable youngsters were happy and completely occupied.

Then, at roughly lunchtime, mum and dad would slowly march over to the edge of the sea, holding their children's hands with enormous affection and then gently jumping over the soft, placid waves. Then they would pack up their belongings, wander into a fish and chip restaurant, mum considerately buying one of those small windmills which always seemed to swirl around in souvenir shops.

Now the Seventies had arrived and our holiday tastes had taken on a distinctly different complexion. Britain had become more ambitious, more expansive, more inquisitive and altogether bolder. For years, the very thought of travelling abroad to another country seemed unthinkable let alone feasible. Most of us thought that Spain, Italy, France, Greece and Turkey were far distant countries that only existed on the Ten o'clock news or a globe at your school.

None of us would ever have believed that one day, you too could fly off to some warm and sunny climate where the sun always shone and the locals would take three hours for lunch. It just seemed inconceivable and how could we ever think that one day it would happen.

So it was that my parents booked 10 days in a newly discovered holiday destination. It was a week in the Spanish sunshine. Quite unexpectedly, Majorca was the packaged holiday of choice for all wildly enthusiastic Brits. After years of so called mundane Margate and allegedly boring Blackpool, here was the lush and tropical Spain.

I'll never forget the weeks leading up to our yearly jaunts to Spain. We would frenetically pack our clothes into several suitcases, squeezing in as many bottles of suntan lotion, shirts, trousers, shorts and sunglasses all tightly packed together. And then the day would arrive or rather I should say evening.

Most of our flights seemed to be at night or in the early evening. A taxi would whisk us off to Luton airport and then we would encounter the airport in all its vastness. To a young 11 year old, an airport was rather like some huge Hollywood studio but without the cameras and film directors.

I can remember being totally enthralled by the whole experience, carrying heavy suitcases onto conveyor belts, the thrill and electric anticipation of it all. People eagerly looking at the notice boards for their flight times, pilots constantly walking across the floor with dutiful air stewards. And then something different. Taxi drivers holding up signs to remind those who may have forgotten that they were the ones who had to be taken home.

It was all utterly crazy, disorganised and haphazard in my eyes. And then after an interminable wait, the call would go out to all the passengers. Would all passengers for flight 68453 to Majorca please proceed to departure gate 15. It was all very puzzling and bemusing and nobody quite knew, least of all me, what we were supposed to be doing. And yet, here we were, my parents and I were about to board a plane for the first time. I think we must have been absolutely beside ourselves.

From what I can remember, the company we were travelling by was called Monarch and the plane itself had Monarch clearly emblazoned across it. Unfortunately, I think Monarch went out of business the following year but still, this was one heck of a plane.

Nervously, we climbed the steps, creeping into the seating area, bending down into our seats and then patiently awaiting that momentous take off moment. But there was something distinctly unsettling and unnerving about it all. I always felt very cramped and claustrophobic while sitting down. There seemed to be little room to move your legs around or stretch out your feet.

In front of your seat, a small table would unfold itself and drop down onto your lap. Then you'd be given those very solemnly expressed directions from the cabin staff. If you were to look under your seat you'd find an oxygen mask, life belt if heaven forbid the plane did something it wasn't supposed to do and what might have seemed to the outsider those rather patronising commands. We had to make sure that, at all times, our safety belts were firmly strapped on in all emergencies.

Then there was the plane food. I have to tell you that plane food was tasteless, revolting and undercooked. It was horribly repugnant, awful and dreadful to the point where most of the passengers would just pretend they were eating it. Those who had paid for the flight must have felt totally robbed and exploited. How could we be expected to eat something that looked dreadfully unappetising?

But for some reason, it was the coffee and tea on the plane itself that left me feeling ever so slightly cold. There never seemed to be any milk or cream so that you often felt you were drinking some beverage that was bitter and abhorrent. Flying though still seemed very luxurious and the last word in comfort.

So there followed two hours of flying above the Iberian clouds, trying unavailingly to nod off to sleep and then waking up feelingly slightly nauseous when I couldn't. The plane seemed to sway elegantly from side to side as if nodding in acknowledgement at the sheer splendour of the journey.

My mum was always very wary and edgy about taking off but was then re-assured when the plane was up in the air. Half way through the journey, the plane would begin to shake and rumble disconcertingly. It was known as turbulence and not what any of us could ever come to terms with.

At long last, the plane would nose its way down inexorably towards Genoa airport. The plane would ease itself onto the runway, softly glide to a halt and then we would disembark. It was all tremendously exciting and all so immensely surprising.

I can particularly remember being excited by the sight of the pinball machine in the reception area. Now the pinball machine was one of those truly unique inventions that I don't think we'll ever see again. It was by some distance, one of the most spellbinding of all sights, an overwhelmingly brilliant game that took my breath away.

Now if memory serves me correctly, the pinball machine was probably a very primitive ancestor to what would now be the Tablet or iPad. This is not to suggest that the pinball bore an uncanny resemblance to them for in complete contrast to the Tablet and iPad, the pinball machine was a huge machine with springs, coils, electrical components, flashing lights, a cacophony of noises and sounds and a number of silver balls.

The pinball machine was a glorious commotion, the ball pinging, whizzing, rolling, shaking, rattling and rolling around some indescribable maze. I struggle to give the pinball machine any kind of description because perhaps it defied description.

Anyway, the fact is that it simply transfixed me in a way that no other toy or game I'd ever seen. I'll always remember that electronic score-board which would invariably award you hundreds and thousands of points if you managed to keep the silver ball in play. It was just the most terrific fun you could ever have on any holiday and gripped my attention as soon as we arrived at our Spanish hotel resort.

I feel sure that there were people who could quite happily have spent their whole holiday on the pinball machine. In those days, the Spanish peseta was the predominant currency so if you wanted to extend your stay on the machine, you had to put in the appropriate amount of money. Needless to say, I always seemed to have more money than perhaps I should have.

Then there were people who, because the machine had got stuck or refused to obey commands, would bash the side mercilessly when the wretched thing wouldn't work. Suddenly, a sign flashed up telling the poor, unsuspecting individual that it was out of order. Quite the funniest sight or so I felt.

In the very early days of packaged holidays, nobody really knew what the expected protocol was in these giant cathedrals of fun. I don't know what other families did during the day but I think there was a genuine sense of blissful innocence about the British abroad.

We all know and knew about the Spanish stereotypes: endless jugs of sangria by the pool, floppy sombrero hats that dangled almost deliriously over our eyes, utterly fearless matadors and toreadors at breath-taking bullfights. And who could ever forget the food, piping hot paellas and yet more sangria to wash it all down.

And yet none of our Spanish friends could quite get their heads around the British culture and mentality. The Spanish, although never averse to a pint of beer or two, were never really interested in excessive booze. They took their time, relaxed in the 90 degree sunshine and then decided to take a break but no ordinary break.

This was the siesta, that three hour lunch period where nobody did anything and everybody indulged in leisure time. All of the shops shut for part of the afternoon and then opened again sometime after 3pm, only to find that most of the Brits had by now dropped off to sleep.

The thing is that none of us, least of all my parents, knew exactly what to do, so we simply went with the flow. I can remember wanting to spend as much time in the pool as I could and being quite content to lay out on a sunbed as and when I'd had enough time splashing about ecstatically in the pool. I think this was a real period of discovery for British holidaymakers, quite literally testing the temperature of the pool so for me this was truly thrilling.

During one visit to the Costa Blanca, I can remember my wonderful dad taking one of those old fashioned tape recorders to the poolside and suddenly being serenaded by the most beautiful sound.

I've no idea why it sticks out in the memory but it was a fabulous moment and one I'll never ever forget. Suddenly, Herb Alpert and his Tiawana band started blaring out across the Iberian peninsula. It was the coolest and most delightful music I'd ever heard. It almost certainly reminded me of some Caribbean island, swaying on a hammock and revelling in that sweet tropical trumpet. It was the most delicious of all feelings.

But I think that there was an overall sense that as brand new British holidaymakers, they were somehow pioneers and possibly ambassadors for our country. We weren't intruders or impostors, just curious observers and reluctant learners. Nobody really knew how to conduct themselves, least of all understand the language.

There was definitely an awkwardness and disorientation about those first years of the Seventies. For instance, the Brits had no idea what to say when it came to meal times. Of course, we were strangers and foreigners but communication became, at times, the most embarrassing of stumbling blocks.

Breakfast, of course, was more or less straightforward. On a huge table, there was the usual breakfast fare of bread rolls, butter, cheese and whatever else took your fancy. But when it came to ordering toast and asking for cereal, it was rather like finding yourself on a desert island. There was a pained silence followed by complete confusion. There followed the wild counting of fingers at waiters and jolly gestures and frustrated attempts at speaking Spanish. All totally ridiculous and completely pointless.

Still, once we'd finished our day of incessant sunbathing by the pool, both my parents and I retreated to our bedrooms. Now what you have to remember is that in Britain, none of us had adequately prepared for any emergency. But quite unexpectedly, I'd found myself in the most unaccustomed pain.

Constant exposure to the hot Spanish sunshine had, quite clearly, burnt most of my stomach, both of my legs, much of my back and, just to make things worse, part of my neck. For the next couple of days or so I walked around in the most unbearable and excruciating pain.

Large red raw burn marks appeared almost immediately. My mum, the compassionate nurse, promptly took out a bottle of Calamine lotion and smeared the cream around the affected parts of the body. I have to tell you it was the most horrendous of experiences and one that I've no intention of repeating again at any point in the future. But this was how we approached holidays abroad.

I think my parents also booked a number of day trips while on our Spanish jaunts. Now days out on the Costa Blanca were as much as revelation to me as they were to my parents. But when I think back, it seems to me that all of us were learning together.

So here's the story. Every time we went on one of these jolly days out, most of the guests were always provided with the same lunch. As we were about to board a coach to say Barcelona, we were all issued with two rather sad looking sandwiches, an egg and an orange.

Now for reasons that were completely beyond me, this lunchtime treat was too small and meagre for words. If you were starving, it might have been considered an insult. Still, I don't suppose any of us minded because this was all very new and in no way reflected the Spanish catering industry.

On the subject of Barcelona, my mind loops back gleefully to one incident that leaves the warmest of glows. It was stupendously hilarious, totally unexpected and just hysterically funny, one of those golden memories that refuses to fade with the passage of time.

Both of my parents decided to do some shopping in a rather impressive and spacious department store in Barcelona. While mooching and browsing, it suddenly happened. There was a massive power cut and the whole shop was plunged into an all-enveloping darkness.

My dad and I had just gone to the toilet and, before you could whistle Y Viva Espana, the lights went out and my dad and I were caught in a rather compromising situation. When the lights go out in a major department store and you find yourself in the loo, there isn't a great deal that can be said although amusement certainly helps to cushion the blow.

The food served up at dinner times was certainly presentable and edible but when it came to dessert, there seemed to be something missing. Maybe it was me but the Spanish waiters and chefs seemed to run out of ideas. Invariably, the dessert consisted of a brownish, rather watery cream caramel or any fruit of your choice. This was a nightly event so it wasn't entirely a surprise. Still, this was my first encounter with Spain, paella, sangria, matadors, baby bull fights and power cuts in Barcelona department stores. Simply magical.

And then there were the other holiday havens, countries we only knew something about through the BBC's holiday programme with Cliff Michelmore and ITV's Judith Chalmers and Chris Kelly. Spain had been our first conquest and the world it seemed would become our oyster.

In both TV holiday programmes, it was almost as if new international frontiers had been opened up and new lands had been discovered. Up until that point, holidaymakers in Britain had only known Pontins, Butlins, and dinner time at 5 in the afternoon. But now, TV had given us detailed analysis on the joys of Majorca, Benidorm, Malaga and Minorca. It was time to kick off our shoes, run into the sun-dappled sea and revel in the Mediterranean.

No longer would our days consist of everything Britain could offer in the way of holiday entertainment. Gone would be the lengthy hours spent idling the hours away with nothing to do, gazing out of the bedroom window forlornly until somebody told us to do the Hokey Cokey in the evening. It was all very predictable and, so it must have seemed at the time, all very tedious. But in a strange kind of a way, Butlins and Pontins were great because none of the kids had seen anything like it before.

Anyway, after a couple of visits to the Costa Blanca and Brava, it was time for my parents to move further afield. Spain had given us something that was inherently exotic and glamorous. It had given us sangria tasting sessions, furry donkeys that would peep sheepishly out of shopping bags, loads of paella and as much cheese as you could eat for breakfast.

Which brings me briefly onto the subject of how the Brits abroad first announced themselves to the rest of the world. You see the point is that because the Brits found it almost impossible to adjust their eating habits when in Spain, it was equally as hard to adapt to their culture.

How could I ever forget the Brits abroad at meal times. It was undoubtedly the most amusing of spectacles. Suddenly, breakfast time would be accompanied by big boxes of Kellogg's Corn Flakes, jars of jam and marmalade from Key Markets and any other produce from a British supermarket shelf.

I always felt that this was ever so slightly territorial behaviour because if the Germans, Italians or French did this at breakfast, they would be mercilessly mocked. But here was Britain, that tiny island, that model of spirited defiance during the War, quite boldly putting its foot down and determined to be British.

Admittedly, we'd all become acutely aware that the Germans had also indulged in a spot of nationalism, one upmanship. For quite a number of years, the Germans had become the subject of much jokey derision. Nobody quite knew why but the Germans suddenly assumed airs and graces, felt superior to the rest of the world and, like Britain, had to make sure that they too could do whatever they liked.

The Germans, with what the rest of the world might have regarded as a presumptuous arrogance, announced themselves shortly before breakfast. While the rest of Spain was tucking into its cheese rolls and Corn Flakes, the Germans, with no regard for the rest of the hotel guests, would do something that both shocked and then just infuriated everybody.

They would wander quite casually to the poolside, grabbing the nearest available set of sun loungers and beds with quite the most stupendous audacity. Here towels would be lovingly laid out on the sun lounger and without a single thought or consideration for the others, the Germans were no longer in control.

Where ever you looked, there were small groups of German families claiming their right to be recognised sunbathers. None of us stood a chance. It was almost as if an invading, marauding army had parked its tanks on large tracts of a war torn land.

Next to the towels were dozens of bottles of sun factor 45 suntan cream, combs to brush wet hair and all of the paraphernalia you would normally associate with sunbathing. There were German newspapers, German paperbacks, German drinks and a sense of German domination. But maybe this is just a personal exaggeration.

Anyway, the fact is that the holidays abroad had now become a worldwide and yearly habit. We could just nip into any travel agency, leaf through the brochures and then just book 10 days in some exotic paradise that had palm trees along the sea front and souvenir shops that sold only fans and flamenco dancers. You simply didn't get that in Brighton or Blackpool.

I think it must have been our third holiday venue and here was another country, currency and another temperament. It was another European country and in many ways a neighbouring tourist retreat. It had the same glamour, the same history, the same allure and much the same attitude to many holidaymakers.

Italy had obviously rich historical connections and a national character that could never be questioned. Italy brought to mind the Roman Empire, the Coliseum, ancient ruins, Florence and Venice. Everything in Italy had the same kind of romantic feel as Spain but if you delved beneath the surface, you were almost privy to much more than met your eye.

I don't think Spain or Italy ever felt they were in direct competition with each other because both were targeting the same tourists and the same demographics. Italy, I think, represented a very real alternative. In many ways, none of us could have known how big and dramatic the impact Spain and Italy would have on the British holidaymaker.

I think it must have been roughly in 1975 that my mum decided to book 10 days in Italy. It was a place called Cattolica, an Italian seaside resort not a million miles away from Rimini. Now this was a country that, to all outward appearances, conducted itself in much the same manner as Spain. But there was something different about Cattolica.

Italy had the lira as its financial currency and nobody could quite have prepared us for the culture shock that was about to befall Italy. Wherever you looked, everything in Italy seemed to be, or certainly sounded, ridiculously expensive. In fact it was expensive on the most extortionate scale.

When my parents and I dropped into a café for a cappuccino, coffee or latte, it was roughly a thousand lira. This was just daylight robbery and beyond belief. It was the most astonishing currency any of us had ever seen. But there was something very agreeable and pleasant about Italy and none of us had any real cause for complaint.

One memory of Cattolica though simply stands out for me. My mum booked a day trip to the gorgeous city of Venice. Venice, of course is one of the most unique of all world cities. Venice, sadly but heartbreakingly, is sinking, slowly, it has to be said, but quite definitely. I think the whole city has just resigned itself to the fact that there can be no turning back. You're disappearing under the water Venice so it's time to get used to the idea. As long as the people are safe then it shouldn't matter.

Anyway, the fact is that Venice was our destination and it was time for a history lesson. First of all we hit the churches, then it was time to admire the stunning architecture, take in the sheer beauty and history of the city and then stroll down the narrow, cobbled back streets. Venice was a geographical gem just waiting for my parents and I.

But if you went to Venice, you had to see the touristy sights and try to take in as much of the city's essence as you could. At that point in my life, I had nothing to compare it with because I had to yet to visit any other part of the world apart from Spain. Still, it was time to venture forwards and uncover the intriguing secrets that Italy may have been hiding.

Once in Venice, we decided to head for St Marks Square, a breath-taking piazza that reminded me of Trafalgar Square in London. St Marks Square was this enormously large open space where the people of the world could stroll at their leisure and admire every sight, sound, murmur and sigh that Venice could muster. You couldn't actually hear what the tourists were saying but I think you could catch the gist of it. The expressions on their faces told of wonderment and awe. How on earth could anything look so geometrically perfect and flawless?

I can still see myself gazing up at the surrounding cathedrals, the shops selling hundreds of ice creams, the souvenir shops doing the briskest of business and the pigeons frantically marching around the square, swarming around pieces of bread on the ground, before flying off to another destination. I can remember eating one of Venice's superbly made ice creams and being totally dumbfounded by the magnificence of it all.

Then my parents took the opportunity to do something they'd always wanted to do in Venice. For years, the long, meandering canals had been Venice's jewel in the crown, a mighty stretch of water encompassing sturdy bridges and the prettiest scenery I'd ever seen. For as far as I could see, there were tiny riverside structures which seemed to bob up and down in time to the musical rhythms of the canal.

So it was that my parents and I delighted on this day of all days. Sitting on our gondola, we cruised almost serenely along the whispering canal, smiling appreciatively at the gondolier and then finding that nothing could match the sheer majesty of everything around us all.

But the best or worst was about to happen. On our way back to the coach, we suddenly noticed that the skies were darkening and the clouds were glowering. It looked as if, at any minute, the heavens would open and the rain would fall in uncontrollable torrents.

Suddenly and quite alarmingly, a sharp flash of lightning lit up the sky followed by the inevitable rumble of thunder. Before we knew it, it rained so heavily and prodigiously that by the time we'd got back to the coach, we were soaked. It was day of light and shade, triumph and drama, all the many contrasts that make life so special.

I haven't been back to Italy since those first tentative steps to the Neapolitan peninsula so it's hard to gauge what exactly the rest of the world was like. Both Italy and Spain were the alternate choices of my parents so I'd no idea what the rest of Europe was like.

So here's an imaginary list of emotions and characteristics of what Europe and the rest of the universe must have looked like. I can only give you surface details but I think this is a more or less accurate portrayal.

France, a country I would first visit with my wife, was, allegedly, snobbish, truly arrogant, dismissive of England, above England, superior to England, utterly contemptuous of Blighty, sticking its nose in the air, fiercely resentful of everything about the English. France fervently believed they produced the best wine, cheese, footballers, rugby union players, singers and baguettes. The French excelled at everything: cooking, eating the best food and producing the greatest of painters and artists.

Magnifique. But we loved France and I love France and so what if they're our cross Channel neighbours.

Then there was Germany. Germany, from a personal viewpoint, arouses strong feelings and passions. Germany, as the history books will always remind us, were the perpetrators of some of the most unforgivable crimes against humanity but that of course was history. During the Second World War, a mad dictator by the name of Adolf Hitler destroyed both physically and mentally the very heart and soul of the world. But with the passing of the generations and decades, the pain has lessened. Germany is forward thinking, purposeful, driven, determined to be accepted for who they are. Germany has a rightful reputation for its thoroughness and efficiency. The Germans are hard-working, meticulous, clean living, punctual and precise. Everything Britain possibly envied. The Germans produced some of the best cars, the finest of hi fi stereos and quite the most orderly and methodical football team. I don't think the Germans ever missed a trick and left anything to chance. They didn't have a sense of humour, or so it was alleged, but they quite certainly had their finger on the pulse.

Russia always seemed to be permanently miserable, depressed, downcast, lugubrious, somehow disheartened by everything and everybody around them. Russia, I felt, never smiled, laughed, joked or, it has to be said, showed any emotion. In Russia, all of the major politicians and civil servants never seemed at ease with themselves, constantly sneering and never completely satisfied with their lot. It snowed a lot during the winter which, quite perversely, decorated the Kremlin. Russia was and still is powerful, enormously well respected, very military, armies always in fine uniform and fettle, straight backed, never sloppy or slovenly. Russia drank their tea from samovars, travelled in wonderful carriages known as troikas and appreciated the Bolshoi ballet. There is a priceless air of formality and nobility about Russia and perhaps always will be. When you go down to their train stations, it is an experience that quite literally takes the breath away. Down in the waiting areas, huge chandeliers hang from the ceiling rather like some high society ballroom. But it seems Russia just isn't interested in happiness or anything that remotely resembles a celebration. Sad perhaps but just a passing observation. I could be wrong but this is how I see the Russians.

Now for just brief mentions of my aforesaid holiday retreats. Spain opened up my eyes to everything I'd always believed in. Spain was daring, full of life, suave, swashbuckling, healthy, hospitable, embracing everything cultural and artistic. Spain was passionate, full of sparkle and wit, swishing flamenco dancers, clattering castanets, bullfighters full of cunning, guile and bravado, At times it almost felt as if they were too bloodthirsty and barbaric but when you thought about it, perhaps this was way the Spaniards conducted themselves.

Italy was, or so the travel books might have had us believe, hot blooded, excitable and apparently temperamental. Italy had that Latin mindset, always on the defensive and decidedly edgy. And yet there was a side to the Italian character that was far more endearing and utterly praiseworthy. The Italians knew and still know how to have a good time, how to throw themselves into rejoicing without any fear of embarrassing themselves. Italy is completely open and not at all self-conscious. The Italians put their cards on the table and let you know exactly what they think of you. Of course, the Italians have a darker side and the Mafia is living proof of that fact. But I'd liken Italy as the land of opera, the land of the sonorous song, pasta, spaghetti, gathering outside restaurants with their families and drinking endless bottles of wine. It is a very closely knit and intimate country that only becomes really demonstrative when the national football team win World Cups. It truly is a country that lives on its emotions and lives for the day. As we all should.

And so we come to the country with whom, as a proud Jew, I've always felt and always will feel an enduring affection for. It is the country that I had to visit, had to embrace, savour and revel in. For as long as I could remember, it was the oppressed, persecuted and downtrodden, the country that could never do anything right, the accused country, the country that was always held to account, trampled over, treated abominably, used and exploited, taken for granted and never given the respect it deserved.

I refer to Israel, the finest of them all, that lovely, peace-loving and joyous country with all of the most honourable intentions and the most admirable force for good. While the rest of the Middle East exploded and imploded, Israel kept to itself and never ever bothered anybody. Israel was rational, understanding and conciliatory, always prepared to listen to the other side rather than being swallowed up by those who were deliberately argumentative and hostile.

Israel was the country of David Ben Gurion and Golda Meir, the State of Israel, steeped in proud history, Jerusalem, Tel Aviv, Haifa, Jaffa, a country of beautiful contrasts and fascinating tales to tell.

But wherever I've been in the world, the messages and themes are more or less the same, that maybe, just maybe, we should all try to get on with each other, that grudges and resentments are completely counter-productive, that nothing can be achieved by hatred and hostility and that whatever may be bugging us can easily be solved by reasoned discussion and constructive negotiation.

We are a nation surrounded by hundreds of other nations, surrounded by continents, oceans, rivers, valleys, seas and fields. But we are bound nonetheless by a solidarity that can only be found in neighbourhoods who stick together. If France falls out with Germany or Italy and Spain have a festering difference of opinion, then how are we to survive, how are we to understand what makes us tick. How can we, in short, communicate with each other when the language barrier seems to be the only barrier?

With the recent arrival of dynamic modern technology, it seems to me that we've never had a better opportunity to discover new angles, to strengthen bonds, establish new links, help each other charitably in times of want and crisis. It almost seems to me that there is within society an almost unreasonable suspicion about anything and everything.

On our holiday jaunts to Spain and Italy, I can remember my mum writing postcards to friends and family back home in England. She would, almost customarily, sit down by the pool, spread out the said postcards on a table and proceed to write down goodwill wishes. It was that familiar mantra of 'Wish You Were Here', the weather was beautiful and the food in the hotel was a combination of the sublime and the ridiculous-sometimes very good but disturbingly shocking at others.

Wind forward to the present day and I find myself where everything seems easier, simpler, more manageable, less hassle, not quite as complicated, laborious and demanding as it used to be.

In the old days, we used to tear a page out of an old A4 exercise book, find a pen or pencil and then write our letters to whomsoever. I suppose what I'm trying to say is that the whole rigmarole of writing something down on a piece of paper seems perhaps antiquated and no longer applicable. Now we write e-mails, text each other on our phones, receive information on the Internet. In a sense there is a great sense of immediacy, easy availability and instant access.

I can remember finding what used to be known as a pen friend on a holiday in Spain. Now this pen friend Terry came from Manchester and I came from London so we had to write to each other by paper and pen. The only trouble I found was that if you made any mistakes, you had to cross it out. Subsequently you were left with a letter that had been completely defaced by words that were crossed out or smudges on the paper.

My wonderful dad kept a diary in his wardrobe for every year until the late 1970s and would meticulously note short messages on important days. Nowadays, we have blogs, social network outlets, message boards and texting. It all seems a long way away from the days of pen, pencil and paper. But on reflection, I suppose this is all a part of the evolution of society. What might have been considered very primitive then is now an everyday part of our lives.

For instance, when I was a kid, I used to go to Gants Hill library for books. Now libraries have to be the most romantic and evocative places you could possibly imagine. It's quiet, civilised, perfectly calm and untroubled. There is an inner sense of order and peace that pervades most of the library. There are no interruptions, no disturbances and you can choose to either read or silently wander around at your leisure.

I took to reading regularly at a much later age than perhaps I should have done but eventually I came to the realisation that in order to improve myself academically, I had to be in command of the facts, figures and details of everyday life. In a way, that reluctance to embrace the English language may just have worked in my favour but I don't suppose I'll ever know.

Libraries were rather like churches or any religious building in that everybody had to acknowledge each other's right to privacy. They were almost like places of academic worship where every so often you would hear the gentle rustling of pages being turned and just occasionally the whispering voice of a librarian. It was all very silent and all very sacred. In many ways, it had something of the air of a monastery or nunnery.

But technology has meant that even libraries have to move with the times. When I was a kid, there was a ticketing system which rubber stamped the book you were looking for. As you reached the exit to the library, you were suddenly faced by whole boxes of files containing names of addresses and the names of the books you were taking out.

On reflection, that whole system now seems rather primitive because now all we have to do is show a plastic card which swipes our book by way of confirmation. The very concept of the old filing system does now seem to belong to another age, although you can still see filing cabinets in some offices.

But as I get older, I find myself increasingly distanced from the things I used to take for granted. I can still go to the supermarket or the local shop without feeling that I've missed out on anything. Now, of course, they've introduced self-service, where the cashier on the till has suddenly become redundant, the sense of excitement and frisson has now gone and everything has become computerised, mechanical and impersonal.

I'll always remember the first Sainsbury's in Gants Hill. It was situated just outside the Tube station and when I look back, it was just so incredibly small. The original Sainsbury's and Tesco were light years away from the way they look now. There was something delightfully quaint and innocent about supermarkets in those days.

The Sainsbury's in Gants Hill was no larger than the original corner shop. The whole shop was divided into two small aisles of food with tins of food stacked neatly in the middle of the shop. There was a cheese and meat counter with cutters that measured them into the precise amount you wanted. Then there were the scales which performed roughly the same function, the genial shop assistants in their white aprons or coats, the sense of community, wives and girlfriends with their shopping bags, everything in its right and proper place. Nobody had to ask where things were in the shop because it was directly in front of you, clearly visible and begging to be bought.

Then there were cash registers at the exit to Sainsbury's, huge, metallic machines with large keys clanking down the price of the product you were buying. I think we must have thought that this was the way it would always be, that nothing would change and everything would be just the way it should be.

But then the corner shop Sainsbury's became the giant supermarket corporate brand, a vast and extremely sociable social club where people congregate, chat, engage with each other, gossip and giggle without a care in the world. Sainsbury's now has become much more than that loyal and reliable friend who always made you feel good.

Sainsbury's is now an industry, a worldwide marketing concept, owned by shareholders no doubt. Sainsbury's, for all I know, is on the Stock Market, an elaborate promotional video and, above all, on Facebook and Twitter. Now even those who hadn't heard of it now knew that Sainsbury's was a force to be reckoned with rather than that the shy child at the back of the classroom.

But it's the sheer size and the spaciousness of the modern supermarket. The Sainsbury's, Key Markets and Tesco's that I had grown up with, were cramped and claustrophobic so to find myself in some huge factory of food with acres of room to walk around in, came as the biggest culture shock I'd ever known.

Part 16:
Now to return to some of those cultural figures I'd grown up with.

During the Seventies, TV programmes on art, history and the sciences always seemed to be stuffy, wooden and stilted. This is not to say I didn't benefit at all from these very instructive and well informed productions but somehow, I couldn't really understand the finer points of their very learned comments.

For instance, towards the end of the 1960s, the BBC, in keeping with its edict to inform, enlighten and educate, reminded us of the space missions to the Moon and other far off planets. They were programmes which made us aware that there was indeed life on other galaxies or constellations, that we had the capacity to land an astronaut on the Moon.

The Apollo missions were quite the most astonishing pieces of TV I'd ever seen. Here, before my very eyes, was a remarkable picture of life on the Moon. Buzz Aldrin and Neil Armstrong had been designated to take up one of the most envied of all jobs. It was quite the most exceptional of all assignments.

For years and years, there had been rumour and speculation on the possibility of man flying up to the Moon via a rocket. Some of the more hardened sceptics poured cold on the water on the project but one July day in 1969, Neil Armstrong, a skilled and very talented astronaut, carefully trod on the surface of the Moon and then seemed to bounce around craters in sheer and unashamed delight. For those on Earth it must have seemed surreal but here was a man floating around on another planet and all we could see were these rather blurred, grainy and black and white images of a man swinging a golf club in outer space. It just looked like some very old and crackly Hollywood movie but reality intruded and some of us were totally breathless. It didn't seem possible but I suppose you had to believe that it was.

The likes of Patrick Moore, brilliantly observant and a man of a wonderfully scientific mind, were absolutely captivating and endlessly intriguing. Some of those Apollo missions were something to behold. They revealed and informed, analysed and dissected on all matters relating to outer space. But I think it was their shrewdness and encyclopaedic knowledge that blew the watching masses away. Here was one event in the history of our times that would make us all look at life in a completely different light. It would change our perceptions and colour our thinking.

And then as we moved into the Seventies, there were other cultural figures who would stand out from the rest of the crowd.

At the beginning of the Seventies, I became aware of the TV arts programmes, quirky documentaries, eccentric figures on the fringes of our consciousness. People we could never really take seriously but who were nonetheless there drifting in and out, floating around in the ether and then claiming our attention.

Aquarius was one of the first arts programmes which highlighted all of everything was extremely clever, amusing and, in a way, entirely unexpected. Introduced by Humphrey Barclay, he gave us a very revealing and honest insight into the world of art.

Barclay comfortably guided us through all of the latest art movements such as Expressionism, Impressionism, Pointillism and Cubism, subjects that had never really been extensively covered on the TV. But Barclay brought all of these movements to vivid life because he felt that the watching public had every right to know about oil and water colours, landscapes and portraits, objects and curiosities.

Aquarius also gave us ground breaking insight into the world of sculpture and sculptors, pottery and potters, the life stories of Cezanne, Degas, Monet, Constable, Turner, David Hockney and Salvador Dahli, he of the beautifully crafted moustache, and Henry Moore, the brilliant sculptor who enchanted and entranced with his completeness and flawlessness, some would have said a technical genius.

Aquarius was almost seamlessly followed by The South Bank Show, another arts programme which simply followed where Aquarius had already been. But the South Bank Show seemed to have rather more depth, detail and even more objectivity.

In a way, it tried to get the heart of matter but would always stand back and admire the scenery. What I'm trying to say is that the South Bank Show was both serious and earnest but it seemed to cultivate a very original documentary style. Like Aquarius, it was neither judgmental nor outspoken, but could be piercing, probing and investigative if it wanted to.

I seem to remember that the South Bank show was highly intelligent and marvellously informative without ever turning its nose up at its viewers. There were programmes about the leading playwrights, plays, West End shows, musicals, theatrical impresarios, film stars with a movie to publicise or just chummy, clubby figures with a joke or a laugh.

The South Bank introduced us to the likes of Harold Pinter, Trevor Nunn and Andrew Lloyd Webber, who would write some of the most famous musicals ever written. I think Lloyd Webber was a lyrical whirlwind and naturally talented wordsmith. Lloyd Webber produced, directed and created a musical in a way that a potter moulds his clay. Every word had its own meaning, sound, point, accent and cadence. For some people, though, Lloyd Webber is almost too good to be true, in some ways full of his own self-importance and maybe detached from the outside world.

Then the South Bank would tell us all about the pop stars of the day, reflecting quite analytically on their private lives, their mannerisms and their motivations. During the Seventies, singers such as Phil Collins, Rick Wakeman, Elton John and Paul McCartney all had their agenda and may well have been obvious subjects for the South Bank Show. They were men with inquiring and receptive minds, with lives that never quite conformed to the way we led ours. Elton John had the outrageous glasses and piano, Wakeman had that dominant keyboard. The South Bank Show tried to get under the skin of those who may have been reluctant to shed theirs.

I have to admit I was never a keen follower of the arts but programmes like Aquarius and the South Bank Show furnished me with an intimate knowledge of what all the latest art galleries and museums were doing. There were features on photographers, photographic exhibitions, features on West End musicals, earnest plays, Shakespearean productions and a full review of all the latest developments in literature.

In many ways, perhaps literature had probably enjoyed its most satisfying period during the 19th and 20th century but that didn't stop Melvyn Bragg from telling you about the latest offerings by Doris Lessing, Stephen King or Tom Clancy. All three had made a significant contribution to the world of literature and who was I to deny them their moment in the sun?

And yet for me, TV still ruled the roost, still produced some of some of the most thought provoking of entertainment. There were programmes such as World in Action, Panorama, Weekend World, Nationwide, Today and the News programmes on both ITV and BBC.

The News programmes at Six, Nine or Ten o'clock in the evening were outstandingly produced and impeccably presented. They also had newsreaders who had established themselves as instantly identifiable figures. They were like comfortable carpets and fireplaces in our living room. People who had all the facts and figures at their disposal, people who knew exactly what was going on in the world and introduced us to places that some of us had never heard of.

The BBC had a whole gallery of newsreaders, gentlemen of the highest distinction and authority, men who dressed for the role they were allotted. Back in the 1950s, men like Michael Aspel and Richard Baker sat at their news desks in the most elegant dinner jacket and bow tie. Most of us, including myself, were both quite taken aback by their remarkable formality of it all. I could never understand why this had to be the case because they hadn't been invited to a Royal Garden party or some very high society dinner party. Still, every day, both Aspel and Baker would obey the very strict BBC dress code, shuffling their papers together on the desk and speak into that very grandiose BBC microphone.

For years, newsreaders of the highest calibre would decorate the hallowed halls of Broadcasting House. They were sharp, highly intelligent broadcasting journalists with a hunger for news stories and a very perceptive eye for breaking stories. They were brave and heroic, inquiring and investigative, cool and detached. They asked all the most penetrating of questions, scraped the skin off a potential scandal and exposed all of the world's gravest injustices. They were completely without prejudice and never biased or so they believed.

Richard Baker and Kenneth Kendall were the first newsreaders who really held my attention. For years, they were my first reference points when the news of the day had to be relayed. At 9.00, they would both quickly shuffle their sheaf of papers, tap them ever so slightly and then tell us about Idi Amin and Uganda, Ian Smith and Rhodesia, the eternal and tribal slanging match between the Tories under Edward Heath and Harold Wilson of the Labour party and his reassuring pipe.

For me though, Richard Baker was the governor, the man who was somehow destined to read the news. I always suspected that he'd followed all of the journalistic rules: accuracy, impartiality and the loveliest of voices and diction. Baker was just in complete command: controlled, measured, utterly disciplined and not a word was mispronounced. Baker was the voice of the Establishment, a man who could convey a news story in a crisp, concise and direct fashion without misleading you. His was a world of honesty, truth and absolute integrity.

I'm convinced that Baker must have gone to some finishing school rather than the school of journalism. I think that he learnt all about posture and body language, how to behave with utter civility and decorum rather than something that was hurried and rushed. Every word, sentence and pregnant pause had to be delivered in such a way that if something was missed out and bungled, he would be the man to put it right. He was a perfectionist, a fanatical perfectionist, somebody who believed that the news was vitally and critically important , utterly sacred and set in stone, on time and never wrong.

Rather like his colleague Richard Baker, it was Kenneth Kendall who also left an enduring impression on me. Kendall was self-assured, self-contained, never ruffled or agitated, always knowing when to speak and when not to. I think there was some in built mechanism which told both Baker and Kendall exactly how to use words. Kendall, though was always admirably composed, flexible when the occasion demanded it and never outwardly emotional. At a royal wedding or funeral, Kendall would be all solemnity and gravitas, somebody you could believe in sincerely.

On the other side, ITV had their own news-reading double act. ITV had sent in their own battalions while the BBC continued in their own prim, proper and puritanical way. It was all very rigid, structured and regimented. Since its earliest days, I think the BBC had begun to think they were somehow in a class of their own, untouchable and invincible. I think they believed that theirs was the official voice, the party line, that eminently trustworthy organisation that had very high standards and qualities that shone through the surrounding scepticism.

Then there was the ITV news, which provided much the same service as the Beeb, but always preceded its news bulletin with the bells of Big Ben, seriousness and the most well-mannered of presentation.

During the 1970s, ITV had their very own artillery: Alistair Burnet and Reginald Bosqanquet. Now the BBC had suddenly found that their supremacy was about to be challenged. They would now find themselves in direct opposition, a television rivalry, an almost tribal rivalry that endured for many a decade.

Now I think it's common knowledge that Reginald Bosanquet was allegedly partial to a drop of alcohol and it was widely assumed that he was never averse to a bottle of lager or several. Bosanquet did, perhaps by his own admission, like his alcohol and many was the occasion that it looked as if some of his news was somewhat amusingly influenced by the hard stuff.

Bosanquet had that red faced, ruddy complexion that owed itself, perhaps unkindly to alcoholic indulgence rather than non-alcoholic tea or coffee. This is not to suggest that Bosanquet was ever outrageously drunk but I think he did enjoy life to the full. His presentational style was never affected by the amount of drink in his bloodstream. But you always felt that he'd somehow spent the best part of the afternoon in the Garrick gentleman's club, happily imbibing several glasses of brandy and smoking boxes of Havanas in that dandyish Raffles way.

Then there was Alistair Burnet, a very precise and punctilious newsreader who always presented the news as if it were a university lecture rather than a news bulletin. Burnet had that rich, velvety voice that drifted languidly across the airwaves rather like some very gentle breeze. Burnet had a marvellous authority, an exquisite correctness and reminded you of the smartest City banker.

What was never really known was that Burnet also gravitated to the pub after a strenuous day in the newsroom. I don't think he was ever a compulsive boozer but if, only to be sociable, would never turn down a drink if offered. He was, though, the most complete and consummate of professionals, always with the safest pair of hands at the ship's tiller. Even if that ship did look ever so steady at times.

There was Sandy Gall, formerly a war and foreign correspondent who braved war torn zones with a courage that perhaps he must have thought was beyond him. Now Sandy Gall was one of those newsreaders who just looked as if nothing would ever disturb his composure or create havoc with his dignity. The voice was quintessentially English, the Queen's English with every word, vowel and consonant superbly and clearly delivered.

Last but not least there was the incomparable Trevor McDonald, undoubtedly one of the finest of all newsreaders. To this day, he continues to convey the news to the watching public with a humour, style and assurance that comes almost naturally. His final story called 'And Finally' is the perfect counterpoint to everything that had come before his bulletin. While the rest of the universe may have been blowing each other to pieces, 'And Finally' is quite the quirkiest and funniest of all news story features. Suddenly, a hilarious story about animals or some offbeat observation about something ridiculous is the perfect last chapter to a day of hard, pragmatic news. It is the soothing antidote to a day of hard hitting politics, war and disaster. Trevor McDonald is that kindly gentlemen with a wonderful sense of impartiality and detachment. I always felt that the official voice of the country was talking.

Part 17:
And now for a brief summary of ITV's coverage of its adverts.

I'd now become aware of cinema's good natured relationship to the world of commerce and advertisements. It was all Pearl and Dean, local businesses advertising their wares and more adverts about shaving cream, after shave lotion, razor blades, shirts, trousers and cinema's love affair with popcorn, Coke and hot dogs. Now television had joined in with the fun, jumping onto the bandwagon with almost gleeful relish.

Throughout my childhood, ITV's adverts veered almost constantly between the sublime and the ridiculous. The adverts were somehow the very glue that held commercial television together. For years before, adverts on advertising hoardings and all the paraphernalia that went with it, was a regular part of our life.

Wherever you went along the street, there were constant references to cigarette brands, the latest cars on the market, soft drinks and all manner of household appliances. It was rather like being surrounded by everything that was relevant to your life. On the walls were huge adverts for everything, screaming out to you and imploring you to buy and buy our product.

On TV, we had a whole repertoire of household favourites. There was Fry's Turkish Delight, a Double Diamond works wonders, Wrigley's Spearmint Gum, Schweppes, you know who, Black Magic, the Esso sign means happy motoring. There was Mclean's toothpaste, R White's secret lemonade drinker, Fray Bentos steak pies, Beans Meanz Heinz, For Mash get Smash potatoes, Homepride bread, the politician Clement Freud and his hang dog, lugubrious face with his take on dog food.

Several of these adverts stand out in my hall of fame. There was the famous Black Magic chocolate advertisement. Black Magic was that dark, very sexy and very desirable box of chocolates. Black Magic had its very own riveting story, a wonderful plot, narrative and was compulsively watchable.

The central character in the Black Magic was this rather heroic James Bond figure who overcame every seemingly impossible hurdle that came his way. Dressed all in black, he would dive headlong into shark infested waters from the tallest of cliffs. Then he would fight off every obstacle that confronted him. Finally he would climb into the bedroom of the woman of his choice, hair soaked and gallantly swept back before effortlessly dropping the box of Black Magic chocolates onto her table. What a man.

Then there were the repeated mentions of alcohol, ringing endorsements of beer and lager. A Double Diamond beer was something very working class and something men drank after a hard day at the office or the warehouse.

Double Diamond had the wittiest of songs and was permanently catchy. By the end of the Sixties, Double Diamond had literally worked wonders and quenched the thirst of an insatiable nation.

Then there was Fry's Turkish delight chocolate, a delicious mix of mystery and exoticism. Fry's Turkish delight was all moody, brooding, mystical, but sumptuously seductive and a treat for the taste buds. The advert itself portrayed what seemed to be Middle Eastern belly dancers swaying and floating around in the most provocative style and clothing. It was all very sultry and suggestive, designed to be swooned over by a very young, impressionable mind.

I'd always been aware of TV's capacity to inform and educate and to that end, both ITV and BBC had achieved their objectives. The programmes were varied, interesting, sometimes too compelling and then downright outrageous. But there were personalities, figures, highly esteemed broadcasters who used all of their years of judgment and wisdom to tell you about things you either knew or perhaps wanted to know more about.

For instance, there was Alan Wicker, one of the most distinguished of all TV figures. Formerly a war correspondent, Wicker developed into one of TV's most polished and adaptable of all presenters. For years, he travelled the globe several times over, interviewing, asking awkward questions with extraordinary intelligence, pestering, badgering, hounding but ultimately getting to the truth of the matter without holding back.

Wicker did everything, saw everything, exposed everything, uncovered everything in a way I would never have thought possible. With that rather casual look and distinctive moustache, Wicker would always seem to be on planes, boats and trains at the same time. He would gaze enraptured out of train carriage windows and stare admiringly. He would rub noses with Maoris in New Zealand, share tea with prime ministers in India, Africa and Australia before slumping back on some comfortable chair on a Sri Lankan tea plantation.

Wicker was never afraid to socialise, schmooze and fraternise with the great and good. There were the corrupt crooks, devious tax dodgers, spivs, chancers, scheming presidents, evil, manipulative characters with shifty eyes and hands. Wicker was a hugely intelligent TV intellectual, totally dedicated to the cause of justice and never less than totally intrigued by those who he felt had something to hide.

My teenage years also gave me a very privileged insight into the stupendous world of David Attenborough. Now the Attenborough family were internationally famous and highly regarded by the very highest. Richard Attenborough had secured an unmistakable place in British hearts.

Dickie Attenborough had been one of the most admired war-time film actors and could also grace a West End stage with his considerable, nay less substantial talents. He was graceful, consistently theatrical, understated at times but never less than a remarkable actor. He appeared in the first production of the famous West End play, The Mousetrap, during the 1950s and would continue to exert a powerful hold in the fields of TV, film and the theatre. Simply a gentleman of the highest order.

But it was his brother David who made me sit up and take notice. David had already become an instrumental figure in the birth of BBC2, taking up an eminently influential and responsible position, a man of upright principles and scholarly learning. But he was also the man who opened up my world, arousing the curiosity of those who wanted to know much more.

David Attenborough was a renowned botanist, anthropologist and animal lover. He suddenly entered my world during my naïve teenage years. Attenborough was academically brilliant, astonishingly well-informed, sympathetic to endangered species and never reluctant to find out about the private lives of insects or how guerrillas in the jungle could interact with human beings. There was an almost instinctive understanding between Attenborough and his animals. You almost felt that Attenborough knew all of his animal's favourite foods and spoke their language. Almost uncanny but possibly true.

But if I delve right back into my childhood, I can remember moments in my life and events that would mould and shape my very young years and adolescence. There were the TV programmes in black and white, the comforting Test Card with its girl in pig tails playing noughts and crosses with a puppet and never finishing the game. There was Peyton Place, Lost in Space, the Beverley Hillbillies, the Avengers, Junior Showtime and so many more.

I don't know why but Peyton Place somehow belongs to that very early age in my childhood. I'll always remember the opening credits to Peyton Place. It was one of the first American soap operas. It chronicled family bust ups and divisions, neighbourhood scandals, saucy, salacious gossip and America wrestling with all of the social issues of the day.

But Peyton Place was my first introduction to what life was like on the other side of the Atlantic. Suddenly you were taken on a behind the scenes tour of America, its post-Vietnam mentality, Barbara Parkin with her rather severe and austere looks, Ryan O'Neal a blossoming young actor and America in all her vastness and unpredictability.

Those opening credits are now imprinted on my mind. There was a small church with a white gabled roof flanked by a couple of wholesome looking trees. But underneath it all, there was that rather sad, sentimental and schmaltzy piece of music that smacked of something worse than melodrama. It sounded like one of those tragic anthems that reminded you of some dreadful event.

Lost in Space was the one childhood programme that would always appear as soon as I got home from my infant school. It was one of the first science fiction telly programmes, a series that was set on board a spacecraft and revolved around the fortunes of a space age family wearing rather odd looking clothes. There was Dr Zachary, a rather comical and deeply misunderstood figure who could never quite understand the machinations of the world as he saw it.

And then there burst onto the screens a programme that gripped me as a kid. It was so dynamically action packed and lively that I must have looked forward to every episode. In fact, because it was shown at roughly eight o'clock in the evening, I would invariably need permission to stay up and watch it.

For reasons that are beyond me, the Avengers was broadcast at 8 o'clock in the evening, far too late for my childish eyes. But because it wasn't too offensive, abusive or violent, my parents would afford me that special hour on Wednesday evening. I don't think the Avengers was in any way dangerous so perhaps allowances could be made.

The Avengers starred Diana Rigg and Patrick Macnee, two very contrasting characters with an appetite for eliminating the baddies and the villains of the piece. Theirs was a partnership based on implicit trust and unswerving loyalty to each other. I thought they complemented each other perfectly, almost reading each other's mind or action.

Patrick Macnee was that typically English gentleman with a bowler hat on his head and an umbrella in his hand. He reminded me of one of those City stockbrokers: smart, sharp, suave and very very dashing. He was cultured, well read, very clipped in his speech and presentable.

Then there was the Diana Rigg figure, Emma Peel, clothed in black, adventurous, ambitious, fiercely feminist perhaps, wonderfully assertive in a room of men, remorseless when she had to be. Diana Rigg high kicked the baddies into the air, pinned them to the wall and confronted them in the most steely fashion. Diana Rigg never stood for any nonsense, never apologised, no prisoners were ever taken, surrender and subjection never being part of her vocabulary.

So in many ways, here I was surrounded by all the sights, sounds, noises, people, characters and attitudes who'd framed my very childish landscape. Everything was very fresh, raw, new, perplexing and, in its way, pleasantly surprising. I never really began to come to terms with what was happening around me, the present day and the possibilities that the future would hold. The present was an indecipherable blur, the past was another country and the future was some golden haze that only the most far sighted or visionary could see.

I now find myself in the concluding chapters of my childhood, while acutely aware that this story does indeed have a successful and encouraging message. It's rather like finding triumph in adversity, redemption in the face of desperation, pure white rather than solemn grey. There was so much to look forward to rather than whatever might have passed.

I think most of us go through our whole lives in some metaphorically busy and crowded room, surrounded by strangers and those we'd like to get to know better. Of course, there is that stable family unit of mother, father, brother, sister, uncle and auntie but for me there was a feeling of hollowness, emptiness and inadequacy because I never knew that there were people out there who cared just as much as my family.

And so there were the childhood memories again re-surfacing like the sun peeping out on a July morning or the magpie on the trees. There was a sudden emergence and re-surgence, a feeling that I'd found that elusive light at the end of the tunnel, a new found source of ecstatic energy and a wonderful zest for life.

When I look back to those early days in Cranley Road in Ilford, the images dance and flicker in my subconscious. There was my parents' kitchen, complete with its Formica brown table, the boiler in the corner with its huge colonies of summer ants bristling in the corner and suitably eye-catching furniture.

I don't know why but I'll never forget the neat row of spices and herbs in a small glass cabinet. We had cute little jars, all very daintily sitting next to each other: Basil, Parsley, Rosemary and Thyme with just a passing acknowledgement to Simon and Garfunkel. For years, these spices and herbs would sit there patiently waiting for somebody to confirm their existence.

And then there was my parent's bread bin. Now I'm not sure whether these were a fashion accessory but bread bins were all the rage while I was growing up. At the time, I seem to remember that Mothers Pride would compete with Sunblest for our culinary affections.

I have to tell you that my introduction to biscuits was one of my earliest and most pleasurable memories. For a number of years, biscuits and cakes of all varieties would hide away tantalisingly in our biscuit tin before eagerly awaited tea times. Ah yes, there was the biscuit tin overflowing with chocolate, cholesterol and fatty substances. But for me this marked the end of the perfect day.

Suddenly, Bourbon chocolate biscuits would mischievously escape from the biscuit tin and all was well with my world. There were Bourbons, Digestive and Chocolate Biscuits, Garibaldi biscuits with mouth wateringly enticing raisins, Nice biscuits with just the most delightful coating of sugar and Jaffa Cakes, those splendid chocolate confections with a layer of orange running adorably through them.

Mention of biscuits and cakes takes me right back to the beginning of my life's journey. In Ilford, my childhood home for over 40 years, there used to be a street called Ley Street. Ley Street was a long, straight road that would take you along a whole row of houses, an old shoe repair shop called Ye Old Cordwainer, a lovely old model railway shop, several greengrocers, one or two newsagents and half way down Ley Street, a huge electronics factory called Plessey's. But this was no ordinarily dull, dowdy and mundane road. This was the road that led inexorably to Ilford.

During my long and extremely unpleasant period of unemployment, I would hear the sound of what I can only assume was the honking sound of a British Rail train. When I woke up in the morning, I would invariably hear this sound. But it was as regular as clockwork, sounding like some distant factory, a remnant of the Industrial Revolution, harsh, grating and mechanical.

Then, as you approached Ilford town centre, you were reminded of just why so many were attracted to Ilford. Right at the very end of Ley Street, there was a small parade of business-like shops, hustling, bustling, haggling and bartering for trade. There was a very modern menswear shop that sold classy, top of the range shirts, T-shirts, sweat shirts and trousers and trainers. Further along was a travel agency that seemed to be there for years, catering to an infant tourist industry taking you to the Costa Brava and much further afield.

But on the corner of the Hainault Bridge off Ley Street, there was a glittering goldmine that I can almost smell. Tucked away unobtrusively and very discreetly, there was the most extraordinary bakery. It was a baker's shop that gave out the most delicious odour. Psychologists and human behaviour experts tell us, with what I assume to be scientific accuracy, that the smells and sights of your childhood are those we can never ever forget.

On our way home from Ilford, my mum and I would always pay a flying visit to this bakery. Here she would always buy a handful of sticky currant buns, perhaps a stick of French bread and something sweet and fragrant for tea.

But the currant buns, I have to tell you, were just out of this world. Not only were they sweet and addictive but to this day, they remind me exactly where I was and what I might have been doing as a child. I seem to remember iced buns and Danish pastries, sugar coated buns dripping and oozing sweetness. I think my childhood was dominated by all of the things that shouldn't have been eaten but were, almost innocently and stealthily. It just seemed to be morally acceptable and if you did put on three stone, then you'd always be allowed to lose that weight, later on in life.

Another fond youthful Ilford memory takes me back to the local Valentines Park. Every Guy Fawkes Night, without fail, Redbridge council would organise its very own fireworks party. Every year, on a muddy field in downtown Ilford, the firework circus would regularly come to town.

But there was an indefinable something about the firework party that gave Ilford an unmistakable identity and status. Before the great pyrotechnical extravaganza, a huge cinematic screen would be carefully set up for the delight and delectation of the children and their families.

Suddenly, this white screen with a projector would emerge in the depths of a dark winter's evening and in front of excited children, there would be a moment of sheer magic. Mickey Mouse would be followed by Donald Duck, an endless sequence of flickering cartoons and short funny films.

But behind this mini Mardis Gras of fun and frivolity, there was something else. There was a raw excitement in the early November air, a tingling anticipation, something good and great about to happen. Indeed it was and how amazing and entirely unexpected.

In one corner of Melbourne Fields, a fairground flared into colourful life. It was a fairground that was noticeably smaller than the one you saw during the summer but a fairground nonetheless. It was loud, buzzy, giggly, occasionally electrifying and atmospheric. Roll up Roll up Ladies and Gentlemen for the coconut shy, the horsey carousel ride that rose up and dropped down insistently, joyously and incessantly. You could jump onto the Dodgem cars that whizzed around at a hundred miles an hour furiously and unstoppably, and tackle the complexities of pink candy floss. You always felt that once you had candy floss in your hand, it would just overwhelm you. Suddenly, there was large sticky mass of flavoured cotton wool, ever so slightly unmanageable, impossible to eat in one go, slippery and elusive.

I can remember wandering aimlessly through the Valentines Park fairground and wondering whether this was what life was really like. Groups of kids huddled together in their own separate gangs, running from one ride to the next like moths to a light, girls light heartedly screaming at the top of their voices, yelling, wailing, scurrying and scampering, comparing notes on their new Adidas T-shirt or Adidas bag. Then the girls would give you substantial chapter and verse on the new David Cassidy single or the new Bay City Rollers album.

Then the boys would step forward, clomping down high streets and through parks in their new platform shoes from Clarks, purposefully pioneering in a way because nobody had ever seen anybody in platform shoes. Of course it was a status symbol and I don't think anybody ever gave it a second thought.

Teenage boys from the Seventies always believed that they knew far more than they were given credit for. Both the girls and boys wrapped scarves around their waist because this somehow indicated that they were far more enlightened and streetwise than their mates. I think the boys of my generation knew just as much about pop music and Ask the Family on the TV than anybody else.

Now there was a TV programme. Ask the Family was rather like one of those deliberately instructive quiz shows that always made you sit up and take notice. It always seemed rather more intense and competitive than perhaps any other programme but you did feel that the entire family could take part. There was a great sense of audience participation about Ask the Family that drew you in.

Ask the Family was introduced by Robert Robinson, a hugely well informed and educated presenter who perhaps should have been a City lawyer rather than a telly broadcaster. Still, Robinson was terrifically well-read and must have studied all the classics.

The whole format of Ask the Family was based on the premise that if you knew more about any given subject than your opponents, then you had to win. I used to love those wonderful moments when both families would desperately press their buttons in trying to answer the questions.

Then there were those whispered conversations between the families when both families would close ranks, father would lean over to mother and the children were almost camouflaged by mum and dad while the deliberations went on. It was almost as if they were like MI5 spies in some secret conspiracy.

On the subject of Robert Robinson and TV quiz shows, you could hardly forget Call My Bluff. Now Call My Bluff was quite unlike any telly programme I'd ever seen. It drew heavily on the English language and all the associations with that very specific genre.

Call My Bluff was an ingenious word game that stretched your vocabulary to the furthermost point. It came out with words you'd never heard of and would probably never use again in any context. But it was utterly absorbing and totally involved you. I suppose I subconsciously drank in all of the words mentioned.

But there was something quintessentially English about Call My Bluff, celebrities of the day cunningly disguising their facial expressions with what seemed to be very convincing descriptions. Each panellist of course had three hidden words on their card and the idea was that you had to guess or second guess these very obscure and grandiose words.

The two captains were great fun. On one side you had Frank Muir and on the other Patrick Campbell. Both Muir and Campbell had that wonderfully Wodehousian and dapper air about them. They were rather like an updated version of Jeeves and Wooster, humorously exchanging bawdy seaside humour, roaring with laughter at the most innocent remark, jesting, joshing, tee-heeing and generally having fun with grammar and words. And then Robert Robinson would ring the bell and both Campbell and Muir would set off on that glorious literary adventure.

Frank Muir wore his best suit, shirt and a bow tie that belonged in some very high society living room next to the crystal decanter. Muir was lovably silly, highly intelligent, quick witted and utterly spontaneous. Suddenly and without any warning, he would pour out some of the wittiest stories and exceptionally clever plays on words. They were little cameos, hilarious insights and vivacious vignettes.

His opposite captain, Patrick Campbell, was equally as funny, a man with a most theatrical take on life, never taking anything seriously. Campbell could be both eccentric and foppish. Campbell was a model of Victorian gentility, a man of standing, a social position in life, repute and renown. Campbell drank the finest malt whisky, smoked the best Havana cigars, read The Times from cover and cover and completed the crossword. Campbell had class, manners and a firm grip on grammar and semantics.

During my most formative childhood years, the 1960s provided the nation with its controversial social observers, commentators who insisted on arguing and debating all matter of subjects. They were moralising, prim and proper, sanctimonious figures who maintained that Britain was going to hell in a handcart, that everything was crumbling under our feet and the whole infrastructure of the country was in a state of complete disrepair.

There was Kenneth Tynan, Malcolm Muggeridge, Gilbert Harding, Germaine Greer, Enoch Powell, Robin Day and numerous others. All poured out their grievances about religion, the Church, the economy, the loose morality, the permissive society, the Pill, abortion, that abominable topic known as under-age sex and the excessive use and abuse of drink and drugs. It was an outrageously and appallingly behaved society and I think all of the aforementioned were just disgusted at the general state of decay and deterioration that Britain had now been reduced to.

Malcolm Muggeridge, to my eyes, always looked very old, wise and very disgruntled with his lot. Muggeridge was one of those very learned and distinguished broadcasters who would spend endless hours in university libraries, swotting up on the Boer War. Muggeridge was, to some, just some grumbling, crotchety old man with nothing better to do with his time than complain, sermonise and criticise the whole of the human race. Muggeridge would sit on discussion TV shows, looking thoroughly fed up and wishing he were somewhere else. It always looked an effort and imposition on his time and you either loved or loathed him.

And then there was Germaine Greer, passionate feminist, ferociously outspoken and never afraid to make her voice heard on any subject. She was controversial, vocal, very talkative, overwhelming at times perhaps but always ready to join in with the most animated of discussions. Greer was never afraid to be disagreeable, determined to rock the boat but only in a light hearted way. Greer was, at times, angry, militant, forceful and dogmatic. She remains one of our foremost campaigners, vociferous, extrovert, apolitical and political on the others. She was neither here or there, ultimately objective but always somehow right and never wrong. Some found her annoying and objectionable but just unavoidable, at times hilariously argumentative.

Then there were the others who were fiercely opposed to the system. Kenneth Tynan was the first TV broadcaster to swear quite freely on the BBC. Tynan was also this old fashioned, allegedly stuffy and archly conservative trouble maker who always stirred the pot and stoked the fires. Tynan was this rather anguished social commentator who never really found any common ground or agreement with the Establishment.

Who could ever forget the one and only David Frost? During the 1960s, Frost became one of the most visible, popular and populist figures on mainstream British TV. What you have to remember is that in the early 1960s, Britain still had only two channels: ITV and BBC1. Frost suddenly entered Britain's living rooms and stayed there for duration of the Sixties and Seventies. He was never intrusive or disruptive but he did have the most remarkable hold on the British public's attention.

That Was The Week That Was first hit our TV screens when I was a mere spring chicken, roughly two or three and if I'd known what all the fuss was all about, it would certainly have been one of the most powerful pieces of TV I'd ever set eyes on.

TW3 was explosively different, ground breaking and revolutionary. It broke down all the barriers, pushed back the boundaries and then rammed the topical issues of the day firmly down our throats. There was an air of anarchy, radicalism, hard-hitting comment and satire about it.

There was something about That Was The Week That Was that was very topical, right up to date and never ever behind the times. TW3 deliberately humiliated, ridiculed and lampooned the whole of the Establishment. It poked fun at the British stiff upper lip: reserve, buttoned up, reticence and the private lives of the rich and the not so rich. The programme savaged and tore apart allegedly daft politicians, exposing fraud and deception at the highest level and then ripped their reputations to shreds.

There were comic sketches from young rebels such as Lance Percival, Roy Kinnear, Kenneth Cope, deeply sarcastic references from David Frost, singular character assassinations of Harold Wilson and the helplessly despairing George Brown, a man, who we were led to believe was not only a political firebrand but also a renowned alcoholic who didn't really know what day it was.

But it was TW3 itself that must have been particularly enthralling because it was shown live. As a young child, I must have wondered exactly how one programme could be watched by millions and millions of people. I can only imagine that the BBC's direct rivals, ITV, must have thrown in the towel and meekly accepted defeat.

For a number of years then, That Was The Week That Was was compulsive watching for those who wanted to be both shocked and amused at the same time. It was astonishing, dramatic, engagingly funny and perhaps cruelly irreverent. It was also shown late at night when the kids were presumably safely tucked up in bed. At times, it was too naughty, too offensive and blasphemous. The language was appalling and it was easy perhaps to imagine the BBC switchboard lighting up with complaints and grumbles.

One notable night of course will go down into the TV archives for all of the right and wrong reasons depending on your viewpoint. It was just another edition of TV3 but on this one occasion, the audience got rather more than they were expecting. For months and years, the programme had dangerously flirted with subjects that were ever so slightly cutting edge and possibly in dubious taste. And yet they seemed to get away with it because this was what the programme was all about it.

TW3 outraged the Establishment, made fun of everybody and everything, making wicked and pungent comments about those who were just ripe for criticism. The Sixties left us with the obvious impression that some of these celebrities in the public eye were asking for it. They were fully deserving of humiliation, exposure and derision so why couldn't a weekly satire TV programme tell it the way it was.

And so we came to that night of all nights. An Indian businessman had been asked to appear on the show to defend his utterly despicable acts of evil and treachery. Apparently, he'd spent the best part of years stealing money from members of the public without a single apology. His company had been deliberately responsible for the most-wicked acts of fraud, deception and embezzlement and now TV had found one of the most horrible villains of all time.

For one memorable evening, the watching audience and the public at home were treated to one of the most spectacular pieces of TV at its most dramatically confrontational. During an almost mesmeric interview David Frost did his utmost to embarrass a man who refused to say sorry. It was as if the lions had been released into the den, attacking and cutting open its prey before hungrily devouring the bones. It was TV at its most bloodthirsty and savage.

Throughout the whole evening, Frost must have felt like one of those high profile barristers in court, taunting and tormenting his victim with ravenous relish. It was the most ferocious cross examination TV had ever heard. Question followed question and fingers were pointed. It reminded you of one of those heated party political debates in the House of Commons. Frost, quite metaphorically, dug his knife into the businessman's heart as if he were privately enjoying the act.

Then the audience seemed to be drawn into this almost hypnotic argument. Voices got louder, opinions almost unanimous in their condemnation and fury that could almost be smelt. It was just electrifying and magnetic. I don't think anybody had seen anything quite like it, certainly not on late night TV. The gloves were off and the punches rained down from all corners. It was a verbal free for all with accusations being fired from all angles and the air was thick with hostility.

Somehow, though, I thought this must have been the real backdrop of my 1960s childhood. There was a Britain that had quite suddenly been confronted with everything that the 1950s had left behind. But here was a Britain that was doing its upmost to forget the Post War years of the late 40s, trying hard to believe that the 1960s could be an utterly sensational decade. It was the decade where every day was like a holiday and nobody ever felt deprived. Here was a chance to throw off those chains of difficulty, suffering and rationing. There was a renewed hope and it was time to grab hold of the Seventies and see how far we could take it.

And so I ventured out into my parents' garden at the beginning of the Seventies and felt a resurgence of something good in the air. Two doors away from my parents' house were an elderly couple with a daughter and son. Now you might think there was anything out of the ordinary about this fact. But there was something that always struck me about this house.

At the bottom of the house, there was a tall weather vane that soared into the air. For years and years, I would look over towards this weather vane and wonder if it could tell me something more about the impending weather. Could it tell me about the warm fronts from the Mediterranean, those funny looking patterns on the weather map called isobars or was it some wonderful looking piece of furniture? I'm not sure whether I could ever figure out why but it did look very impressive.

I'm not sure now but I would always see their son with a pipe in his mouth and whose main hobby in life was chess. Cranley Road in Ilford, in its way, was always unpredictable and unsuspecting. Sure people went to work in the morning, came home in the evening and the whole neighbourhood seemed to be at ease with itself.

But I did make one or two observations about Cranley Road, which I have to say were completely mystifying and, looking back, almost characteristic of the whole road. There were the kids with the summer holiday bikes, dashing and darting out of houses and then frantically climbing back onto the bikes again.

There was a very decent and law-abiding family but there was something about them that I just couldn't understand. Whenever you walked past this house, the family car seemed to have been dismantled, pulled to pieces and was now almost completely beyond recognition. I'm not sure why but the car was simply a skeleton. The engine seemed to have been taken out, the wheels removed and there was nothing that even remotely resembled a car.

As I say, I'm sure they were a lovely family with nothing to hide but this is one childhood reminiscence that sticks indelibly in the mind.

I'm not sure whether this applied to most of Cranley Road because it did have the same set of roofs, the same dark brown tiles in front of their house. As the Seventies arrived and progressed, the pebble dashed look would be replaced by crazy paving. Then TV aerials would stubbornly cling onto chimney stacks and it all looked very attractive, very decorative. The living room curtains would eventually give way to blinds and the aerials would be replaced by Sky boxes.

In those days, people were very house proud and many was the time I would pass painters in white overalls, carefully applying a whiter than white emulsion to the front of the house. And then a year later, another colour would appear and the following year an even more daring choice. But there they would be, seemingly summer after summer, regularly slapping all the colours of the rainbow onto a house that was now accustomed to paint.

Then you'd hear it from miles around you, ringing, tinkling and singing at times, the ice-cream van with that same delightful inevitability. You were never given a warning but it did seem that most of the parents knew instinctively when it was going to happen.

Just before tea-time though, another sound came to define the arrival of tea time. On the other side of the road, all had been relative calm throughout the day. Until it happened. As regular as clockwork, there was the barking of the dogs. As the years passed by, this was something my young mind had grown to expect.

I don't quite know why but at the same time every day, I would hear the same barking, the same pitiful yapping, maybe a disgruntled dog who had yet to be taken out for a walk. I think there were a couple of our canine friends because they all seemed to be calling out to each other and responding at the same time. Perhaps they simply wanted to escape from Peyton Place or maybe they were simply being lovable members of your family.

But it was the essential character of Cranley Road that made you think and comment. I think we all felt that our house had something that stood out from the rest, not exactly superior to others but something that marked it out. I can't remember whether this was the case but I'm sure that we had some of the most ornate ornaments on the sill of our living room window.

There were the colourful glass dolphins, the stunning tramp on the park bench, the family photographs going way back when and an assortment of curios. There was the onyx green cigarette lighter, candlesticks for the Jewish menorah, all snugly keeping each other company throughout the seasons.

I'll always remember my parents' neighbours two doors away from us because they were the ones who brought a different dimension to a day in the garden. They were always friendly, chatty and forthcoming on all subjects but there was something else that I couldn't help but notice.

During the summer, they would invariably hold bonfires at the bottom of the garden. Nothing unusual you might say. But suddenly they would appear, huge clouds of smoke leaping into the air, crackling, drifting, blowing in the wind, reaching into the blue sky and clutching at the tips of the tree branches.

It was quite the most magnificent sight and one that I can still hear and smell to this very day. Great memories.

I think you can appreciate that although a very private and reclusive teenager, I could still feel as though I belonged in the same company, the same social group, the same level and never at all feel excluded.

Further down Cranley Road, there was a lovely family: wife, husband and two sons. Now I always thought they were one of the most intellectual families I'd ever met. Day after day, week after week, month after month and year after year, theirs was the existence I'd always admired: it was intensive study, incessant reading, listening to classical records and a life of private contemplation.

Both parents were determined to give their children the best possible of all starts in life, instilling all the values of dignity and humility that they thought were somehow fitting. They were thoughtful, exceptionally academic, well-educated, and deeply respected and respectable.

Whenever I walked past their house, it was rather like looking at some very grand looking school tucked away in some orderly neighbourhood. For what must have seemed an indeterminate period of time, the two sons would always be heard on either the violin or the piano. It was rather like listening to some glorious and melodious orchestra, perfectly in tune and at one with nature. You felt privileged to be one of their neighbours because you knew that their sons were both musically gifted, emotionally stable and always polite. Which is not to say that you weren't but the fact of the matter was that they seemed to be intellectually mature years before I was.

Without fail, I would hear that very placid classical piano and violin, a sound so sweet and angelic that you'd be forgiven for thinking that the Royal Albert Hall had moved into Cranley Road. It was a sound of polish, scholarship, delicacy and craftsmanship. It was a sound that had a real sense of learning and academia about it, a sound that was the end product of years and years of dedication and devotion, love and care.

How those two sons must have been gently taught that music was indeed the food of love, the gateway to some promised land, and a passport to wherever they wanted to be in the world. Music would open up new frontiers to them, classical music had energy, vibrancy and passion, sadness and melancholy at times, regret and remorse at others. But essentially, classical music was full of drive and ambition, a noble calling and a profession that more or less guaranteed work at all times. How could they possibly fail?

Which brings me rather neatly back to my relationship with music. Now classical music never really appeared on my radar. Classical music was always too sombre, solemn and miserably melancholy. There was something very haunting, dramatic and pessimistic about it. There were the long silences in the middle of a piece and a stern finality about the piano. But there were the redeeming instruments. You had the soothing violins with their reminders that all was well in the world, the flutes and recorders with their jolly playfulness and the heavenly harp which always sounded angelic.

I have to admit to a complete ignorance about classical music and acknowledge that our neighbour's sons were masters of their craft, culturally learned and always seeking improvement, a somehow unattainable perfection. And yet it wasn't unattainable because they'd already reached the heights, the summit I could never hope to get to.

Everybody had heard about the classical maestros, the likes of Beethoven, Mozart, Bizet, Tchaikovsky, Strauss, Wagner, Debussy, Brahms and many others but I always felt that there was something about these giants of their field that didn't quite make the desired impact on me that it should have done.

Of course, both Beethoven and Mozart were some of the greatest composers that the world would ever know. And yet, from a personal point of view, theirs was the music that didn't quite have the ring and resonance that I might have been looking for in music. True, it was a music that had both power and muscularity. Admittedly, it also had decisiveness, a clear vision and authority. You could never argue with classical music because it knew where it was going and was determined to get there. When the orchestra struck up, it was absolutely sure of itself, never hesitating, quite honest in its intentions. Maybe that's why I didn't understand classical music. Perhaps the music I was interested in had a very different purpose and maybe I just couldn't see what that purpose was. It would remain to be seen.

Part 18:
And now for a look at those famous moments in time when the world seemed to stand still.

Throughout my life, I'd been surrounded by some of the most dramatic events in history, moments that made us stand still, caught us on the hop, made our hair stand on end, took our breath away, confronted us with a moral dilemma, caused us to question why, how and when, intrigued us and then simply moved us onto the next chapter.

It's amazing how the smallest things, the most trivial of things, even the most obvious things can leave us breathless, lost for words, mystified and then asking more questions. These are the events that stop us in our tracks, make us wonder why we behave in the way we do, thinking too deeply and then analysing what might have been. Looking back and with the benefit of hindsight maybe we should have been done more to influence the direction our life had taken us.

But then we become realistic, we become accepting of our fate, philosophical about the setbacks but glad of the chance to have another go. My dad, bless him, believed very fervently in fate and always said that what will be, will be. There are no guide books or psychological manuals which tell us what to do and how to conduct ourselves. I think we are simply at the behest of whatever life can offer.

Anyway, now for those definitive events in life which made history, shaped history, moulded history, simply occurred quite unexpectedly without any knowing why. They were earth shaking moments, the radio announcements, the breaking news moments, those vividly momentous occasions when nobody knew what would happen next.

It does seem somewhat ironic that the assassination of President John F. Kennedy took place on the day before my first birthday. Now I'm sure there was a perfectly logical explanation for this most dramatic and traumatic day. Here was a man loved and adored by his nation but somebody must have forgotten to tell America that it was my birthday.

So what possessed a warped and twisted mind to point a gun at a President's head literally hours before the celebration of my first year on the planet? My mum had gone to all of the trouble to make that special cake and here was the most powerful man on the planet being shot at for no apparent reason, killed for nothing, with no ulterior motive and to all outward appearances, a victim of circumstances, going about his daily business as usual.

And yet this was that shocking and tragic day which changed the course of political history, shifted the balance of world power, turned the world on its axis and then pointed accusing fingers at murderers, hardened crooks and shady characters.

The assassination of John F. Kennedy not only changed our perceptions, it also put the spotlight on much deeper issues, made us all aware of how precious our own lives were, how we should be grateful that none of us would ever have to live our lives out in the public domain.

For instance, what were you doing when that went gun off on November 22nd 1963? Were you innocently checking the post at work, searching through filing cabinets for some important document? Were you shuffling through papers, tidying up your desk or talking to somebody on one of those big, black phones? Were you on your way to a business matter, tying up a deal, negotiating with another reputable company or just walking down the road or street in all innocence.

Presumably the main topic of discussion would have revolved around matters that bore no relation to American politics. Perhaps you were still raving and waxing lyrical about the relatively new Dr Who with Patrick Troughton. Or maybe you were recalling that year's Cup Final between Manchester United and Leicester City, a game which United were expected to win and, to all of their fanatical supporters, quite naturally did.

Maybe you were just sitting in your garden, walking the dog, or twisting the night away in some West End club. Perhaps you were travelling on one of those lovely old Route Master buses and wishing you were one of the Beatles, a pop band who would become a cultural phenomenon.

And then it a happened. In downtown Texas, the most famous man in the world wound his way through the streets in the largest open topped limousine you'd ever seen. Sitting next to his wife, Jackie, Mr President swept back his hair, grinned for his idolatrous American public and bang bang. There followed a sharp intake of breath, a horrified moment of silence and then the looks and shouts of horror. The president had been shot dead, there was a suspension of belief and then disbelief. America was aghast, reviled, amazed, heartbroken, completely traumatised. For some reason humanity was at a loss, unable to take in the sheer scale and magnitude of what it had just seen.

But it was the sheer suddenness and appalling wretchedness of that day that seem to reverberate around the world. It was almost as if the world had lost one of the kindest, most generous and revered men who ever lived. President Kennedy had won the hearts and minds of every neighbourhood, town, city and village throughout the world. He was a giant of a man, full of wit, wisdom, animal magnetism and incredibly popular. He was the man committed to world peace, who genuinely felt that the world could be a better place if only we sat down and talked. And yet on a November day in 1963, that man and his principles were snuffed out, shot down in cold blood.

What about the day of the Coronation of our Queen Elizabeth the Second in June 1953. I have to tell you that my written account can never be accurate but I'd like to think that there was something in the air that must have been truly breath-taking, like nothing we were ever likely to see again in our lifetime.

When, in all fairness would the country ever see a Coronation in their life? It really didn't seem possible and yet it was.

It's been fairly well documented that the Coronation was the first big public occasion in colour. Up until then, the world had been a rather sinister shade of grey and black and white, very pale and drained looking. The War had only been over for eight years but we were raw, injured, damaged, still recovering from the madness, mayhem, noise and carnage.

Our houses and buildings were in blackened heaps of ash and smoke, our morale had been battered into submission and we were longing for something to look forward to. There had been rationing, deprivation, hardship and trembling grief. Now there was a technicolor, all dancing, all singing Coronation of a monarch. It was quite the most spectacular show on earth, full of pomp and circumstance, glittering and shimmering with gold carriages and royalty in all its magnificent finery. What a day it must have been. It was time to roll out the tables for street parties, jam sandwiches, balloons, uninhibited kids having a ball, families and streets in perfect unity, linking arms, joking and laughing, singing and serenading, energy and overflowing exuberance. A day to truly treasure.

But where were we on that day of all days. It was the beginning of a new era, a new chapter in our lives, a passage of time that held so much promise and potential. Suddenly the nation had a new young Queen, the monarchy had undergone a radical makeover and Britain was ready, willing to welcome and just agog with excitement. It was as if the world had temporarily stopped for a couple of seconds and swallowed a sharp intake of breath.

On that early June day in 1953, by way of sheer coincidence, the world was also witnessing something that too many must have been quite exceptional. Edmund Hilary and his faithful mountaineering team had just conquered Mount Everest. In itself, this was undoubtedly one of humanity's greatest achievements but, to all intents and purposes, it was something that nobody could possibly have anticipated.

Then there was the famous Derby victory at Epsom in which Sir Gordon Richards had delivered a winning horse in the most civil and dutiful fashion. It was as if Richards knew that June 1953 was that time for the Coronation and the Queen would be immensely pleased. He was always the most obliging and gracious of jockeys.

At home, most of us were crowding around six inch TV sets, which looked rather like gold fish bowls but served the purpose quite admirably. Mum, complete in bright kitchen apron and nicely turned out appearance, would rush in and out of the kitchen, scurrying around the living room, plumping up the cushions, dusting the tables, straightening the curtains, adjusting the antimacassar draped over the sofa, busying herself constantly.

Mum was in her element, buttering the cheese, egg and fish paste sandwiches, filling up the kettle, boiling it incessantly for cups of tea and then tidying up newspaper souvenir copies of the Coronation. Then, the beautifully huge radio would be switched on to the Home Service or the Light Programme, dials gleaming with light and power.

Then Mum would endearingly move dad's glasses, his pristine copy of the Sporting Life folded to the point of absolute precision. And then, the little TV would spark into life in that quaint corner of the living room. There was the grainy, black and white imagery, horses fabulously attired, stirrups that were somehow bejewelled with the most expensive jewellery, nodding and acknowledging their human audience.

Later in the afternoon, mum, dad, son, daughter, uncle, auntie, neighbours and close friends huddle around the TV in the most intimate circle. It was almost as if they were watching something that 10 years before, not even in their wildest dreams would they have regarded as even remotely feasible. And yet, here they were, all fascinated, all transfixed, maybe sceptical but eager to embrace the sheer beauty and artistry of the day. It was a day when royalty and millions of admirers would gather for a united celebration. The bells would ring out resoundingly and a new Queen would take her place serenely in history.

On another distant day, something happened that represented quite clearly the end of the era. It was almost as if part of us had also lost something, waved a fond farewell and never had time to say our goodbyes. It was the final, conclusive, comprehensive full stop and punctuation mark of our lives. One man had left us permanently, never to show the trademark two fingered salute, the cigar in his mouth, his heroic Wartime legacy.

Winston Churchill was one of the greatest Prime Ministers and military figures Britain had ever known. Through the darkest days of the Second World War, Churchill was the one man who rescued the nation, salvaged it from near certain defeat, despair, tragedy, obscurity and oblivion. While the bombs exploded, buildings burnt to the ground and the people trembled for their life, our Winston stood firmly, defiantly, stubbornly in the face of catastrophe. He called the nation to order, settled shattered nerves and made the most heart-warming and conciliatory of speeches. Everything would be fine, Britain and the rest of the world could breathe again.

But on January 30th 1965, the world paid its final respects to Sir Winston Churchill. Churchill had passed away peacefully at a ripe old age, naturally and most regrettably. It was the grandest of all sending's off, a parting of ways with our most amiable friend, the man who was so representative of everything Britain had stood for in the world.

On a late January day, the State Funeral wound its way respectfully around the City and the streets of London. It was the most sombre, solemn and introspective day in the history of Great Britain. It was a day Britain bowed its head in remembrance, taking off their caps and watching with an air of deepest reverence. Slowly but surely, the hats came off, and that very English sense of gravitas and sorrow reigned supreme. It was the ultimate outpouring of grief. Here was the finest of all statesmen lying in restful state.

More recently, the world also seemed to celebrate the one event in its history that hardly seemed possible but always looked as if it might happen. It was that most victorious of occasions, the day two countries finally met up with each other, faced each other bravely and then shook hands with strong hands and no hard feelings.

This was the day that East Germany and West Germany were reunited with each other, reconciled after all these years, clinking huge steins of foaming beer and slapping themselves in utter self-congratulation. It was almost as if the tensions, stresses, rivalries and bitter resentments had vanished overnight. It somehow seemed that two countries had buried their differences, smoothed over the obvious divisions and just seen common-sense.

It was the night when the old Berlin Wall came crashing to the ground and a nation revelled in its unity. The Berlin Wall was that rather grey, bleak and formidable barrier that had so regrettably and physically, kept two countries apart. For years, politicians bickered and squabbled about all matters of trivia before ultimately deciding that there was no point in hating each other's guts.

And so it was that in November 1989, ecstatic students, husbands, children and wives all came together and cheered a crumbling wall. Never has one wall assumed so much worldwide significance, never has the demolition of one brick wall meant so much to so many people.

But it did and we saw it with the evidence of our own eyes. It broke into a million pieces, shattered and crumbled into dust and decay never to be seen again. In many ways, the collective sense of relief that the Germans felt must have been reflected in every German house, flat, school, hospital and shop. Quite wondrously, East and West Germany could talk again to each other and with each other, free from the constraints of pettiness and regional arguments. It had to stop sooner rather than later.

I can even remember where I was on the night the Berlin Wall came tumbling down. It was a family holiday in Switzerland and quite the most scenic of all locations. Our hotel was overlooked by the most beautiful mountain range anybody had ever seen. It was white, jagged and breath-takingly undulating, almost framing our hotel in some giant picture postcard.

At roughly tea time, a group of Germans in our hotel, by now uncontrollably elated and jumping for joy, celebrated with understandable passion. Gathering around a small table, they lit a candle in the centre of their table, ordered several breweries of beer and ate enthusiastically, heartily and boy did they did have a good time. I can still see that symbolic candle, a small gesture, but the candle signified diplomacy, sense, intelligence and civility. The battle between East and West Germany had been sensibly curtailed, knocked on the head, remedied and rectified. It must have been the day and night Germany must have thought they'd never ever see in any lifetime. But they did and that must have felt so good.

I now take you back to my pet subject of football and the 1996 European Championship in England. For over 40 years, Britain has mourned and lamented the fate of the English football team, rather like some lovable old uncle. Year after year, we yearn for something to cling onto, some shred of hope, the misguided belief that one day the country would win the World Cup. It is safe to say that most of us are just delusional, resigned to the fact that it may never happen again, not even the remotest of chances but in the face of it all, we dig out our dusty rosettes, wave our Union Jacks and just look on with that knowing air of sadness and despondency.

Still we did have the 1996 European Championship in England and after all the fanfares, medieval opening ceremony and everything that made us swell with patriotism, the rest of England and I fell into the most deceptive of traps.

Come the Semi Final at Wembley, England met their oldest of footballing of foes Germany. It was football at its most melodramatic, intense and unbearable. Perhaps we should have gone to the cinema or bingo hall during the evening because in retrospect it just wasn't worth the hassle or aggravation.

The 1966 World Cup Final had been bad enough but this was just ridiculous. Still the law of averages insisted that it had to be our turn. Nobody could deny or begrudge us and those Germans deserved to lose again. Not because of what happened during the War but essentially because we were the superior nation, we were technically brilliant, good in possession, controlled, organised and rigorously disciplined. The Germans had none of those qualities. Or so we thought.

When the final whistle with the score at 1-1, the whole nation gasped and headed straight for the kettle. Time for refreshment and rejuvenation, it was merely a matter of time, the inevitable had been delayed. Little did we know that the very qualities we thought we'd possessed had been hijacked by those cunning Germans.

At full time we were level pegging and whatever emotional and physical resources England might have had were now in the hands of Fate. To be perfectly honest, everybody looked shattered, knackered, totally drained and empty. England had simply run out of petrol and were now playing the kind of game that played straight into Germans hands.

Those golden, halcyon 90 minutes were now seeping away into total ineffectiveness. It was almost as though somebody had pulled the plug on the electricity. England were as lifeless, tired and lethargic as some well beaten army on the retreat. They'd run out of ideas, the spirit had ebbed away and then Gazza missed that wonderful chance to win the Cup. If only that despairing leg had been a telescope.

I suppose we should have known better though. The Germans had movement, idealism, structure, togetherness and flexibility. The Germans knew they had the beating of the English. They did warn us years before when hundreds of British holidaymakers helplessly watched them with their sun towels by the pool. It was the clearest of warnings and, painfully, we just watched them and ignored them. The Germans won the European Championship against the Czech Republic and England manager Terry Venables somehow wished that the Germans would just go away and never darken our corridors again. Still, we did our best and nobody could deny that.

And so I move on to the Royal Weddings, those stunning state occasions which brought the nation together for just a day. Gradually we watched the days unfold, the Queen's daughter Princess Anne to Captain Mark Philips in 1973, the Queen's son Prince Charles to Princess Diana, doomed to disaster, the Queen's son Andrew to Sarah Ferguson, sadly a marriage not made in heaven and the Queen's son Edward to Sophie.

On reflection, I suppose, royal weddings seemed to figure prominently in our minds throughout good and bad times. They provided us with a temporary escape route from the usual workaday chores of life. But the one marriage that really stood head and shoulders above the rest was Prince Charles to Princess Diana. After all, it was my mum's birthday so how much of a coincidence was that. Perhaps they'd wave to my mum while in their golden carriage.

But that now best forgotten day back in late July 1981, we all felt that everything around was just right, brilliant, perfect and flawless. What could possibly go wrong? The future king was about to marry his Princess, so everything was just idyllic. Diana looked so feminine, pretty, sweet, winsome and just angelic. You half expected the angels to strike up something on the harp.

Sadly, though, as the passage of time would prove, the relationship between Charles and Diana would hit so many hard rocks that eventually something had to give. Little did we know that Diana would become haunted, hounded, tormented and tortured by those who professed to have her support.

Then the years would pass and the horrible cracks would suddenly become irreparable and poor Diana was devoured not only by her inner demons but ripped to shreds by the vultures ominously hovering over her. It was a gruesome, unsightly sequence of events, rather like some revolting horror movie.

There were the dark, grisly episodes that have been horribly well documented: the bulimia, the eating disorders, the behind the scenes rows with her husband and the day when poor Diana hurled herself down stairs. It was frightful, distressing and harrowing and yet in hindsight, none of us ever knew the full story.

And yet that day in July 1981 should be preserved in some amazing time warp. It should be lovingly stored away in some very comfortable place in our memory. On that day, the nation abandoned itself to street parties, knees ups around Buckingham Palace, sheer delight that something good had happened for a change and the full knowledge that subconsciously, we were an essential part of the Royal Wedding. We were moved and entranced by the whole day, active participants in everything that happened that day.

I got the impression that we must have felt we'd planned the whole wedding, catered amply for all the guests and then finally turned up at St Paul's Cathedral in our Sunday best. You had to look very presentable for the Queen in your Saville Row suit, shirt and tie, that gorgeously prepossessing dress with just the right amount of flowers on them.

But then we found ourselves back in our living room with its simple, straightforward sofas, its brightly coloured wall paper and photos on the table of emerging pop icons, Spandau Ballet, ABC and the Human League. There was something very startlingly original and unique about 1981. You almost felt that somehow, you had become so emotionally involved in the day that maybe you'd forgotten to feed the cat or spoken to your neighbour that day. It was easy to forget who we were that day because somehow we'd been removed, almost temporarily from reality and transported to some wonderful fantasy land where only good things happen.

I seem to remember working for a shipping company called Sealink at the time and never being sure just how much of an impact the Royal Wedding was having. I was doing some meaninglessly inconsequential Youth Opportunites scheme and being paid a pittance for it. I must have felt so devalued and demeaned at the time because there was no immediate prospect of full employment and that whole period was moreorless a complete waste of time.

Still July 1981 was the best of all months, one of our happiest days as a nation and who was I to spoil the occasion by being sullen, sulking and disillusioned by everything about me? In many ways, that Royal Wedding made us sit up and straight, reminded us that the monarchy was still functioning and flourishing. It was a day set in some floating, dreamy, ethereal world where everybody smiles at you and shakes you vigorously by the hand. I'm convinced that in that far off day back in 1981, we were all ecstatic, elated and bowled over by everything it meant. It was a day that had a deeply religious flavour and a spirituality all of its own.

But then we stared out of the window the following day and discovered the same landscape, the same mood, the same people, the same temperaments, the same families and the same friends. Nothing had changed; I was still that very shy, petrified late teenager with nowhere to go. My parents were still there to guide and coax me as best they could and everybody must have felt that from July 1981 onwards, we would get on with the business of our lives as if that Royal Wedding day had never happened. But it did and we witnessed it.

Realistically, the scenery outside hadn't moved, the postman and milkman would still do their daily rounds, the housewives would still put the washing on the line, both sons and daughters would still go to college, wives and husbands would go out to work and the 1980s would proceed in much the way that previous decades had. We would all have designated roles in life and most of us would come to realise that nothing was noticeably different.

We still had three TV channels, New Romantic music was about to replace Glam Rock in the charts and Robin Day still wore that amusing bow tie. It was a time when, ever so slightly, fashions and reactions would change, the rebels would deliberately stick two fingers up at the system and Boy George would look like a girl. All very confusing but, in its way, very revealing. It said so much about who we were and where we were coming from.

Mrs Thatcher was about to upset quite a few people and basically it was as it always was. There was an ordered uniformity about the early Eighties which would only unravel for the worst in later years. You could almost feel and smell a significant revolution in the air. But at the time, we simply dismissed the feeling from our mind.

It was on the day after the Royal Wedding that I began to notice everything was in exactly in the same place as it always had been. I looked out of my parents' living room and there they were in stark relief, all of those domestic certainties and practicalities. There was the early morning paper boy randomly pushing copies of the Sun, Daily Mail and Mirror through our letterboxes, mothers diligently scrubbing their doorsteps, window cleaners thoroughly wiping windows and builders at the top of their ladders carefully repairing tiles or roofs.

For the rest of the nation, I saw it all as clearly as a day. Life was all about sameness and repetition, predictability and relentlessness. All we could hear were the humming factories, the seething industrial chimneys, belching and blustering, forever active, always visible, the supermarkets in the high street, overflowing with people, spilling out into the streets, chatting, gossiping, confiding, never able to stop and talk.

Indeed, this was the way it had always been since that fateful day in July 1981 when a handsome Prince met her lovely Princess. It looked and felt as it had always done. The sound of cash registers still made that distinctive ringing sound, a sound that made sure that your transaction had been made and it was yours to take home.

Above all, there was that familiar pace about life: bustling, hurrying, rushing, urgent, harum scarum, never pausing to stop, always conscious that even if we did miss the bus or train, another would almost invariably follow.

But for me, life was much as it had always been wedding or no wedding. How could I even begin to contemplate what life would be like in August 1981 or September 1982? I would find out in the goodness of time.

The Royal Family though had been the glue that held the nation together, the binding influence, who gave the nation the strongest moral foundation. It hardly seemed right to overlook the part they'd played in our lives. They were the people who stood strong while the rest of the world looked on with despair on its faces. They were the ones who always held the fort when all seemed out of control but above all they were sturdy, loyal, and devoted to the cause, never panicking, never uptight or anxious.

Besides, the Queen was always there for us as a nation. She was naturally gracious, noble, regal, calm in a crisis and imperious. She had that wonderful air of serenity, self-possession and an ability to stand back from the chaotic crowds and just take the heat out of potentially explosive situations. When everything seemed unfair or just plain unsavoury, Her Majesty had the right posture, carriage and position, neither judging, passing comment nor expressing a very debatable point. She was impartiality personified and that's why I think we should have the most unqualified admiration for her.

And yet Ilford was still there, my earliest recollections and reference points, that point of the compass that was neither north, south, east or west. There was something of a suburban neatness and composure about Ilford that had always been there. It was sleepy, undemanding, modest, self-effacing and genuinely glad to be alive. Ilford was completely happy with its station and never frightened of progress.

But Ilford did lack any kind of manufacturing industry. It was never renowned for its shoes, steel, cotton or wool. Sadly, it was never famous for anything real or concrete but it did have its warmth, compassion and generosity. Everybody stopped to talk to you in the street, congratulated you on your birthday or commiserated on a personal disappointment.

Ilford did though once have a thriving brewing factory in nearby Manor Park, an alcoholic paradise in our neck of the woods. The thirsty tongues of the Ilford populace finally had the answer to the prayers. If memory serves me correctly, I think it was a Mackesons factory and although now long since gone, I'm sure you can still smell the rich odours of yeast, hops and bottles of lager by the crate load.

As previously mentioned, there used to be a C & A, but historians will happily tell you that C & A used to be a Super Cinema in another incarnation. It is hard to imagine what Ilford must have looked like before I was born. But for the sake of poetic licence I think I'll try.

Apart from the early 20th century horses and carts, there were the barrow boys proudly marching their fruits and vegetables to Ilford market. Wearing their neatly pressed shirt and cap on their heads, they would push their carts patiently, albeit painstakingly up hills and down. It would be a long, hard gruelling day of labour and toil of unrelieved hard graft but worthwhile and financially rewarding.

But I can almost hear the audible sigh of relief when the 1950s, 60s and 70s arrived. By then, local shopping centres looked and felt very architecturally different. The awnings, those canopies which used to hang over the tops of shop fronts, had now gone and the severe, business-like air that they had, was perhaps a thing of the past.

Shops like Bodgers, Fairheads and Harrison Gibsons, which had up until that point looked so hidden away and secretive, now looked open, free and welcoming. It was almost as if Ilford had been locked away, trapped by some imaginary feeling of claustrophobia, frightened that people would talk about it or gossip.

Once the 1950s arrived, I think Ilford just came out of its shell, bursting into colour, released from the shackles of the Second World War. There was a leaner, fitter and stronger look about Ilford that quite clearly showed. Now the shop windows had bright red summer and winter sales signs on them. Now the Ilford shops could crack jokes with their customers, laugh at their humour, stop to look at those splendid lights in the Harrisons Gibsons shop window. Ilford had now discovered a new voice, a more confident projection and the most lovable character. It was unashamedly, quite inimitably the Ilford we knew we'd see one day.

Soon the horse and carts were consigned quite literally to the scrap heap of history and now a new method of transport had found its way onto the streets of Ilford. It was almost as if Ilford had re-invented itself, re-branded itself and quite literally risen from the ashes. It was so good to see that the 1960s was the decade when everything looked brighter, lighter, quite clearly noticeable and not so repressed and self-conscious. Those awnings were beginning to get in our way and in a sense their disappearance was almost the beginning of something new. Perhaps the renaissance had arrived in Ilford. You could ring the chapel bells now and then dance around the maypole. Suburban Essex was a great place and still is.

Suddenly, there were trolley buses and trams, Route Masters and lorries, cars and vans. Although the streets of Ilford still had that rather harsh and grating sound, I think there must have been a point when the sunshine came out during a very early Mrs Dale's Diary or the Archers. Perhaps British society had just flung open its doors and expressed its gratitude. On second thoughts, perhaps the Kinks had just discovered that lazy sunny afternoon. Or Bob Monkhouse had just picked up the phone on the Golden Shot. I do know that it was a defining and seminal moment in British cultural history. You had to be there to see it. It made for marvellous viewing.

No longer did we have to dwell on the misfortunes of Tony Hancock, the foggy pea soupers that descended on the capital city of London, those dreary, boring days when Hancock complained that there was nothing to do on a Sunday afternoon. No longer did we find ourselves at a loose end when there were only two TV channels. There was something, Ilford felt, that must have been soul destroying when all you had was Family Favourites on the radio, Educating Archie and spam fritters for late tea.

Still, they were good times, satisfying tea times, family supper times, light hearted discussions and witty banter. There were the jokes made by Arthur Askey and Tommy Trinder, glorious tittle tattle from Jimmy Edwards and his handlebar moustache, knock about fun from Tommy Handley and splendid radio comedy from the Goons. There were the silly middle class accents and oratory from the marvellously pompous Kenneth Williams and classic character observations from Sellers and Milligan. It was all very hilariously simple and blissfully easy to understand. Now pass me the ABC cafe sugar basin please.

As a family, I can still remember eating all of our meals in the kitchen but, across the nation, Britain had now moved into the glamorous world of the living room with its large glass oval shaped table and very fashionable lights that hung from the ceiling like some miniature version of St Paul's Cathedral. It was a white dome that seemed to dominate my teenage years. Then there was some wonderful orange glass ornament that looked as though it should have been in the Tate Modern but was nonetheless very striking.

And yet how I must have sympathised with the likes of Tony Hancock. During the 1950s, you almost felt as if there was, quite literally, nothing to do on a Sunday afternoon, that the world had shut down, that nobody was doing anything or working, that society was on permanent strike, that wherever you looked, the world was empty, desolate, grey, despondent, frustrated, almost ridiculously bored.

But the 1960s were different for my generation, the dull monochrome colours of the 1950s had all but disappeared. Somebody had the foresight to do something about this tedium. I can just imagine some talented visionary from the world of art taking out his palette of reds, blues, greens, yellows and oranges and carefully building up a series of great images and dramatic scenery.

So what happened when the black and white days of Muggeridge, Tynan, Educating Archie and Mrs Dale's Diary gave way to those bright, bold and dancing colours that came in all shades? Suddenly we had Frost, Joan

Bakewell, Dudley Moore and Peter Cook, the hugely learned Dr Jonathan Miller, and John Pilger, the campaigning investigative journalist who was always interested in politics, poverty and discrimination.

We knew that they were the characters with their fingers on the pulse of the nation. While I was growing up, I always knew that the Sunday newspapers were passing righteous judgments, running their hypercritical eye over those who were loose, morally corrupt, deviant and devious.

The News of the World, now no longer with us, used to be the one paper that exposed all of those outrageous aristocrats who lived their crazy lives, those who burnt the candle at both ends, who lived life to the full and completely cut themselves off from the society we were brought up in.

The world, according to the News of the World, was peopled by vicars with so called hookers, tax dodgers who always bucked the system, hardened criminals with stubble on their chins and a society in total confusion in the most horrible state of decay. Those highly esteemed Victorian values were now gone forever, consigned to the dustbin of history. It was rather like watching a metaphorical Berlin Wall crashing to the ground.

I suppose, though, the Cambridge Footlights comics could still lighten up our lives because they were the ones who saw the world we were living in and realised that anything was possible. Britain could still be made fun of, still ridiculed without any long term harm and lampooned because somehow the country lent itself to that kind of humour.

I have to say I did like Dudley Moore and Peter Cook. They must have just been delightful company in the BBC bar or in some West End club. Moore and Cook created a world that was not only funny but was singularly without boundaries or taboos. There was nothing that was off limits, no character or situation that couldn't be discussed or scrutinised.

Moore and Cook were two of the most creative and insightful comedians of the 1960s and very few of their contemporaries could ever touch them for inventiveness. Their wonderfully observant sketches, hilariously accurate one liners and general air of matiness gave you the impression that there was something very instinctive about their delivery that never ever disappointed.

The two come to mind and will go down in the history of TV comedy and may stay there for ever more. I'd like to think of them as works of art that will appreciate in value in years to come, gold plated gems that always gleamed and moments that are affectionately preserved in our minds.

How about the one where Dudley Moore and Peter Cook meet up with each other in an art gallery and quite by accident, strike up a dialogue that had us all in gales of laughter. It was simply exquisite and yet absolutely on the nail, a perfect summary of British humour from two of the most exciting comedians of the time.

So this is the scene. Peter Cook, in dirty, crumpled coat, sits down in the aforesaid art gallery and bumps into Dudley Moore, a complete stranger and yet a man of like mind. For the next couple of minutes we are treated to the kind of comedy that maybe will never ever be reproduced again. It is an absolute joy.

Cook, in all his artistic wisdom, turns to Moore and delivers some of the finest lines in the history of comedy. It is splendidly pretentious, gloriously silly but in its way designed to make you laugh and laugh.

Moore is then subjected to a never ending stream of Cook's very deliberate analysis of some unknown painting. Cook then rattles on almost indefinitely about stuff and nonsense, the great Impressionists and how landscape paintings had made a very definite impression on him

Cook then launches into a story that bears no relevance to art or artists. It is simple, almost as if Cook had forgotten why he was in the art gallery in the first place. The look on Cook's face and that repressed smile will live with me forever and a day.

Meanwhile Moore, also in grubby and shabby coat, gets out his lunch and starts eating his sandwiches. Moore, desperately trying to control his laughter, chews on his sandwich all the while praying that the giggling will somehow remain a giggle. And yet here was comedy at its masterly best, both Cook and Moore, interacting, reacting and feeding off each other before delivering that decisive punch line.

By this time Moore, smiling broadly with a sandwich in his mouth finds Cook, straight faced and emotionless, impassive and yet acutely aware that what he was doing was genius, simplicity and absolutely intentional. And then there was the moment.

Cook, in the middle of a rambling dialogue with Moore, suddenly drifts into the world of both the sublime and the ridiculous. He tells us, quite openly, that one night he was sitting in his kitchen minding his own business when there was tapping on the window and it was Brigitte Bardot, the film star with a passion for cats.

Now the likelihood was that Ms Bardot may never heard of the British comic Peter Cook but it's safe to assume that when she was informed, she may have well have been highly amused.

And yet by the end of the Sixties, I suppose Britain had become more or less together again despite everything that might have been considered slightly wrong or remiss. There was a sense that life bubbled along at its own leisurely pace without any real interference from those who wanted to ruin everything.

Towards the end of the Sixties, there was Woodstock, that huge pop music festival in America that told us all that people could get on with each other, that although the consumption of drugs was still common, it had yet to reach epidemic proportions.

There were the classic Woodstock images of men and women in strange costumes called kaftans, colourful beads around the neck and just a hint of cannabis in the air. There they were, swaying their bodies to the infectious beat of the music and deep in the land of meditation and silent appreciation.

These were the hippies, the beatniks, the happy people, groovy man, way out, men and women who witnessed the full beauty and panoply of the Sixties. They had long hair, rebellious urges and weird, mystical thoughts. But they always looked content with their lot. The Sixties had neither affected or damaged them. It was OK to be in the moment and just be who you were and what you were.

There was the brilliantly thought provoking Bob Dylan, one of the world's most imaginative of lyricists, a song writer of immense, renown, gifts, pedigree and substance. Dylan had written everything from thoughtful folk to gritty middle of the road music without ever forgetting his musical roots. Dylan was a natural wordsmith and the words in his music were rather like a book of decorative illustrations. You could feel the hurt, pain and suffering in his songs, the power and force of the voice and that subtle blend of raw melody and lyricism.

Throughout that period, America had quite evidently led the way in technology and innovation. Years and years before anybody else, the Americans were one of the first nations to bring colour TV into their living rooms. The Americans seemed to invent TV dinners and for as long as I can remember, America was always way ahead of any other nation in the world.

Americans had also produced some of the most entertaining TV chat shows, shows that drew their audiences in like flies to a moth. Possibly one of the most high profile and skilful of all chat show hosts, was undoubtedly a master of his craft, leading light and one of the best exponents of the genre.

Johnny Carson was, for ages, widely acclaimed as a chat show host supremo. Carson was America's darling, a true professional who regularly attracted weekly or nightly audiences that ran into several millions. Carson was stylish, riotously funny, honest and direct but never crossed the line. Carson knew exactly when he'd said too much and was rightly diplomatic for that reason alone.

I always felt that here was this man with a wonderful gift of the gab who was made for prime-time TV. You can see all of his guests of that purple 1960s period just filing into the studio and plonking themselves onto the sofa next to him. America had always revelled in its celebrity culture and Carson was almost spoilt for choice.

There was the wonderfully eccentric Woody Allen, frequent appearances from the Hollywood powerhouses such as Jimmy Stewart, James Cagney, Burt Lancaster, George Burns who lived to a ripe old age and always smoked a cigar, the biting and acerbic wit of Lenny Bruce and a whole gallery of the great and the good.

But Carson, Larry King, Jay Leno and all of those witty inquisitors decorated American TV with their incessant joking, side splitting humour and slapstick fun. In Britain, we were about to be introduced to a man who, in many ways, would rival Johnny Carson for sheer likeability and geniality.

For a number of years, Michael Parkinson had been the serious news and current affairs presenter with a notable turn of phrase and tongue in cheek presentation. He'd dominated the 1960s with human interest news stories and sharp observations on British society with all its strengths, weaknesses, foibles and occasional idiosyncrasies.

Saturday nights were compulsively watchable TV nights. Parkinson was the man who sat in one of those essentially 1970s chairs, crossed his legs, adjusted his clip board and then grilled the celebrities for all their worth. Parkinson had that unique delivery, that intimate understanding of the chat show rule book. He would hold his hand on his cheek, stare at Hollywood in the face and then listen attentively.

There were frequent moments when I often wondered whether he'd perhaps gone too far with the intensity of his questioning. But I think he brought the very best out of all of his guests because that was the way you did things as an interviewer. You gently chipped away at your guests defences, scraped away at all of those tender sensitivities, before digging into territory that perhaps they didn't want you to venture into.

There was the famous Parkinson interview with the legendary actor Robert Mitchum. During the whole interview, it became almost embarrassingly clear that Mitchum just didn't want to be part of the whole experience. The whole of the interview consisted of Mitchum, dreadfully long silences and tongue tied moments that seemed to go on forever. Mitchum was being almost spitefully unco-operative, awkward, monosyllabic and totally unreasonable. To this day, I'm not sure how Michael Parkinson ever survived this ordeal without feeling that his reputation had been destroyed overnight.

In the first couple of years, Parkinson, although an essential part of the Saturday night furniture, needed somebody to challenge his supremacy. I'd grown up with his tough interviewing style, that no-nonsense, uncompromising approach that most of us could readily recognise. But there had to be an alternative, another angle, something that came from somewhere else, somebody who gave the art of interviewing a radically different look and complexion.

Russell Harty, almost overnight, appeared on our weekend TV screens on London Weekend Television. Harty was hugely intelligent, a huge intellectual from a British university and splendidly articulate. Harty had an almost peerless command of the English language, Harty was wordy, grammatically correct, clearly pronouncing every vowel and consonant and treating his interviewers with the most enormous respect. At no point did Harty appear to be snobbish, patronising, rude or abrupt.

Harty, I felt, was never deliberately critical or tactless although there might have been one or two occasions when the truth had to be told. Harty would humorously flirt with his interviewees and, on one memorable moment, paid for that flirtation with a vengeance. And yet it seemed to the audience that Harty had done nothing to offend or upset.

Harty had invited onto his show a lady by the name of Grace Jones. Now Ms Jones had established herself as one of the world's most glamorous singers and fashion models. But what none of us could have expected was quite the most astounding displays of naked aggression, unnecessary violence and shameful behaviour.

Without provocation, Harty, now deep in discussion with the noble Sir Ralph Richardson, turned his back on Ms Jones. It was quite the most innocent of all acts and yet it was enough to bring out the darker and sinister side of Ms. Jones, promptly lashing out at Harty with her bag, all the while childishly slapping Harty on the shoulder with utter hatred and wild indignation. It was, I suppose, one of those historic, must see again moments in TV history and yet had I been Harty, I'm sure I'd have been absolutely petrified.

As the 1980s progressed, TV interviewers came and went. Des O'Connor had been one of Britain's most loved of all national treasures, a natural entertainer, performer, singer, comedian and general nice guy. To all intents and purposes, O'Connor would never have been an obvious choice for the role of TV interrogator.

And yet Des O' Connor, as if by magic, had become transformed into a natural chat show host with his own prime time slot. Throughout, O'Connor pinned down the chat show and monopolised the very best in the celebrity interviews. In keeping with his comic roots, he would be the one who cornered the market in laugh out loud encounters. At the end, he would throw his body about in some weird motion, heaving himself to one side before just collapsing in laughter. It would be safe to assume that 1970s pop culture had done more than enough to keep me both amused and well informed.

Part 19:
Motorway service stations, hotels, trains, boats, planes and much more.

When I was a young kid, motorway service stations were those strange and bizarre places that were always ever present and would in years to come multiply. It was a time in my life when nothing of any great moment and note ever seemed to happen and even the most insignificant buildings would somehow claim my interest.

When my dad took us out all on a Sunday afternoon, it was a journey laden with a sense of the surprise and the unexpected. It was normally the West End during the winter but with the arrival of summer, it was either Westcliff, Southend or strawberry picking in Upminster, Essex.

Now these trips to Upminster or Essex were invariably enjoyable and there was a real feeling of family togetherness. Along the Southend Road, there was a liberal sprinkling of both egg and potato farms where you could buy an indeterminate amount of eggs, potatoes and a whole variety of other food stuff.

But then my dad would drive us back home from our day in salubrious Southend, that healthy and outgoing seaside resort that became my parents' summer haven. Suddenly, my dad would pull over to the side of the Southend Road and take us into a restaurant that bore a resemblance to a motorway service station but never really looked like one.

Back in the 1970s, there were literally hundreds of Little Chefs by the side of all motorways and in a way, this eatery seemed to fulfil the same function. It served well cooked, hot meals, with all the trimmings. What you have to remember is that most restaurants during the 1970s still observed the Chicken in a Basket rule, whereby every menu seemed to contain the same chicken in a basket, a Black Forest Gateau and perhaps a glass of Rose wine just to wash down that gastronomic work of art. For art it most certainly was, the plate overflowing with everything the British palate could possibly want.

Then there were the English hotels with their quaint customs and enduring traditions, lovely old fashioned establishments that seemed to have been there for years and years. It can hardly be denied that everything about the English hotel has been carefully preserved and somehow accepted for what they are.

I can remember going to Margate and being vaguely aware of all these little clusters of bed and breakfasts somehow sloping down to the sea front. They always looked meticulously clean, small, well contained, spotless and respectable. There was an air of timeless gentility about these B and B's that reminded you of that golden Victorian age. An age when the English were a dominant force in the days of the Empire. And just for good measure, Margate had and still has as far as I know the most enchanting sweet shop, an old fashioned sweet shop served by staff with Victorian dress and Victorian charm.

Walk down the average road and you'll find an English breakfast hotel in all its finery. There are the immaculately washed curtains in the window, the smallest lamp with the prettiest lamp shade in the tiniest of lounges. But it was the interior of the hotel that made you feel glad to be alive.

As you walked into the reception area, you were confronted with what can only be described as a quintessentially English scene. On the desk or a rack are some of the greatest literature known to mankind. Neatly arranged are all the touristy leaflets and guides to the local town.

In those guides, you'll find everything you could possibly want to know about the local seaside town. There's information about anything else from village fetes, ancient castles, craft and pottery centres and wonderfully historic market towns. It's all very informative and revealing, essential reading material for those who like their hotels to be quaint.

There is something about an English bed and breakfast that illustrates perfectly what the English think about themselves. There's no fuss, commotion or any hint of anxiety. It's all very quiet, sleepy, refined and unhurried. You almost feel as though that none of these peaceful havens will ever change.

There are the re-assuring rituals: the bulging and groaning full English breakfasts, huge plates of sausages, eggs, bacon and hashed browns in no particular order. There are the cleanly cut and civilised families quietly sitting down to their breakfast, two racks of toasts on the table, cups and saucers of tea and coffee nestling snugly, ready to be used and consumed as and when appropriate.

And then there's that rather narrow and awkward staircase that took you up to your bedroom. You lug your suitcases laboriously up to your hotel bedrooms, stairs creaking and squeaking like some protesting campaigner. And yet your footsteps were soft, steady and deliberate as if the merest noise would wake up the whole of Blackpool, Southend, Brighton or Bournemouth.

Downstairs in the tiniest lounges are a small selection of daily newspapers, both local and national, the smallest of coffee tables, the thickest of carpets and perhaps the family cat or dog just to make you feel right at home. There is a military precision to everything about the hotel, from the receptionists politely presenting you with your bedroom key, the hushed tranquillity and a hardly noticeable bookcase with cheap paperbacks.

But there was this unwritten agreement whereby the hotel owner will insist, that wherever you go for your evening meal, you have to be back by 10 or 11 in the evening. The reason given is that they have to lock up and go to bed. So the fact remains that unless you've got a key to the hotel, you would have to find alternative accommodation.

Now the fact is that I don't think my family would have been too pleased if we'd stayed out to the midnight hour because if we did, we'd have to sleep on the beach. It all seems a long time ago but those were the days when even English hotels had a natural civility, a longing to be normal and just intent on killing with you kindness.

I'll never forget those early wake-up calls in our hotel. Suddenly, there was a gentle tap on the door, a voice from the land of Crossroads and the whole breakfast paraphernalia. A quietly spoken member of staff would place the tray of cups, saucers and the pot of tea ever so silently on our bedside tables. And then there were the two small cubes of Tate and Lyle sugar, snugly cosy on the edge of the saucer, excited and ready for the day.

These were my Tate and Lyle childhood days, sweetly honeyed, idyllically and quite undoubtedly the best of all years. I was growing, developing, discovering and expanding my knowledge of the world before reaching that train platform known as teenage maturity. I was curious but slightly bewildered, poised to embark on a journey that never quite reached its destination at first but then jumped onto another steam locomotive. Finally, I would pull into another station, grateful that things would eventually turn out for the best.

But then I looked back to my childhood and thought of all those metaphorical hopes and dreams in my life. How would my life take shape and blossom? Maybe it would be that heather or gorse covered hillside of a Scottish glen, or the flowers and plants around us. Perhaps it would be the happy hibiscus flower, the euphoric eucalyptus climbing the wall of some Far Eastern garden. What about the jolly jacaranda, all very perky and spritely on a summer's day or the bubbly, buoyant bougainvillea just happy to be alive.

I remain convinced that my life would still move ahead, surging into the front, commanding a place in the sun, laying back in my deckchair and finding that nothing would ever disturb the idyll. And then I would bathe in all of that splendid imagery quite without any prompting.

I would eat that sumptuous dinner on the terrace of a Spanish country house, rocking back and forth in my wicker chair in splendid isolation, casually leafing through Proust for the 20th time or sipping a languid cocktail or two while parakeets twittered sweetly. And then the most divine intervention of a guitar, drifting but somehow very decorous in the silent breeze.

Or perhaps I'd find myself on that romantic yacht in some wide, expansive sea, gazing at those far off mountains, sea gulls wheeling and swooping for joy, hundreds of birds darting and floating in the whispering breeze. The moments are precious, indelibly printed on my mind.

There I would find myself in a Somerset Maugham short story, striding through some dense Borneo rain forest, sipping a tequila sunrise, mixing sociably with the Malayan colonials, flicking away the mosquitoes, staring up at the heavy skies and then waiting for the soaking monsoons to pass. These would be the most delightful sensations rather than a minor inconvenience.

Maybe it would be that beautifully hot and dusty summer's afternoon on an Indian cricket pitch where the sun always set on the Empire. On a dustbowl of a pitch the two captains, complete in green caps and just a hint of a bandana, would meet in the middle, toss a coin and then engage in that unique summer pursuit.

Far away would be those shimmering pavilions in the mid-day heat, Noel

Coward singing the praises of the mid-day sun with perfect understatement. Cricket was that magical piece of summer symbolism. There was the gentle crack of ball against willow bat, varnished and forever shining. The gossiping pigeons would gather at cover point for an afternoon conference and the fielder down at the third man would prowl the boundary with an almost leisurely air.

And then we would all retire to that elusive pavilion where tea and cucumber sandwiches would be served with traditional grace. The punkah fans on the ceiling would whirl around freely and very subtly at times, thick cigar smoke samba dancing in the breeze, curling and twisting into the air with an almost reckless abandon,

I would think it highly likely that that marvellous game of cricket would peter out into an honourable draw and all appetites would be amply satisfied. I would stare out into the distance, hands in my safari jacket pocket and binoculars loosely hung around my neck. I would then entertain some of the civic dignitaries with tales of Boycott and Compton in their pomp, Sobers simply lofting his sixes to all four points of the compass, Bradman conquering the world, towering and dignified cricketers with a simple aim; to take cricket onto another planet, decorate and embellish the game as if it were some delicious cream cake.

Or maybe my life reminded you of an FA Cup Final, a day of riotous celebration, huge colourful club rosettes on our shirts and coats, flags and banners with jokey messages, Wembley Stadium just immovable and indestructible. In those long gone days, we had the Twin Towers now sadly departed and much mourned and yet during my 1960s childhood, absolutely essential to the whole plot of the day.

In an imaginary world, I'd always wanted to be at that FA Cup Final, that day, singing along Wembley Way, joking with the lads and girls, sharing their humour, dancing their dances. I wanted everything that they had: confidence, attachment, loyalty to the cause, a sense of being part of something, connected, sympathetic, receptive and ultimately cheering for my team.

When the fans started swaying from side to side and holding their scarves in the air, I felt as if that should have been me. I was looking for recognition and approval in the fans' world. I needed to feel part of that collective unit. There was a sense of brother and sisterhood that I perhaps envied. Wembley on Cup Final day was a tight knit neighbourhood, a communal day where all the fans seemed to share a common bond and similar interests. And all I wanted was to be there with them.

Who cared? You may have thought me selfish and self-indulgent but I longed to be at Wembley Stadium because that was the day when the whole of the footballing community came out for that golden day in May. There was the fresh, beautifully cut and well-manicured Wembley grass, the rousing brass bands before the game, the players on the pitch in their immaculate suits, programmes in their hands, carefully surveying their land as if it were their personal garden.

I would have loved to have been an impartial observer of every Cup Final regardless of the teams. Cup Finals you see were magical and mystical and that's how I would have liked my life to be. To be full of surprises, atmospheric, eventful and gloriously momentous. And yet, as a shy teenager, I still felt an outsider, held back and burdened by my own insecurities, excluded from the party.

I still felt that I could join in with that wonderful pre Cup Final song, Abide With Me. In fact, I wanted to be up there on that big platform, the rostrum from which that gentleman bellowed out that lovely old song. In fact, I'd have been tempted to take that baton and conduct the fans in Abide With Me. I have to admit that I would have given anything to be the conductor of an orchestra, to lead the way, to be in the forefront of events rather than feeling as though I'd been left behind.

And so the players would emerge from the tunnel just before the kick-off. Both teams would march out into the late spring sunshine, the crowd would be in full and raucous voice and there I would be, milking the applause and accepting the adulation. Wembley would be my opportunity to be the leader of the pack, finally noticed and possibly judged. But I wanted to be the driving force behind the whole operation, the creator and producer of the whole day, the whole reason for Cup Final day. I would be the inventor, innovator, the instigator, the man who made it all possible. Call me vain but hey after all those years and years of loneliness and introspection, it was about time that Wembley and Cup Final day were the metaphor for my life.

But if I couldn't have Wembley as my imaginary life, then I'd happily settle for Brazil. Brazil had colour, carnival, imagery, a life force of its own, vim and vitality. It had vivid patterns, swirling shapes, music and the samba. It stayed up all night, experienced life in its all glory and then almost grudgingly went to sleep. Brazil was the land of dreams, the land of absolute fantasy, the country who gave us beautiful football and, above all, Copacabana beach.

That was the way I believed life should have been. There was the Copacabana with its hundreds of holidaymakers, nut brown boys playing beach football or volleyball, loose limbed, elastic, stretching out for the ball, trapping the ball with their chest and knee before balancing it on their head while all the time keeping the ball up in the air with thrilling ease.

That was me, flexible and athletic in my ball possession, somersaulting with the ball and toying with the ball rather like that lovable seal in the zoo. I'll admit it I, too, wanted to be an exhibitionist revelling in the game of football as it should be played. Brazil was the land of inviting opportunities, breath taking sights, glorious heat and Sugar Loaf Mountain lapping up the warmth in the summer sunshine.

Brazil was exotic, fascinating, religious, warm hearted and benevolent. All of the boys on the beach kindly asked you to play football because that's the kind of nation it is. Brazil was everything you'd hoped and imagined it would be because there was something very intriguing and mysterious about it, something deeply embedded in its culture. You had to find out more and I'd always believed that Brazil would be the way I'd have lived life as a kid growing up in Ilford. I'd play football all day on the Copacabana, and hold the World Cup aloft in the Maracana stadium. A truly defining moment

Or maybe I'd imagined life would be similar to some Caribbean island where the sun not only shone but touched my soul in a way that no other country could possibly have touched. The Caribbean, in my mind's eye, was a heavenly paradise, so blissfully perfect and idyllic that you could hardly have believed that any other country could match it.

The Caribbean had palm trees on all its islands, hundreds of palm trees impeccably behaved and gently waving at its visitors with a hospitable nod. There was Jamaica, Barbados, Bahamas, the Dominican Republic, all resplendent with their gorgeous beaches, acres of sand and much, much more.

There were the banana plantations with their fruitful harvest, the sheer prodigious volume of coconuts and coconut water. But above all, there was Caribbean rum, harmlessly inoffensive alcohol and starry, tropical nights that ended with back breaking limbo. For hour upon hour, I would join in with quite the most magnificent limbo, bending my back rather awkwardly before squeezing my body under the bar. But this was all in my imagination. And then the music Caribbean style. Hour upon hour of soulful ska and reggae, Bob Marley in perfect harmony with his many friends. And then you'd see the triumphant carnivals with its whistles, the clashing, clattering oil drums, utterly musical and sweet.

And so I move to the very last and concluding chapters. Once again, I find myself back at the home I was brought up in. I'm back at Cranley Road, Ilford, standing outside the house with its crazy paved walls, that cute little dog carved in stone and the solid black tiles, capable of withstanding anything that was thrown at it. I can see the black painted gate, slightly rusty and withered but nonetheless a fundamental part of what made our family home a home from home.

And then there were the pavements in Cranley Road, for the most part smooth and regular but when you weren't looking they would deliberately catch you out. Quite unexpectedly, you would trip up on one of the paving stones and then tell yourself off, chastise yourself for your own carelessness, your accident-prone nature, your sheer negligence and foolhardiness.

Because those pavements were cracked, broken and jutting, I wondered whether they were privately chuckling at my temporary air of vulnerability. It was never ineptitude but occasionally I used to trip up on one of those paving stones and was never given an adequate explanation.

Cranley Road was never at the heart of the manufacturing industry but it still had its well to do businessmen, its industrious shopkeepers and conscientious office workers, people cut from the finest cloth, honest, hardworking, people with a purpose and strength of character. They were Ilford's newsagents, menswear shops, boutiques, the fruit and vegetable stalls, permanently cheerful and humorous. Ilford had grocers, department stores, hustle, bustle, harum scarum, busy and talkative.

There was that charming old gentleman who stood on his soapbox every Saturday afternoon. He was a larger than life man with the loudest of voices, a thick grey beard and an admirable philosophy on life. He was the voice of Ilford on a Saturday afternoon, booming, clearly heard and just very visible.

Standing on his orange crate in the centre of Ilford High Road, he would suddenly throw his arms about, gesturing, gesticulating, posturing and pontificating. His sole mission in life, it seemed, was to sell as many Bibles as he could. Next to him were huge piles of the Bible and then the Saturday afternoon sermon, a gentleman convinced that the Messiah would come one day. It was quite the most remarkable sight I'd ever seen.

As the afternoon progressed, I began to wonder whether this constant stream of religious wisdom would ever stop. To be honest, it didn't seem to matter as such because here was a man who believed that everything he was saying carried a very real sense of authenticity, the complete truth and nothing but the truth. You could say he was the Bible Man, the man of Genesis, Leviticus and Deuteronomy.

But the early days and those awkward teenage moments accompanied me all the way to the age of 20. There were those warm and blissful days at Valentines Park Lido when every family in Ilford flooded through the turnstiles. Inside the Lido, there were those youthful yelps, repeated screams and that childhood zest for life.

Throughout the day, all you could see were those remarkably fit lifeguards, sitting very comfortably on the rails next to the pool, surveying their Empire in the most responsible fashion. Now from what I can gather, most of them were impeccably well-qualified and always available should something have gone terribly wrong.

Hour after hour, they would perch themselves onto the blue railings with a whistle around their neck, every so often twiddling it around their finger with an almost casual air of indifference. But it was the scene inside the Lido that held me rapt with attention.

There were acres and acres of blankets, towels, wonderfully enthusiastic children, families with packed lunches, pushchairs by what seemed to be the hundred and humanity at its most vocal. This was that summer of 1976, the heatwave that started in April and didn't leave us until the August Bank Holiday.

Inside the Lido there was the fountain, forever gushing and overflowing, almost hypnotic at times and very striking. Next to the fountain, forever eager and exuberant, was the café with its snaking queue for ice-creams, lollies, Coca Colas and those juicily sweet blocks of flavoured ice called Jubblies.

What immediately struck was the slide and diving board inside the pool. Now the slide and diving board were almost incessantly used by excited kids. Every so often, you would see daring youngsters throwing themselves off the board, somersaulting in mid-air with all the aplomb of a Tom Daley. But both the diving board and slide were extremely dangerous and perhaps nobody really gave it another thought. Eventually though, the board and slide were taken down for ever.

But still the families turned up with the most re-assuring regularity, kids chasing each other around the pool loudly and volubly, almost beside themselves with untrammelled joy. It was somehow inevitable though that the 1970s would burn itself out, collapse with exhaustion, slump over the finishing line and then pretend that it just couldn't cope with the sheer energy and intensity of it all.

Maybe the 1970s in Ilford was rather like any Essex suburb, maybe Ilford had seen so much and experienced so much that it was just blasé, seen it all and done it all. Maybe Ilford was much like any suburb, market town, fishing harbour, village or coastal seaside resort. Perhaps Ilford conducted itself in much the way that its neighbours Redbridge, Wanstead, Gants Hill or Barkingside did.

Like Ilford, Redbridge, Wanstead, Gants Hill and Barkingside could also boast its commendable landmarks. Redbridge had its Red House pub, Wanstead had its villagey, rural air and Gants Hill had its roundabout. None of these Essex suburbs were in any way captivating or arresting but they must have had the most attractive character. They were hard working, respectable suburbs just getting on with the business of living.

I always had the impression that all of the entire borough of Redbridge just wanted to be modest, humble and unassuming. It simply hankered after the quiet life, never bothering anybody and just pursued a life of utter simplicity and commercial stability. The shops that had always been there just looked for an easy going prosperity and moderate profit margins.

I can remember being taken to Clarks shoe shop off the Ilford High Road by my mum. It must have been during the school summer holidays and I can remember being struck at the way that nobody ever panicked or indeed looked flustered. Every July, my mum and I would make our yearly appointment in Clarks. Here, I would place my feet on that measuring device and find out whether I needed a size 8,9,10 or 11. I think they must have used a tape measure but for the life of me there didn't seem to be any logic to the whole exercise.

When my social life began to take off, I suddenly became aware of the pub. Rather like any other place in Ilford and Gants Hill, there seemed to be loads of pubs. In fact, Brentford football club has got a pub situated on every corner of the ground. These drinking hostelries have been very much part of the British fabric for as long as time itself.

Some pubs of course are medieval looking, some very small and claustrophobic with little room to hold a pint let alone do anything else. Some are community pubs with beer gardens outside and benches to sit down on. And then again, there are the modern wine bars which look like pubs but somehow feel different. Essentially, they are pubs but now of course they serve good, wholesome food and are much more family oriented.

Anyway, the fact was that I'd suddenly discovered the pub, the boozer, the watering hole. I'd developed a partiality for alcohol, crisps and refreshments. In years gone by, I couldn't have dreamt that this was the kind of place I could walk into in all innocence without feeling like some lost sheep.

Opposite Gants Hill station, there is the Valentine pub which has always been there and had been for quite a number of centuries I suspect. It was just that I hadn't really noticed and this was a reminder to me that drinking lager in moderation was acceptable, that meeting friends for an evening chat was perfectly natural and nobody would question my motives. In a way, this represented the astonishing progress I'd made since childhood. Now I was participating in the kind of activities that, had I been totally honest, I wouldn't have thought about 15-20 years earlier.

Towards the end of the 1980s, I'd become friendly with a guy who'd I met at Barkingside Youth Club when I first started going there. He suggested that we meet up for a drink in the Valentine and just spend a pleasant evening, joking, chatting and observing all human life.

At this point in my life, I didn't really know a great deal about pubs and the whole environment around them. I knew they were meant to be places of relaxation after work but didn't know that either you had to buy a round of drinks or your friends did. Suffice it to say, I was ever slightly baffled by this rather weird ritual. It was some bizarre rigmarole that didn't seem to make any sense.

Anyway, throughout the evening, I found that my friend had a strong liking for either Guinness or lager. Suddenly, he would chuckle heartily at what must have been the most inoffensive joke or comment I'd make. To my utter astonishment, I'd made another human being laugh or appreciate who I was. Now there was full acceptance of the adult I'd always hoped to be, a smile on the face on the friend I never thought I'd make.

So this was my breakthrough moment. The Valentine pub circa 1987 was my entrance to the big, wide world. Here I was surrounded by other families, men and women from all backgrounds enjoying a night out among people they knew. They sat around tables, animatedly chattering away, roaring out with laughter when the mood took them and playing all manner of both verbal games. I occasionally looked around me subconsciously taking it all in and just wondering why I hadn't done this so much earlier.

Once inside the Valentine pub, there was so much to see: the body language, the men standing by the bar, the whole movement and dynamic of the pub, the families sitting at the table in private groups, the orderly queue of people waiting to be served. It was very much a learning curve and one I took to gradually but eagerly. And then the Valentine exploded into action.

At roughly nine in the evening, there would be music, a live band, the stage was set and the Valentine would become this mini rock concert venue. The speakers would be hauled onto the stage, microphones manoeuvred into place, guitars tuned to a perfect pitch, organ sound checked and the Valentine was somehow reformed and transformed. Whereas before there had been the low babble of conversation, now there was pounding rock music.

From that moment onwards, all you could hear were loud guitars and even louder drums, relentlessly shaking the floor, cracking the ceiling and bursting at the seams. It was noisy, overwhelming and, to some of the residents, perhaps too much. If an order for noise pollution had been issued, then none of us would have been surprised but hey, this was our night of the week and let's hear it for the Led Zeppelin look alike band. It was all very harmless and just the way it had always been perhaps.

The other pub which I used to drink in was the Kings Head in Chigwell.

Now the Kings Head was quite literally a medieval pub and once you saw the pub, it was easy to see why. As you walked into the Kings Head, all you could see was a complete throwback to both another distant century and another age.

Outside were these wonderful timber beams criss-crossing the front of the pub. Now here was a pub to reckon with. It was a delightful pub that somehow reminded you of King Arthur and The Knights of the Round Table, court jesters dancing on tables, flagons of beer and mead, so called peasants begging for a crumb of bread. But inside, the pub there would be low timber beams that you had to bend down to. The Kings Head was richly medieval, a pub with a very definite character and warmth.

All pubs, of course, cling on almost loyally to the age old traditions that have sustained them through all of those unstable times when life must have been extremely hard. Pubs still have their games of dominoes, a game consisting of a whole box load of black and white dots in the shape of counters, shove ha'penny, a game of pennies, skill and accuracy and one that required endless concentration. Dominoes and shove ha'penny are still played on the pub tables of Britain and for those who take part in these games, it is quite the most absorbing of all sights.

In Gants Hill itself, there is the King George 5th in the Cranbrook Road. I have to admit that this is one pub which I haven't had personal experience of. It looks much the same as all the rest of the pubs in the area and I seem to remember seeing the chirpy Bobby George, one of Britain's finest darts players, in the King George.

Darts was the ultimate pub game, a game that used to be played by gentlemen with pints of Guinness in their hands and a crafty fag for good measure. I've never been able to get my head around the game of darts and maybe I never will. Of course it's simple and uncomplicated but it just seems to lack any kind of finesse. There's nothing, in my eyes, that looks remotely skilful nor could it be said that appeals to any of my senses.

Now I know my darts enthusiasts may shoot me down in flames and attack my ignorance but darts has nothing to recommend it aesthetically. There is no grace, no beauty and no sensuality about the game. There is no art or artistry about it, nor does make it feel as though you've experienced something that is deeply profound.

This is just my opinion but when the likes of Eric Bristow pick up those three tungsten arrows, move forward to the oche and stare intently at a dart board, I have to tell you that there is something in me that doesn't respond or react. Then Bristow clenches the darts in between his fingers, bites his lips nervously before throwing the arrows at his target.

I have to tell you that when I saw Bobby George playing darts, all of the stereotypes came flooding into the mind. There were the abundant supply of beers, the fags, the crisps, the silk shirts worn by the darts players and the working class Britishness of it all.

After the shots had been released, most of the darts players, I suspect, would pick up their Sun newspapers, wolf down the last of the cheese and onion crisps or crack the dirtiest joke. All very British and patriotically so.

Next to the darts board would be, and still is, the small black board with all of the latest scores affectionately chalked on to the player's scores. I suspect that the King George is not unlike most of our great British pubs in as much that it is democratic, completely without any discrimination, always willing to let you into its premises in the most amicable of fashions.

On the subject of Gants Hill, may I take you back to the library in the Cranbrook Road. Now I know nothing about architecture or anything relating to architecture but Gants Hill library had the most distinctive entrance of any library in the country. Whereas Ilford library could be reached via the town hall, Gants Hill had something that marked it out for attention.

As you walked up to the front doors of Gants Hill library, there were two truly superlative white columns. Nothing out of the ordinary you might have thought but columns were something you'd find in churches or stately homes. But there they were decorating the library doorway or perhaps just an unexpected adornment.

To this day, those columns remain where they've always been, white, solid and unyielding and trustworthy. Admittedly, they look somewhat worse for wear now but for as long as I can remember, they've always been there. I wonder how they must have felt when Geoff Hurst raced away to score that final winning goal in the 1966 World Cup Final. Perhaps they raised a toast and celebrated with a bottle of plonk. It's the fondest of thoughts.

And so I wind my happy way to those final paragraphs of my childhood and my story so far. From the quiet, suburban serenity of Gants Hill with its columned library, its magnificent car park, the King George 5th pub, the very compact sports shop next to the pub and all that associated itself with my childhood, this was my journey.

I've painted a picture of this humble, grateful, modest, quiet and thoughtful child. I've given my very personal observations because now seemed the opportune time to tell you that my childhood was great, memorable and brilliant. It was the childhood of the 1960s when the society I'd grown up in had no secrets, no deceits, no inhibitions and very few hang ups.

I think and hope I've succeeded in telling you how nice, amiable and gentle we all were. I hope I've conveyed to you all of the childhood dreams which became fruitful ambitions: the teenage fears and anxieties that simply melted away, the moments and events that shaped and moulded me, the cares and troubles that became ecstasy and laughter, the insecurities of those very early years that became certainties and finalities.

When I look back on my life, a life of pleasure, happiness, achievement and private rejoicing, I can now live with myself, recognise that the bad times were bad but not so bad as I thought as they were going to be. I can see now through that darkness, greyness and despair as merely a temporary period of my life.

I can now reflect on how I coped with the disappointments and rationalise all of those setbacks and drawbacks that seemed beyond resolution. I can now begin to understand much more about the person I was as a child rather than dwell on the teenager I became.

After all, these were my teenage difficulties, traumas, trials and tribulations and maybe they were stepping stones, a preparation for better times, a gentle introduction as to what was to follow in later years.

There's a part of me that feels as if I've found a definitive solution to why I behaved in the way that I did as a teenager, a sense perhaps that there was a reason for that painful immaturity, that reluctance to join the rest of my generation, sharing their life. It would be true that along the way, this has been the most therapeutic journey, a journey that showed me the way, guiding, encouraging, coaxing and cajoling me, smoothing the rough edges and shepherding me into the path of glory, splendour and contentment.

It was a journey that was undeniably bumpy, crashing into and then colliding with all the congested traffic of my teenage years. It was a journey that might have ended up in some disastrous back alley, darkened doorway or anonymous street corner. How I must have yearned for things to go right, how I must have searched relentlessly for a way out of my teenage crisis, how I must have struggled and toiled to find that majestic sunset, that ocean liner sailing gloriously over the horizon.

In many ways this, I feel sure, is undoubtedly a happy ever after story. It was a story where all the early obstacles in life were successfully conquered, all of those school years of anguish and turmoil that were part of the growing up process and maybe just maybe a story of complete triumph over adversity.

But the background figures of my life will always be there, my wonderful late dad, the deep and enduring love for him, my mum and brother who were always there for me. Of course there were arguments and disagreements but perhaps they were common to all families. Perhaps everything that happens to us in life is meant for a purpose and fated to happen.

Perhaps my childhood followed a similar route to that of my friend's generation. Or simply they managed their problems in a way that I couldn't. I try to make sense of my teenage life and find that there is some momentous event that shapes us without us even knowing.

And here I stand at the entrance of some mythical Yellow Brick Road where everything blossoms into all the colours of the sun. Admittedly, there is no Tin Man or any of his other acquaintances but this is the place where I want to be. This is the point at which I want to run into the garden, smell the roses, skip through the corn fields, touch the tips of the tulips and embrace the sun flowers.

This is not wishful thinking or some expensive, big budget Hollywood movie where fantasy comes face to face with illusion and everything is just imagined. There is no grand plan or scheme to any of our lives, nothing that is destined to happen or pre-ordained about it. I'd like to think of my life as one gigantic foundation stone with all of the supporting pillars that held everything together and remained a constant. Occasionally, there were dusty cracks in those pillars that may just have threatened to give way and fade into irremediable dust.

But I remained defiantly strong, obstinately determined, and firmly confident in the knowledge that everything would fit and join up. Of course, there were those islands of pessimism, fields of negativity, those huge strips of land where nothing ever happened and uncertainty reigns. And yet there are redeeming lights at the end of tunnel and those were the lights which drove me forward and salvaged the diamonds from the debris.

And so I bid farewell to those balmy, hazy, lazy days of summer, winter, spring, autumn when childhood was something we quite possibly took for granted. We had no idea what was in store, we were never far sighted, visionary or indeed capable of seeing into the future.

I look back to those far off days of Sunday trips to Westcliff with my parents, being chased by my grand-ma around my parents' garden because I'd just trampled all over my mum's apple tree and simply accepting these memories for what they were. They were part of the whole growing up process, my development as a young boy into a teenager.

There can be no bitterness or regret for what happened during my teenage years because that's what happened to me. I can't pretend that it was easy because it wasn't. But as I look back, I can now put my life into a very sober perspective, pulling back the camera lens and viewing my present with sensible, realistic eyes.

It's true to say that none of us can ever imagine what might happen to us in any given time frame. We're all endowed with different personalities and the things that take place in our life are often self-fulfilling prophecies. I'm inclined to think that without being aware of it at the time, most of us have got a pretty good idea that fate is bound to intervene. In other words, quite literally what will be will be.

Part 20:
My day at Speakers Corner.

I have to be honest with you. My day at Speakers Corner was quite the most satisfying day you can have with a crazy book in your hand. Some people get their kicks out of bungee jumping or crossword puzzles but on one glorious Sunday afternoon, yours truly delivered the most stunning performance of his life.

For nigh on three hours, I pontificated endlessly on the joys of life, nature and how my splendidly unique book would leave you spellbound.

Now for those who have ever been part of this unique Sunday institution, Speakers Corner is one of the most remarkable tourist attractions in London. It remains part of our great British heritage and has been one of the most permanent landmarks since way back when.

But for the first time in my life, I decided to throw caution to the wind, unashamedly rattling on for three hours on British eccentricity and Victorian life. I kid you not, it was the most bizarre experience I've ever had and it has to be said, highly enjoyable.

At roughly 1.45, I arrived at the entrance to Hyde Park Corner, complete with nothing but an unrehearsed script and no idea of what to say. After a roughly half an hour walk to Speakers Corner, I settled on a spot where I knew I could be seen and heard.

I then proceeded to launch into the greatest three hour speech ever heard. I must have gone through every gesture and mannerism you could think of. How I managed not to break into hysterical laughter is beyond me.

There was the theatrical arm waving, references to Victorian morality and decency, the valiant attempts at humour and, above all, the incessant talking. But this was a perfect opportunity to open up and express my innermost feelings.

I've never been the outgoing or extrovert type but somehow I'd found my own space, a platform for the controversial and articulate.

Here, I was in the middle of one of London's most famous and democratic of stages. This was the spot where freedom of speech found its most natural voice, the place where every frustrated after dinner speaker could finally make their presence felt.

Without any inhibitions, I embarked on the kind of verbal journey that must have come as a complete shock to my system. I had no idea of just how good it felt to be so out of character. I'd suddenly become one of Speakers Corner finest, dare I say it, actors. I was expansive, flamboyant, bristling with wit and humour.

They say that the British are notoriously repressed and reserved, renowned for their stiff upper lip. But for me, this Sunday afternoon was an almost therapeutic experience. It was almost as if somebody had released a valve, flicked a switch or just given me a ticket to Disneyland.

Suddenly, I could be somebody I could only have dreamt. This was a completely different Joe Morris, a positive, confident and vibrant Joe Morris. I'll admit it, I did feel liberated and so utterly carefree, rather like the kid in the toy shop who suddenly finds their favourite train set.

With my wonderfully loving and supportive family behind me, I was at peace with the world. Life for me is beautiful, cherishable and so utterly sweet. I'd suddenly found a torrent of words and language that simply electrified and galvanised me.

Before I knew it, I was sermonising, joking and jesting with the best of them. On either side of me, there were the traditional representatives from the world of religion and politics. They would holler into their microphones, belt out their rhetoric and then, unsuccessfully preach to the converted.

It is, I believe, the most surreal and extraordinary way of spending a Sunday afternoon in late Spring. Who could possibly have asked for any more out of life? The trees were completely green, the birds were merrily chirping away and nature was just ecstatically happy. It was rather like being serenaded by a choir.

The point is that talking to the masses on a Sunday afternoon at Speakers Corner was everything I thought it would be. I too, could feel like the ring master in a circus, the Prime Minister in charge of a country, the leader of the pack. This was no ego trip by any means but I did feel as though I'd climbed the highest mountain.

Nobody will ever give me the Pulitzer Prize, the Nobel Peace prize for literature but this was a towering achievement. I was a bon vivant, outstanding raconteur, the most dapper of dressers. Victorian Madness Lyrics was the culmination of years of hard literary graft, a festival of words and, its own unique way, peerlessly poetic. I should know because it was the book I wrote.

Yes, I can honestly say that this was indeed the greatest contribution to world literature since Dickens was knee high to a grasshopper and reading the Pall Mall Gazette. I'm not one to boast but Victorian Madness Lyrics will go down in history as one of the most spellbinding works of art.

I must have been half way through my stirring narrative when I was suddenly joined by my tourist friend. Now I have to extend my heartfelt gratitude to this very learned gentleman. I'm not sure why but I'm sure he identified with me. He sidled up to me and started quoting Shakespearean lines and witty verse.

Between the great outbursts of sheer lyricism, I toiled and sweated for Queen and country. After another eruption of lunacy and silliness, I asked in all seriousness whether my new friend could get me a cup of tea, anything to soothe my fevered brow.

A couple of minutes later, my new acquaintance returned with a welcome bottle of water. Never have I been so grateful for a drink. The sheer exhaustion on my face told its own story. Now I know how market traders must feel after a day of shouting 'Apples, Pears, Oranges, half a pound for a quid'.

I think I must have spoken on more or less every subject I could think of. Before you could say anything contentious, yours truly launched into the most bewildering literary references. I quoted Chaucer, Dickens, Hardy and anything else that remotely resembled an intellectual comment.

So I continued, almost ceaselessly it seemed, only pausing for breath when the cameras started clicking. Oh yes, there were the enraptured crowds, smiling, sympathising, totally confused. I had to explain to them that I was on a personal crusade, a mission to change. Maybe I'm just a revolutionary seeking to upset the Establishment or the Government.

You see Victorian Madness Lyrics was my brainchild, a labour of love verbal exuberance on the grandest scale. I expounded on everything and everybody. This was my stage, rather like one of those Roman emperors in the Coliseum. Friends, Romans and countrymen I give you Victorian Madness Lyrics, a glorious homage to the finest ska band of all time.

At 4.30, with the evening upon us, it suddenly occurred to me that my message had been conveyed. My pronouncement had been delivered. There was nothing else to say on this literary wonder of the world, this sterling contribution to English literature. Hyde Park I thank you.

Part 21:
Sport in my life- My memories of Tennis

It hardly seems possible but Wimbledon fortnight is with us again in a couple of weeks' time. Summertime sport in England was always genteel and refined, rather like its summer cousin, cricket.

Of course, when the umpires take their chair and the players begin to swing their rackets, most of us will be enthralled. Tennis at Wimbledon is one of those endearing traditions that never loses its appeal. Year after year, they converge on SW19 as if Wimbledon were the most popular rock concert venue in London.

This is the time of year when we take up full time residence of our local park courts. We flourish our forehand winners, put heart and soul into our serves and then sit down to watch a Rafa Nadal art exhibition.

Rafa Nadal and Roger Federer and that genius called Djokovic have consistently demonstrated the game in its finest colours. In recent years, the game of tennis has rarely known such a rich canvas. One of these days, they may have to put down their paint brushes and some of us will simply acknowledge sporting excellence.

Year after year, the seething Wimbledon crowds turn up at SW19 with that marvellous sense of almost inflated expectation. Finally, our Andy Murray presented us with our first Wimbledon men's singles champion since the days of Flappers and the Charleston.

Of course we had every right to expect that one day, surely one day one of our British players will do the business. I mean how hard is it to win the famous tennis tournament? All you have to do is to turn up on Centre Court, negotiate the first week, and then toil your way through at least 20 five set thrillers. Not much to ask surely. Or so you would have thought.

But in Britain, we do things the hard way and when it comes to Wimbledon, there always seemed to be insurmountable obstacles. Throughout we've seen them all. They look the part and, bless their cotton socks, they do make a determined effort. Until Andy Murray that is.

Sadly though, gallantry very rarely wins sports trophies and coming second is rather like winning the booby prize in a raffle. British tennis players have come and gone rather like passing ships in the night and some of us have now lost count.

Back in the early 1970s, there was Roger Taylor, that smart and very personable Yorkshireman, a man of guts and gung-ho spirit. Taylor, of course, like his predecessors, knew exactly what the British public were hoping for. But Taylor, for all his charm and approachability, just couldn't find that five star performance when it mattered. We bowed our head and shuffled dejectedly away into the distance. Perhaps next year hey!

We did keep trying and were never deterred because the Brits never give up. Taylor kept coming back to South West London but all he seemed to get was a punnet of strawberries. Still you had to admire his persistence and sheer will to win.

Then of course there was a lion hearted Brit who looked as though he'd stepped out of a Dan Dare comic. His name was Buster Mottram, a bullish bruiser of a player full of fire and aggression. Mottram, we thought, would be the answer to our prayers.

But Mottram was rather like the sparkler in a firework box. He fizzed and flickered but then simply petered out. This is not to say that Mottram was just another poor spirited British tennis player who simply tried their best. It's just that when it came to the decisive crunch, they simply lacked that vital cutting edge.

The 1980s represented another period of failure and mediocrity. True they did turn up for that Wimbledon party but none ever seriously threatened the big boys.

There were the Lloyd brothers, John and David. Now John and David Lloyd are extremely compatible tennis players. They remain two of the best ambassadors to the sport of all time. Perhaps somebody ought to give them a carriage clock as a reward for their services.

I seem to remember that both the Lloyd brothers were always well-behaved and good to their mother. They were never troublesome and disruptive. They would never dream of swearing at umpires and when the crowd became ever so slightly impatient, they would just get on with it and smile for the camera.

Then there was that unforgettable British tennis player who almost cracked the Wimbledon code. In fact, he was so close to winning it that some of us genuinely believed that he had. Perhaps we weren't watching and it was just a hallucination.

Even so, Tim Henman seemed to have everything the British public had long yearned. He had touch, technique and the softest of tennis hands. Henman was the nicest, kindest and gentlest of all sportsman. He would casually saunter around Wimbledon, politely signing autographs and winking cheekily at the crowds. It was at this point however that Henman forgot his lines.

Somebody should have told him that there was an important tennis tournament to be won. Henman should have been told quite firmly that no British men's singles player had ever won Wimbledon for over 70 years and it was about time that they did.

But we were very tolerant and understanding as a nation. We knew that no British player throughout that period looked remotely like a potential winner. So Henman was told to pull up his socks and give it everything.

Sadly though, Henman was all effort, whole hearted exertion and British tenacity. True, Henman did get to a Wimbledon semi-final and he did take Goran Ivanisevic to five glorious sets. But he never quite reached the finishing line and you can only imagine that Henman was never fated to win Wimbledon.

Maybe it had something to do with Henman's background. Yes, he did come from Oxfordshire and he did mind his Ps and Qs. He did sit up at the dinner table, and always said thank you. Some would have you believe that this was his downfall.

Henman was, quite possibly, too polite and proper, maybe even meek and submissive. The snotty critics told us that Henman lacked fire in his belly. Others simply assumed that he came from a middle class background and was just very self-conscious. Tim was, to all outward appearances, too reserved and repressed. The stiff upper lip, they said, would never win Wimbledon. Our Tim had to be more of a fighter, a devil on the court. But Tim did strive and sweat for every point and set, a man who did his utmost for his country.

And so we move onto the next great British pretender to the Wimbledon throne. Here is a man who looked the genuine article, the man who was convinced that one day, he will become the greatest Brit ever to win the men's singles at Wimbledon.

Andy Murray was one of the notable survivors of the tragedy that was Dunblane. Murray, it should be remarked, also has a rather special gift for the game of tennis. He seems to have a natural aptitude for the sport and was quite unlike anybody we'd ever seen at SW19.

Murray is tough, ruthless, hungry and ferociously competitive, a player who growls and snarls when points are lost. Murray is totally focussed and driven, a man who never knows when he is beaten. Murray is full of energy, bristling with desire and forever seeking that perfect forehand winner.

Murray is indeed almost ridiculously ambitious but then perhaps he's entitled to be. He now had a Grand Slam in his pocket and the US Open title may just have been his crowning moment of glory. But Murray finally brought to the nation what has to be surely its finest moment. He won the Men's Singles Final at Wimbledon and Britain cheered from the rafters. It was undoubtedly an iconic moment.

The only obstacles though to Murray's progress are Spanish, Croatian and quite possibly Swiss. Rafael Nadal is undoubtedly one of the most sublime tennis players of all time. Nadal is one of those compelling sportsmen who just seem to get better by the month. He will always be assured of a place in the Tennis Hall of Fame.

And so we come to a man who quite simply oozes class and magisterial authority. This was the man who brought the definitive Midas touch to tennis. To this day, he continues to produce some of the sweetest forehands and backhands tennis has ever seen.

His name is Roger Federer and in Federer, Switzerland has given us one of the most accomplished tennis players of all time. With his cool demeanour and unmistakable suavity, Federer is everything tennis could possibly have hoped for. Federer, it has to be said, is simply imperious, stateliness personified, the very model of dignity and good manners. In fact, he reminds of you that famous Swede from the 1970s.

Bjorn Borg undoubtedly belongs in that elite group of tennis players who glided effortlessly across the green acres of Wimbledon. So light was Borg on his feet that it almost seemed as if the man played in his slippers.

Borg dominated Wimbledon for five successive years and won the men's singles Final as if by memory. His five Wimbledon titles will linger in the mind like a favourite song. Truly, there will never be a player quite like Bjorn Borg.

I'm sure that few players will ever conduct themselves with as much prim propriety as the Iceberg from Sweden. Borg had, it seemed, the lot. He had a nerveless composure that only the best tennis players possess and a classic racket action that the purists would drool over.

During the Seventies, both Borg and the American pin up boy, Jimmy Connors, were fierce rivals on court and infectiously chummy off it. For most of the Seventies, Borg and Connors were players of sumptuous gifts and honest to goodness friends.

Jimmy Connors was the original all American icon. He was fresh faced, cherubic and joyfully amusing. In the old days, American tennis players always looked as if they'd stepped straight out of a Fifties western. Connors reminded you of one of those yee-hah cowboys, galloping into town on the back of a horse.

Then there was that marvellous Romanian who was pure Wimbledon gold. Somehow the Seventies SW19 played host to a whole cartoon strip of characters. For one Romanian though, Wimbledon was rather like somebody from the pages of Beano. He charmed his way into the Wimbledon fans' hearts and always gave the SW19 crowds some of its most hilarious moments.

Ilie Nastase was far by the most comical showman. If Nastase had jumped onto stage at the Comedy Club, the chances are that his audience would have demanded more and more.

Nastase, you see, sneered disdainfully at authority, paid no heed to convention and stuck two fingers up at every umpire in the land. But when Nastase played tennis, the whole world applauded thunderously. There can be no doubt that some of Nastase's groundstrokes and whipped cross court returns were delivered from another galaxy.

But the jovial Romanian did humour at Wimbledon in a way that very few of his successors were able to match. Before one serve, it was Nastase who pinched a policeman's hat without a moment's thought. On another occasion, he would casually sit next to the crowd before sharing giggly jokes with the ball boys and girls.

I'd like to think that if somebody does write his autobiography, then this would be the flattering picture of his life. It might be said that Nastase was the cheeky kid, always mischievously sneaking out of school early and forever chucking paper aeroplanes at respectable teachers.

But then that was the Wimbledon from my Seventies childhood. There were the Woodies, the doubles brothers who were known as the Woodies, so precise and harmonious. Vitas Gerulaitis who had a brother whose name I can't remember. There was the very religious Vijay Armritaj, an Indian player who would always cross himself between points followed by lovely gallery of European tennis maestros.

There was Ivan Lendl, once the superb coach of one Andy Murray. It was always believed that Lendl was by far and away the unluckiest tennis player never to win Wimbledon. I seem to remember that Lendl was curtly dismissed as the one player who could never play on grass and therefore had no right to the men's singles trophy.

Still I do hope that Lendl is included in a list of all time tennis greats because the man could still set the pulses racing. It would be a desperate shame if he is forgotten for I still think that Lendl was never given the credit that he deserved.

Then and not to be forgotten of course were the ladies. The Wimbledon ladies were the very model of femininity. Of course they wore the prettiest of dresses and skirts, for this was their day to shine and show off. It was their day to flirt outrageously and then serve in the most demure fashion.

There was Chris Evert, by some distance one of the most graceful tennis players the United States has ever produced. When Chris Evert walked onto Centre Court, it was almost as if a member of royalty had appeared.

Chris Evert had that splendid air of nobility that only the very best players seemed to have. She had that wonderful aura of graciousness about her that spanned the generations.

With both hands clenched tightly to her racket and eyes firmly fixed on her opponent, she radiated serenity. Whenever she lost or won a vital set point, nothing would disturb her concentration or train of thought.

Whenever Chris Evert appeared at Wimbledon, there was almost a ceremonial air about the place. Trumpets were blown and a very important person had made their presence felt.

She was the one with poise, polish and a perfect posture. She had, quite possibly, a certain refinement about her that other players could only envy. You somehow suspect that her home was immaculate with every table and chair in its proper place.

There was Martina Navratilova, a Czech player who became a naturalised American. Now Martina became one of the most celebrated tennis players of all, notching up nine Wimbledon titles without apparently breaking sweat.

Navratilova was just a master of her craft, a player who may well have been given a racquet for her third birthday party. She swept into the gates of SW19 as a youngster and just crushed her opponents into the ground.

It would be no exaggeration to say that Martina Navratilova has cemented her place in the record books, a player who Wimbledon reluctantly embraced but then discovered could play like a dream.

Navratilova had a guts, strength and athleticism on court that was somehow unquestioned. She was feisty, ruthless and utterly fearless. Navratilova had a stubborn will to win that was somehow contagious, a player who would stop at nothing to win tennis matches.

Then of course there were the poster girls of Wimbledon. Rosie Casals oozed sweetness and light, an American who had a certain innocence and daintiness about her. It was almost as if she felt like an intruder at an English tea party. It looked as if she was apologising for being there. Casals though, like Chris Evert, was all delicate forehands and an almost innate command of the baseline.

I also recall, perhaps wistfully, of the one occasion when Britain did produce a winner at Wimbledon. Her name was Virginia Wade and she won the ladies singles title in 1977. Now there was a sentence I didn't think I'd ever write.

But in the year of our Queen's Silver Jubilee, Virginia Wade presented the nation with a jewel in the sporting crown. I'll always remember Virginia Wade because she always wore a cardigan before and after matches. But Virginia was somehow the quintessence of Englishness and she deserved to be successful.

After toiling through the rounds that year, she finally reached the Wimbledon Final. She always reminded you of one of those typical English ladies who sip tea with the landed gentry. Or one of those middle class types who regularly watch polo matches. Now she was about to find her own station in life.

Facing a Dutch woman by the name of Betty Stove in the Wimbledon ladies singles Final, Virginia Wade achieved what many had thought impossible. She won the Wimbledon Final trophy and some of us just had to pinch ourselves. Surely it was a figment of our imagination, just a made up fairy tale.

But no Britain had, and not before time, clinched its first major sporting trophy since a famous blond hair chap by the name of Bobby Moore lifted a certain football trophy called the World Cup.

I mustn't forget those other charmers and stylists of Wimbledon's distant past. The names were like famous lines from a Shakespeare play or that rousing overture by Beethoven. They were the genuine characters who gave Wimbledon its meaning and purpose.

There was Tom Okker and Jan Kodes, two sturdy but entertaining players who definitely knew their way around a tennis court. Okker and Kodes were players of rugged masculinity and whole hearted machismo. I got the impression that all of their opponents knew they'd been in a match when they met these two.

I'm sure you'll remember those two French musketeers from yesteryear. French tennis had rarely troubled the Grand Slams but two men from across the Channel set quite a female hearts a flutter in recent years.

There was Henri Lecomte, a lovely and fluent player who brought undoubted artistry to the wide green acres of SW19. Lecomte was the original D'Artagnan, flashing his sword before drilling home his forehand winner. So dramatic and so enthralling.

Then we had Guy Forget who, like his French compatriot, always gave full value for money wherever he went. Forget was neat, methodical and utterly engaging company. When Forget played the game of tennis, you knew you were watching a major event.

Two more players from yesteryear also leave a pleasant imprint on my mind. They were two Australians with an almost inborn talent for tennis. Perhaps they were given tennis rackets at birth and simply told to learn the game.

There was Ken Rosewall, always nice, kind and, you felt, accessible. Rosewall always seemed calm, controlled and somehow imperturbable. If there was a raging tornado or hurricane in the neighbourhood, Rosewall would probably shrug his shoulders and continue playing.

I'm sure Ken Rosewall was somehow destined to play tennis. Rather like Bjorn Borg, he never looked flustered or troubled. There was that slight tug at the shirt before serving, a gentle bounce of the ball and then the explosive serve that was totally emphatic.

Then there was Rod Laver, a man who strode onto Centre Court with the all-conquering air of a gladiator. Laver was one of those supreme and silky tennis players who knew he was good. Laver just seemed to ooze a superior air and I feel sure that all of his opponents were psychologically beaten before the game.

Suffice it to say Laver was just the most technically adept tennis player of all time. He would prowl the baseline like the most predatory of all tennis players, clout back his forehand returns with prodigious power and then smoothly comb his hair.

So Wimbledon throughout the years has given us everything we could want out of an annual tennis tournament. It has been sad, poignant, moving and utterly unique. Surely there is no other sporting event that can take us quite literally to the soaring heights and beyond.

Wimbledon is not only about expensive punnets of strawberries and cream and refreshing glasses of Pimms. It is about players with their lovely mannerisms and idiosyncrasies. It is about stone faced and judgemental umpires who sit on high. There are the ball boys and girls who are forever scurrying about the courts. It is without a doubt one of sport's most arresting sights.

Whether it be Andy Murray, Novak Djokovic or a complete unknown, you can be sure that Wimbledon will wear its most fashionable clothes and bow to the Royal Box. It will don its nattiest hats, wave the Union Jack and then laugh at the sheer sparkling spectacle before them.

Part 22: Cricket –
It's cricket and the 1970s.

This is Ashes year, cricket's answer to football's four yearly World Cup, the Lions rugby union summit meeting or the FA Cup Final at Wembley Stadium.

The meeting of England against Australia is sports finest, most compelling and allegedly antagonistic of cricket matches. It is cricket at its most competitive and allegedly confrontational. Some would have you believe that its cricket at its so called, nastiest and most vindictive. The truth is that England and Australia supposedly hate each other's guts and will continue to do so for as long as we live.

Every couple of years we gather at Lords, Trent Bridge, Headingly, Old Trafford, The Oval and more recently Cardiff's Sophia Gardens for a battle royale, fiercest rivals and sworn enemies.

In fact, there can be few countries who, some would have you believe, so passionately detest each other. Personally, I think it's just hyped up friendly rivalry. Still it still tickles my funny bone.

This year, the Ashes will provide us with an England side who may be one of the best and most cohesive units for many a year. True, there were the legendary names from way back when but, to all intents and purposes, this current Australian side are rather like one of those poor cousins who used to be extremely prosperous.

It can't be denied that the Australian cricket side of 2013 are no longer the force of old. Back in the Seventies, Australia had one of the strongest, hungriest and most aggressive sides in the world. They were battle hardened, destructive and more or less unbeatable.

My mind takes me back to two of Australia's most decorated quick bowlers. Fast bowlers are normally known as quickies but these gentlemen were given strict instructions to terrorise England. No English cricket team has ever left the field quite literally trembling with fear.

Jeff Thompson and Dennis Lillee were two of Australia's most powerful and lethal fast bowlers. I'm sure that both Thompson and Lillee were gun toting cowboys in another life. It was safe to assume that England always drunk in the Last Chance Saloon.

Jeff Thompson was one of those cold eyed assassins on the cricket pitch who never gave an inch. He was tall, leggy and absolutely merciless. Thompson, shirt flapping and blond hair flying, was the most terrifying sight in any Ashes series.

He would slowly trundle his way back to the pavilion, rub the ball vigorously on his trousers and then hurtle his way back to the bowler's crease with all the menacing intent of some evil pantomime villain. He was never hurtful or cruel but Thompson had all the ammunition he needed.

Thompson would then seem to open up his arms at a wide angle, feet were splayed out and the ball would simply fly out of his hand like a catapult. It always looked as if the man had a permanent grudge and refused to apologise for his actions.

Sportsmen and women love to announce themselves as soon as they walk out onto the field of play. Sometimes it's a loud proclamation and sometimes an irritable tantrum. For Jeff Thompson, it was always the quiet whisper followed by the most explosive bouncer in the world. Perhaps Thompson was simply getting it off his chest.

I'd like to think that most sportsman have their very own personalised gimmick or perhaps some cunning marketing ploy. Perhaps they rehearse for hours on end pacing up and down in the dressing room like some restless actor.

For Dennis Lillee, the game of cricket was just as important. Lillee would prowl around a cricket field as if he'd just lost his last fiver on the horses. Lillee was equally as dangerous as Thompson and would make no secret of the fact.

With his thick brown hair and equally as thick moustache, Lillee would wind himself up and then charge into some poor helpless batsman with all the fury he could possibly muster.

Lillee had those enormous thighs that had power written all over them. He bounded into bowl as if his life depended on it and then just released all of his pent up anger.

Sometimes sport can drive sportspeople to utter despair and frustration. For Dennis Lillee, cricket was simply another way of letting go, of making your voice heard and your presence felt.

Lillee walked out onto a cricket pitch in much the way that a Prime Minister or President steps up to a microphone. There is a statement to be made, a point to be expressed and a purpose in their manner. For Dennis Lillee had to be noticed, had to be acknowledged and never ignored. He was a man on a mission, snarling and sneering at the English with an almost personal grudge. Perhaps you felt Lillee had got out of the bed on the wrong side. Such behaviour, we felt, was utterly outrageous and had to be condemned. But that of course was Dennis Lillee.

Then, of course, there were the lesser known but no less effective Aussie warriors. What about Rick McCosker, an opening bat who without setting the world alight, always knew how to compile an innings? He would patiently wait for the short ball, adjust his bat to the right angle and then crack the ball through the covers for the most superlative of fours. McCosker was never a natural show boater but never less than smart and presentable.

McCosker, as I seem to remember, was inevitably followed by the Chappell brothers, Ian and Greg. Now the Chappells oozed class and charisma. Their partnership as the spine of the Aussie batting line-up was something to behold.

They were lethal hitters of the ball and utterly compatible. I'm sure they had the same taste in their choice of breakfast cereal.

Who could ever forget wicket-keeper Rodney Marsh. Now here was a man who must have done the chat show circuit. Marsh was one of the cheeky, crafty characters who never left a cricket pitch without a smile on his face. Never short of an opinion or comment, Marsh was playful, unpredictable and simply hilarious. You suspect that for Marsh, the tapestry of life was indeed a rich one.

England of course were also over stocked with cricketers never afraid to put on a show. It almost seems like the Seventies was scripted to be a golden era for English cricket. Certainly there can be few who would deny that they were there to see it.

England's foremost opening batsman for most of the Seventies was one Sir Geoffrey Boycott. When Geoff Boycott came bouncing out of the pavilion at Headingley, it was rather like watching a City worker putting in a strenuous twelve hour shift.

I feel sure that Boycott, on arrival at the wicket, would also take out a lease on the crease. You felt absolutely certain that Boycott was at the wicket for the duration of the day. In fact, Boycott was such an immovable force that by the afternoon of an Ashes match, some of us were just mesmerised.

You often get the impression that even a bulldozer wouldn't have been able to move Boycott. Boycott was everything English cricket had hoped for. He was a study in concentration, stern and unforgiving off the back and front foot, a steady accumulator of runs, a wonderful stickler for technique and touch.

A century for Boycott was like the conquest of Mount Everest. By the end of the day, Boycott, although tired, was never less than sociable. He would shake the hand of one of his colleagues with firmness and gusto, buy them a well-deserved drink and then quietly reflect on his stunning achievements.

Boycott would then be followed by two very solid and upright gentlemen, men who wouldn't have looked out of a place in a bank. I suspect both men were in possession of a smart black suit and bowler hat. Oh and we mustn't forget the Financial Times. It would have been an absolute necessity.

Suffice it to say that Denis Amiss of Warwickshire and John Edrich of Surrey were as English as red pillar boxes and steak and kidney pies. In fact, Amiss and Edrich were the very essence of Englishness. They were its representatives and ambassadors.

Amiss was a genial, at times bold and conscientious batsman. He was the kind of man who knew what he had to do and simply got on with the job in hand. Dennis Amiss never complained, argued, interrupted or disrupted. It was an honest day's work and that's how he liked it.

Amiss was the very personification of hard graft and good old fashioned commitment. Somehow, he was made for the rigours of Test cricket. It is easy to believe that Dennis Amiss was made for the game. With a flick of the wrists, or a gentle forward defensive prod to gully, Amiss had every conceivable shot in the book. Truly a cricketer to treasure.

English cricketing followers will always have a kind word to say about

Alan Knott. Now wicket- keepers always seem to bear the most unenviable of responsibilities. Rather like goal-keepers, they regularly face up to the most thankless of sporting tasks. It is in their gloved hands that the outcome of a Test Match can vitally depend.

Alan Knott, though, was one of those characters who just seemed to ooze dependability. With those big red gloves and a rapturous reception from his adoring fans, Knott was just enchanting. He would jump up and down, stretch his arms and then move his neck from side to side. It was, without a doubt, one of the most unusual sights cricket has ever seen.

We all know that sportspeople have their own habits and superstitions. But with Knott, you always had the feeling that he was auditioning for some theatrical production. When he crouched down in readiness for the first ball of the day, Knott looked in complete control. Personally I will always remember the Knott handkerchief.

Now I'm not sure why he needed a handkerchief but Alan Knott would always start a Test match complete with a ready supply of hankies. Nobody knew why but come the Test Match, a tissue would be seen sticking out of the Knott trousers. Kent have very rarely boasted such a fine and upstanding wicket-keeper.

Then there were England's spin brigade. I've vague recollections of Ray Illingworth but they were always good ones. Illingworth brought the Ashes back to England at the end of the Sixties. It was the first time in what seemed like several centuries.

Illingworth, though, had professionalism and dedication seeping out of his body. He had that smooth, leisurely air that commanded respect. He was never ruffled or flustered and when the chips were down, he would simply get on with the business in hand.

He was one of those devious spinners with several tricks up his sleeve. He trundled in from the Kirkstall Lane End with a gentle, deliberate trot. They were frequently mixed up with cunning deliveries that nipped back off the seam and then just confused the batsman.

Two other spinners also jump into my sporting consciousness. There was Derek Underwood and Tony Greig, two honest to goodness spin masters who relished their craft. You can imagine them in the nets just flipping the ball into unsuspecting batsman, mischief and menace in every over.

Derek Underwood was one of my favourite spinners. I don't know why Underwood was a very appealing character. There was nothing out of the ordinary about him but he just seemed to exude assurance as soon as he stepped up to bowl. He would roll up his shirt sleeves and with careful steps, roll up to the wicket and twirl his fiendish fingers. A sheer and peerless genius.

Tony Greig, another spinner supreme, was unmistakable and if you passed him in the street he could hardly be missed. He was tall, leggy and utterly imposing. Greig wore his England cap with immense distinction.

You always felt that Greig would have been far more at home on a basketball court. At well over 6ft, Greig loped in to bowl with a hop, skip and a jump. He became one of England's most distinguished of captains, a man with a strategic cricketing brain and plenty to offer the game of cricket.

And then there was Ian Botham. In 1981, Ian Botham would become one of English cricket's favourite sons of all time. In fact, he should have been the given the freedom of Britain, such was the magnitude of his achievement.

For years and years, English cricket had laboured desperately to win back the Ashes. Botham answered the call of the nation and the summer of 1981 was the year English cricket finally found its knight in shining armour. Botham saved us from utter indignity and how we revered him for it.

It is believed that nobody had ever seen a cricketer quite like Ian Botham. I'm sure he was the one man who knocked at the door at Lord's one day and asked whether he could transform England into a winning side.

There were the inevitable cynics who just sniggered and couldn't accept Botham as the saviour. Besides, England hadn't won the Ashes for decades and Beefy was just a pretender. But the man from Somerset changed our perceptions, shook the sport to its senses and, or so it seemed, trampled all over the opposition.

It can be said with some certainty that Botham was by far and away the most terrifying quickie bowler England would ever confront. He was bold, remarkably fast and truly decisive. Botham knew what he wanted to do and by the end of an over, our antipodean friends looked utterly relieved. Botham was the man English cricketing fans had been searching and yearning for.

Truly, here was a man destined to be included in every England squad for a number of years. He was a colossus of a sportsman, the man who, overnight, brought certainty and stability to English cricket. Botham remained convinced that nothing was impossible, that if England tried hard enough they could be the best.

Even in retirement, Ian Botham is still a publicist's dream. You must have seen him. One minute he's walking for charity and the next, contributing positively to Test Match Special.

Botham is the nice man, the caring, benevolent humanitarian with a heart of gold. His regular walks from Lands' End to John O' Groats are of course legendary. But here you have a man who has lived life to the full and never regretted anything. I think we should take our hat off to him and lavish him with compliments.

And so on to the subjects of politics and sport. There is a school of thought that the two should never mix. In fact, they are rather like two well matched heavyweight boxers who threaten to cause chaos.

Politicians never make any secret of their sporting passions. This is thoroughly noteworthy and, to all intents and purposes, extremely comforting to know.

Politicians, they may tell us, are those opinionated and forthright characters, always telling us who to vote for. Throughout the ages, they have stood up in the Houses of Parliament, shuffled their pieces of paper and then poured out well-rehearsed speeches about the State of the Nation.

But, and this has to be true, many a politician has much more on his or her mind than you might think. True, they're professionals with many a neat turn of phrase. But, for all their rousing rhetoric, politicians still long for a place on the football terrace or a starting block in the 100m Olympic Final.

For instance, some of us may well know that Harold Wilson occasionally had rather more pressing issues on his mind than politics. Wilson was one of the most influential and important Prime Ministers of modern times. But Mr Wilson occasionally seemed slightly pre-occupied with football.

Harold Wilson was a confirmed Huddersfield supporter and happily sang the praises of the Yorkshire club. He must have, at some point, watched Huddersfield. If he did, then he must have known that a certain Herbert Chapman was their manager. Chapman of course was the chief orchestrator of Huddersfield's League Championship winning symphonies. I'd like to think that Chapman also played the piano.

Anyway, when Wilson wasn't welcoming in the age of White Heat technology, he could also be seen waving his Huddersfield scarf. I'd like to think that he was the most versatile Prime Minister for many a decade.

Wilson's successor, Edward Heath, never really shared the same footballing interests as his eminent predecessor. But Heath did like life on the ocean wave and much preferred the bracing sea.

Heath was the much respected sailor on board the good boat Morning Cloud. He could have enjoyed watching the likes of George Best and Jimmy Greaves but Heath opted for the challenging waves of the Channel. He was a man of a nautical persuasion.

A brief mention perhaps should be made for possibly the most visible and remarkable Prime Minister of recent times. She was highly regarded by those who knew her and unfairly despised by others.

Margaret Thatcher was the first woman Prime Minister Britain had. The unions hated her, her Cabinet had, until her final years, nothing but unqualified admiration for her and Dennis, her husband, it is to be assumed, idolised her.

But Thatcher was never the sporting type and by her own admission, an afternoon at Stamford Bridge would have been totally mis-spent. I think she might have found lacrosse or badminton to be somewhat less hectic.

I do recall her being appointed as President at Blackburn Rovers but she would have been the first person to admit that football wasn't uppermost in her mind. Perhaps she felt that Rovers were not the force they used to be.

If we move forward a decade or so, we found ourselves at the most misunderstood Prime Minister British politics ever had. Somehow I don't think John Major ever quite knew what he'd done wrong but the public were never sure what to make of him.

What we do know is that Major was a passionate Chelsea fan and loved his cricket. For all the cheap jokes at Major's expense and all the vicious criticism, Major was very much a sporting enthusiast. He is a wise observer of Surrey County Cricket Club and proudly takes his place at the Oval.

In 1997, Labour finally became the Government of the day. Tony Blair became Prime Minister and the nation invited a new face into their homes. Blair was clever, rational, forward thinking and refreshingly progressive. Blair was determined to be both popular and a Man of The People.

On all matters from housing, education, transport and the Economy, Blair's voice had a rich clarity to it. It was a voice of conviction and unquestionable authority.

But for Tony Blair, Saturday, Sunday or Mondays were all about Newcastle United. It is not known whether the likes of Jackie Milburn, Len Shackleton or Malcolm Mcdonald ever featured prominently in his debates but for one weekend, Tony Blair was a St James' Park fan supporting the black and white shirt of Newcastle.

I always felt rather sorry for Gordon Brown because nobody really acknowledged his contribution to mainstream politics. He reminded me of the little lad at the back of the class who everybody ignored. Brown had plenty of good ideas as Prime Minister but could never assert himself at critical moments. Still, he did like his football and he did have an abiding passion for rugby union.

Gordon Brown supports Raith Rovers, a club unfortunately rooted in anonymity but still followed by a former Prime Minister. You always felt nothing but pity for clubs in the lower Leagues. How could Gordon possibly get excited about a team that regularly attracts only 500 odd Raith fans. But I think his devotion to his local team deserves rather more than a medal.

And so we move forward to the present day. Nowadays Prime Ministers tend to use sport as rather an attractive public relations stunt. Throughout the ages, all of our most recent PMs have used sport as a kind of extension of their personalities.

But before I mention our current PM, I think it's only fair that I make one or two more brief references to those Prime Ministers of another vintage.

Before the 1980 European football championships, Margaret Thatcher, who allegedly had no time for the Beautiful Game, was photographed outside 10 Downing Street smiling dutifully with the England players. The image of Emlyn Hughes and Kevin Keegan on either side of the Iron Lady is one I will cherish.

Then there was poor John Major who nobody really knew. Major would often be seen in magic cricketing poses. Major took every opportunity to correct what might have seemed to be a distorted public image.

He would, quite frequently, be seen at The Oval watching his beloved Surrey. Wearing the smart club blazer and tie, Major would be totally transfixed by the much acclaimed Surrey batsman Graham Roope, a very consistent England player.

Major would also tell you in loving detail about Jim Laker, the England spinner, a man of sterling service for Surrey and a man who once took 19 wickets in a Test Match for England.

If we cross the Atlantic, we may well find a man whose interest in English football may well have gone completely unnoticed. Our friends from the United States would love to be better acquainted with the nuances of English football. Still they do have a President who supposedly supports West Ham United.

Barack Obama is a man of taste and discrimination for this is the team that

I follow. It has to be said of Mr President that when it comes to English football, you will always be a very shrewd and knowledgeable man. If I do happen to see you at Upton Park one day, it is to be hoped that we can share the friendliest of conversations. You are extremely welcome at Upton Park.

The new football season is literally on our doorstep again and for what must seem like the umpteenth time, football supporters will be ironing their scarves, oiling their vocal chords and preparing to travel the length and breadth of the country.

Football is that yearly mid-August ritual where hundreds and thousands of men, women and children jump onto an emotional roller coaster. They are the fanatical ones. They are the ones who sacrifice everything just to make sure that their team either wins the League or avoids relegation.

In the season of 2013-14, football will offer us an enriching diet of breathtaking goals, nervous managers and referees who always make the wrong decisions. The Premier League is a crazy, hectic nine month marathon where egos, temperaments and reputations are constantly monitored.

Of course, the new season will present us with all of our old friends: arguments, controversies, argy bargy and the players. We mustn't forget the players. The players are the ones who make it all possible. The players are the cogs and wheels. They're the components in the machine. The Premier League, you suspect, is their bread and butter, their theatre.

When the likes of Wayne Rooney, Theo Walcott, Juan Mata and Carlos Tevez step out into those billiard table green pitches, we will all feel that thrilling sense of anticipation, a sense that it might be our year. Or perhaps next year.

Sadly, football has no time for soppy sentiment or silly fantasies; it has no time for your fond hopes and ridiculous optimism. If you support one of the teams in the lower Leagues, you may have to content yourself with crumbs and leftovers. Is there no justice in the world? One of these days, League 2 will retaliate with a vengeance. Mark my words.

The fact is that the Premier League are just a money grabbing gang of mercenaries who simply want world domination. Well I'm here to tell you that this will simply not do. One of these days, Torquay United, Rochdale, Grimsby and Northampton will launch a sustained attack on those Premier League know-alls. How dare they get ideas above the station?

Still, we all know that the little fish of the Football League are the very fabric of English football. They were the teams who make the world go around. Somehow they will always remain upright pillars of the community, hardworking and forever downtrodden.

But football fans will climb onto their buses and coaches, sing their ageless football chants and just bubble over with enthusiasm. It is one of those marvellous routines that have stood the test of time for as long as I can remember.

If your team just happen to be at the other end of the country, then these are the procedures all football supporters have to go through. Maybe this is something that comes as naturally as puberty or maturity.

But for most of us, supporting your local team will remain one of the most frustrating of pre-occupations. We often ask ourselves the same questions season after season. Why support a team who are highly unlikely to win anything or indeed why bother?

My sympathies will always be with the likes of Torquay United, Rochdale, Grimsby or Northampton. I suspect they will never know what it's like to be victorious or glorious. They will never, I suspect, ever win the FA Cup or the Premier League so they may find themselves questioning their existence. I do hope that, one day, a rich sugar daddy comes along and guides to them the dizzy heights. Oh I wish they would.

Still, as long as they're happy with who they are and where they are, then that should be the status quo. This is their fate and destiny in life and perhaps they should simply resign themselves to whatever will be.

But whatever their status or location, football teams will continue to provide the focal point for most of their supporters. You can imagine what it would be like if they had no football to look forward to. Instead, they would have to go shopping with their wives or girlfriends every Saturday and Sunday. Perhaps that may be a good thing.

Now this might seem like the most convenient of arrangements for the female gender but I somehow think that most men would get severe withdrawal symptoms. For men, football is their foremost priority and spending a Saturday afternoon in Marks and Spencer would drive most of the male population over the edge.

No, the fact is that football is a man's weekly fix, the signature at the end of the letter, the main reference point. They meet up with their family, pals and colleagues in what appears to be the liveliest of union meetings. They shout vociferously and claim unswerving loyalty to the team.

The more traditional of supporters will insist on that most traditional of football lunches. Burgers will be ravenously consumed, songs will be chanted rather like church psalms and vulgar profanities hurled at the opposition. Of course, these are just idle threats but you can't help but wonder why they behave in the way they do.

Still, this is the way football, at times, wishes to conduct itself and maybe always will be. There is an inherent tribalism among football supporters that is somehow in their blood. From a young age, they're taught that if you don't stand up for yourself on the terraces, you're bound to be attacked or seriously injured.

I did have one slightly unnerving experiences at Upton Park in the late Seventies which still sends a shiver down my spine. You would stand on the South Bank for the best part of two half and hours and by kick off, feel just a touch traumatised.

This had nothing to do with the ground or the players on the pitch but the away supporters made it abundantly clear that your presence was, how shall I put it, troubling them. When the London clubs came to Upton Park, the whole of the away section next to me would voice their considerable disapproval.

But the rivalry, although very personal, did give the match a spicy flavour.

When either Chelsea or Spurs came to the Boleyn Ground, the atmosphere could almost be felt and touched. There were the familiar songs, the incessant clapping and the same old harmless insults. After all, this is what being a football supporter is all about.

Above all though, football should be about sport at its most sporting. It is about respect for the opposition, learning to lose without ill feeling and a warm kinship with each other. Perhaps this is wishful thinking but I can't help but feel that football supporters and the game itself will always have soft spot for each other.

It may be a cliché but yes, football matches have always had an air of electricity about them. There is an undercurrent about it, an ever present drama, a sense perhaps that there were underlying issues that had to be resolved.

I always feel that football supporters have a certain social position in life in the great football hierarchy. They are the ones who, week after week, month and month, give an unswervingly emotional commitment to their lifelong team. It is the closest thing you'll get to footballing idolatry.

It's almost as if all the events that had already taken place, pale into utter significance. This is the day of the needle derby and this is the day that counts. This is that moment in the week when everything and anything is conveniently forgotten: bills, the mortgage, the grass that hasn't been mown for ages and that shelf you had every intention of putting up.

For the millions who watch football, this is their chance to be somebody else, a different persona with a different outlook on life. Premier League or Championship football give their lives an altogether new meaning, perhaps another attitude. It might be a good idea to think in the positive rather than negative.

I'm inclined to think that when the likes of Manchester United, Chelsea or Arsenal walk out of the tunnel, most supporters believe that their lives are somehow complete. Saturday, Sunday and Mondays gave them an utter sense of fulfilment and reward, days with a fresh faced complexion and substance.

Back in the 1950s and 60s, of course football was the predominantly working class game. It was played out before factory workers in their cloth caps or the horribly exploited shop worker. Of course, they waved their scarves, of course they rattled their rattles but sadly, it seems, football has lost both its meaning and innocence.

The days of £100 a week players and managers in bowler hats now belong to another distant period in history. It's rather like rummaging around in a dusty old attic and finding nothing of any value.

Surely, you felt football was far more civilised and highly regarded by those in the know. True the tackling could be savage and maybe the passing did leave a lot to be desired. But football was our game, the game we played on the streets with jumpers for goalposts. Football was the game we looked up to, felt we had something in common with, sympathised with when it wasn't feeling well. We had a genuine understanding of the sport and a warm rapport with the people on the terraces.

I'd like to think that I'll always be part of football's enormous family, that nothing will ever match that priceless sensation when the final whistle blows and your team has won. The fact is that football will always be the most pleasant of companions wherever you are in the world.

Television, of course, was never likely to left out of any of football's equations. Then again, you could hardly have expected otherwise. We knew that sooner or later TV would come knocking on the door and demanding a king's ransom.

Nowadays, most of us are subjected to a hearty diet of football highlights on a Saturday night and much more. A certain Australian tycoon by the name of Rupert Murdoch stormed football's very brittle barricades and changed the whole face of TV football.

The Sky Sports channel was football's very own plaything, a simple toy that Murdoch could play with and then discard if the mood took him. Thankfully, football became Murdoch's most treasured possession and the game is more or less a daily occurrence.

In the old days, we had Brian Moore and London Weekend Television's most prized asset called the Big Match. The Big Match at Sunday lunchtime was football's most nutritious meal. Highlights of Saturday's games were mixed up with panels of experts and well informed comment.

The BBC, in their infinite wisdom, had an almost inevitable head start on ITV. Since 1964, Match of the Day had become that well established fixture, something meaty to chew on while you were having your tea.

Match of the Day may have been in black and white in the early days but there always seemed to be something colourful about its presentation. Football was something you could now watch without having to leave your armchair.

The first episode of Match of the Day was shown on BBC2 and was somehow a template for what was to follow. Kenneth Wolstenholme was a friendly, avuncular figure who spoke with a very clipped English accent. Wolstenholme was a throwback to the days when BBC newsreaders wore dinner jackets and spoke into huge BBC microphones.

The match itself was predictably mouth-watering and appetising. In fact, I don't think the BBC could have picked a game so loaded with lip smacking possibilities. It had potential written all over it.

Liverpool, under the adored Bill Shankly, were about to hit the big time. The city, itself of course, had just given birth to a group called the Beatles. Merseyside was fit and flourishing and Anfield was the most atmospheric ground in the old First Division.

The fact is that, on that famous day back in 1964, football and TV were married in sickness and in health. Match of the Day was the blushing bride and football took its lifelong vows.

Liverpool played Arsenal at Anfield and Kenneth Wolstenholme introduced the programme with that deeply elegant air about him. He welcomed the captive TV audience with an almost suave authority and, it has to be said, football never really looked back. Welcome to Anfield, Liverpool and Beatleville, Wolstenholme said in almost portentous tones.

Two years later, Wolstenholme would feature in one of this country's finest sporting victories of all times. Looking back, it almost seems like the most improbable of all historic events. One day, we felt, we would rub our eyes and convince ourselves that it was just a daydream. But it happened and sometimes you to believe the evidence of your eyes.

The 1966 World Cup Final was the one occasion when a whole nation simply abandoned itself to one joyous party. England did indeed win the World Cup. No seriously, we did win the most precious piece of silverware you could imagine. It was the best feeling in the world for a country now swollen with pride and a real sense of patriotism.

It had taken us long enough but on a July afternoon in the middle of the Swinging Sixties, England were acclaimed World Champions. Forget about the Second World War and the interim period. England had won another battle and this time the score-line was different.

When the final whistle went, to mark the end of the 1966 World Cup, England, I feel sure, entered a new era both culturally and psychologically. It must have felt as though a burden had been lifted from the shoulders. For the first time in ages, we could celebrate and socialise with each other in a way that wouldn't have been possible perhaps 10 or 15 years before.

It surely is amazing how the likes of Bobby Moore, Geoff Hurst, Martin Peters, Alan Ball and Bobby Charlton suddenly transformed the whole mood of the country.

Of course the 1950s may have been seen as idyllic to some but somehow the Sixties had its very own personality. As a nation, England could once again express itself. At long last we had the capacity to discover, invent and create. We were the revolutionaries, the artists, fashion designers and pop stars.

I'm sure it must have been the case that before the 1966 World Cup Final, England must have felt very stifled and perhaps frightened in a way. Maybe we didn't think we would ever find new horizons or new philosophies. Even as a young child, it might have seemed that we were reluctant to enjoy ourselves.

But quite by chance, we did let go of what seemed like the severe and stern Fifties. Perhaps we just wanted to colour in the Sixties because the Fifties were interminably black and white.

Yes, the Fifties did give its generation everything it must have longed for. There were the mesmerising juke boxes in every London coffee bar, rock and roll music that almost seemed to define the decade.

But the Sixties had something even more identifiable about it. It had clarity, endless energy and a sense of immediacy about it. It was happening now. It had freshness, directness and a glorious originality.

To my young mind, the Sixties may have been just another decade but I think some of the images from that time will never be erased. It seemed to be rather like a permanent amusement arcade. Perhaps people felt they were being rewarded in some way. Maybe the Sixties was a time when anything and everything seemed possible and viable.

If we'd looked hard, everything was brightly and vividly coloured, flashing, glittering, pounding and throbbing. It had a life, magic, a sense of the unexpected and the utterly unpredictable. You could literally be anybody you wanted to be without feeling the slightest twinge of embarrassment. Go on, let yourself assume any persona.

Perhaps Prime Minister for the day or even a member of the Royal Family. Nobody could stop you or hinder your progress. You were in charge and you were the architect of your future. This, I feel sure, was your time, your place, your chance to be as creative as you wanted. Your moment to make your mark.

Of course, the Sixties gave us its very own iconic days and special occasions. There was the Profumo scandal, that shocking and rather sleazy episode that shook the Establishment to its foundations. Politicians of all shades shamefully bowed their heads and pretended they had no knowledge of the incident.

Still, we were the children of the Sixties, the children who saw the likes of the sensual Tom Jones, a singer of some pedigree and stature. We also witnessed the dynamic Lulu, a Scottish chanteuse who literally belted out her feisty lyrics. Engelbert Humperdinck always looked like the smartest City bank manager you could possibly imagine. Humperdinck always seemed to sing in pine striped suits but never a bowler hat.

All of the aforementioned were my Sixties entertainers although all of them honed their skills in War ravaged Britain. There was Dusty Springfield, who always seemed to write songs about heartache and rejection. Poor Dusty.

Then there was Sandy Shaw, a product of London's East End. Now Sandy Shaw was the one girl who brought a devil may care wit and impudence to the world of show business. She was the girl who once appeared in the Eurovision Song Contest without any shoes on. That had never happened before and at the time was highly unusual and almost without precedent. Nobody in the world of music knew that a professional singer could just shimmy onto a stage bare-footed and still belt out a well-crafted song.

The Sixties though was all about possibilities and probabilities, a time when the whole world was desperate to find out much more about itself. It was a time when we all felt ready to carry out our obligations and make a fresh start.

During the Sixties, one woman stood out from the rest of the crowd and made her presence felt. She stepped on to her platform and told us everything we wanted to know about the family unit, morality, purity and the appalling obscenities she'd heard on the television. It would never ever do.

On one notable occasion, Mary Whitehouse stood up in front of a feverish and fervent gathering of women and made her case. She made it quite clear that yesterday evening, her whole family had been shocked and horrified by the language used in an otherwise ordinary TV programme. Still that was life and from a child's perspective, this must have seemed like the norm.

Anyway, while I was growing up in Ilford during the Sixties, I suddenly became aware of my surroundings. There was a very profound consciousness that Ilford had its own shopping centre with its own department stores and specialist shops.

For instance, there was Bodgers, one of the most enduring and most prominent of department stores in Ilford. Bodgers was rather like an extended member of your family: comfortable, reliable and deeply respected by all who shopped in it.

Bodgers had a sedateness and elegance that spanned the decades and generations. Bodgers sold the kind of objects that were always useful, practical, applicable and appropriate. It was the kind of store that extended the warmest of invitations even when you weren't feeling well. Bodgers was homely, lovable, down to earth and completely without airs or graces. It had none of the pomposity or pretension of other shops. Bodgers was admired by the masses because it never really felt either superior or inferior.

What made Bodgers so special, I suppose, was its timeless charm, its air of regal stability and permanence. It had served its customers throughout the decades and generations generously and unquestioningly. No questions were ever asked, nothing was ever much trouble and there were never any lingering disputes or long held grudges.

Bodgers was a pillar of respectability, a shining beacon of civility and gentility. You felt an eternal debt of gratitude to Bodgers because wherever you went in the store, the staff bent over backwards to help you.

Bodgers, indeed, never had any delusions of grandeur, a sense of guilt and shame. There was an air of simplicity and gentle innocence about Bodgers. It was unashamedly quaint and straightforward. It was always there for you, regardless of the consequences, forever mindful of its wonderful sense of duty and responsibility. It was helpful, dignified, at ease with the rest of the world, awfully charming, permanently obliging and splendidly co-operative.

I always felt that Bodgers had this innate sympathy that none of the others could ever boast. Not only was it sympathetic, kind and generous, it also offered some of the finest products on the market. Some might have regarded it as old fashioned and behind the times but there were times when it did give off a rather faded magnificence.

But when it looked as though Bodgers was on the point of bankruptcy and extinction, something deep within the Ilford public cried out for its survival. Bodgers was the people's shop, a shop without any prejudice or favouritism. I'm sure that Bodgers happily greeted everybody who passed through their doors. Bodgers was old school and traditional but always ready to be flexible when the occasion warranted.

Surely they felt Bodgers was richly deserving of another chance, an opportunity to re-build from scratch, a time for re-construction and resurrection, to rise from the ashes. Bodgers was always dignified, noble, upstanding, a genuine pleasure to all and sundry.

But it was the whole experience of Bodgers that always filled the people with enormous pride. Bodgers sold everything. I was always particularly taken by the first floor and all of its paraphernalia. You had to see it to believe it.

In one complete area of the ground floor, there were simply acres of huge and impressive carpets and more carpets. You could see them scattered everywhere. There were rolls and more rolls of enormous shag carpets, rugs from all over the world and settees that somehow belonged in the 1950s.

The staff at Bodgers couldn't have been more agreeable or personable and I always felt that most of them had attended classes for courtesy and chivalry. Indeed, the customer was always right and I always believed that there was something undeniably proper and correct about it.

Apart from the carpets, rugs and settees, there were innumerable wardrobes and cupboards of the finest vintage. Goodness knows how long they'd been there but they were there for your continued viewing pleasure and delectation.

There was a well ordered formality about those cupboards and wardrobes that was simply admirable. Nothing was ever out of place and there was a general air of streamlined symmetry about that floor.

When you went upstairs at Bodgers, you felt as though the whole world was at its fingertips. On bright, glistening shelves were everything the housewife could possibly want.

Before your spellbound eyes were everything your living room and kitchen could possibly desire. There were knife sharpeners galore, dinner plates by the dozen, knives, forks and spoons in neatly arranged rows, glassware, beautifully decorated bowls, casserole dishes, crystal decanters of sheer sumptuousness, cups and saucers, pressure cookers that catered for all tastes and shelf upon shelf of everything that looked pretty, rosy and enticing.

Then there was the greasy café on Bodgers first floor, a secret corner of shop that at times looked both apologetic and remorseful. It hadn't committed any crime nor had it done anything wicked or corrupt. But there was something about the café that didn't quite fit in with the rest of the store's décor.

The staff were always kind and welcoming but there was a lived in, traditional look about it that had few if any redeeming features. I seem to remember eating their toasted cheese sandwiches and their splendid jacket potatoes with baked beans or coleslaw. It was quite the most mouth-watering of all feasts.

But I always felt that Bodgers had a riveting triumphalism about it. It had survived two World Wars, innumerable recessions, all manner of economic crises and still came up smelling of roses. It had a hardiness, strength of character, amazing powers of endurance, a determination to forge ahead with complete confidence.

As you walked into the store, several features took the eye almost immediately. I think the shop was designed in just the way the architects and builders had hoped for. This had Ilford written all over it, rubber stamped for eternity and posterity.

In front of the shop, there was a sweet counter serving the finest in chocolates, sweets and cigarettes. I'd always assumed that all of the rush-hour commuters would rush in there for a packet of chewing gum and a bar of chocolate. But it always had a busy liveliness about it that always struck me as very appealing.

Bodgers was though, cosy, domesticated, traditional and re-assuringly profitable. I don't think it was a goldmine but they did have their regular clientele. Bodgers was permanently approachable, never rude or obnoxious and simply delighted to see you.

There was a buzz and vibrancy about Bodgers that made you feel glad to be associated with it. Bodgers was richly historic, proud of its roots and origins, completely in charge of its destiny. It had a masterful authority about it that could never be challenged.

Some high street shops simply refuse to move with the times but Bodgers, in a sense, had to follow the latest trends. It had been there since the late 19th century and the store had prestige, an honourable place in Ilford folklore and the wholehearted love of its inhabitants.

Bodgers was part of Ilford's heritage, an unmistakable link with everything that had gone before. There was a warmth and radiance about the shop that made you feel wanted. For years, there was a steadiness, sturdiness and an impressive presence about Bodgers. It stood to attention every morning and proudly surveyed the British Empire.

Bodgers meant something to all classes, all ages, all backgrounds, kindly beckoning you inside and rolling out the red carpet. It was a considerable part of our lives, substantial, a major influence, democratic, never snobbish and richly layered. It had floors, departments within departments, a small but compact lift and all manner of surprises.

On the first floor, Bodgers also had that wonderful air of femininity. Women from all over Redbridge would flock to the perfume counters spread right across one half of the front of the shop.

Here, women in smartly-pressed uniforms with excessive make up, would stand behind their counter, smiling devotedly for their female customers. It was daily, it was predictable but never less than fascinating. With a small bottle of perfume, members of staff would delicately dab Coco Channel onto the demure wrists of girlfriends or wives. Bodgers had, and will never lose, its old fashioned delicacy and duty.

Deeper into Ilford, there was Fairheads in the Cranbrook Road. Now Fairheads had real class, breeding, good posture, an essentially Victorian sense and sensibility. Fairheads was roughly the same age as Bodgers. In the late 19th century, Fairheads opened its elegant doors to a resounding fanfare of trumpets.

For the next 150 years, Fairheads was all things to all people, an unmistakably huge building that reeked of the English aristocracy. It was easy to imagine titled women and upper class gentlemen swanning into the shop with that faintly disapproving air. But things have changed most dramatically since then and now, sadly, Fairheads just couldn't keep up with modernity.

Sadly Fairheads is no longer with us but was very much the friend of the people. Fairheads was the home of lace and thousands upon thousands of rich fabric, lacy material, lace curtains, an abundance of cotton reels, needles and pins in the smallest boxes. It also offered all of the essentials that every woman could possibly desire.

Fairheads had grace, a timeless charm and sociability. It had its very own position and station in life. Nobody ever disturbed or disrupted its peace of mind, its rightful place in the hierarchy. There was something very knowing, worldly and intricately woven about it. Rather like Bodgers, Fairheads was immaculately tidy, methodical, everything had to be just right, orderly, precise, unfailingly polite. Fairheads had an unwritten code of conduct. It had manners, protocol, effortless simplicity, none of the hardnosed commercialism of other shops. Fairheads was refined, a model of fairness, integrity and probity. Highly regarded by all and sundry.

In the heart of Ilford High Road, there were the other trustworthy institutions, commercial high street giants. They were the shops that gave something to Ilford that was unique and irreplaceable. Every suburb, town and city has its outstanding qualities, traits that none of its counterparts could claim as their own.

Harrison Gibsons was that stern, upright, no-nonsense and pragmatic department store. It towered over Ilford High Street with all of the majesty it could possibly muster. Harrison Gibsons was dependable, remarkable, always there in times of stress and adversity, a lifelong ally when all seemed to be lost.

What struck me was the sheer size, the sheer immensity of it. It really was an architectural wonder, quite the most astonishing creation I'd ever seen. Huge concrete blocks seemed to soar into the air, its rooftop nestling in the sky in a perfect collaboration with the rest of the world.

Harrison Gibsons was that splendid store that gave its public the greatest lighting department in Western Civilisation. Whenever I walked past Harrison Gibsons, you were almost taken back by its electrifying presence, its ever present illumination, a feeling that everything around the store was permanently light and bright.

But Harrison Gibsons had lifts, remarkable lifts, lifts, if memory serves me, that had gates and shutters. Or maybe this was an exaggeration. But these were lifts that had personality, posture and the most elevated of social positions. These were lifts that were almost a throwback to another age, 1920s or 30s lifts where gentlemen doffed their bowler hats and ladies stepped daintily out onto the floor with a parasol in one hand and prim innocence in the other.

But above all, Harrison Gibsons had carpets, vast rolls of carpet standing to attention, ever respectful of its traditions, mindful of its standing in society. Harrison Gibsons was rather like your living room, an extension of who you were, your dining room chairs, your fixtures and fittings.

There is something about these grand old shops that is timeless and unchanging. I'd learnt that during the Sixties, Harrison Gibsons had been the unwitting victim of a serious fire. But undaunted and undeterred, it soldiered on regardless, roaring back into life as if nothing had happened. It was determined to carry on, completely unaffected, imperturbable, determined to hold on to a stubborn independence.

Then there was Room on the Top, a nightclub in the Ilford High Road with an air of obvious style and sophistication. The Room at the Top was one of those nightclubs that always seemed totally at odds with me. I knew that I'd never aspire to be a party animal so therefore the Room at the Top was unsuitable and inaccessible. Best left alone.

I could hardly forget Downtown, that incredible record shop in the Ilford

High Road. There were record shops and record shops but Downtown had a certain warmth and symbolism. This was the shop all of the hip teenagers flocked to from miles away. There was something about Downtown that stood out from the rest of the crowd.

I'm not sure why but Downtown was the one place you could go into and never feel left out or excluded. Many was the happy hour you would spend idly flicking through the huge racks of LPs, singles and tapes with complete freedom and impunity.

Whenever you walked into Downtown, you never felt people were looking at you, sneering at you or following you. Besides, most of my generation bought all of the latest hit singles and albums in there so there was never any sense that the staff were somehow staring or sniggering at you.

I started buying some of my records at that pivotal moment in pop music history when the world of cinema met up with music on the friendliest of terms. I think it must have been the summer of 1977 when two films hurtled almost uncontrollably into the dizzy world of dance and disco.

Saturday Night Fever and Grease were two of the most outstanding and energetic summer block-busters anybody had ever set eyes open. They were joyous, uninhibited and staggeringly happy clappy. They made you want to run out in the street, grab hold of a complete stranger and samba into the small hours.

Both Saturday Night Fever and Grease were, I feel sure, two of the most popular albums ever sold in Downtown. I think that both albums somehow ideally catered to most members of your family but particularly those who believed that the 1950s had never gone away.

Downtown, though, was Ilford's goldmine, an entry into a musical dreamland. The shop assistants always seemed to have long hair, cowboy style waistcoats and that devil may care attitude. In fact, their attitude was the attitude of the day, perhaps the attitude of the Seventies. But a positive one with no grudges, no spite and no recriminations.

When you walked into Downtown record shop, you felt an innate sense of belonging, a feeling that the music you followed was the music others followed. There was a real connection, rapport and kinship.

There was one other landmark in Ilford which still tickles my funny bone. I'm not sure why but it was the one venue that somehow sent a warm glow down my spine. Every so often, I would pass it and feel as though I'd seen it a hundred times before in some other environment.

It was the Green Gate pub in the Eastern Avenue which may sound like any other pub you'd ever heard but this was different. It was a pub like no other and I remain convinced that it was the kind of a pub that nobody had seen ever before.

Outside the Green Gate pub were parked some of the biggest bikes in the history of motor bikes. They were giant-sized, monumental bikes which gleamed in the late, fading summer sunshine, chrome frames spotlessly clean and a credit to their proud owners.

Then they would emerge from the pub in all of their finery, stocky, well-muscled men who looked as if they'd just stepped out of a Dan Dare comic. They had thick beards, thick hair, prominent tattoos on their shoulders and a pint or three of the best in their hands.

This, I feel sure, was the Ilford branch of the Hells Angels, fine, upstanding gentlemen and women who quite clearly resembled those nightclub bouncers regularly standing guard outside adult establishments.

But these were no sneering or snarling beasts with menacing knuckle dusters. These guys and girls were peace loving, innocent pussycats who wouldn't have hurt a fly. They were quite, conciliatory characters who just wanted to be friendly, talkative and inoffensive.

Meanwhile, life at home for yours truly continued in much the way that it had for most of the Eighties. It was aimless, directionless, perhaps unnatural in the eyes of some but still looking for a way into the heady society and people of like minds and interests.

There was an ever-present feeling of weakness, brittleness and fragility about my life that seemed to follow me everywhere. I always felt that if somebody so much as touched me, I would fall backwards into some hellish black hole and never emerge.

Every Rosh Hashanah, the Jewish New Year, I would accompany my late dad to Beehive Lane synagogue and stare longingly at all of the teenage girls, knowing full well that I had no idea who they were or why I was looking at them.

Of course, I had the same male hormones and, of course, that insatiable male curiosity. But for me, these girls may just well have been aliens from another planet or members perhaps of some faraway tribe. There was a sense that I'd missed out on those first years of being a socially adept teenager and there was no way back now.

It almost seemed the last train, bus or plane had disappeared into the distance and you were left on your own. Adolescence, for me, had now been replaced by suspicion, cynicism and painful naivety. There was a genuine reluctance to do the things that came naturally to other kids.

I don't think why but there was an irrational fear that something dark and sinister would happen to me if I did join in with the other kids' activities. Perhaps it was some deep rooted psychological barrier that became impossible to dislodge.

Did I perhaps think that some evil force would overwhelm me, sweeping me off my feet and dropping me into a tank of piranhas. I knew subconsciously that these raging terrors and that trembling trepidation was all in the mind. Unreal and imaginary but real nonetheless.

Throughout my teenage years, I wandered far and wide, roaming piteously, never homeless but apart and sadly alone. There was a painful remoteness and indistinctness about my life. I always felt as if everything was completely out of reach, far away on some bleak moorland, where nobody lived or existed.

Gradually, I began to feel as though I was locked away in the darkest of cupboards, whimpering away like some shabby tramp with only a shopping bag for company. Everything about my life was completely without plan, method or purpose. There were no foundation stones or building blocks, no hammers, shovels or cement to build it with.

Suddenly, I was confronted by misty, foggy horizons, haunting tunnels and caves, ghosts from a lonely past, tattered and ragged garments of my existence.

It all seemed very pointless and haphazard and yet I had to find a way out of this complex maze, this faceless oblivion. And so it was that I found Ilford B'nai Brith, an international Jewish charitable organisation with a heart of gold. The sound of silence was about to be broken by the most delightful musical.

And so it was that on an early January evening in 1983 that I took my first nervous, but brave steps, into a world that up until then had been very enclosed and somehow off limits. I think I must have felt that had I moved ever so stealthily towards this next stage, something terrible would happen to me.

But it was the all-inclusive, all singing and dancing group who overnight who made all those years of emptiness seem like a distant, unspeakable nightmare. It's hard to describe how emotionally difficult that period of my life was but what I knew that from now on was that I would no longer feel like an outsider looking in. I would never ever feel excluded again.

I can never adequately put into words the enormous gratitude that I have for B'nai Brith. That evening, I think we discussed new ideas, new possibilities, events and suggestions for what we thought would be the right things to do in the future.

It was an undoubtedly nerve racking but very critical turning point in my whole outlook. No longer would I be that rather sad, pathetic individual who could only speak when asked to or when the mood took me.

True, I never became an animated conversationalist and there were frequent moments when I would just hideaway silently in the corner without a single word passing my lips. I was still very much the quiet, strong and silent type perhaps, but there was a very real sense that I could, if I'd wanted to, make a purposeful and lasting contribution to society.

We would meet every Sunday evening and engage in some of the liveliest of debates, debates on everything from the latest news stories of the week to Judaism and being Jewish. Of course, there were disagreements and yes, there were arguments but surely that was what life was about.

Then we would find a middle ground and consensus, where one member would reach a negotiated settlement. Yes, perhaps you were wrong or maybe you were right. There was an ease and sense of diplomacy about the group. Everybody had their very specific opinions on any subject but it was open for discussion.

Shortly after I joined Ilford B'nai Brith, one of the members had told me about the group's brand new magazine called Baby Rolfid. Now Baby Rolfid was an anagram for Ilford B'nai Brith and I was asked, given my passion for writing, whether I'd be interested in doing any articles for the group.

Now I have to tell you that at this moment, I must have felt like a child in the proverbial sweet shop. I didn't really know what to write but at the back of my mind, there was some bizarre association with words and literature.

And then it came to me in a flash. What about poetry? Now deep within my mind there was a nagging urge to write something very clever, very imaginative and something my friends would inevitably remark upon.

So it was that I put pen to paper and found these untapped reserves of very wordy and immensely descriptive pieces of verse. Somehow, I knew that I'd created something that most of the members of the group would have to remember me by.

The wordy verse, which it undoubtedly was, went by the title of Summer. Summer was very much my first, if rather tentative venture into the world of descriptive prose and one that I'm not sure whether I could ever repeat again.

Summer was all about the 'stateliness and majesty of clouds' or something that was reminiscent to of how we perceived summer. It was all about those endless blue skies, sheets blowing majestically on the washing line, summer in her finest finery.

Anyway, the fact was that I'd arrived and I was here to say. I can't remember what we did as a group in 1983 but it must have been completely satisfying and engrossing.

By the end of 1983, I could now look back on the year with an almost indefinable satisfaction. I knew that I was very much an integral part of a Jewish charitable organisation. I was still very muted and subdued at times but I did feel wanted and connected.

I'm sure it was close to the end of 1983 when the group announced its intention to go on a short winter Christmas break. 10 years earlier, the very thought of joining people of my age on any kind of holiday would have filled me dread.

But here it was the opportunity of a lifetime. The venue was Coventry and a short stay at what used to be a monastery but had now been converted into a youth hostel. It was an intriguing prospect but one that I had to embrace with open arms.

So it was that a small group of us all drove down to Coventry for a short stay in a youth hostel. I'll always remember what we did on Christmas Eve. After settling down for the evening and unpacking our belongings, we then proceeded to what seemed to constitute fun and relaxation. Anyway we thought it was.

Shortly before lights were switched out for the night, there was distinct giggling and chuckling. Without any reason whatever, somebody decided to chuck a pillow at the other person. There was definitely an air of light heartedness and frivolity about the hostel as pillows were flung, inhibitions flung out of the window and we began to behave rather like those irrepressible school children at St. Trinians. I could hardly believe what was happening to me but it had to be the best year of my life up until that point. Nobody cared, we were happy and that was all that mattered.

I've a vague recollection of what happened during that break in Coventry but I do know that those recollections are now gold plated. I seem to remember that on our first day, party games were organised outside and the whole holiday had a structure and timetable to it.

Now I've no idea why and it may have lost something in my powers of recall but I do remember what we had for Christmas Day lunch. It was the most unexpected and unconventional Christmas Day lunch. Something that I don't think would have figured too prominently in the homes of most families across the nation.

Christmas Day lunch for the visitors of Ilford B'nai Brith consisted of tripe or some ghastly creation from the kitchens of a Coventry youth hostel. I don't know why we were served trip and to this day I can't remember whether we ate it or not but tripe it was and some of us must have reluctantly consumed it. Who needed turkey and all of the trimmings? Some of us were just determined to have the best time of our lives.

I think it must have been Boxing Day when the decision had been made fairly unanimously to go to Stratford upon Avon. Stratford upon Avon was of course the home of one of England's greatest poets and playwrights, William Shakespeare. But I suppose the closest I'd ever come to Stratford was Stratford, East London when my dad used to pass it on the way to the West End.

The main theme of our day in Shakespeare country was a treasure hunt. Shortly after lunch, we all drove to a remote spot in the land of the Bard. The cars were parked, maps unrolled out and suddenly a group of young Jewish people were seen traipsing through muddy fields, desperately seeking shelter and wondering quite naturally what we were supposed to be doing.

At the end of the day, we all slumped into our chairs back at the hostel, breathless but uplifted, laughing and totally exhilarated. Nobody knew who had won the treasure hunt but, in all honesty, it didn't seem to matter. There was a sense of lovely absurdity and improvisation to the day that none of us had anticipated. There were no rules, no time limits and nobody was declared the outright winner. It was all made up, haphazard and it was the festive season.

So it was that we returned to Ilford exhausted, drained but quite elated. We'd set out to do whatever we liked, we knew that nobody could ever criticise us for what we had done and, above all, nobody could pass judgment on us. We were grown up, consenting adults and in moderation, we could be whoever we wanted to be and enjoy life to the full without a single pang of guilt or conscience. We behaved in much the way that most civilised adults would be expected to behave. We watched the telly, played board games, listened to music, played the games that spanned all ages and then just cheered loudly when the bells of Coventry cathedral tolled.

At long last I'd found a safe harbour, a comfortable seat overlooking the eternally sun dappled bay, its rays bouncing off the yachts, a timeless jewel that would never fade into obscurity.

I'd found people with the same interests as me, the same hopes and ambitions, the same dreams and fantasies. It was almost as if my life had found an entirely new set of circumstances, episodes and series. It was simply a case of gently peeling away the wrapper and finding something absolutely priceless and joyous.

Now I'd found my kind of people, people who were naturally articulate, confident, driven and ambitious. They were everything I would now try to emulate and compete with and yet I insisted at first in hiding away in corners where nobody could spot me.

I have to admit it was scary, terrifying, overwhelmingly different and yet gradually I began to find that even if I made the smallest contribution to a Sunday evening, it was still a valid and valued one. Nobody would laugh at me, demean or degrade me, find fault with me nor would they take me to task.

It was just a wonderful feeling to be part of their lives, a privileged observer at some very important meeting and gathering. Ilford B'nai Brith had now given me the perfect opportunity to be as opinionated or indeed as balanced as I wanted to be. Nobody would ever shoot me down in flames, criticising, condemning or at any time humiliating me. They were understanding, considerate, receptive and just totally inspirational.

Whole Sunday evenings would be spent chatting, sharing the latest news of the week, laughing at the idiosyncrasies of our noble yet flawed politicians and then poking fun at the B List celebrities.

At first, it was difficult to take all in, fully absorbing what they had to say and wondering whether I deserved to be part of their world, their discussion. And yet, there was never a problem, no impediment, no holds barred. I too could join in, gently engage and participate in something that.10 years before would have been completely beyond me.

This was a world of friendly argument, democracy at work, me on the outside looking in and yet completely at ease with my surroundings. I was still on the edge, still on the periphery but ironically fully aware of the wonder and magnitude of it all.

I felt rather like a nervous kitten, tentatively dipping its paws into a river for the first time. It suddenly occurred to me that gradually, step by step, I could make that giant leap of faith, a complete transition to the world of a properly functioning and communicating adult.

That Christmas 1983 break to Coventry had turned my life around. It had given me permission to somebody I would never have thought I could be. I'd suddenly discovered that there was nothing to be frightened of, nothing to get agitated about and above all, here was the place I wanted to be.

Of course, I should have been in gainful employment by then and maybe there was a sense that maybe I didn't belong. All of the members of Ilford B'nai Brith were in steady work and good jobs. And yet throughout that period, it didn't seem to matter that much because, in the bigger picture, I had different priorities.

And besides, I was never looked down upon or patronised at any time by the guys and girls at Ilford B'nai Brith. Understandably, they were wary and unsure of why I couldn't find work. After all, I had showed my literary prowess with my summer poem for the magazine so perhaps they might have thought I was some late developer who'd graduated from college and had briefly lost their way in life.

But I was never snubbed, overlooked, rejected, denounced or singled out as in any way different. Ilford B'nai Brith gave me a firm platform from which to redress the balance of my life, to strike out and find untapped resources and use my initiatives rather than be dependent on others to look for them.

Because that was the way it had to be. By now, I'd been given a position on the B'nai Brith committee with the sole responsibility of coming up with new ideas for the group. I think I'd felt I'd been given a substantial role in life. Now people would listen to me, take on board whatever I thought would be suitable or constructive for future events. I had to admit it was the greatest feeling in the world. I truly felt wanted, recognised, acknowledged and confirmed as a regular guy. No more lonely streets, dark corners, alienation or could shouldered ostracism. I'd passed my first interviews, I'd been selected as the candidate for my constituency for the best party in the land. Ilford B'nai Brith, I can never thank you enough. You were the turning point, the fresh start, the kick start, the new beginning, the catalyst for dramatic change.

Part 23:
And now for some more final childhood memories.

I can still see it, remember it quite vividly, hear it, loud, cheering voices in the distance, occasionally muffled by some low and inexplicable roar. For as long as I can remember, it was rather like some very noisy neighbour but a neighbour who knew when to keep the volume down. Still I had no complaints whatsoever.

It was the home of Ilford Football Club, my local football team and, for me, Saturday afternoon heroes. Or supposedly so. Back in the 1950s, English football sneaked its way into our consciousness by way of the Charles Buchan football manual, a glorious fascination with the game and, for some, the cigarette card method.

Now let me see. My local team were Ilford Football Club, conveniently situated at the bottom of my road. Well almost. Ilford's ground was off Ley Street and first came to my attention during my teenage years.

I'd always been aware of the football club because you knew that it was geographically opposite the Ilford Laundry. This may have been an idyllic spot for the team's washing. How those virile and masculine Ilford lads must have longed for clean shirts and socks.

But Ilford were never a big time club nor were they a club with wealthy owners and a substantial bank balance. Ilford were a small, humble, non-League club with no promises and no pretensions. Ilford just minded their own business at the bottom of our road.

Ilford played in what you used to be known as the Isthmian League, a tight, compact league with hundreds of devoted supporters. They were life-long supporters who presumably worked in either Bodgers, Fairheads or Harrison Gibson's.

I would like to think that they were hard working members of the public who just wanted to spend a hassle free, relaxed afternoon off Ley Street.

I never had the privilege to be part of the whole Ilford football experience and I fear I may regret it now. Because Ilford, although Saturday afternoon must have been a very special and magical time, had to be an almost therapeutic experience for those who just wanted to wind down. It was a time to get rid of all that stress, sing heartily from the terraces and indulge themselves in 90 minutes of happiness.

The Ilford ground, itself, always looked like one of those very old, rickety grounds that must have creaked every time you walked past it. The seats, I suspect, were painfully wooden, the stands and terraces reeking of hot dogs, burgers and endless cigarette smoke.

259

Every so often, out of sheer curiosity, I would lean out of my bedroom window somewhat precariously and stare at Ilford's floodlights. It was here that I heard my first football chants, the first sustained hand clapping, rousing applause when goals were scored and by what can only be described as communal singing.

To the outside observer, Ilford football club, now at Dellow Close, may have seemed a creaking and crumbling relic. But regardless of its age, the terraces were always very much alive.

Of course, the roofs were rusty and rapidly decaying by the day. But I felt there was an old fashioned solidity about that corrugated roof that was part of the club's character. Ilford football club was strong, community minded and identifiable.

Ilford's supporters had a very close knit and intimate relationship with both the club and its very homely roots. Nobody was ever going to be bigger than the club because that was never its style.

I suspect that after Ilford's matches, their fans would ecstatically trudge back to their homes in Ley Street for their tea-time plate of wholesome fish and chips and the inevitable cup of tea. It would be the most traditional of rituals but then they would look at their Pools coupons just in case they'd won a couple of hundred quid.

On reflection I suppose, I should have seen more of Ilford football club. I should have slipped on a pair of tough shoes, wrapped an Ilford scarf around my neck and loyally cheer on this lovely old suburban Essex club.

The story was that Ilford football club had an excellent record in the FA Amateur Cup. I seem to remember hearing that Ilford had won this highly regarded Cup. Along with Bishop's Stortford, they were one of the most successful teams in Cup competitions, a team with its very own social status and local charm.

But I bet Bishop's Stortford didn't have a laundry or fire station on their doorstep. I bet they'd have been hard pressed to find a local bakery that sold mouth-watering cheese sandwiches. Nor could they boast a timber merchants with its abundant supply of wood.

One year, or so legend had it, Ilford won the FA Amateur Cup way back when I can only imagine that the local mayor must have insisted that the team parade their trophy on the town hall balcony. Perhaps they were implored to do an open top bus ride along Ilford High Street. What delightful and historic days they must have been for Ilford.

Eventually, though, the floodlights that I could see from my bedroom window sadly went out and Ilford football club that used to live in my neck of the woods, faded and then vanished into thin air.

One day, the circus packed up and moved to allegedly greener pastures. Where would those local newsagents go for their Saturday afternoon thrills and spills, thick winter coats on, scarf warmly wrapped around the neck and all of the 1950s paraphernalia? What would happen to that gentle joking on the open Ilford terraces, the cosy camaraderie, father and son, mother and daughter, uncle and aunt? Whole families and neighbourhoods.

What would happen to Ilford's football supporters? Would they wander off to the Valentines Park bowling green, another leisurely swim in the very animated Lido? Would they jump onto a distinctive 169 Route Master bus for an afternoon's shopping in Gants Hill or Barkingside. Or would they just sit on the park benches next to the café. Maybe they'd spend a very modest sum on the tiny pitch and putt golf course.

Maybe those same Ilford football supporters take themselves down to the Cranbrook Road end of Valentines Park. Perhaps they'd head for the enchanting budgerigar cage where sweet whistles and chirpy cheeping would drift languidly across Essex.

Or would those same football supporters just change their sporting allegiance and walk back to those very English games of cricket. Essex always played some of their matches at a well built and furnished ground at the Cranbrook Road end of Valentines Park.

You could also play cricket on another well-kept Valentines Park field. The field would take those by now converted football supporters into hidden paths and thick bush land. These now eager cricket fans would now swallow a much needed bottle of re-invigorating water or a bottle of Coca Cola.

Isn't it strange how my childhood experiences always take me back to Valentines Park? There is a very homely grandeur about the park, a timeless magnetism, a deeply romantic hold on me that may fade with the passage of time but always be there, hovering, floating and drifting in the air.

I will never ever forget, for instance, the squirrels in Valentines Park, scurrying and scampering surreptitiously between the trees darting into a dark bush where nobody could ever find them.

There was one summer when the Valentines Park squirrels almost took up permanent residence in the whole of the park. I'm not sure but these tiny creatures took up full time occupation in every hiding place they could find.

Summertime though, for me in Valentines Park, had its very own life and vibrancy, its identification with the simple and natural things in my world. Everything was easy, undemanding, brighter, more hopeful, and endlessly optimistic.

For instance, there were the tennis courts at opposite ends of Valentines Park. On my frequent runs around the park, I would occasionally look up at the by now heavily populated courts.

Why, I asked, were these glowing testimonies to health and fitness so joyously full during the Wimbledon fortnight? There had to be a reason why all of these tennis courts resounded to the cracking and thwacking of yellow tennis balls over the net.

I can still see those loosely flapping nets, the fading tramlines, the hard concrete ground. There was something delectably and timelessly English about this scene. And yet none of the players on court never ever took tennis seriously, which in a way is how it should always be. It should be light-hearted fun and never bickered over. Because that is the essence of life and sport.

And then my teenage eyes took me inevitably back to the Valentines Park cricket ground where Essex took up bat and pad during a heady week in early

June. I've mentioned the one and only John Lever and Ken McEwen, Ray East and Keith Fletcher but there were numerous cricketing characters that just happened to catch my fascinated eyes.

During the Seventies, England enjoyed its most purple period of prosperity. Those were the days when cricket seemed to acknowledge some of its greatest players with a gentle, appreciative smile. It was the County Championship, overflowing with gems, little nuggets and gleaming treasures.

At Kent, there was that most sturdy of Kent batsmen, Brian Luckhurst, a high scoring, powerful and robust stroke maker, a player with all of the most correct of strokes off the front and back foot. Luckhurst was tidy, efficient, capable of a long innings and infinite patience.

Back at Essex, there was Mike Denness, cool, stylish and a polished captain and batsman. Denness was never fancy or ostentatious, nor was he too thoughtful and introspective. He just got on with the task at hand, rolling his wrists when he had to make those handsome strokes, head held high and poised for action. He knuckled down to the task in hand and made the most of both his strengths and limitations.

Cricket was also, for me, all about the bowlers, the men who slogged their way through the day from morning to early evening without a single complaint or grievance.

This, I think, is English cricket in its finest appearance and conduct. The bowlers are the men who shape their team's innings, the purveyors of mischief and mayhem, the men responsible for the single handed destruction of the opposition.

Every summer's morning, English bowlers clock on for their early morning work rather like those industrious men at the local factory. Theirs is a life of uncomplaining toil and industry. They are the men who go through those same arduous and repetitive routines all day, over after over, minute after minute, hour after hour. It is undoubtedly stimulating to watch and unashamedly English.

For me, there was John Snow, formerly of Sussex and a bowler of remarkable stamina and endurance. Snow, from my earliest memories, was quite the most amazing sight in all English cricket.

He was the one, who without any grumbling or any hint of protest in his makeup, would bowl all day unquestioningly and unconcerned by outside distractions. Snow, I felt sure, deliberately cut out all the peripheral noise around him and got on with it.

With or without pullover, Snow would jog in at Lord's, Edgbaston or Headingley with that very neat and purposeful air. There was something very straight backed, honest but calculating, about the Snow bowling action.

Snow was very determined and yet, perversely, there was something very delicate about the Snow bowling action. Slowly, he would walk back to the pavilion, rub the ball very vigorously on his trousers and then hurtle into the bowling crease with menace on his mind.

It was the Snow bowling delivery, never hostile or angry, simply clean and clinical, bouncing gingerly into the bowler's crease, ball tucked safely into his hands and then almost exploding destructively into the batsman with the ball that swung and moved violently in the air. Snow was never an assassin but he did know how to hit the ground running.

Snow belonged to that golden generation of English bowlers during the 1970s. There was something about Snow that was typical of the man. Snow, I suspect, was very proud of his profession, his trade and craft. He always looked humble, tidy, well organised and utterly sincere.

I'd like to think that in his humble retirement, Snow has taken himself back to his South Coast home and reflected wistfully on those heady, halcyon days with the England team. He would remember the days when he would be the main architect of the West Indies or Australia downfall.

He would probably settle down very happily by a fishing bank and sling his rod into some very fertile river. He would perhaps take a brisk and invigorating walk along some very craggy coastline, heartily sniffing the salty and salubrious air of Hastings or maybe Eastbourne.

Perhaps Snow is a publican, a genial host in his local watering house and inviting all of his old Sussex team mates in for a swift half or two. Perhaps, he is an accomplished artist, painting all of those wonderfully majestic South Coast gulls, swooping and dancing between the rocks.

Then there was Geoff Arnold, another personal favourite. Arnold played his cricket for both England and Surrey. It was hard to know what was going through Arnold's mind. Perhaps he was rehearsing his bowling action, thinking deeply about all manner of devious plots with his fingers.

Arnold was Surrey through and through. This meant that he played most of his cricket at the Oval, which is one of the spiritual homes of cricket. The Oval has very little of the majesty of Lord's but it does have a huge and very impressive presence.

Because Arnold played for Surrey, it is easy to think of all of those tiresome county stereotypes. Surrey of course is a stockbroker belt which probably means that it's very wealthy, very upper class and very patronising. But this is quite clearly not true because Surrey is very quiet, friendly and easy going.

Surrey offers you in for a cup of tea, a slice of cake and biscuit. How neighbourly and community minded is that. You had to believe that both Arnold and Surrey were both decent and fair minded.

Arnold, though, was a superb bowler for both England and Surrey. Like John Snow, his partner in crime, Arnold had one of those distinctive bowling actions that live forever in the mind.

Arnold was one of those business-like, highly principled, persistent and hard working bowlers. Rather like Snow, Arnold was strong, purposeful, hungry, forceful, never aggressive but nagging, insistent, a model of raw, fired up perseverance. He would almost tip toe to the bowler's crease as if he was ever so slightly afraid that he would hurt somebody.

Arnold would spend long, bowling stints, marching back to the pavilion at either Old Trafford, Trent Bridge or his local Oval, pounding away with over after over of medium pace bowling and an air of full blooded intensity.

Geoff Arnold, although never menacing or sinister, still reminded you of somebody completely unconnected to cricket. He was rather like one of those prim and proper footmen in some grand Victorian house. He would ask you if he could take your coat and top hat and then take you kindly to your seat for dinner.

Arnold, I always believed, looked too nice and inoffensive to hurl down cricketing missiles into terrified batsman. Arnold should have worked in a bank perhaps, leafing through five and ten pound notes with meticulous care. Arnold should have worked in an insurance office or maybe as one of those pillars of the community who always had time for the elderly and never shirked his civic duties.

For me, both John Snow and Geoff Arnold were outstanding cricketers, generous men, good men, top of the class, men of honour and men of upright standing. John Snow occupied very important places in my personal estimation. They were men of high repute, highly valued, thoroughly estimable and above all my teenage cricketing personalities. I can pay them no higher compliment. Thanks gents.

And so I find myself back in the neighbourhood that shaped me, gave body and soul to my very earliest years. Cranley Road was where it all started.

Cranley Road, with its straight laced windows, our pebble dashed back garden wall, my dad sitting in the sun hour after hour, sun glasses perched hilariously on his bronzed forehead, staring into a blameless blue summer sky, while his old buddy in the background, Frank Sinatra, wrapped his vocal chords around I've Got You Under My Skin with an almost inordinate passion.

Cranley Road, or so it seemed to see, was somehow completely unaffected by events in war torn Cambodia and the rantings of Enoch Powell at his full throttle political pomp. Cranley Road had no interest in the private lives of Lord Lucan, Edward Heath or the Pope. There may have been a passing curiosity in what these distinguished individuals may have been doing but, from a personal point of view, they may just as well have been bit parts in a Shakespearean tragedy or the latest cast in a Harold Pinter play.

I was never sure what my neighbours must have thought about the 1970s or the people who made it tick. Every evening, they would watch Alistair Burnet, Sandy Gall, Reginald Bosanquet, Kenneth Kendall, Peter Woods and Richard Baker all weave together the very complicated strands of the day's news.

TV newscasters were our window on the society around us but these celebrities or household names were just very distant, faraway figures. They were like unrelated, fuzzy and obscure who seemed to be living on some desolate wasteland, totally cut off from civilisation, fading away and then receding into some black hole.

Cranley Road in Ilford will always be Cranley Road though, naturally inquisitive because that's what people do, funny, buoyant and contented since this is the way it always was.

You may be sure that if anybody was ever hurt in Cranley Road, that the good neighbours would always rally around in large, very sympathetic clusters. An ambulance would be called for immediately, concerns would be expressed and the poorly patient would be fussed over very compassionately and solicitously. Because the neighbours of Cranley Road in Ilford were always there to help and come to your aid.

There was always something wonderfully idiosyncratic about Ilford Town Centre on a Saturday afternoon. I always knew that something completely out of the ordinary and unexpected would suddenly burst out of a box, leap out of a hidden corner or pounce on you with that beaming grin on its face. But I was proud of where I came from. Ilford had undoubted class.

For what seemed the latter end of the Eighties, one gentleman, with no prompting at all and little shame or self-consciousness, would steal the show. Every so often, there comes a time when even the most daring among us would think twice about doing something that we might find is completely out of character.

The fact is that a very elderly gentleman, regular as clockwork, would quietly appear in the middle of the town centre in Ilford. I say he was elderly because that was the impression he gave most of us.

He was grey-haired, of medium height but he did have the most remarkable voice. Above all, he had the thickest and longest grey beard you were ever likely to see. To all outward appearances, he looked Jewish and looked in complete control of proceedings.

Saturday after Saturday, he would climb onto his soap box, stand very rigidly on his favoured spot and then deliver his Saturday sermon. It was quite the most moving sight. He was loud, he was powerful, utterly persuasive and, at times, very convincing.

To all intents and purposes, he was a preacher, a religious, passionate man who believed that one day, the Messiah would come. He had an almost captivating charisma that left most of his observers open mouthed and gasping.

There he was week after week, with his towering pile of Bibles, preaching to the converted, shouting, waving frantically and pointing to all four points of the compass. But he was never shaken, deterred or discouraged by those who disbelieved him.

Every Saturday, he was vocal, strong willed, adamant that he was right and completely gripping. He roared like the proverbial lion in the jungle, getting louder and louder until Ilford began to sound like its very own version of Speakers Corner.

He was neither pompous nor dogmatic, nor was he some frightening fascist with dangerous views. But he was very safely enthralling, almost encouraging at times. So what must this fascinating gentleman have been thinking when he got up on a Saturday morning?

Did he wake up in his Ilford property with a clear idea of what exactly he was going to talk about? Perhaps he just sat there in his bed, thoroughly rehearsing his grand delivery to his people. Perhaps he mulled over those very controversial statements that he was about to make and decide that, maybe, some of it was slightly inappropriate or contentious.

What paper would he have been reading on Saturday morning? I feel sure that it had to be some very opinionated publication with very definite views on everything. I can only guess that it was either the Telegraph or the Guardian, which is not to say that either paper is anti-everything, merely just guesswork on my part.

I can now see him in his pyjamas, mooching and pottering around his kitchen, deep in thought, before dressing very precisely. He would gulp down his third tea, bite very disinterestedly on his piece of toast before spluttering with rage at the wars around his world.

Then he would slip on his white shirt, iron his trousers very meticulously and then climb into those trousers very methodically. For, of course, everything had to be very methodical because this was what made this gentleman tick.

He would then pull on his long black coat, tying the laces on his shoes with rigorous attention to detail and combing his flowing grey hair with extraordinary attention to detail.

I imagine he would jump onto the 169 bus to Ilford Town Hall with a very spritely spring in his step. Then he would get off at his destination, the curtain and bed linen shop on the corner of Ilford High Road, poised, ready, controlled and exceptionally well-informed.

For a while, he would loiter outside the old Maison Riche department store with its abundant choice, silently composing himself, remembering all of those momentous words, mixing and matching, weighing up their meaning and influence, adjusting his vocal chords and then editing what was right and wrong.

In the mind of our Ilford preacher, this would be the afternoon like no other. And what an afternoon that would be, filled with gravity and gravitas, heartfelt and deeply heartening. For our man with the thick beard, Saturdays were always heartfelt and heartening.

And so I reach the end of my story, the story so far if you like. Of course, there have been highs and lows, peaks and troughs, fluctuations and moments of very heartening steadiness. At no point have I ever despaired or doubted. All of us are subject to the dramas, hazards and ecstasies that are much more than the rich tapestry of life. It is believing against the odds that it can still work out for the best. It can still work in your favour even though there are times when you may think this is highly unlikely.

So there it is. My life journey so far. It is best summarised by the charming little doctor's surgery at the bottom of Cranley Road in Ilford. Unfortunately, it is no longer there to lovingly tend to the ailments and aches of the local residents. But I can still see Dr Clarke and the highly esteemed and personable Dr Eliott. They were men who commanded your respect and with that distinguished grey beard and grey hair, Dr Eliott had at his disposal all of the medical knowledge that made him the man he was.

I feel sure that these were the places and people who put my life into a much clearer perspective than I would ever have thought possible had they never been there. Yes, Ilford, society, life and football and family life were very much part of me, part of my life journey so far. I feel immensely honoured. Always.

Lightning Source UK Ltd.
Milton Keynes UK
UKOW02f1847160115

244637UK00001B/111/P